Praise for The Vampire Le
by Laurence A. Rickels

"I am quite amazed by many of Laurence Rickels's observations in *The Vampire Lectures,* but above all I'm honored to be included as a subject for study.... It's the ultimate book to give to anyone who makes fun of you for liking vampire novels or films. I recommend it. It is incredibly rich and thought-provoking. I'm grateful for it."

—Anne Rice

"What began as a small lecture ten years ago has grown into a blockbuster. The whole nine yards is covered in this tell-all: eyewitness accounts of vampire attacks to medieval folklore 'truths.' It's an interesting, wild, and very informative cutting-edge read for those sleepless nights at home ... alone ... in the dark."

— *Village Voice*

"From embalming practices to pop culture, Rickels draws on every possible vampire metaphor to make his points.... He returns repeatedly to Stoker's *Dracula* to illustrate our psychodynamic reality, filled with death wishes, erotic substitution, and symbolic meanings.... A sophisticated survey of vampire culture."

— *Publishers Weekly*

"*The Vampire Lectures* is engrossing, challenging, and—like the death, sex, and AIDS that it evokes—morbidly fascinating."

— *Gadfly*

"This vigorous contribution to literary and paranormal theory collections will enhance the pursuit of often remote scholarship into mythology and sorcery."

— *Library Journal*

"*The Vampire Lectures* ranges widely and loosely through fang-filled literature and film and argues that our relations to the dead, including the ghostly stains that the Other leaves on the psyche, fuel pop culture's continued fascination with the undead. Quite fun to read."

— *Bookforum*

The Devil Notebooks

The Devil Notebooks

LAURENCE A. RICKELS

UNIVERSITY OF MINNESOTA PRESS

MINNEAPOLIS · LONDON

Frontispiece: *Devil Father Mine*, 2005. Photograph by Nancy Barton.

Copyright 2008 by the Regents of the University of Minnesota

Published by the University of Minnesota Press
111 Third Avenue South, Suite 290
Minneapolis, MN 55401-2520
http://www.upress.umn.edu

Library of Congress Cataloging-in-Publication Data

Rickels, Laurence A.
  The devil notebooks / Laurence A. Rickels.
    p.   cm.
  Includes bibliographical references.
  ISBN 978-0-8166-5051-4 (hc : alk. paper) — ISBN 978-0-8166-5052-1 (pb :
alk. paper)
  1. Devil. 2. Devil—Psychology. 3. Psychoanalysis. I. Title.
  BF1548.R53   2008
  133.4'22—dc22   2008006868

Printed in the United States of America on acid-free paper

The University of Minnesota is an equal-opportunity educator and employer.

15 14 13 12 11 10 09 08   10 9 8 7 6 5 4 3 2 1

CONTENTS

PLEASE ALLOW ME TO INTRODUCE MYSELF • ix

DEVIL FATHER

NOTEBOOK ONE • 3

Intro/Limbo or *Satan's School for Girls*—*Race with the Devil*—Murder in Isla Vista, Santana, and Santee—Dare Devil Aleister Crowley—*The Devil Rides Out*

NOTEBOOK TWO • 19

The Devil in Freud or the Father's Same Body—*The Other Side* and *Communications from the Memoirs of Satan*

NOTEBOOK THREE • 34

More of the Same Body—Wolfman and Fraternities of Satan

NOTEBOOK FOUR • 45

Metropolis, California—The Satanic Cult of the Built Body

NOTEBOOK FIVE • 60

Prints of Darkness in Freud, Goethe, Flusser, and Reisner—First Circle of the Seven Deadly Sins

NOTEBOOK SIX • 70

Second Circle of *Seven* and the Deadly Sins—*The Evil Within*

NOTEBOOK SEVEN • 86

Freud's Dying Days and *The Wild Ass's Skin*—Sweet Nothing or *Needful Things*

NOTEBOOK EIGHT · 99

Angel Heart in the Right Place—*Demons* Projections—*Falling Angel* Takes Heart—Demonic Phallus—*Walpurgis Night*

NOTEBOOK NINE · 112

Sounds of Satan—The Wagner before the Horse—Banality or Evil

NOTEBOOK TEN · 131

Satan and Golem, Inc.—*Childhood's End* and *Beyond the Pleasure Principle* on Purpose—What's the Sexual Difference between Techno Survival and Mass Suicide?

NOTEBOOK ELEVEN · 154

Demonic Bodies of Work between *Satan: His Psychotherapy and Cure* and *Event Horizon*

NOTEBOOK TWELVE · 163

Revelations of Evolution in *Memnoch the Devil*—*Inferno*—Keep Away from Apeling—*Dancing in the Light*

NOTEBOOK THIRTEEN · 176

Possession by Demons or the Dead in *The Amityville Horror, Witchboard,* and *The Exorcist*

NOTEBOOK FOURTEEN · 194

The Exorcism of Anneliese Michel and *The Possession of Joel Delaney*

NOTEBOOK FIFTEEN · 201

"The Call of Cthuluh" or The Craft of Disgust

NOTEBOOK SIXTEEN · 211

My Bad or *The Damned*—Spiritualism—*To the Devil a Daughter* and *The Sentinel*—My Evil

MINE

NOTEBOOK SEVENTEEN · 233

Paradise Lost—Hearst Castle—*The Black Cat*—*The Coming Race*—*Peter Schlemiel*

NOTEBOOK EIGHTEEN · 250

"The Mines of Falun"

NOTEBOOK NINETEEN · 258

Swedish Tourism and German Romanticism

NOTEBOOK TWENTY · 276

The Devil's Elixirs and *The Monk*

DEVIL FATHER MINE

NOTEBOOK TWENTY-ONE · 293

Please Allow Me to Introduce Myself, Part II—From Ferenczi to Derrida, or Faith without Redemption

NOTEBOOK TWENTY-TWO · 310

The Witch Metapsychology in Freud, *My Mother: Demonology*, and Anton LaVey

NOTEBOOK TWENTY-THREE · 331

Freud and the Devil, or Appetite Comes with Eating

NOTEBOOK TWENTY-FOUR · 343

The Devil and His Grandmother, or Rear View Mirrors

NOTEBOOK TWENTY-FIVE · 353

Michelle Remembers, or Rhyme Word Death

NOTEBOOK TWENTY-SIX · 360

Hitting Bottom in *The Club Dumas, The Omen*, and "Reading the Lack of the Body"

REFERENCES · 369

FILMOGRAPHY · 377

PLEASE ALLOW ME TO INTRODUCE MYSELF

I once led a field trip through the Falun mines with students of the Konsthögskolan at Umeå Universitet following our compact seminar on a famous incident that transmitted a certain mining complex of techno unmourning to and through German Romanticism first, then psychoanalysis. Here's looking back with you, kids. It was right after our Last Supper in Falun, in some provincial restaurant, after it became evident that our immediate environs doubled on weekends, after dinner, as disco for teenagers, that we visited the ultimate level of our Falun mine excavations. What was mine was now yours: the recent past, which is always the most primal, repressed, and catastrophic past, had flashed back before your eyes. This was the disco setting of your own adolescent grouping, groping, responding. And you cruised the dance floor with some sense of what it means to have survived yourself, to be a ghost at a familiar scene. It was time to remember the mass killer of Falun, the adolescent army boy, who had no doubt been a regular visitor to those disco exchanges in which teen volatility, confusion, idealism must be metabolized, doubled, and contained. He chose not to be a ghost visiting the scene of his time past, but to visit upon the survivors of those he murdered scenes of crime and haunting.

Several years later I started wrapping my work of compilation (and resistance) dedicated to the Devil around the kernel of this excavation project (which enjoyed a shelf life prior to this Devil frame). Now that my infernal framework is a wrap, I remember with gratitude my Devil course clients, both the undergraduate students at University of California, Santa Barbara, and Universität zu Köln and the graduate students at

Art Center College of Design and European Graduate School. Thanks for another work of teaching, a sequel of sorts to *The Vampire Lectures.*

I first proposed my new class on Satan for the 2000 summer session at UC Santa Barbara. I knew it would give me the opportunity of catching up with a piece of my own resistance. Thus I initiated research into the Prince of all occult figures—and the only occult figure I had to that date avoided interpreting with Freud. Of course I knew the Devil in the corner of the Faust tradition, but my focus there was always fixed on the superhuman dimension of all that striving—as on the installment plan of Faust's suicide. I also knew that there were precedents for distinguishing or choosing between the rule of the Devil and undead realms not subsumable by that rule. In *The Satanic Bible* Anton LaVey calls "vampire" another name for the passive aggressive in our midst—the one, you know the one, who, just like a parasite, sucks up all our energy. Anne Rice's vampire Lestat, as we will see, takes affirmative action against the Devil in the Nietzschean mode. Nietzsche, however, cast vampirism in the pejorative mode (although he certainly affirmed writing with blood—which is not the same thing as signing in blood). But Nietzsche's Zarathustra also dismisses the Devil, borrowing his nimbus and name (in "Of Great Events") to identify among the various diseases of the earth's skin more modern "fire-dogs" or subversive and revolutionary devils: they are bitter, deceitful, superficial. Perhaps it is Milton's Lucifer, the Devil as freedom fighter, who is the cursed precursor of this targeted tradition of acting out in groups. Zarathustra teaches that we must unlearn belief in "great events" (such as the resounding acts of liberation); the world revolves instead inaudibly on the discursive feat of introduction of new values.

Zarathustra anticipates with dread that his superman will be identified as the Devil, probably. When Freud recast Nietzsche's superman as belonging in the primal past rather than coming toward us out of the future, he wasn't being contrary but in fact, like another X-man, was proffering a way out of certain appropriations of the future. Nietzsche withdrew the superman identification from men of resentment by projecting his thought experiment into the uncontrollable, unforeseeable future. In the meantime, however, these very resentful types could lay claim, in Freud's day, to Nietzsche's future, now present going on past, as their time of the superman's realization. Freud therefore shoots the superman back into the primal past underneath multiple layerings of commemoration and mourning.

The primal father, or rather the primal father in early development, or, in other words, the pre-Oedipal father, is the model for this study's understanding of the Devil in psychoanalysis and its fantasy syndications. The study also submits for consideration the importance in psychic life at large of the pre-Oedipal father's brief stint before time's up with the arrival of the Oedipal father. Following the First World War, Freud recalculated the lump sum of what the supremes (realized supermen or racist demigods, the Prince of Darkness, the primal father) could inflict. He consequently placed them—all of them, all of them demonic possessors—in the personalized past of our recovery on the couch of his science.

In my course of amassing materials upon materials to make out the case of the Devil, I found the rule (according to the Standard Edition of psychoanalytic figures dedicated to the father's death) in my place of exception. The Devil turned out not to belong to the network of haunted occult mediatic relations I had explored before over various undead bodies. In my series of occult media studies I took exception to the rule that the father's death is the content or discontent of every haunting. Occult figures, like vampires, for example, get a rise out of unmournable losses that, in these cases (for the creature or for the victim), have not been contained by the father's death. Behind every vampire, mummy, werewolf, and so on, we can find—missing—the unmournable loss of mother, child, or sibling. But the Devil represents the exception to this rule (one that proves its own rule). The Devil represents the father, an early image of or fantasy about the father, which we will be designating throughout as "Dad certainty."

In all the other occult scenarios, the father and the father's death provide a diversion leading far away from the crypt of unmournable loss.

But if the father takes center stage in Devil fictions, it's not as Oedipal father. The substitution that the Oedipal father introduces as third person is also always commemorative: to substitute for a loss, withdrawal, or lack is to keep in touch with it as loss, as lost. (Desire sparks in these dark shadows, a guilty survivor inside the Oedipus complex.) Down the pages of this study, we will assemble the composite picture of the Devil father. For now let's just say again that the infernal Prince represents the pre-Oedipal father, the primal father in our early lives. (The funky desire we may encounter here is one-way and at this father's disposal.) To obtain the Devil's psychoanalytic portrait we will proceed, then, by process of elimination (but elimination in every possible sense).

Let's keep turning up the contrast between the undead—the un-Dad—and the Devil father. The Devil does not grant the fulfillment of the get-well or be-dead wishes of immortality neurotics. The Devil doesn't give immortality—while every other occult figure extends life to the point of unsettling boundaries between life and death. The Devil gives a certain amount of time and the deadline. Artists, thinkers, even professors (like Dr. Faust) are given to appreciate the Devil's grants of quality time, of a span of time uninterrupted by the randomness of death or by any other suddenly pressing inhibition. In Thomas Mann's *Doctor Faustus* the Devil's offer assumes the guise of the immortalizing side effect of deadly diagnosis: the Devil gives composer Adrian Leverkühn more-of-the-same time, but time controlled and intensified by the certain deadline contained in his syphilitic infection. The Devil only gives time at once immersed in finitude and "immortalized" by an appointed end. Leverkühn in turn will die only of this certain death—and no other fatality, no accident, will intervene to cut short the time that is given. The Devil gives a diagnosis and that gives time, time to work, time to break through to a lament that rings true through the history of music and man, which, as we will see, is the double history of the Devil.

This book began as lecture notes. But the notes scribbled for lecture were in turn largely based on the notes I took down as dictation from a host of gadget lovers and other experts. Is there a single key Devil fiction or study considered here that wasn't recommended to me by students, friends, and colleagues?

The handful of premature publications of portions of this Devil notesbook could perhaps be excavated but can no longer be recognized in the new mix. Beware of raising the ghosts of improper burial—recycling, plagiarism, the unread works—in the precincts of the infernal Prince!

Devil Father

NOTEBOOK ONE

The Devil is an institutional figure, the kind you negotiate with and bind yourself to by contract that will be observed down to the fine print. In honor of this book's origin down the corridors of an institution of higher yearning, let us take our Prince back to school. A good introduction to the Devil of an exception is the 1973 TV movie *Satan's School for Girls* (produced by Aaron Spelling). The onset is a slasher chase scene. The camera's unidentified POV relentlessly pursues a breathless young woman. When another person enters the picture, the POV drops its stare, and we are confronted with the possibility that this is the one. But each time it's a near miss. Increasingly we get the picture that either we are on the edge of this woman's delusional world or her pursuer is somehow supernatural (while humanoid enough to share its uncanniness with innocent bystanders). The POV catches up with her. Her name is Martha. Her death is ruled a suicide. Her sister, Elizabeth, doesn't believe it, certainly doesn't understand it, won't stand for it. Martha attended Salem Academy. Elizabeth decides to enroll there as a new student, under cover of an assumed surname, to investigate causes and conditions of her sister's state of mind.

The movie bases its subsequent suspense buildup on the easy assumption that of the two instructors at the school we are introduced to as the transferential bookends of Salem Academy, it has to be the behavioral psychologist, Dr. Delacroix, who is the force of evil behind suicides that by number three look like murder. The experimental rat maze he hovers over like his control panel in class to the terrified amazement of unfocused pupils is, in your typical horror setting, a dead giveaway (namely, every horror film's self-reflexive moment when, beside itself, it moves to contain itself). In contrast to this mad scientist, there's the art instructor, Dr. Clampett, whose class we first visit. He is clearly everyone's favorite, a real Oedi-pal. He works the transference for the thing called love ("a special kind of love," as Roberta, one of his groupies, will describe it down the halls of this TV movie). He makes his point with an abstract op-art piece about the interchangeability of reality and illusion. "Illusion and reality are different but also very much the same. What we think we see is as real as what we really see." If the girls just "hang loose," and look at it first this way and then that, they will agree that the shapes look now like they're advancing, now like they're receding. The new girl, Elizabeth, doesn't get it. He points out that she was concentrating on something and therefore locked into her mind the very first image she saw. The artist must "dare to see things unlike anyone has seen them before."

Dr. Clampett works the transference, but in a certain way. All is illusion and reality—except the grades the girls will get at the end of the term. But a friendly reminder that they will meet again tonight at his wine party follows this assertion of a difference that he alone wields. Earlier during art class, while reviewing student work, Dr. Clampett gags on the "gloomy" goth painting by Debby: he hopes she'll get over the phase; maybe a new boyfriend is in order? He's the easy-going type for whom inhibition knows one cure-all. In contrast to the all-or-nothing playful abstraction of the demo artwork, Debby's painting represents and re-presses an object that can be lost and found. We see a recognizable but unidentified cryptlike room that contains the portrait of a girl who went to the school, namely Martha. Elizabeth will carry this representation around the basement chambers until she finds the fitting room. But first Elizabeth wants to know more about the room. Debby: "It's like a room I saw a long, long time ago." "Where?" "Here, here in this building." Her rodent-identified panic is on the rise. It belongs to the recent past, the most repressed past, the era of identifiable losses, of losses with which one identifies. Elizabeth goes to the classroom building next door and picks up the painting (we hear the rodents in Dr. Delacroix's classroom as we pass down the hallway). In the dormitory cellar she finds the room. She notices that someone is there. We see Dr. Delacroix. She rushes back upstairs to tell Debby: "I found the room in your painting." Debby flips her id.

Roberta and Jody slip into the hallway to reassure Elizabeth that the cross Debby must bear in mind is history: It's just some creepy legend about the school. During the Salem witch trials there were eight young women who were accused of witchcraft and hung in the cellar. "There was someone in that room tonight. I saw him!" "Don't tell Debby." Next day Elizabeth is pretty sure it was Dr. Delacroix.

Debby is one of the charges without parents who cannot readily let go of losses or find substitutions that successfully fill in for what's missing. By contrast, Roberta will say that she, too, like the three suicides, doesn't have parents—but you don't see her killing herself over it. She can replace what she has lost without complications.

The film plays as one kind of horror film until mad scientist Dr. Delacroix files for victim status: running away from "him" or "it," he ends up falling into a pond and, as students form a circle around the spot he's in and silently push him away from the banks with long poles, drowns as casualty of what looks (especially at that time) like a Manson-style kill-in.

So it turns out that back when Dr. Delacroix seemed to be harassing Debby in his class (to the point of her going into rat-in-a-maze convulsions in the hallway), we now recognize that he was trying to reach her, show her a way out of a maze not of their making. But the lesson he taught was spot off: terror, which motivates anger, even killing, gradually breaks you down. The result would be the passivity Debby embodies in her zomboid way. But Debby is one of the orphans resisting the Devil's offer. But not out of choice: melancholia is Debby's condition not caused by her free will. In other words, she flunks the Devil's test because her will isn't free but must first pass through the missing other. When we see Debby rush off to what will turn out to be her rendezvous with death or suicide, she clearly is giggly and pleased in anticipation. Although her jolly self is perhaps the very measure of her depression, the point to be made still is that Debby at least seems to want to join the Devil's groupies.

What Dr. Delacroix identifies as terror instills in those who are not neurotically inhibited, not stuck on some loss in this world, a spell of certainty, submission, invulnerability, and a special kind of love. Thus, Roberta answers Dr. Delacroix in class that the purpose of the experiment is to drive the rat (totemic stand-in for missing children and siblings) crazy. But that is another way of saying that Roberta cannot be caught in the maze.

Though Roberta arrived at the academy depressed, Dr. Clampett gave her the power never to feel vulnerable again. He gives you all that and more. But to benefit from his gift you can't fight him, can't resist him. Indeed, now Roberta can see and say that her being without parents was the price she gladly paid for this prize: it has to be that way to receive Dr. Clampett's gift of invulnerability. Why should I resist him, Elizabeth asks rhetorico-ecstatically. But you still have your family, don't you, Roberta inquires. Elizabeth admits that she's Martha's sister. Roberta: "Dr. Clampett tried to help her." Now Elizabeth's the one, the missing eighth person needed to carry out the reversal of the sentencing and execution of the seventeenth-century coven.

If you could imagine viewing the 2000 presidential election as another made-for-TV horror movie otherwise unspecified, while watching it (for the first time) you would most likely assume that Gore, even in name, was the psycho killer, the mad scientist, the vampire or vampiroid. Just to see him was to know his burden of mega repression. Especially when the cameras shot him from behind, from the way his hair was cut straight across the back of his neck to his posture, the fit of the pants, the backside was just vacant and in its vacancy shouted repression. Of course we know that he had been getting it—his sense or direction— from his politician father all his life. If Gore seemed relieved, almost relaxed, almost healthy when he conceded the second time, it is because by both winning the election and yet not having to go through with being president he both satisfied his father's decree and circumvented it. But the more we watched this horror film, the clearer it became that this was, specifically, a horror movie about the Devil. It was Oedi-pal Bush, and not the neurotic-to-psychotic Gore, who filled and fulfilled the Devil role.

He seemed openly non-neurotic (or psychopathic) to the extent, for ex-ample, that there was no transference, no ghost, not the least shadow of an influence, conflicted or otherwise, passing from senior to junior. The first president Bush was a neurotic, specifically a war neurotic, whose trau-matic crash course in World War II went untreated but achieved sympto-matic simulcasting as the Gulf War. But the second Bush was uninhibited. His decision to finish his father's war for him just wasn't a problem. When it was age and era appropriate (in the 1980s), he was a partygoer, getting into and out of trouble as big as Texas. Born-again Christianity allegedly put a stop to that. Sure! He's so likable. He'd probably hug me. And why not? In retrospect Gore's zombie behavior betokened resistance to the Devil; it would have been easy to fake his suicide.

When it looks like Debby, too, committed suicide, Elizabeth fills in the blank: you can't believe all three girls killed themselves?! It's either a Hell of a coincidence or they're all rats in a maze. In losing Debby in spite of her best efforts, Elizabeth loses Martha again, too, but this time on her own turf of well wishes, which means that mourning or unmourn-ing can take over where the investigations will leave off. Now it's time for discoveries—and closure.

Somewhere between cult suicide and occult crossover, but with con-viction and certainty, Satan's schoolgirls follow the Devil father who takes them down in flames. Was it all a mistake, do they all just commit sui-cide after all? This moment of undecidability marks Devil fictions and fantasies in the Christian setting of faith: is it group suicide or entrance into a new supernatural (or evolutionarily mutational) form of existence?

In the end all but the three girls without parents (plus Elizabeth makes four) have joined the Clampett family, with Roberta at the front of the line. Elizabeth sits this one out. Dr. Clampett: "Eight of my girls died here. Now I've found eight to take their place, abandoned like them. I welcome what man rejects." "You don't believe that—that he's Satan!" "Tonight they will sacrifice their immortal souls and will return with me. Come with me willingly." Why should Elizabeth prove to be a joiner, unlike her dead sister? But then Satan hit on Martha also by mis-take: she wasn't alone in the world. Was the sibling relationship one of discord, the kind that located Elizabeth in a nice home while Martha had to stay away at school? The sibling bond of unmourning undoes Satan's best-laid plans. This is one of Satan's recurring miscalculations: he fixes his focus, hit or missing, on the child's relationship to parental—really, paternal—guidance, as the crack where he can get his foot or hoof in the door and work the black magic of substitution (or rebellion).

In two Devil films, *Fertilize the Blaspheming Bombshell* and *Constantine,* Satan and his minions try to replace or displace the dynamic between identical twins to make room for infernal victory. The first film opens with one twin driving in couple formation to visit the other twin, an anthropology professor. "Where's your sense of adventure?" "In a big soft bed in Vegas." Last call between twins. But the one lost in the desert mumbles the hard to recognize or remember name of the town. She's cut off before she can spell it out. The place name isn't even on the map. That's because it's the mirror reversal of "Satanville." Their car runs out of gas a few miles out of town. I guess the gas station attendant emptied the tank. "They didn't want us to get very far." Torch bearers in a row, row, row. Chanting. The boyfriend is set aflame and dropped off the cliff. "Lucifer! Hail!" High priest wearing ram's head rapes her. With this sacrifice they "promise to draw all the people of this land into all the evil that we can." The other twin feels long distance the pangs of the knife markings her sister endures. Next day the surviving twin is looking for her sister in the desert region known as "Devil's Playground." She soon finds the abandoned car and a scene marked by a burned pentagram, "a Satanic sign of evil," and by the broken crucifix left behind: "the symbol of sacrifice." "It's like Sandy's calling me from somewhere." She walks in on the Satanic service. "Come in my dear. We've been expecting you." Looks like it's going to be a repeat performance: even the victim to be sacrificed is last night's look-alike. "There is no God but Satan. Kneel, you impertinent slut!" "Fuck you!" "Yes, that's what you'll do until you bear Satan's offspring." Off to the pentagram they go, torches in a row. They get her goat. Toad's blood gives potency to fertilize the blaspheming slut. "Now you shall know the hardon of sin." She escapes. All the men's torches couldn't put him in her again. The Satanic monks keep chasing her and she keeps killing them, all of them.

Constantine lets roll three plot lines. The Spear of Destiny is circulating again; exorcist Constantine pulls a "soldier demon" out of a possessed girl ("We're finger puppets to them—but they can't come through!"); Angela, an LAPD officer, just knows that her twin sister, Isabel, did not kill herself. On the surveillance tape Isabel utters "Constantine!" before taking the plunge. Isabel was labeled psychotic: but she was clairvoyant. Angela represents the norm. "I don't believe in the Devil." "You should, he believes in you." That was Constantine, who is trying to reverse the Hell sentence he received when his own clairvoyance drove him to attempt suicide. Constantine discovers that Satan's son has his own plans. He needs a clairvoyant (Isabel or, it turns out, Angela), and he needs God's assistance (which the Spear supplies). By coming out as another clairvoyant, Angela admits her betrayal of Isabel and opens up prospects for mourning. The rebellion of the son was settled out of the father's court, in which we still find ourselves. Following the twin lines of mourning, Constantine asks that Isabel be released from Hell. In exchange he will go right away with Lucifer to keep his appointment in Hell. Done. But when it's time to go, Lucifer misses a beat, senses gravity in his feat, and thus must recognize defeat. The last wish granted Constantine on the dead twin's behalf amounted to self-sacrifice, which wiped the suicide slate clean. Lucifer removes the cancer and tar from Constantine's chain-smoked lungs to give him more time, in which to sin or sign again.

At the very end of *Satan's School for Girls*, when the Devil pops up, parting shot, as signature effect on the sidelines of the group burning (where he was last caught making the scene) before going up (again?) in smoke, he's smoking a cigarette. We know that he is supernaturally exempt from mortal limit (where the girls were most likely let off). But we also know that, by occupying the ready position to transgress and spite the NO in his smoking face, he's a teenager. When it's poof and he's gone, he leaves behind a smoking charred spot, like the burned ending of a cigarette, also known as the butt.

You need a neurotic-to-psychotic psyche, one that's inhibited, as in stuck on missing objects, to take the leap of faith called God or to cultivate more personalized occult relations with undeath. The psyche that signs up with the Devil is uninhibited and non-neurotic (or psychopathic passing as non-neurotic). One major proviso: while in all its purity Christianity undoes both death and life in order to secure eternity for one and all, most Christians smuggle into the afterlife an identifiable continuity shot dedicated to the ones they love and with whom they identify. The terrorism that indwells (the fine print of) Christianity's relationship to the dead is not the platform that (consciously) appeals to believers seeking shelter and comfort when death otherwise appears to have dominion.

Race with the Devil is a good example of the psychic difference distinguishing Satanists by process of elimination. A couple of neurotic couples must escape a vast network of Devil worshippers who fit right in with the Middle America of RV parks, Western-style saloons, swimming pools. The older couple (boss and the wife) has not reproduced; instead a younger couple has been adopted, not as progeny, but as a couple of doubles that help deny that there's a father along for the ride or race among them. The boss couple has acquired in the RV a self-contained world to maintain the fantasy of doubling where otherwise generations divide. The boss says: "We're self-contained, babe." That's right: a self-contained babe. When the boss discovers that the younger double of his couple brought the dog along, the self-containment already begins to crack: the dog will require pit stops that will interrupt the self-contained drive.

Skipping the father, the gap between generations, the couples enter a mode of automobility, of mobility of the *autos* or self, which is self-reflexively a trailer. A trailer advertises film in or as film. Like the projection of a medium that shares its origin with that of the printing press, the trailer or RV moves slowly like a new covered wagon entering and claiming new frontiers. Younger couple and older couple sitting in one RV, d - r - i - n - k - i - n - g. The boss is toasting getting toasted: "We pulled our lives together, we've made it. Here's to best friends." Do the neurotic math: It's really four couples. The girls hang together in the RV while the boys take the celebration outside. The buddy movie is in the foreground. But there's only one pair of binoculars. The guys take turns watching (through their shared pair of bi-noculars) the nude young women that fold out from what turns out to be a Satanic ritual. What a contrast between happy hours: the neurotic couples border on libidinal danger zones from the distance of drunken sentimentality; the Satanists observe ritual practices that demarcate, punctuate, and release unabashed ecstasy. But wait, they're knifing one of the nudes. Then the older wife opens the RV door and nags the boys to call it a night. She throws light on the witnesses to murder. Close the door! Too late. The sacrificial logic on this side is unexpressed, but it translates as: you stupid bitch, I could kill you. Lay the projective blame on the wife for turning the lights on them! And from that point fast forward the neurotically doubled couples must flee the Satanists, who by the end, just when the fourpack thinks it's safe now, burn, baby, burn them up in their self-contained RV. They become the sacrifice they interrupted.

While this study waits until the closing part and parting to give the inside view of film as Devil's medium, this much should be noted here in advance, as we advance, right here from the start, via fast clips of Devil fiction. Film that immerses itself in and then exceeds its self-reflexivity in order to include or release the violence it otherwise self-contains is infernal. Thus, Devil movies are most closely related in their special effect—violence—to the horror medium of slasher and splatter films, which moreover in the course of a given title's serialization or repetition compulsion regularly admits a Devil theme to come out in the watch of the ever-renewable Mass of murder.

Slasher films can prove traumatic. But they also harbor—at the latest in their recourse to repetitive remaking of the crime—therapeutic closure. Devil fiction parts company with the control release mechanism of slasher horror whereby the disconnection from the maternal mirror gaze, the ultimate horror in your face, can over time, in group or mass format, be consumed. Devil fiction digs instead the gaze of the primal father—which must indeed be dug up, by contrast and elimination, out from under its overlayering by the maternal spookulations disturbed or summoned whenever we touch on the canned violence of our mass-media culture. Devil fiction can provide, underneath it all, a form of radical stabilization, but this stripped-down submission to the father in our face or fate should not be confused with therapeutic reabsorption, redistribution, and controlled release of violence.

Devil fiction inhabits the medium of projection (where all the other occult fictions are at home) not in order to put an identifiable projection to rest but to reclaim for further use its metabolism before it contains or exhausts itself. In other words, there is a "creative" principle in projection to which Devil fiction addresses itself. As Freud laid it out along the bottom line (in *Beyond the Pleasure Principle*), what we call projection is our only possible *relationship* to inner over-stimuli, which, unlike external stimuli, cannot be met, on first contact, with a protective boundary. Thus, internal stimuli, which can convey traumatizing shocks in the breach, are automatically projected outward where, at one psychic or artificial but irreversible remove, they are framed by the external direction of our defense screening. The long and the shot of it is that Devil film knows it inhabits the loop of our intake and outtake of worlds of our own making. But to the uninhibited this knowledge is preamble to the how to rule it over others.

That's why Devil fictions adhere to the repress release of violence between or behind the headlines. When "Satan in German Literature and Beyond," at the time my new big course on campus, had its official school-year premiere in winter quarter 2001, a series of current events scored either a direct hit with the logic we were developing in class for the identification of, in, and with Devil fictions, or the kind of near miss that was just the same instructive. In first place was the case of David Attias, the eighteen-year-old freshman who during party time in the college student town of Isla Vista (right next to the UC Santa Barbara campus) ran down his fellow students in his revved-up car. Once his car was stopped in the tracks of impact, he jumped out and up and down among the dead, the dying, the hurt yelling, "This is the dark side" (Mozingo, "Witness"), "You deserved to die," and "I am the angel of death" (Mozingo, "Freshman"). The Thursday night before Death Drive, "Attias came to the room of Katie Brownstein, 18, down the hall. Brownstein said Attias told her he was a prophet who wanted to spread good through the world. He also spoke of God, the Devil, the supernatural, and said he was going to die" (Mozingo, "Freshman"). He was looking to void the void with certainty.

The automobile, the mobility of *autos*, of what in Greek spells "the self," was the move or movie David made to obtain a certain closure of imprisonment and set his relationship to his father in headlines over his own condemned (but contained) body and psyche. The Attias father was identified as film and TV director, who had directed episodes of *Ally McBeal*, *The Practice*, and *The Sopranos*. But his son, a film studies student, drove home the film he needed to see. In making this deadline, David hoped to reverse the Saab story that was his life. Apparently (and I want you to hear "parent" in this throwaway adverb of semblance) the father had threatened to repossess the Saab *autos* if his son did not agree to see a psychiatrist (instead of a counselor). Two fellow-student witnesses reported that David "had recently ranted about problems with his family" and, in particular, had "cursed his father" for the letter threatening removal of the *autos*. But the present tension between "Crazy Dave" (his nickname among peers) and his parents went way back: "A woman who said she often baby-sat for Attias in the early 1990s called the family warm and close, not 'a typical Hollywood family. I can't say enough good things about his parents,' Gina Longo, 40, said Tuesday. 'They were such a lovely family.' Longo added that David Attias was always jittery and that she found him difficult to deal with. 'They tried hard, but I think they were scared of him too,' she said of the family. 'They walked on eggshells. They had more than they could handle'" (Mozingo, "Parents").

In the Attias media event, the mother figured as uncontained and overflowing dump site. At the arraignment the father asked, on his better behalf, for forgiveness. "'On behalf of my wife I'd like to say how devastated and heartbroken we are for everyone affected by this horrible event,' he said, choking up. His wife clasped her mouth with a pained expression and cried" (Mozingo, "Parents"). You can see how David might have thought of himself, bottom line, as nothing or, on an upbeat, as mega destructive in his own rights. Attias was isolated at school, perhaps shunned. But then the Isla Vista in-crowd was forced to take notice: one witness remarked that Attias, whose "'eyes were wide open'" as he sparred with and shouted at bystanders, "'looked so ominous, even though he was so little'" (Mozingo, "Witness"). It was not his small man on campus standing that occupied or cathected the drive seat of his murderous acting out all the way to its external containment.

In the case of Charles Andrew Williams, who went on a shooting binge at Satan, I mean Santana, High School, the reactive rebound of his local reception—only bullies for him in Southern California (whereas back home in Maryland, in contrast, he enjoyed support)—cuts in before we can conclude that he danced with the Devil. If it's not already on the tip of our tongues, then let's cite it from *The Last Boy Scout*: the daughter's wordplay in seasonal homework, which already raised Hell at school, gets father's attention right before he discovers his wife's lover in the bedroom closet: "Satan Claus." What thus inhabits Santa should add fine print to the surname and designate the clause and clauses of the will (to evil).

The Charles Andrew Williams shoot was, however, a Dad reckoning, to the extent that his father, who had brought him west, at longer distance from the mother (the parents were divorced), had failed him. The move to California more than doubled the mother's own move with stepson to South Carolina, which Andy could only interpret as abandonment, but which all became the father's fault when he made his bigger move. Soon it was time to take stock. From day one in Southern Cal father and son were the local laughing stock—and soon the stock of a smoking gun. During this period of isolation in Satan, I mean Santee, all he could do was hope "to form a heavy metal band called Army of the Wicked" (Wride and Zamichow). But when he also hoped out loud to have gun, will punish tormentors, his bystander audience (soon to be captive) laughed off this tall order as another tall story. But he chose to begin the shoot inside the restroom and from there fired around the campus courtyard. He was finally cornered in the restroom where the shooting began. The boy known as Andy "surrendered meekly, just minutes after he fired his first shot, officials said. 'It's only me,' he told sheriff's deputies, who had been concerned that there might be a second gunman" (Gold, Ellingwood, and Reza). Every restroom is a paramilitary outfit organized around the containment of sexual difference. Andy's choice of this frame for his shoot at least does overlaps with some of the features and centers of the Devil fantasy. It is reported that he hated his Dad (Smolowe et al.). Shortly before the murderous incident Andy had broken up with his twelve-year-old girlfriend, a loss that, however it was cut, could only double the pressure on the fault line—the transmission of substitution—between son and father.

The case of Aleister Crowley serves as final opening demo for our course of study. Not because he was a Satanist. He wasn't, even though he included Devil worship within his polymorphous remix of paganisms. He was known as "the Beast," but only to the extent that his mother named him that but with a horror he effortlessly turned into a badge of honor. Already this reversal of the mother's horror movie points the way to Crowley's mascot status in the worship or study of the Devil. In *The Confessions of Aleister Crowley. An Autohagiography,* Crowley, writing down his early years in the third person, identifies himself as his father's son. This continuity shot could only come about after the fact of the father's death. This death was doubled or determined in line with the son's wish. On the night of the father's death, he was dreaming this same death. To fix the quality of this connection, he turns up the contrast with his mother's death. He keeps on dreaming that she's dead but she's still there. Eventually a dream death coincides with her passing. And this time, Crowley recalls, the dream had that special quality control he had sensed the one and only time he dreamed up the dead father. The mother's life or death position is uncontainable within the dream series; until, that is, the father's death is finally built up out of the repetition and catches up with the traumatic uncontrollability of the maternal body's presence and absence. Dad certainty originally gave Crowley first personal relations with himself, the world, his life, in evil. If there is, then, maternal, material resistance to this self-certainty, it is nonetheless described, spectacularly without any identification whatsoever on Crowley's part, as the bouncing, escaping fallout from his wishes, which he followed relentlessly until one day the mother, over and out, was subsumed within Dad certainty.

> In the case of Alick, he was the only son of a father who was naturally a leader of men. In him, therefore, this spirit grew unchecked. He knew no superior but his father. . . . In looking back over his life up to May 1886, he can find little consecution and practically no coherence in his recollections. But from that month onwards there is a change. It is as if the event which occurred at that time created a new faculty in his mind. A new factor had arisen and its name was death. . . . the boy— away at school—dreamed that his father was dead. There was no reason for this in the ordinary way. . . . The boy remembers the quality of the dream was entirely different from anything that he had known. . . . During the years that followed, the boy—and the man—dreamed repeatedly that his mother was dead; but on the day of her death he— then three thousand miles away—had the same dream, save that it differed from the others by possessing this peculiar indescribable but unmistakable quality that he remembered in connection with the death of his father. . . . From the moment of the [father's] funeral the boy's life entered on an entirely new phase. The change was radical. Within three weeks of his return to school he got into trouble for the first time. . . . Previous to the death of Edward Crowley, the recollections of his son . . . appear to him strangely impersonal. . . . It is only from this point that he begins to think of himself in the first person. From this point, however, he does so; and is able to continue this auto-hagiography in a more conventional style by speaking of himself as I. (52–53)

Even though "he was the only son of a father who was naturally a leader of men," who passes on to his son, "unchecked," "this spirit," Crowley also admits that this period is indeed checked and not resolved or integrated in the Oedipal mode of inheritance. It is a period in which, "in his recollections," "he can find little consecution and practically no coherence." A "new factor" or, indeed, "new faculty"—of death, of the father's death, that is, of the simultaneity of the son's dream of this death and its occurrence—gives Crowley the consequences of a pact with the Devil. This pact is not signed in the name of the third person—that impersonal check upon Crowley's spirit—but is dyadic in structure, in exchange. But unlike the dyad with the pre-Oedipal mother, which, sealed over and over again in vampirism, for example, via the recycling of blood, promises to extend life indefinitely, the pact relationship with the Devil father, which is signed with an excremental spot or scrap of otherwise wasted blood, grants a certain deadline and, in exchange, a finite quantity of quality time, time unhaunted by missing persons. As soon as the new faculty in his mind loses the Oedipal father, Crowley starts throwing the same fit with his mother, too, until he succeeds in shaking the hold of the missing body.

In Terence Fisher's *The Devil Rides Out* obedience to the Devil grants the followers a newly charged relationship to linear time. On certain dates, initiations or baptisms can take place. Grimoires bring about a "transference of souls" that allows all the characters to occupy interchangeable places—like doubles—not only in magic but also in time and thus in relation to the dead. At the right time sacrifice can act as transfer for the recently deceased, thereby gaining some more time for the deceased who comes back to complete the required number of celebrants at the Satanic gathering. The Satanic priest can even summon the ultimate embodiment of the deadline, the Angel of Death, who, even when repulsed by the Christians inside the holy circle, cannot go without a victim. In the end, time is completely reversed for those who have defeated the Devil: one victim even gets to start over where before she had died. The time line recoils now against the Satanic priest, who must fulfill the requirement that the Angel of Death can return only by making a deadline.

The opening crisis concerns a young man without his father who is captivated by Satanist McCarter (who calls him his "son"). The Satanist is modeled, in look if not in person, on the historical figure Aleister Crowley, whose pagan career was grounded, as we already witnessed, in the timing of his father's death. However, Crowley's one idea was his lazy-fair affirmation of human free will. These Luciferian aspirations are left out or covered over in the film's presentation of the Satanist as hypnotist with the power to impose a following in the tight spot of his wish, his command.

A friend of the young man's deceased father (who happens to be an accomplished Devil buster) comes to the rescue of the heir head. But after the first round has been won, one young girl is at risk and one young woman has died. Why were these two innocent bystanders not inside the protective circle? A neurotic offering up for sacrifice of two targets of mixed feelings that just had to be split off must still be reversed. In the meantime the Satanic group embraces blood sacrifice as the way to bring back Tanna, the young woman who died outside the Christian circle. When Tanna is brought back after all through the reversal of time and McCarter's substitution along for the ride of the Angel of Death, a surprise party for the faithful overtakes their former acceptance of her parting.

NOTEBOOK TWO

Dogs don't take to evil types. But the spooky lady looking for a bitch that has proved herself a breeder is as interested in dogs as is the local supplier for lab experimentation. The whining dog has to "stay" inside the pentagram. "One thousand years we've waited since you were chained to the gates of the bowels of the earth. We have followed the law. Send your seed! Send your beast!" Thus begins *Devil Dog*. One day the perfect couple is home from work, and Skipper lies dead in the road, hit and run. The children can't be comforted. Today is the daughter's birthday from Hell. "If something happened to me, would you say, just get another daughter?" The siblings go outside and meet a produce seller with a litter of puppies in the back of his van. Now the girl who couldn't get over it skips right over Skipper's loss and loves one of the puppies. "This is my best birthday ever." The ease with which Lucky slips into the empty space of Skipper is a Dad giveaway, especially when coupled with the natural antagonism between the new family dog and the Oedipal father. Lucky trains the children first. When they return to their rooms from the attic where they hold Satanic services, they find their mother picking up items or, in short, snooping around. "Leave our things alone and get out of here and forget all about it. I mean it!" But then they suddenly turn back into their more recognizable "Aw come on, Mom" typecasting. But mother tells her husband they need to talk about the children. Home alone with Lucky, the mother reads a magazine while she waits. Each time she looks up from the page, Lucky is noticeably slightly closer to where she sits, watching her. When her husband's home wanting to know what problems she's having with the kids, she brushes that off with the same hand that grabs him seductively. By the time the father notices that he's out of the loop, the fears he confides to the family doctor earn him a tranquilizer prescription. "It's as though an evil power has moved into my house. Betty is so cold—she's somebody else. There's been a conspiracy against me ever since we got the new dog." Doctor: "I believe you believe it." "It's not me—it's them, my wife, my kids, that dog." When the medical practitioner can't help, he turns to the local bookstore owner, who (of course! who else!?) knows all about the occult. "Hold a mirror to the sleeping person to see the true state of the soul." When he tries it out on his sleeping daughter, the one who swapped her fifteen minutes of loss for the best pet ever, he faces a reflection looking like Regan in *The Exorcist* after the long haul of possession. Finally he finds the shaman who knows how to draw the sign in his palm that can stop and stop up the demon dog's eye beam so the demon will be consumed by its own fire and go back to its master. When it's all over, the son, back in the Oedipal fold again, asks father to uphold the law to the litter: "There were ten pups in the litter—where do you suppose the other nine are?"

The Devil has two points of entry in Freud's science. He is along for the aside in which Freud, in your dreams, addresses philosophy and music. But then he also takes center stage when Freud analyzes cases of possession, in delusions and in dreams. Both frames of Devil reference already appear in *The Interpretation of Dreams*. In the chapter seven stretch of philosophical interrogation of reality, Freud makes reference to the Devil in Tartini's dream. The composer Tartini dreamed up the sale of his soul to the Devil, who, in this dream, then seized a violin and played the sonata the composer took back with him into the waking state. The Devil dream is an ornamental and parenthetical illustration dangling from the preceding paragraph in which precisely nothing was concluded about true reality: "The unconscious is the true psychical reality; *in its innermost nature it is as much unknown to us as the reality of the external world, and it is as incompletely presented by the data of consciousness as is the external world by the communications of our sense organs*" (*SE* 5: 613).

Freud's example of Devil dream possession in *The Interpretation of Dreams* is cited from the record of a nineteenth-century French pediatrician: the record shows a thirteen-year-old boy whose "sleep became disturbed and was interrupted almost once a week by severe attacks of anxiety accompanied by hallucinations":

> He always retained a very clear recollection of these dreams. He said that the Devil had shouted at him: "Now we've got you, now we've got you!"... He woke up from the dream in terror, and at first could not cry out. When he had found his voice he was clearly heard to say: "No, no, not me; I've not done anything!" or "Please not! I won't do it again!" or sometimes: "Albert never did that!" (*SE* 5: 585–86).

Freud interprets the dream delusion as, one, referring to masturbation in the past, interrupted by denial and threatened punishment; two, as responding in the present to increased temptation arising, arousing with the onset of adolescence; and, three, as reflecting the present tension, what Freud terms the "struggle for repression," which transforms the suppressed libido into anxiety, and thus presses it into the service of punishment. There is an audio portion on the record that emerges with the loss of the boy's voice, which, once regained, belongs, at least in one instance, to a third-person party. While he is afflicted by the Devil of a nightmare, the possession seems to intervene after the dream crisis, which is first alleviated by the takeover of the boy's voice by some other's voice.

Two items in the original record that Freud leaves out of his sexological interpretation help fill in the blanks drawn between one voice and that of the other. The boy's father makes an appearance in the hypothesis that "a past syphilitic infection in his father" (*SE* 5: 587) may have deposited in the boy's brain predisposition to mental illness. But the boy also describes how his nerves were overexcited to the point that he even contemplated the release afforded by "jumping out of the dormitory window" (*SE* 5: 586). This prospect of suicidal flight from the Devil, which the boy was able to counter and contain, is framed by an institutional inference that at age thirteen the boy was separated from his parents, including the father with the evil legacy to bear in his son's mind. When he was subsequently sent to the country, he was—given time and greater separation from parental guidance—completely cured. The boy thus went with the Devil down the fast lane of self-recovery.

Serial dreaming stuck in the groove of traumatic impact, evidence presented by accident and war neurotics, first guided Freud beyond the bottom line of wish fulfillment in his interpretation of dreams. Serial dreams introduce repetition as that which lies beyond or before the pleasure principle and represent the first and, last but not least, the entrenched attempt to build up a protective layer against mega-traumatizing stimuli. The compulsion to repeat opens up a new habitat for Devil reference in *Beyond the Pleasure Principle.* When the compulsion to repeat manifests itself in strict opposition to the pleasure principle, it assumes the aspect of a demonic force. "The manifestations of a compulsion to repeat (which we have described as occurring in the early activities of infantile mental life as well as among the events of psychoanalytic treatment) exhibit to a high degree an instinctual character and, when they act in opposition to the pleasure principle, give the appearance of some 'demonic' force at work" (*SE* 18: 35). This new focus can be fixed in and on the analytic session: "It may be presumed, too, that when people unfamiliar with analysis feel an obscure fear—a dread of rousing something that, so they feel, is better left sleeping—what they are afraid of at bottom is the emergence of this compulsion with its hint of possession by some 'demonic' power" (*SE* 18: 36). Once in analysis, this demonic force pops up within the transference as foreign body.

> In the case of a person in analysis, . . . the compulsion to repeat the events of his childhood in the transference evidently disregards the pleasure principle in every way. The patient behaves in a purely infantile fashion and thus shows us that the repressed memory-traces of his primaeval experiences are not present in him in a bound state and are indeed in a sense incapable of obeying the secondary process. It is to this fact of not being bound, moreover, that they owe their capacity for forming, in conjunction with the residues of the previous day, a wishful phantasy that emerges in a dream. This same compulsion to repeat frequently meets us as an obstacle to our treatment when at the end of an analysis we try to induce the patient to detach himself completely from his physician. (*SE* 18: 36)

Repetition compulsion or the demonic appears as a decontextualized and sealed-off momentum in the transference, in the in-session doubling of the duo dynamic that Freud found, at least at first contact, haunting. Transference raises ghosts between the two of you. It owes its metabolism to mourning. Hence the example Freud gives above of repetition compulsion preventing termination of analysis. Repetition compulsion in the transference raises Hell over a foreign body or antibody inaccessible to the transference dynamic of mourning (or unmourning). But it lends itself just the same to an attachment to a figure out of sight, to the side and behind you, who watches your back.

The publication date of Freud's "A Seventeenth-Century Demonological Neurosis" sets the case study deep inside the second system that opened up around *Beyond the Pleasure Principle*. We're thus given ears to hear what's in the name of the monastery where exorcism was performed not once, but twice. In its name, Mariazell places Mary, ambiguous figure of immaculate reproduction, alongside the single cell or *Zelle*. The subsidized mode of existence the painter finds in the end as alternative to the Devil pact still splits its share with the leader of the pact in relation to the *Zelle*, the monastery's social unit, but also in name the unicellular organism of replication that transmits the fantasy of body-based relations with father. Nine years of leader and the pact time equals, says Freud, nine months of pregnancy. To sign oneself over to your partner in pact, *sich verschreiben*, also means, same words, to make a mistake in writing, to commit a lapsus. It is in the phrasing of their contract that Freud discerns the fine print of their exchange: the painter vows to be the Devil's *leibeigener Sohn*. This can or should be translated as "bound son," as in duty-bound, beholden, or owned serf-style. Literally the modifier means "of one's own body."

According to Luther's counsel for a depressed friend, the Devil is a manipulator who uses syllogisms to tempt souls or psyches already depressed. The Devil "can make the oddest syllogisms: 'You have sinned. God is angry with sinners. Therefore despair!'" (275). Luther therefore counsels avoidance of the desperate state of being all alone with the letter of the law. Luther cites Moses for speaking of the upper and lower mill-stones of the teachings of law, which give us our daily grind. But from the New Testament perspective Luther can reverse the sentence and begin and end with the lower millstone, the gospel, which is quiet. Watch out when the Devil turns the gospel (back) into the law. But implicit in Luther's diagnostic criteria is the existence of cases of depression that are constitutively more open to the Devil's legal binding than to the gospel's genuine articles of faith and forgiveness. For these cases, to be grounded in the strictly legal bond with Father, taking it at word and to the letter, is far better than contemplating the leap of faith.

Rudolf Payer-Thurn first brought the materials on the painter Haitzmann's deal with the Devil to Freud's attention with the proposal that they collaborate on a study. But it's hard to cosign onto work with or on the Devil. Payer-Thurn published his own essay, "Faust in Mariazell," in a local Goethe club journal. Payer-Thurn sets out to account for the Catholic pageantry attending the closing "salvation" or "rescue" of Faust in Goethe—a foreign body in the Protestant tradition, story, or history of Dr. Faust, who was damned not saved—by following the pact element of the legend into its prehistory and settling down in and around the documentation of Haitzmann for a continuity shot at or as the explain-all of influence. On its own, however, the Haitzmann story remains a near miss: too Catholic by half. Payer-Thurn digs deeper in the archives of Mariazell to find the "bridge" that another Devil's client, about forty years after the release of Haitzmann, represents between the hyper-Protestant setting of the Faust legend and the Catholic culture of Maria-zell. This bridge case features a Protestant citizen who conjured the Devil in order to cut a deal that would give him nine years of fun and funding. This entry within the Mariazell archives turns up a contrast with the story of Haitzmann that reaffirms Freud's readings of the particulars of the painter's case. The Protestant conjurer, Krueger was his name, is forced to negotiate with a Devil who is loath to commit for nine years. The Devil agrees to five years, then seven, finally the nine requested. And yet the Devil never meant to observe these negotiated boundaries. Before the deadline the Devil, grown tired of the service, places his client at his disposal, flying him high and dropping him when he calls out "Jesus Maria." Krueger ends up with a broken body—but also a broken contract. In double recovery, then, he pledges conversion to Catholicism and then, once his health is restored, travels to Mariazell to renew his vows. The specialness of the offer of nine years is thus recorded. The offer of body and soul doesn't fly the literal standard of servitude as "same body." Let the record show that the pact was worded differently: according to Krueger's recall recorded in the archives he allowed: "I Johann Krueger sign *[unterschreibe]* myself with my own blood to give you as deposit my body and soul, for which you will serve me faithfully for nine years, after which time you can do with me what you will."

In the fifteenth century the couple of authors responsible for the *Malleus Maleficarum* hammered the same-body connection the witch's way, which makes small change in one gender, which we can discount, since the Devil is not a broad:

> Moreover it is useless to argue that any result of witchcraft may be a phantasy and unreal, because such a phantasy cannot be procured without resort to the power of the Devil, and it is necessary that there should be made a contract with the Devil, by which contract the witch truly and actually binds herself to be the servant of the Devil and devotes herself to the Devil, and this is not done in any dream or under any illusion, but she herself bodily and truly cooperates with, and conjoins herself to, the Devil. (Sprenger and Institoris, 7)

In *On the Nightmare* Ernest Jones concluded that if even the legends give incest as the principal ritual crime committed at Witches' Sabbaths, then the bottom line for the Inquisitioning mind (as in the tract above) that grounds all conjoining oneself (and not just herself) to the Devil is incestuous in significance (165–66).

In person the Devil gives us a certain father, a blood bonded father. The Latin phrase in the archival documents that gives time or cause for the painter's dealings with the Devil, *ex morte parentis*, refers to the death of his "parent." Freud translates "death of the father" and thus performs in short hand his interpretation. (On the displacement track, the *Standard Edition* of Freud replaces *Vatermord*, or "patricide," in the title of the Dostoyevsky essay with "parricide," the murder that results, of course, in ex-parents.) As Freud underscores in his reading of the seventeenth-century case of relations with the Devil, the painter receives no sensational benefits in exchange for his immortal soul but gets instead a paternal replacement for the parent he had lost: a bodily father, yes, a father with maternal attributes, but not subsumable by the mother, not this time, nor by her missing place. Even when pumped up with breasts, the Devil is still the father who alone can cancel the painter's adoption of the deferred obedience plan. The painter's difficulties in earning a livelihood following the death of his parent belatedly obey the father's veto of the son's wish to be an artist or, and it's never too late, administer punishment for the son's transgression. Exorcism of the Devil's hold over him, of a holding pattern that for a time served to stabilize the painter, leads, the second time around (and by doubling as the painter's initiation into a church order) to an artist's life in a culture of subvention, beginning with the immediate care given by the Church Fathers at the monastery named Mariazell.

According to Freud, the painter comes back for more exorcism treatment of yet another pact relationship because the Church Fathers let him go the first time around without making any referrals to support groups—for losers. Incapacitating depression could be deferred for the nine years of service to the Devil father in the form of some kind of low-maintenance adjustment disorder. The first exorcism, the missing half of treatment via pact or possession (Freud treats them as therapeutically interchangeable), shook free his lust for life. However, he's in no position (he's not having funds yet) to compete for booty with the young blades of more means. He's also living with his married sister in overstimulation city. Now it's holy figures that harass him while he has himself retrofitted for the transition from Devil father service to life with Church Fathers. What he gets with the second exorcism is the free gift of referral to his support grouping as member of a Church-fathered organization. It's not quite the same outfit that the holy visions extolled. But the exorcising Fathers at Mariazell caught the drift and assisted the painter in cutting his losses once more with renunciation or low maintenance.

Haitzmann's illustrations of his dealings with the Devil, which were painted during his second recovery at Mariazell, demonstrate a resurgence of investment and interest in his art (through which the Oedipal organization of depression following his parents' deaths had driven the stake). The pictorial supplement as working-through in the painter's case is left hanging in Freud's study. However, it is possible to suspend it via Hanns Sachs's review of Alfred Kubin's 1909 novel *The Other Side.* Sachs identifies the work, which the author in fact dedicated to his deceased father, as mourning over a loss that doubled as the loss at which he was with painting, his main medium, the mother of his media. Once the literary work was completed, he could again pick up or feel the brush of painting—as demonstrated by the illustrations with which he supplemented the novel.

Kubin first met his father when he was a two-year-old; the father's military service caused this delay that announced his interruptus of the dyad right on schedule but also without prep work. He met his father for the first time in Salzburg, which is where the protagonist of *The Other Side* met his friend Pateras (= pater), who enjoins him to emigrate with his wife to the utopian community of Pateras's own making in Asia. "Dream City" is assembled entirely out of collectibles dating to the 1860s, the era in which Kubin's parents wed. The protagonist, Kubin's representative in this work of metabolization and interpretation, is married in the 1860s to a woman who dies, like Kubin's own mother, of TB (or not) before her time, the time of acceptance. This (double) loss is anticipated but pushed back—over and again cheated as close call—until its excruciating staggering or staging proves unbearable. Once she's dead, the fresh widower represses as such what the melodrama of leave-taking had also displaced: that night, under the roof of a concerned neighbor, he sleeps with his host's "demonic" wife.

For the artist protagonist, who makes up his mind to renew relations with this friend and accept his phantastic offer of citizenship in the Dream State while perusing his photograph, relations with Pateras are close up and up close—but also, at the same time, long distant. Pateras is in a sense already the dead father and ancestral spirit. He comes alive—as object that can be lost—in his all-out conflict with "the American," the showdown that concludes the protagonist's survival of "the other side." Sachs closely follows Jones's reading of the Devil (in *On the Nightmare*) when he notes the fluid exchange between father and son identifications in their demonic merger and murders. The American makes his exit as the atrophying appendage of his member, which sloughs the body of its attribution while slithering away as snake. There is, just the same, something chthonic and maternal-medusoid about this body, which the father-and-son relationship circumscribes as off-limits via the diversion of castration and Oedipal rivalry/desire from pre-Oedipal regression or embodiment. This spot of "pater" 's overdetermination is marked by a certain "Uhrbann," a towering structure that pronounces a "ban" that bears a "clock" *(Uhr)* in earshot of time that is "primal" *(Ur)*. The cock tower has his and hers entrances and chambers. In his chamber the protagonist learns to stare at the wall right in front of him over which water flows ceaselessly and announce: "Here I stand before you!" Then it's time to exit again. The central ritual of the dream society is performed regularly at certain times. This excremental or urinal impression is marked as repressed—as pointlessly or senselessly determined—via the ban, which renders the ritual compatible with neurotic obsessive-compulsive behavior. The love that Kubin works through to "the other side," that of his and hers outlets, is identified in the closing paragraph as, bottom line, immersed in toilets and latrines.

The Devil's first appearance to Haitzmann is as the kindly paternal figure of a middle-aged gentleman accompanied by his dog, the *Hund* that in German is just the aspirated version of *und*, the "and" of connection and belonging. A dog is also always the representative of our outgrown and discarded nose to the ground, to the anus. (Mephistopheles pops up out of the poodle that followed Faust home. He undergoes the transformation at or as the end of Faust's free translation of *logos*, after four tries, as "act" or "deed," both in the sense of push-button performative immediacy and, as it turns out, as deed of writing and purchase.) The subsequent Devil appearances or apparitions, which mix up gender traits and mythological references (and which Freud interprets in the Oedipal terms of feminization and castration), evidence metabolization of the significance of the father down regression tracks all the way to pre-Oedipal parenting. At the same time it is important to emphasize that these visions do not accompany the nine years of same-body sonhood the painter apparently received in exchange for signing up.

Wilhelm Hauff's excerpts from Satan's memoirs—*Mitteilungen aus den Memoiren des Satan*—ended up reformulating the Faustian prospect of the second time around with the pact in terms of doubling of names. When the first volume appeared in 1825, the author's name was given as xxxxf. Like the extension of quality time into doubled but finite lifetime that one obtains from the Devil, this name gives a small crowd of signatory placeholders that is extended once over, rather than indefinitely, as in ff. The second volume appeared under Hauff's proper name. (The first volume, however, was the only one of his books to be reprinted in his own lifetime.)

When we first encounter the internal author of these memoirs, Herr von Natas, he is hosting a reception for which he has selected the music. While the music plays, Natas observes his guests. Later he analyzes each one of them—their "inclinations and drives"—based quite simply on his observation of how he or she listened to which piece of music. In the meantime, each person in attendance is convinced that he or she knew the same man, only years earlier in some other place under another name. Soon this sense of already knowing Natas takes the downward turn of widespread belief that he had wronged them one and all. The spell is interrupted when one of them spells the name backwards: Satan (358).

Natas or Satan and the narrator establish contact in an exchange about the state of letters. The narrator admits that he has published some work, but not in his own writing: he translated certain "immortal works of foreign nations for the dear German public" (361):

> He praised my modest resignation, as he called it, and asked me whether I might agree to translate [*zu übersetzen*] the memoirs of a famous man, which have been available to date only as manuscript? Assuming that you can decipher, it would be an easy task for you, as

> I would give you the key to it and the manuscript is composed in good
> German. (362)

Though earmarked earlier in the narrative for the circulation of immortal works or words, Satan extends "translation" to cover the decipher-
ment of his encoded messages.

The labor of decryptment soon makes our translator or editor fear
for his senses as though beset by unwitting incantations.

> Who could guarantee, however, that these written traces would not
> creep through my eyes into my mind and drive me mad; and couldn't
> I be inscribing myself unconsciously into his service *[seine Leibeigen-
> schaft]* precisely through the act of deciphering and copying out Satan's
> words? (363)

However, he soon discovers no haunting effects in the papers and nothing spooking in his proximity since commencing the decryptment on
Monday.

Thanks for the memoirs upon memoirs it appears that that's all the
Germans wrote for the last twelve years. In the corner of every "I was
there" documentary of German letters: Satan or Natas was there. He
bumps into E. T. A. Hoffmann. After they bump along, Natas tells his
editor, decoder, or translator—in short, the narrator—that he introduced
the special doubling effects that got Hoffmann going. He visits various
gatherings of men of letters with the Wandering Jew. Later on Natas and
narrator visit Goethe. Natas is a Goethe fan, even though he's still pissed
about his portrait as Mephistopheles (440). When they prepare to leave,
Goethe extends an invitation to Natas to return soon. Natas jokingly ponders that Goethe thus summons the Devil. *Zitieren,* which means to cite
text as well as summon guests, ghosts, demons, or the Devil, is the verb
that skewers the Goethe standing invitation on top of all the other literary encounters inside the work and up above in the vicinity of Hauff's
proper name. When literary life isn't being cited, sighted, sited between
autobiography and fiction, tall tales of protagonists, who are doubles, lay
out lives cite-specifically in literature only. A quote from Jean Paul fills
in for Natas's inability to describe a love scene. *Don Quixote* keeps doing

double time. But what alone is continued at length in or as volume two is the second trend, which culminates in a symposium in Purgatory where delegates of European cultures relate their literature-conditioned autobiographies.

The time between volumes one and two, the time of Hauff's unnamed success and anticipated continued success, is fictionalized as legal dispute stuck on the name of the author and subject of these memoirs. The name Devil, or *Teufel,* is credited by the court with being an identifiable subject's family name: Satan, however, can only be an arbitrary name, since no one is allowed to carry two names (469). Did Hauff, like Faust, seek to sign up, via the Devil's memoirs, for more life (of the rich and famous), finite but doubled life (f rather than ff)? He achieved this wish with the first volume's second printing. But his turn to a second volume or second pact, this one in his own name (ff), released Hauff from the Devil's service.

In *Asylum of Satan* the Devil does not accept Dr. Specter's offer of the neurotic virgin songstress in exchange for his own "continued eternal life." Dr. Specter sacrificed various clients who came to him for miracle cures, the woman who can't walk and the blind woman to insects and reptiles, respectively and respectfully, as promised. The Devil shows up for the final service. Dr. Specter has kept his little pretty under lock and key and had her virgin status checked on regularly. To keep the watch hands-on but not too obvious, he impersonates his own female assistant, Martine, who praises, in German accent, Lucina's soft white flesh unblemished by sin (while gliding blood-red nails down her back). Dr. Specter is at the end of his once-already renewed life span. His second contact or contract, which asks not just for more life, but for continued eternal life, releases him from his infernal bond. The Devil isn't interested in the internal or eternal dimension of immortality neurosis. Twice is enough.

In her study of the development of psychoanalysis out of exorcism, Monique Schneider contemplates the revue of guises the Devil assumes in relation to the painter, from benign father transference to "mythological" phantasm. "The order of succession of the diverse forms follows the inverse order of that which, according to Freud, one encounters in the course of the psychoanalytic cure" (15). But her reservation is confirmed when she compares this lineup with what is described in the documentation of the mass possession of nuns in Loudun. In particular, the metamorphoses Grandier undergoes as Devil prove the exception to the therapeutic order to be the rule in this occult genre (59). This inversion characterizes Freud's shifting analogization of psychoanalysis with different functions of this genre. Freud shifts between recognition of the affinity of his science with exorcism, even with the interventions of the Inquisition, and insistence on the importance of the Devil's psychotherapy, the intervention that precedes the proper therapy of exorcism. In addition to an official power of purification and elimination, there is an occult power surge whereby all the aspects of the vision that were interdicted return and regroup (24–25). This metabolic process lies at the center of both the possession and the therapy supposed to put an end to it—and it corresponds to a pivotal function in the interior of the psychoanalytic cure (27).

The relationship to the Devil is, for Haitzmann, a phase in his work of mourning or unmourning that proceeds in fits and starts, starting overs, never rising to the issue of substitution whether as mourning or in the Devil's name. He opts for a low-maintenance life in subvention, a refunctionalized variation on inhibition or fixation. At the remove of the protagonist's removal from the list of prospective Devil clients the medium of projection nevertheless introduces dying for nothing or for sure as the medium's limit concept or turning point for its revaluation.

In *End of Days* the Devil must couple with his designated bride (when she was born in 1979, the Pope decreed that the Devil's baby boomer must be protected, not destroyed). In the end, as the millennium countdown is about to begin, the security guard who is protecting the chosen woman is the Devil's last chance to corporealize and copulate. But this man, we know, is haunted by the deaths of his wife and child. In the beginning of the film he's about to kill himself. His suicide gets deferred for the duration of the film. Even when the Devil takes possession of him, he is able to resist for the time it takes for the woman to run away and for him to impale himself on the sword of a sculpted warrior (on the point at the end of the sentence suicide hands down to its deferral). In his Devil-possessed voice, as he began to mount the bride, the guard called out to the altar painting of the crucifixion: "You died for nothing!" But if the guard remembers himself and stops the Devil inside him, it is because he is not going to die for nothing. What flashes before his dying eyes are the ghostly figures of wife and child come back for him. He gets the afterlife of immortal souls and family reunion. But what he in fact sees are the ghosts that all long haunted him and that made him the least likely candidate for the Devil's same-body bonding in Dad certainty. My favorite postcard find all my days in Santa Barbara displayed sunset on the beach with a logo that I'm sure, Dad sure, was supposed to caption the image as "Day's End in Santa Barbara." However, someone left out one diacritical mark, and it proclaimed instead: "Days End in Santa Barbara." During the big fire in the 1980s I remember someone describing Santa Barbara as "paradise in Hell."

NOTEBOOK THREE

In a letter dated June 18, 1911, Freud comments to Oskar Pfister on the interpretation the latter gave of a young man's vision or hallucination of the Devil. As recycled in his 1927 study *Religious Studies and Psychoanalysis (Religionswissenschaft und Psychoanalyse)*, Pfister recounts (12–13) how his patient, as teenager, had been drawn while on his way home to gaze upon a mighty oak. Suddenly a large dark figure stepped toward him from behind the tree. The figure "rubbed his hands against me, as though wanting to wash them. At the same time I heard a clap of thunder." He was rooted to the spot. Finally he ran away horrified. After a few questions, we discover that this naked Devil with dark kinky hair resembled his worst enemy at that time. His foe spread the rumor that he had impregnated a local girl. The scandal was resolved in Pfister's patient's favor through the intercession of his own father. A physician was asked to examine the girl in question. The physician certified that she was "pure." For libel, the kinky-haired kid had to pay a fine. One more detail comes up at the end of the questioning: the Devil's nose was not that of his enemy (his was "significantly larger") but rather had the "remarkably small nose" of the pure girl. Pfister interprets the Devil incarnation of the patient's foe as violent wish that his enemy be turned into a demon, humbled in the nude, rubbing hands that he could never wash clean, wearing the nose of the girl he defamed. Freud: "That the Devil carries the nose of the innocent young girl in his face 'as visible sign of his libel,' is probably too tame and too unified an interpretation." It's way more likely that out of conflicting thoughts or wishes this vision emerged with certain features having gained in the struggle the upper hand. "Then the Devil would be a hybrid figure; he is really also the girl, and his nudity can be better explained as means of seduction than as, on the other side, the sign of his humiliation." It would be hard to comprehend, Freud argues, how the Devil would be punished by the acquisition of a nose that is surely attractive. The interchangeability of nose and genitalia would help explain why the girl's nose appears on the (naked) Devil's face. Freud stops short here, suggesting to Pfister that he hasn't yet interpreted the boy's vision and that his treatment would benefit from careful indication of the "probabilities" influencing this representation of the Devil.

Who desired the pure girl? She was still a virgin. The bully plainly found her attractive enough to use in his defamation of the boy's own purity. The kinky-haired guy is the sexual figure here, in the buff. He is joined, between or behind the lines, by the boy's father. Was it a pure privilege and honor for father figures (I'm including the doctor and the magistrate) to discover that the boy simply couldn't have impregnated the girl? The illicit makeup of the bully as Devil, as creator in the medium of excrement, tracks back to an early reception of the father as holder of the monopoly in sexual penetration, and advances through the intermediary figure of the girl with whom the boy identifies. The Devil father and bully acquire the pure nose or genitalia by entering the boy/girl from behind: the nose is the sign that he wasn't just passing through but parked instead in the rear.

The Brotherhood II. Young Warlocks takes us to the back lot of a Calvin Klein underwear shoot and calls it a private school campus. The survivor of contact with the Devil's agent is the narrator, who is needed, right from the start, to introduce us to the different cliques on campus, the in and the out groups. The narrator plus two equals the rebel group that fits in neither with the authorities nor with the in-group (jocks and their groupies). The jock group rules outsiders (notably the rebels) by maintaining relations of uncertainty. Is seemingly benign contact with a jock at any given time a neutral gear in everyday life or another setup on the way to the out-group member's humiliation? One of the rebels has started jogging, not to make a statement or put on a show (as in the case of the jocks he runs into) but as a move toward recovery (he needs to quit smoking). The jocks praise him, set him above and apart from his loser associates. They include him in their pack run and finish with him right down the line through the locker to the showers. Acceptance? Initiation? "What's that?" It's a permanent marker. He's the fall guy after all. The jocks surround him like in some prison rape scene. The leader proposes writing "my pussy" over the smoker's butt (the leader is kneeling face level with the rebel buns). But then the new guy on campus intervenes. The jocks are humiliated, and the rebel, saved, rushes back to get his two friends to come with him to meet what a great guy. They meet by the pool. Soon they're frolicking in the water, passing around a jug of alcohol. The new guy introduces himself as Devil's agent. "I'm a student of the soul. You all have something in common — you want something you can't have. I can help out." He can make them all local stars. They just have to break the Ten Commandments. Even murder? Symbolic murder, of course. To seal the deal they must taste their agent's tears. "You drink tears, your mind opens up." The pool scene gives support, certainty — in contrast to the shower scene of initiation into sexual difference as permanent marking, torment, and secret pleasure. Rather than the rip and tear of castration that we were invited to imagine shoved up the young man's asshole, the three are offered tears, the outpouring of benign excremental communion.

Christianity and the Devil, in it together, help Wolfman overcome his desire to surrender to his big bad but beloved father, the potent corporeal figure and pathogenic force of sexuality in his immediate family. Little Wolfman's seduction by his sister carries out at one remove the paternal p-unitive trauma, love it or live it. He took care to breathe in the Holy Spirit but always to breathe out evil spirits. The breathing-out exercise was also required whenever he saw any figures he would not like to be like. These "beggars, or cripples, or ugly, old, or wretched-looking people" (*SE* 17: 67) followed the downbeat of how he saw his father. But heavy breathing, hot off the audio track of the primal scene, was also a resource for positive identification of or with the father. In

neurotic disorders affecting breathing, for example, some early representation of digestion is responsible for anxieties about taking in something
toxic or losing something good when breathing in and out. The passageways of air intake and outtake and the digestive tract passing right
through you remain the vulnerable points of our most direct contact
with the world.

But then one day, a German tutor changed the frame of the teen's
demonizations and idealizations when he introduced his charge to the
freethinking stance at attention. The military thus came to uniform Wolfman's teen spirit. But the breathing rituals weren't stopped in these marching steps. And whenever Wolfman saw three heaps of dung, he still had
to think of the Holy Trinity. A caterpillar dream Freud interprets recalls
the tutor's influence: he had helped Wolfman overcome his sadism toward small animals. But this brings back, at least in Freud's narrative,
recollection of one Devil of a dream. Even while this dream is assigned
to the period before the tutor's influence, it is nevertheless brought back
in association with the tutor. And it is brought back to be exorcised
within the analysis, and within the analytic and transferential relationship to Freud. The German tutor's influence is responsible for Wolfman's
fond rapport with all things German, and that's a fact, Freud adds, "which
was incidentally of great advantage to the transference during the treatment" (SE 17: 69). In the earlier dream the Devil was pointing to a gigantic snail, image of childhood sexual research. Based on popularized high-
cultural reference to the Devil (a composite of the poem "The Demon"
by Lermontov, a poet prized by Wolfman's sister, and of a popular picture representing the Demon in a love scene [SE 17: 69]), Wolfman's
dream representation includes the father's (and his own) idealization
of the daughter/sister, whose accomplishments were read off the legend
of the middlebrow map of high culture. This Devil father furthermore
promises the complete answer withheld from the little boy when he was
witness to the primal scene. The sister in the Devil father is on her role as
transmitter of the father's influence or seduction and as intercessor between father and son, whereby she took the brunt of the grunting father.

"When he heard that Christ had once cast out some evil spirits into a herd of swine which then rushed down a precipice, he thought of how his sister in the earliest years of her childhood, before he could remember, had rolled down on to the beach from the cliff-path above the harbor" (*SE* 17: 67). The later caterpillar dream, the one that brought back, by contrast and association, the Devil and the snail dream, benefits from the switch from passivity to activity (in a military setting).

But then Wolfman remembers the waking experience of riding by a father asleep with his son in the fields. The son wakes his father, who shouts at Wolfman as though his look at them was illicit, improper. The passive, feminine, or homosexual submission to the father had, then, really only been repressed. His psychoanalysis gave Wolfman access to this repressed portion of his libido, each piece of which upon being set free sought out some sublimated goal or concern. But the tutorial in father-and-sonhood taken with Freud is the cover for his continued service to, for, as his undead sister. The Devil represented the father as blocked for Wolfman by his sister. He was the contained, certain father. But the complications in the Wolfman case, which lie in his relations with his sister, cannot contain themselves in the father. Schreber occupies through his older brother, who like Wolfman's older sister committed suicide, the same uncontained projection booth of idealization and demonization with regard to his own father, the mad scientist who experimented on his sons. Just the same the Wolfman case shows how the fantasy of the certain father refers to a pre-Oedipal father, the father who holds the primally abusive monopoly of sexual difference (or, simply, of sex). At the time of the third person's first interruption of the dyad, there is only one "difference," and it belongs to the father. Little boy, little girl, and mother can only offer a back end deal to obtain, sure thing, the father's penetrating certitude.

In *Omen III (The Final Conflict)* we catch Damien in the act of father worship (he welcomes the coming "paradise of pain") in the private parts of his residence. He climbs stairs but in a sense descends into an underworld crypt just beneath a white abstract observatory orb (with its crack down the middle). What opens up as long-distance vision is the techno sublimation of the lower bodily senses and orifices. In the secret chapel the idol of the crucified Nazarene is in reverse, backside showing. Damien, born of Jackal and not of man, that is, woman (specifically, "the gaping wound of woman"), embraces the Christ figure whose back is turned toward him and squeezes the crown of thorns until red juices begin to flow. He excrementalizes the Christ figure in his performance of the rear view of the crucifixion.

It's lonely as a top, I mean at the top, especially when you're son of Satan (in *Damien: Omen II*). Damien and his stepparents watch an old movie in their home theater. Mark, Damien's closest friend, is manning the projector. When the film flickers, Damien jokingly admonishes the "projectionist." Mark: "Drop dead." While rewinding the film in the family projection booth, Mark overhears when one of the good citizens in league against Damien confronts the stepfather—the brother of Damien's first "father," who was shot just as he was about to put a ritual end to the boy—the truth about his (and his dead brother's) stepson. Stepfather Thorn is still protesting these charges but not Mark. A projective tension in his relations with Damien is pressing the panic button. In bed he reads the Bible. The next morning Mark goes off for a walk. Damien follows. "Why are you running away from me, Mark?" "I know who you are." "I love you Mark. You're like my brother. You are my brother." "The Beast doesn't have a brother." "Come with me Mark, I can take you with me. Look at me, Mark. Please come with me." Mark dies of some internal attack while Damien is caught between faking and revealing pain.

The Devil father excludes no outlet from his multipronged dong of penetration. While Devil clients must be nonphobic about the risk, under orgy conditions, of contributing a span of lifetime to or through reproduction or of engaging in homosexual acts, they are otherwise Devil-Dad set against both reproduction (as the Christian couple's proof of purpose) and homosexuality (because it is a crystallization of inhibition that restricts, on averages, the range of a client's influence over others). In *Satan's Children*, for example, Bobby is the ambiguously placed boy in a stepfamily where the tyrant father treats him as cinder-fella while his stepsister delights in his humiliation. When he runs away from home, he runs right into a club of shit kickers who treat him to anal rape. Before he is discovered on the border of Satan's summer camp, we listen in on two girls arguing about lesbianism. One just can't help herself. The other, Sherry, warns her to start trying to like guys before Simon finds out she's a samer. While Simon, Satan's representative at camp, is away, Sherry maintains discipline in the breach she opens when she falls for Bobby. Joshua challenges her: even if Bobby was raped, that just makes it worse; the master doesn't like victims. But when Simon himself challenges Bobby as loser, it proves to be a paradoxical intervention. Surely, Simon says, Bobby is just the type who likes to turn the other cheek. But then Bobby stops feeling sorry for himself and takes revenge: he executes the rapists, puts his father in his former place, and turns his stepsister into his fuck dolly (she folds up nice and neat in the backseat of the car). Bobby proves Joshua wrong. While Bobby and Sherry are getting it on, we intercut to the scene of the lesbian's crucifixion.

Wolfman's double Devil dream precedes the section on "Anal Eroticism and the Castration Complex," in which Freud spells out the smear tactics of certitude. It begins with the in-session duo dynamic, with a form of resistance that in German embraces the sense of "two" *(zwei)*, namely *Zweifel* ("doubt").

We know how important doubt is to the physician who is analyzing an obsessional neurosis. It is the patient's strongest weapon, the favorite expedient of his resistance. This same doubt enabled our patient to lie entrenched behind a respectful indifference and to allow the efforts of the treatment to slip past him for years together. Nothing changed, and there was no way of convincing him. At last I recognized the importance of the intestinal trouble for my purposes; it represented the small trait of hysteria which is regularly to be found at the root of an obsessional neurosis. I promised the patient a complete recovery of his intestinal activity, and by means of this promise made his incredulity manifest. I then had the satisfaction of seeing his doubt dwindle away, as in the course of the work his bowel began, like a hysterically affected organ, to "join in the conversation," and in a few weeks' time recovered its normal functions after their long impairment. (*SE* 17: 75–76).

Thus Freud establishes contact with Wolfman through the anal underworld and gets the patient to address him on transferential turf as old fart, the father as farter. Wolfman's gastration complex was indeed established early on. The bottom symptom layer belongs to a shameful and depressed identification with his mother, which replaced what had been just the year before his open and happy defiance expressed by the mess he would make whenever he and his beloved Nanya had to share the bedroom of the obnoxious English governess. "A year later (when he was four and a half), during the anxiety period, he happened to make a mess in his knickerbockers in the daytime. He was terribly ashamed of himself, and as he was being cleaned he moaned that he could not go on living like that. So that in the meantime something had changed; and by following up his lament we came upon the traces of this something. It turned out that the words 'he could not go on living like that' were repeated from someone else" (*SE* 17: 76). It was his mother who had complained of her own sickness in these words to the doctor, "without imagining that the child whose hand she was holding would keep them in his memory" (77).

The identification with the mother is the legacy of the primal scene that established Father as public enema number one: "Under the influence of the primal scene he came to the conclusion that his mother had been made ill by what his father had done to her; and his dread of having blood in his stool, of being as ill as his mother, was his repudiation of being identified with her in this sexual scene. . . . But the dread was also proof that in his later elaboration of the primal scene he had put himself in his mother's place and had envied her this relation with his father. The organ by which his identification with women, his passive homosexual attitude to men, was able to express itself was the anal zone. The disorders in the function of this zone had acquired the significance of feminine impulses of tenderness, and they retained it during the later illness as well" (78).

His initiation into the realities of sexual difference couldn't unblock his primal inside view of the sexual relation. The sister who seduced him (and thus repeated, according to Nicolas Abraham and Maria Torok, the fondling that the father had encouraged her to perform on his person) represents both the new order of sexual difference (between siblings) and the old order of father's controlling interest in sexual difference (if only to the extent that as the father's favorite everything coming from her was from the father passing through her). "He rejected what was new... and clung fast to what was old. He decided in favor of the intestine against the vagina, just as, for similar motives, he later on took his father's side against God. He rejected the new information and clung to the old theory. The latter must have provided the material for his identification with women, which made its appearance later as a dread of death in connection with the bowels, and for his first religious scruples, about whether Christ had had a behind, and so on. It is not that his new insight remained without any effect; quite the reverse" (79).

Like his doubting or doubling patient, Freud only now admits "that one portion of the content of the primal scene has been kept back." He's been holding the portion back but can now allow it to enter into the conversation: "The child finally interrupted his parents' intercourse by passing a stool, which gave him an excuse for screaming" (80). Moving from the specifics to the generic, Freud explores the medium and significance of fecal matter (mater):

> At the same time, like every other child, he was making use of the content of the intestines in one of its earliest and most primitive meanings. Feces are the child's first gift, the first sacrifice on behalf of his affection, a portion of his own body which he is ready to part with, but only for the sake of some one he loves. To use feces as an expression of defiance, as our patient did against the governess when he was three and a half, is merely to turn this earlier "gift" meaning into the negative.... At a later stage of sexual development feces take on the meaning of a baby. For babies, like feces, are born through the anus. The "gift" meaning of feces readily admits of this transformation. It is a

common usage to speak of a baby as a "gift." The more frequent expression is that the woman has "given" the man a baby; but in the usage of the unconscious equal attention is justly paid to the other aspect of the relation, namely, to the woman having "received" [in German "conceived" and "received" are the same word] the baby as gift from the man. The meaning of feces as money branches off from the "gift" meaning in another direction. (82)

The pre-Oedipal father is the agent of the anal theory of birth. The young child accepts this theory as certain. Soon anal babies come rapidly down its assembly line. To comprehend the true nature of reproductive relations would require—or will require—a leap of faith. The anal-theoretical reservations about the true theory of birth are confirmed by acts of finite doubling, like cloning, or like the specifically demonic way in which one obtains one more lifetime in exchange for the sacrifice of the embodied life of one victim. To possess a body, demons or the Devil must enter the body from behind to save face or, rather, recycle it.

In *The Brotherhood of Satan* the designated coven struggles to double finite lifetimes, passing finite quality time with certain deadline as torch, not the internal kind flaming with mourning, but from sacrificed generation to the doubled continuity shot. A nuclear family passes through an indefinite relay of flashbacks, not necessarily their own, until they discover the children are needed to complete the required number of thirteen that will replace the oldies. Is it possible to bridge the two worlds? Followers hope that life will be renewed in Satan. "Enter for yet another lifetime—in the brotherhood of Satan." At that point, at the latest, we as viewers of the film, as inhabitants of familiar flashbacks, as believers in our own immortality at the sacrificial expense of the oldies, have been welcomed, too.

In his 1908 reflections on character formation based on anal eroticism, Freud notes how Devil's gold turns to shit. The Devil is linked through anal relations specifically to sexual curiosity. That's why the Devil digs the contents of the bowels of mother earth. For the Devil as for his followers and clients, the excavation is not about the dead or undead. The cutting edge of anal, diabolical curiosity is specifically sadistic rather than largely melancholic. At the society meeting of March 4, 1908, Freud referred to the case of a young man whose excessive kindness was aimed at undoing the fact of life that at age five he concluded a pact with the Devil whereupon he performed all kinds of sadistic acts. The cut of sadism, the cut of curiosity, is not the cut of loss. It belongs to the great health of childhood. Let us take literally Freud's analogy (in "Analysis Terminable and Interminable") between the way in which children resist or disbelieve in the true story of reproduction, even or especially after it has been revealed to them, and the tendency of the heathen to go back to their idols after Christianity was first imposed on them.

NOTEBOOK FOUR

In 1933 Karl Kraus composed *Third Walpurgis Night,* the third strike of a match with Goethe's two Walpurgis nights in *Faust* I and II, and he was out of satire. His practice, which peaked around the First World War, was to slip the bloody reference that the journalistic phrase openly hid and bracketed out back into circulation between or behind the lines of satire, which, as lines given in art or fiction, were automatically granted a more open and less defended span of attention. Once swallowed and its provenance revealed, this one bit of coverage stuck there, a catch in the throat, the catch to the insurance policy the press takes out against the shock of the news. Now you don't see it, now you gag on it. Hitler's rise to power raised mediated language to the power of murder machine. There was no longer any gap or overlap into which Kraus could insert his surprise interventions. But he writes just the same, picks apart the Nazi screed in newspapers, if only to demonstrate that he is not pleased with his predictive powers nor convinced that one can arrest history on the laurels of proven prophecy.

In *The Case of California* I argued that the West Coast was the toast of all reunions of the legacies of "Germany," California's other coast, the other "Back East." Much of this argument concerned the era of German exiles on Main Street, California, their psychoanalytic and sociological influence, in particular on what the critical record could show with regard to California's own "culture industry." Bringing this discursive coupling into the present—and staging it as forced marriage—I even suggested that there was a symptomatic relationship of displacement between the fall of the Berlin wall and the rising up of a "wall" from the collapsed bridge of the San Francisco earthquake. On stretches such as these academics cited me for contempt of history. Where are they now that my discourse has flexed powers of prophecy? Around the time of Arnold Schwarzenegger's triumph (of my will or testament), I was invited to introduce a screening at UC Santa Barbara of the recently restored version of Fritz Lang's *Metropolis*. The case of Lang, to which I have revisitation rights, turned out to be the setting in which something could cross my mind about Schwarzenegger.

Metropolis, which first screened in 1927, has already gone down in history, now as the first serious science fiction film, now as the greatest silent ever made. But first it did time in Hollywood horror movies of the 1930s (which employed many of the same people who worked in the German film industry the decade before, even, like Karl Freund, on *Metropolis*). The monstrous scenes of animation or reanimation in James Whale's Frankenstein films, for example, get their spark from the lab procedure in *Metropolis* whereby a woman's doubled image is imprinted onto a robot that comes in her life size. (Whale got the monster's body from another German film, *The Golem: How He Came into the World*.) *Metropolis* returned from this underworld sojourn in the 1980s and 1990s, replicating itself in countless music videos and sci-fi and superhero films as an identifiable look of the future hovering between the recent past and "today." At some point in this span of the film's renewed popularity, Disneyland rebuilt Tomorrowland to look like a *Metropolis* set.

What has become in the world revealed by Hollywood the most iconic film by far was originally commissioned as German blockbuster to compete with the Hollywood products that were already monopolizing the international screen. But by the time Lang finished the most expensive film the German industry had ever before made, the company that got Lang started had been bought up by Paramount. Between affiliations, historical moments, and audiences, the film, shot straight from the hype, fell way short of expectations.

Since 1984 the irretrievably lost original has been flickering in our faces in supplemented versions of the American cut to which the original was sacrificed shortly after its premiere in Berlin. Often only stills had to fill in for all that didn't survive the sweep of the cutting room floor. The 2002 version covers the original story and loses the supplementary status of the inserts. Consider two stills of a commemorative monument or grave standing in for the otherwise missing melancholic trajectory of the film that lowers the doom in the prehistory of the story we watch on screen. In the restored version this monument is placed in a niche behind curtains, and displayed and glimpsed in the time it takes to open and close the curtain. The images thus lose their status as stills and become moments of stillness in a motion picture. The monument holds the missing place of Hel, the woman wooed by two men, mad scientist Rotwang and Fredersen, ruler of Metropolis, whom she married. She died giving birth to Freder (and granting Metropolis heir time). Rotwang constructs a robot woman to be the vehicle for Hel's return (if not to life then at least into his life).

Now, a version or cut can be just another original. The American version prompts us to interpret Lang's *Metropolis* via an exclusion, which is also just another form of implication and emphasis. The mission of the American cut was to shorten the Lang version. If we keep this economy in mind, the cut of the subplot involving *der Schmale*, or "Slim," a detective plot of surveillance and intrigue, even though it showcased Lang's stylistic mastery of this genre, was one large chunk of reel changes that could go if the film had to lose almost half its wait in the old version. Such logic overdetermines, by contrast, the exclusion of Hel's unburial plot.

The total removal of Hel, in image as in name, was the work of American playwright Channing Pollock, who, hired to rewrite the film's titles, of course influenced, even guided the editing process. Pollock decided that, in English, the proximity of the name Hel to Hell would divert Americans at attention span away from the movie, either in shocked disapproval or onto the laugh track. But if Pollock proclaimed that his revision of the film gave it, for the first time, meaning, then I can concur, but only to the extent that he in effect created an after-the-fact momentum of questions and excavations that redoubled *Metropolis* back onto the missing place of Hel.

The removal of Hel from the original that at the same time re-programmed her as the return of the repressed is not, however, extraneous to the film. Hel's exile or return cannot, in other words, be confined to one man's phobic intervention in what's in a name. For, what remains ambiguous even in the 2002 version is how the figure Maria is made to fit or shift the Hel position that the robot was built to assume. Even with reference to Hel up and running, we are pulled in two directions regarding Maria's introduction into the funereal techno fantasy plot of replication and reanimation. The standard rendition of this plot twist is that Fredersen discovers that the workers are rallying behind somebody called Maria at the same time that Rotwang reveals to him the invention of the cyborg. Fredersen convinces Rotwang to drop whatever plans he had in store for the techno body that does not yet resemble a woman, dead or alive. He should instead, temporarily, give it the image of Maria, so that with this body double Fredersen can undermine the real Maria's message and mission. But why does Maria enter Freder's life early in the film as mother figure surrounded by workers' children she refers to as his brothers? It is the establishing shot for Freder's mother complex, to be sure. If Freder is to make it to the future of substitution in coupling, then the body of Maria must be doubled and divided, divided and conquered. The extreme representation of her sexual threat, which includes the castrative edge she assumes for Freder when he sees her lascivious robot version in his father's embrace, must be destroyed. At the same time, the real Maria must suffer, too, so that Freder can rescue her from the humiliation and torment. The pedestal of the complex that raised Maria into Freder's line of sight, his love at first sight—but also fortified the distance of idealization or demonization into which his love must fall short of the off-limits object—thus gets knocked out of the running of Freder's stunted love life.

It is to turn up the contrast, then, that the story of Hel (or rather that of Rotwang's techno-substitution for this missing person) is offered. It is the cautionary tale of one mad scientist's inability to find a living substitute for an absence that death only doubles: just like a mother she chose another suitor, the third person who thus interrupted Rotwang's duo dynamic. But it is also possible that we have two stories here that cannot be reconciled; in all likelihood the Oedipal story of Freder's working his way out of the complex that repressed incest fantasies build serves as a diversion away from the entrance to the crypt or the tech-no-future in which the mother's missing body remains hidden and preserved. Why else would Rotwang, apparently, even if at seeming odds with the story line, hallucinate Hel in place of Maria, whom he guards while the robot double is out in the underworld on her anarchic mission. There is a third story or plot breaking through here, too, at this intersection of irreconcilable and nonsuperimposable complexes. Freder's psychosis-compatible castration at the sight of "Maria" sexualized in his father's arms also marks the introduction of the robot, which Freder is Oedipally bound not to recognize. The full hallucination releases the cathedral sculptures of the Seven Deadly Sins that are animated now to march forward, following a skeletal figure of Death as their leader, presumably marching toward Freder with the swinging scythe at the front of their line dance. The leader of the mortal sins is, of course, the Devil on his own volition relating to us via the very sins through which we metabolize the world of our creation. While the castrative threat performs the unrepresentability of death (that is, one's own death), the overall allegorical momentum assigns certainty and finitude to the Devil's sway over the deadline.

Up to a point (the turning point of his psychotic break at the end of the film), Rotwang would be content with his Hel replacement. The robot as substitution without complications, as new and improved outcome of a loss that can be written off as deduction with benefits, belongs to the province of the pre-Oedipal or primal father, whose monopolization of sexual difference whereby he alone can plug into the interchangeable backsides of mother and children, circumscribes our relationship to the Devil that takes off from and returns to this anal underworld. In striking contrast to the reality of reproduction (that would require of little one, certainly in the early years of sexual research, a major leap of faith), the anal theory of birth is always the first inside view of creation because it makes evident sense. And we continue, at some level, to make anal babies simply because we can keep on making more and more of them.

The sexualization of the robot woman derives from her anal-phase significance as receptacle to empty or fill at your disposal. According to Melanie Klein, early relations with the breast are right away extended to include preoccupation with the mother's insides, in particular with the feces and father's penis incorporated therein. In Ira Levin's *The Stepford Wives*, the men in town form a coven for the necromantic replacement of their wives by enhanced robot doubles. When Walter, after spending his first late night at the men's club, joins his wife, Joanna, in bed, he wakes her up with his frantic masturbation. When they next make love, she registers his passion at an all-time high. "What did they do, . . . show you dirty movies or something?"(14–16). No, not quite. Instead we can assume that the men explored with Walter the benefits of replacing the wife with a fuck dolly. In Bryan Forbes's 1975 movie version, the experience of doubling is grounded in the abyssal bottom the heroine hits in the transference during her first session with the female psychoanalyst, and which sparks outside session whenever she overhears one of the perfect wives moaning too much (me thinks) with a pleasure she deems unimaginable given what could only be the meager efforts of the pathetic husband. If we leave the Devil fiction behind for science fiction in this film, then we have also exchanged uninhibited one-way fun for psychosis-compatible inside views of replication.

A refrain in *Metropolis* that then places its refraining order on the conclusion of the film is that there's a blank between the brain and the hands that must be filled as mediation, with heart, if Metropolis, for example, is not to succumb to self-destruction. Freder ends up in the foreground as the mediating heart everyone was looking for. But what is also missing between brains and hands is Hel, not as heart but as the womb, the maternal body or the body as mother. Lang later disowned the ending, benefiting from his coauthorship of the screenplay to lay the blame on his better half, Thea von Harbou, his wife back then. But when Lang left Germany, he found he hadn't only separated from Germany under Hitler: von Harbou remained behind in a new partnership with the Nazi

German future she cosigned. Lang thus later reflected regarding the conclusion of *Metropolis:* "One cannot make a socially conscious film in which one says the mediator between hand and brain is the heart— I mean, that is a fairytale, really. But I was interested in machines" (Bogdanovich, 178).

But a concluding frame of reference that is essentially Christian does not get in the way of—nor is it contradicted by—an overriding interest in machines. Hitler was a big fan of Lang's *Metropolis.* He, for one, saw no problem in the situation of machines running life's transmission—or live transmission—within a Christian field of representation that had also already, there's no way around it, admitted demonic aspirations and powers. Lang came to think of himself, as film director, as working like or as a psychoanalyst. But just the same he found out that he could be constructed as Hitler's representative.

In *The Testament of Dr. Mabuse,* Lang thought he was implicating the Nazis through his depiction of an underworld organized around a phantom with telehypnotic powers who, pretending to be alive, communicates with his minions through or as media only, from typewritten orders to audiences with the Dr. in person in a basement, where only his shadow shape is discernible through the curtain or screen while the phonograph plays his commands. The film was banned in Nazi Germany—but only because it failed to include representation of the Nazi takeover as rescue party that must follow the anarchy of crime. At the same time Joseph Goebbels invited Lang to occupy the chief directorial post for a new era of German filmmaking. By this time Lang must have been so freaked by his equal access to the same wavelengths from which he otherwise sought to keep his distance he just had to split the scene.

Lang had all along been a medium who sleepwalked and sleeptalked with the same assurance that Hitler boasted of when it came to forecasting trends. World War I shell shock inspired both Lang and Hitler to become mediums or media. (In both cases partial and/or hysterical blindness held interchangeable places with projection.) While before the war Lang was pushing painted postcards to support his pursuit—against his father's wish that he become an architect—of the art of painting, Hitler sold hand-painted postcards to finance his own artistic vocation. While Lang's turn to film would achieve a displaced following or negative representation of the paternal order, Hitler's eventual career did the same to his own father, who was on the Austrian border patrol. (It would not be far off the mark to see Hitler as also having entered the film medium as director or leader, not only via Leni Riefenstahl, whose occasions, sets, and extras he provided, but through his own editorial supervision of the dailies coming in for his nightly viewing from the many fronts of his total war.)

Lang couldn't sustain a double legacy, that of the two most famous Austrians of the twentieth century, Freud and Hitler. In *You Only Live Once* "what Americans call a 'three-time loser'" "is hunted and . . . fights all alone against the power that menaces society, but he must fight" (Lang, 29). Lang, rather than add to his duo dynamic, split it—for California. But the Lang and the short of it is that the doubling that shadowed or guided him as an uncanny synchronization between his moves or movies and political events could not of course be taken interpersonally, was not restricted to his person, and indeed continues to come full circle. The experiment is on, only in California, no other place, concept, or field of representation could sustain it, to combine, incorporate, synthesize, or overcome the extremities named Freud and Hitler in an assembly line of intermediaries. Currently at the front of this line, Governor Arnold Schwarzenegger is the third famous Austrian—and we're out of the running of extremes that are at the same time up and running in one corpus. Schwarzenegger recounts his initiation into the synthesis of foreign corpora to be built. "He put on the music from *Exodus*. At first, I was embarrassed. I had to laugh. I couldn't pose to that. He urged me to try. He showed me how to hit the best, most dramatic poses during the high points of the music and how to do the less dramatic, more subtle poses during the quieter parts. He taught me to move and turn with rhythm and flow. . . . After two days I ended up with an entirely different posing routine" (Schwarzenegger and Hall, 58). Even at first sight Schwarzenegger's career movies could be summarized as the construction—on his own person or cinematic corpus—of an ambivalent maternal introject capable of hosting the cohabitation or juxtaposition of "opposites." The first two *Terminator* films book the ends of the tension that Schwarzenegger's techno-fantastic body can contain.

What I prefer to refer to as the bosom body is that built body that is all bosom or, if you prefer, buttocks. This body thus derives both from first contact with the breast tumescent with milk and, turned around to the primal father's penetrating monopolization of distinction or certainty, from the anal outlet storage of sexual difference. *Junior* takes it literally, up the forward displacement of the anal theory into an heir pocket in Schwarzenegger's abdomen, where baby—all gastrointestinal systems are go—has room to grow. But he cut this wide birth from developments with which he was ever keeping abreast. In 1974 Schwarzenegger noted that he was not stuck on or in his exhibition body. In fact, unflexed, the built body remained hidden, internalized: "My body doesn't look massive when I'm standing relaxed.... I never tried to tense it up, to get muscle bound. However, when I posed my... body would open up... and my muscles would appear.... I could make my chest expand so dramatically it shocked people; they didn't know where it came from" (70–71). The appeal of the enhanced body is double: the fuck dolly of the anal theory of birth wraps around the Oedipal or Christian body. But this double whammy, too, is a wrap: what can be found on the inside is the mother's body, which, because it can only be found missing, cannot be deemed superseded or redeemed by the twofold body.

According to Klaus Theweleit's interpretation (in *Male Fantasies*) of the upward mobilization of the German psyche between the world wars, training of the focus on militarization began with boy bodies that father, school, and state rewired and rebuilt as killer machines that took one pleasure, the only one that was left to live or die for: cutting into despised amorphous swamp things with the phallic steel that sent them to (and at) the front. Under cover of jumping the gun, these built bodies could also steal the pleasure of suicidal merger with the maternal body. The lawn sprinkler to which their heterosexuality was reduced for low maintenance watered the sister, both as nurse and sibling. The sister thus doubled as the other boy body either at one remove from the brother in arms or in denial of her own proximity to the maternal blob. *Male Fantasies* fixes us up with its focus on its German materials. However, the polymorphous visuals give a more sweeping diagnosis. Thus we find Captain Marvel on one of the pages of Theweleit's study. Certainly there is a tendency in cultural studies (one that Theweleit does not cosign in his own writing) to line up the Nazi German bodies as on one "armored" continuum with, say, the American superheroes. The problem with loud and clear interpretations of the fascist psyche is that they run the risk of universalization. Certain readings of fascism can thus, upon wide-ranging application, become fascist in turn. This also holds true of those readings that follow Elias Canetti in viewing Daniel Paul Schreber—Freud's favorite psycho whose fantasy destiny was becoming woman at the same time as s/he would also become robot—as Nazi *avant la lettre*.

Novelist Michael Chabon popularized the historical setting of American superheroics that pits, for example, two American Jewish teenagers, the creators of Superman in the 1930s, against the Nazi German interpretations and appropriations of Nietzsche's overman. (Chabon's further alignment of American superheroes with the Golem legend is interesting or even true—but only to the extent that Superman must sit then on the same shelf next to the Barbie doll, who also embodies a minority's ambivalent relations with assimilation.) Superman, Batman, Wonder Woman, Tarzan (specifically the films starring Johnny Weissmuller), and even James Bond are addressed by Theweleit's reading of the fascist metabolization of post-natural embodiment but only in one of their aspects, the side they struggle (all "American" superheroes are defined by conflict tracking back to a traumatic past) to overcome in its one-sidedness.

In *Beyond the Pleasure Principle* Freud raises the question of the superman in the language of drive: Is there not a drive toward perfection that promises us the superman? No. Not as long as we owe so much to repression:

> The repressed instinct never ceases to strive for complete satisfaction, which would consist in the repetition of a primary experience of satisfaction. No substitutive or reactive formations and no sublimations

will suffice to remove the repressed instinct's persisting tension; and it is the difference in amount between the pleasure of satisfaction which is demanded and that which is actually achieved that provides the driving factor which will permit of no halting at any position attained, but, in the poet's words, "presses ever forward unsubdued." The backward path that leads to complete satisfaction is as a rule obstructed by the resistances which maintain the repressions. So there is no alternative but to advance in the direction in which growth is still free—though with no prospect of bringing the process to a conclusion or of being able to reach the goal. The processes involved in the formation of a neurotic phobia, which is nothing else than an attempt at flight from the satisfaction of an instinct, present us with a model of the manner of origin of this suppositious "instinct towards perfection." (*SE* 18: 42)

Freud's reading of the impossibility of "superhuman" perfectibility does not contradict the American side—the inside of Nietzsche's reading—but offers a cautionary tally to Germanic readings of superhumanity that err on the side of self-identity. Thus, Faustian striving for the highest satisfaction refers to what was primally repressed. Since Freud postulates primal repression (of the mother's body) as the one repression not even the superman nor the most accomplished psychopath could ever get around, it is the building block or blockage that guarantees self-difference as the bottom line of selfhood (that throws self for a loop through the other).

Walter Benjamin concluded that allegory is always also Christian in frame. (This claim holds interchangeable places with the charge that secularization inheres in Christianity as its half-life.) Christianity certainly cathected allegorization not only in order to recontextualize certain pagan symbols (like the unicorn) and demonize the rest but also, and more importantly, as the mode of appropriating the Old Testament. The cross is just another sign, to be sure. But thanks to Christianity (conceived as the saturation-interpretation of all words and worlds out there in terms of its "other story") every sign in the meantime bears association with the Christian cross.

The allegories that Benjamin contemplated are typically in ruins; the "modern" allegorist, according to Benjamin, maintains all the metaphysical frames of reference as defunct or dead but rescued (not redeemed).

Thus, Christianity in Benjamin's reading, too, becomes nihilism, the busy interchange to which, however, the melancholic sensibility Benjamin also summons to his interpretation of allegory cannot be relegated.

In "On the 'Uncanny'" and *Beyond the Pleasure Principle*, Freud entered a battlefield of doubling and nothing. The repetition compulsion evidenced in the serial dreaming of soldiers suffering from shell shock who kept flashing back to the scene of traumatic impact modeled Freud's revalorization of psychic reality. Freud formulated his new theory of the drives in a setting as modern as the technologization advanced to the fronts of the Great War and as ancient as Christianity. While addressing the "demonic" aspect of the repetition compulsion, Freud formulated as "Devil's advocate" a series of scenarios in which the relationship between life and death is reconceived as the drive to defer the end, on one side, and—on the other side—the drive to rush to the end ASAP. *Metropolis* also shows a stricken world of the future ruled or driven by doubling or repetition. It is hyper-modern in its setting but also seeks its definition or conclusion home on the Christian range of meaning.

In *On the Nightmare*, which was in the first place his psychoanalytic study of occult figures, Jones drops a reference to a goddess of death named Hel who, according to certain legends, was the Devil's mother. The portion of Jones's study that contains this reference to Hel, namely part 2, was first published in 1912 in German as a monograph in a recognizable psychoanalytic series. The technologization of our relationship to the end (in a word, drive theory) belongs in *Metropolis* to the mad scientist Rotwang, whose mix of gadget-loving science and black magic is the secret source of the techno-modernity of Metropolis. Rotwang is at home with the mix: his laboratory, which is his home, is the only ancient building in the upper city other than the cathedral. Inside it offers a rapid-fire shortcut down into the underworld to which it at the same time belongs. Fredersen turns to Rotwang to solve a problem he is having as ruler with the political unrest of the workers or "hands." The robot is ready and waiting to be turned on to turn the ruler's wish into command. But the city, too, with its central machine called heart machine, its upper world of conscious thought, and its underworld of repressed hands, is itself a built body, an artificial life-form, ready and waiting to be pressed into service, a service that proves, however, hard to contain or maintain. This is Rotwang's legacy, and it, too, lives on at or as the end, and not according to the plan that serves as the official ending: the father-and-son reconciliation over the woman's cleansed or uncanny-proofed body, an at once Christian and Oedipal legacy of substitution. The robot was attached to Rotwang, who took a robot hand to replace his own, lost in the course of constructing the replica android. The robot reconstitutes this dead woman, and the bond between techno woman and her robot builder is the hand he had offered her in marriage, which could not be accepted alive, only live. Even when the heart joins hand and brain at the close of the film in a marriage ceremony that reconciles all citizens of Metropolis, there's a secret handshake along for the union. The closing gesture of reconciliation is but the repetition of the exchange of hands between the robot and its creator, a bond of incorporation that joins the tower city and its underworld, where workers appear to labor solely to generate the electricity that illumines and animates *Metropolis*, both the city and the film.

Christian Oedipality and the Devil's pre-Oedipality differ only in the links and limits of their media. When it comes to the dead woman Hel, the ability to ditch the missing woman and live on is cosigned by Freder and Rotwang. But Rotwang's madness is the exception to what rules at the end. His madness also takes exception to the ends Rotwang initially sought for himself and the robot. Thus, when he enters the hallucinatory space in which Maria and the robot are not so much interchangeable as equally beside the point of the sudden continuity of Hel's existence, Rotwang also again touches the film medium but this time in such a way that we don't have to hand it to him. Lang intended to accompany or extend Rotwang's leap off the deep end with the animation of "ghosts and ghouls and beasties" (Bogdanovich, 179) that would stream out of the cathedral at the moment the total destruction of the city must double as the beginning of its redemption. While the scene puts

Christianity and demonic "ghouls and beasties" in their (same) place, the "ghosts" make an exception. In contrast to both Christian immediation (the medium as message, the word made flesh) and the Devil's dad certainty, "ghosts" are resolutely mediatic, mediational, medium-dependent. They are not, then, the so-called ghosts of unfinished business or those holographic messages or messengers from the Christian afterlife, but the ghosts that rebound from, resound within our dead-ication to the other, both in primal time and in the uncontrollable time to come.

When Schwarzenegger played Conan the Barbarian as blond beast struggling against monstrous figures of Christianity or nihilism, he explicitly entered Nietzsche's texts right where the philosopher presented us with the new stakes of misreading—and this was his ultimate test of or for our superhumanity—which are precisely life or death. In *Terminator 2* and *Last Action Hero* the Schwarzenegger protagonists put themselves to this test until, by the end of the projection, they also put themselves to rest. Both through the contact and the subsequent withdrawal, the protagonists upgrade formerly non-nurturing mothers in the estimation of their sons. But as terminator, because he has left behind a part of his android hand crunched in the machine and can at any time be replicated, he is also the missing link (the link with the missing) that loops future through past ad infinitum. Thus, the "good enough" Oedipal mother meets match and maker in the internalized—eternalized—good breast of pre-Oedipal, pre-Christian provenance. As *End of Days* and *The Terminator* showed, evil marks the damn spot this breast is in, which won't come out in the course of Christian reversals of good and bad.

The experiment is on in California. Its parameters appear futural or interminable. As projection, however, it can also be interpreted in reverse: as referring to its past achievement, realization, or result to which we now relate in the mode of recovery. To recycle Karl Kraus's verdict on psychoanalysis, Governor Schwarzenegger is the embodiment of an illness for which he is also the anti-bodiment or cure. He always wanted to be really, really big.

"I dreamed of big deltoids, big pecs, big thighs, big calves; I wanted every muscle to explode and be huge. I dreamed about being gigantic"

(17). But then he discovered (while *Exodus* played in the background) that he was all along sharing a fantasy: "Even though I was a newcomer, they wanted Arnold. It had to do with having a big body, being spectacular. People could identify more closely with a huge body than with a perfect body" (59).

NOTEBOOK FIVE

With the onset of his second system (in works encrusted with quotations from Goethe's *Faust* propping up discussions of the superego, for example), Freud cycles between ultimately demonic repetition as expression of the inertia in organic life and the combo energies of libido. But then repetition reemerges as the egoic and unicellular prospect of replication: immortality on the spot we're in with reproduction or death. The cycle of Freud's speculations in *Beyond the Pleasure Principle* passes through the metabolism of our worldly relations with or in the Devil as set out in 1965 by Vilém Flusser, mortal sin by mortal sin, within a lexicon adapted, for the duration of his *History of the Devil*, to and from psychoanalysis.

Flusser was born in Prague in 1920. He published what I've translated as *History of the Devil* in Brazil in Portuguese translation. The German original did not appear until 1993. By the late 1980s Flusser had more or less established himself in the makeshift world of art magazine writing—all about the future now of media influences in theory, on art. But even though the leading international art magazines supported him, he remained a figure on the margin, who was codepent on the notion of making it big. Published, as usual, by European Photography, a small press that seemed to exist only to have Flusser's books on list, his 1991 *A Conversation* was based on an interview Klaus Nüchtern conducted with Flusser the year before at the arts festival in Graz, Austria. The subject is Flusser's account of the nomadic impulse, as presented in his plenary lecture the night before, and which is situated in the course of the interview as rivaling many well-known philosophical investigations in the receiving area of techno media. His collected works address photography, vampirism, the future of writing in an age of techno visualization, and a couple of plays. In 1991, he was described as living and writing in Southern France. He died in 1992. Friedrich Kittler wrote a somewhat reluctant intro, I mean, obit for *Kunstforum international*. He agreed with Flusser that his strength did not lie in mathematics and then let Flusser make the claim that he was a thinker instead. More recent publications seeking to collect his work and give it the completion of biographical and autobiographical supplements place a study in linguistics in the place of Flusser's first book and moreover suggest that Flusser insisted at the time on conducting his life and work in his new language. Otherwise the Devil book is listed in these necrospectives but never glossed or in any way commented upon. It is a true foreign body. Unfazed by these more recent displacements, I still count *The History of the Devil* as Flusser's first book, which, completely out of context with his condensed all-out effort to be recognized many years later, remains his best by far. It is the only work in which he seeks a fit with Freud, though from a distance of the rationalization that the deadly sins required consultation with a sex theorist. But to his credit, it is the fit with Jung that would be noted by most scholars as most likely to proceed from an inquiry into the Devil.

The Devil is one immortal figure who, however, also has a history. Human history is the history of the Devil. The Devil's job or purpose is to keep the world in this time, in time we keep with history's momentum. The complete defeat of the Devil means the world would cease to exist. In another *The History of the Devil* (to which we owe the superegoic dictum about death and taxes), Daniel Defoe puts this period at the end of a sentence that the Devil's dominion must "deliver" to mankind:

> The homage and worship the Devil has from the world is an usurpation; and this will have an end, because the world itself will have an end; and all mankind, as they had a beginning in time, so must expire, and be removed, before the end of time. (293)

This sense of an ending comes from God. We are therefore—as the living or as the dead and undead—more closely related to the Devil than to God. From the witch's flying broomstick to magic elixirs, the Devil's way has been one of enhancement or extension of our bodily existence.

The Devil's hallmark means of getting a rise out of this world, by drugs or drug-lubed broomstick-dildo, never depart the worldly sin of Lust.

Relations with the Devil begin or begin again in Lust, already inside the protoplasmic form from which life first evolved or again evolves. The cell is immortal; it takes in life, moves in time, and then divides or doubles itself, replicates itself. The multicellular organism by contrast is mortal, not by accident, which is the relationship of protozoa to death, but by plan, by law. Soul or psyche arises out of inhibitions, limitations, frustrations of our lustful striving to develop, to evolve, to rise to every occasion. To be more or less free of inhibition, either in the mode of great health or in the conscience-free condition of psychopathy, is to stand closer to the Devil than to God and His soul strain of inhibited, neurotic followers. Humans are, after all, essentially erotically uninhibited: human sexuality is not limited to the purpose of reproduction. This is the bottom line of human sinfulness. Our desires—self-sex, same-sex, unisex, fetish sex, self-play, and foreplay—are perverse, that is, not by a money shot reproductive party to future generations. However, Flusser warns, if free love could be realized on this polymorphous basis, it would be the end of human being. But when it's time for an example, Flusser points to the unlimited passion plays of nationalism, particularly in Europe, each brand or flaming up coming complete with its own underlying love of the mother tongue.

The second Deadly Sin, Anger, breaks limits and inhibitions and thus frees up passion. Laws, rules, regulations breed Anger. In other words, the law transforms the world of the senses into the world or word of Anger, of power. In Lust and Anger we desire reality, we want our desires realized. But we end up—for example, in the development of science out of lustful curiosity and angry transgression—in danger of losing, precisely, our sense of reality.

As essential as lustful propagation, for example, is number three, the sin of Gluttony, of identificatory ingestion and digestion. We live in the excrement of human intake of the world. The world is subjected thus, in the first place, to a rear view and a reversal, the kind that leaves itself behind, where it remains. This logic of the backside covers fecal matter in at once irreversibly mediatic terms or turns. Once the mirror image reverses what it reflects, it can never be reclaimed by or as world. The same goes for what passes through our gastro-industrial system. It sticks so close to but so far away from that which was consumed and reversed. At one decisive remove from the world, excrement results from our most direct or intimate contact with the world: the world passes through us via channels lined in membranes designed for absorption rather than for egoic defense. These channels—together with the passageways of breathing that are unconsciously aligned with the former— are therefore the preferred sites of symptom formation. Excrement is the first model or experience both of loss (the body falling away from itself) and of creation or production. Excrement falls away from or grows out of the body it outlives, however briefly and technically.

In *Prince of Darkness,* the team of scientists and experts (including a radiologist and a translator) summoned to the site of an unidentified phenomenon in the basement of a church is confronted with the outside chance that the Devil is beaming up down there (for the time being still inside a bubbly green test tube, electronic monitor, or cathode tube). Technically, it's Satan's father who is being summoned to break through. Christ was an extraterrestrial, but humanlike, who gave us the warning. But he had to wait seven million years until our science and technology could explain it.

The test tube in the church basement vomits forth a chain reaction of spewing its same substance into humans, who throw it up into more human receptacles. The research team members are all dreaming the same dream. The dream, as one of the researchers reports, is prerecorded and not part of his subconscious: the dream or premonition is making room for itself. One resister of this fantastic hybrid of belief and technology tells it like it is: "This is caca." As one scientist explains, every particle has its negative side. Our technology can now confirm this, namely the materiality of evil. Or, in other words, everything, right down to every subatomic particle, has a backside.

In addition to the chain of receptacles—including the homeless surrounding the downtown church who were immediately transformed into uncanny zombies, into the *Unheimlich,* the "unhoused"—one team member has contracted the scar she eventually becomes as walking, seeing-eyeballs raw meat."One will be chosen." By chance she checks herself out in a compact mirror and thus releases the mirror contact or touch through which the Devil's father begins crossing over from the dark side.

The first team member to admit this chance or change in the scientific format of the group inquiry—the interdisciplinary cohabitation of belief and technology—is the woman physicist who is one out of two delegates of our identification. She dies at the end according to the sacrificial logic of near miss (Christ, remember, was a Carpenter) that requires that the man in her life, another physicist on the team, face loss, even while losing it, in the mode of catastrophe survival. In other words, she dies so the group—and by proxy the world—can be saved. (She throws her weight against the Devil's father—the Devil father—passing through the mirror portal that shuts down on both of them.) In the parallel or alternate ending, the survivor dreams the same old dream again—but this time it's the sacrificed woman who turns the corner rearmarked for the Devil or his father to turn around.

While the team player was still being set up for the fall, she is the first to admit the Devil hypothesis: "So it's really Old Scratch himself knocking at the door." From that scratch, the scratch of writing on the ancient text, the scratch of etching, the scratch of media like gramophone, typewriter, photography—*prints* of darkness—current scientific and media analogues accompany or double our understanding of the menace in the basement. The Devil mobilizes all the ways in which the world is held together, represented, let go, controlled, transmitted, realized, and mediatized. The scratch-and-sniff essence from which Old Scratch as media mascot develops is the excremental liquid that turns everything it enters into one of the stations along its line of waste production.

In this media Sensurround reality is to be receiving transmissions from the future. What starts from scratch in the church basement transmits in identical dreams all the research team members start having. What if dreams, they now wonder, are messages sent as photographs or radio signals from the future to warn them about present spans of tension that the Devil is trying to break through. When we see the dreams of/from the future, we get a camera view, one, it turns out, we can change, like a channel. We pick up the first impressions or scratches of techno contact contained in photography and which here give rise to the Devil's movement but which, at the digital tape future ends of technologization, also bounce back as future warning.

In *The Eighteenth Angel* the triumphant return of Lucifer is solicited through beautiful angels. Lucifer will be enticed to merge with one of the eighteen beauties and thus materialize. A genetic researcher has created "human blanks," clones, for the Devil's embodiment. But the appetizer for merger, a beautiful face, is what the dark order dedicated to Lucifer's return is trying to select and win by the skin of the victim's chin. One of the finalists is a daughter in conflict with her father following the mother's death. The mother was the ruler of the family and the focus of her daughter's ambivalence. The father's attempt to fill her two shoes ends up substituting for the original father-and-daughter relationship. The father penetrates the dark order's monastery and finds the cloning scientist, who has been silenced. His zombie state embodies links and limits of the alliance between the Devil and science. He can only scratch three 6s in a row, another cloning series. But the father goes forth and multiplies: 18. The eighteen clones are "blanks" to be filled with one and the same substance. They are anal babies. The same body connection is put through with excrement, the other blood bond. But the face must be grafted from the living difference: the mother is in the face.

In *Resurrection* we face an overly zealous psycho Christian. In the offices of law enforcement one agent notes with disgust that the newspapers are showing "pictorials of the crime scenes." Soon they'll be offering guided tours. Society worships at the Mass of murder. The Detective who is the match for the psycho who tries to make him fit a suicide plan is stuck on the loss of his son. The one piece missing from the body of Christ that psycho is building up out of parts he removes from his victims while they are

paralyzed but alive to the pain (like Christ on the cross) is the heart of a
baby boy born on Christ's big day to a mother named Mary. The stitched-
together body still minus the heart is discovered in one of the closed-off
crime scenes. The agents are forced to their knees in vomiting recognition
of life as excrement. Each body part to this date has belonged to a thirty-
three-year-old. The baby boy is psycho's human shield; the detective can't
risk the life of a son, of his son. But psycho overshoots his plan. "Time for us
to die," he proclaims. But he goes alone. The son is saved. Mourning can begin.

Because of its metabolic proximity to and remove from nature, shit rather
than earth or clay is the Devil's creative medium. By passing through
creature and creation first, shit is in a sense artificial, a repetition and a
production, and as product it is moreover a blended mass of sameness.
It is this world, according to Flusser, which protects us against the natural
world of accident—and against God. The digested and excreted world
has a purpose, that of serving mankind. The world thus becomes real
again, believable. But what then finally is the difference between the
undigested world of nature and the digested world of technology? We
know as little about the future evolution of our machines as we know
about the future development of any animal. What we do know is that
machines develop or evolve more quickly than animals or plants. That's
what makes our world so horrific. We eat the world to excrete the machines that overtake and devour us. We will die out and be replaced by
technology just as we replaced and erased our missing-link connection
with the primates.

At the core of his study of representations or projections of the
demonic, *The Demon and His Image (Der Dämon und sein Bild)*, Erwin
Reisner investigates the fundamental choice between good and evil as
the choice of what to eat, the question raised already under the trees of
knowledge and of life. Unlike Flusser, Reisner registers certain pleasures
or highs—such as nationalism—as belonging to the techno order of
Gluttony that asks us to choose our poison.

"The masses, the machine, and the scientifically applied antitoxin
are all expressions of the same demonism, approximations of the split,

broken, and, in short, profoundly poisoned spirit" (193). Nourishment that finds its reflection in poison is a specific kind of poison, an anti-toxin. "*Condensation and splitting* thus produce poison or rather two poisons, one's own poison and the alien poison, which however, in spite of all apparent animosity, are finally blood brothers" (174). The former poison is narcotic; the latter, which is Dionysian, aims at getting high.

According to Reisner, nationalism is a form of "word poison" whereby the foreigner is demonized. This is how radical a Christian frame of reference can be: the Jewish God is essentially the poison that every nationalism spreads. But lay off the Jews: to persecute the Jews is to become contaminated by this very poison. No one passes the multiple chosenness test.

Reisner's demon study is part of a postwar German world that divides the losses it cuts with Flusser's survival. Between the two schol-ars we can take measurements of the body count of intelligent life that National Socialism and World War II brain drained from the German word. They provide a fitting frame for the portrait of the Devil as Prince of the middlebrow culture (phantasmatically) at the controls of mass society. Reisner died shortly after the appearance of his 1966 book, *The Jews and the German Empire (Die Juden und das Deutsche Reich)*. In this work, Reisner responds to the postwar German discourse of working through and resolving—putting to rest—the recent past by underscoring our relationship of identification with the past. According to Reisner, to identify with the past means to acknowledge it as one's own. But identi-fication with the past means that what would appear to be mine comes to (and through) me via the other. The guilt of our fathers is still our re-sponsibility, whether we're the children of Nazi persecutors of the Jews or, skipping the beat of the recent past via the Christian sense of what's proper or properly my own, we're modern Jews still responsible for Christ's death (243). "To the question, who carries the responsibility for anti-Semitism, one must answer: the Jews if they raise the question, and also the Christians or those who hold themselves to be Christians, if they inquire about it" (68). "Thus the judgment that befalls Germans and Jews is the *judgment of fallen Adam as such*" (11).

According to *The Demon and His Image,* our closest affiliation with the Devil whereby we took the fall is the drugs we still take even though we know the risk and recognize their proximity to death. It's a demonic form of cannibalism: "In drug-induced euphoria one divides oneself into a demon and a corpse" (183). But there is not only the high that brings us to the point of dissolution: a mild toxin can give rise instead to a memory of what was lost. Hence the social drunks still sing in the choir. The hard drinking loner "enjoys and affirms the negation of his own ego, he seeks his life in death, and only thus does the pleasure taken in poison become black magic, cult of the Devil" (189).

Whereas before the Fall the tree of knowledge was, essentially, the poison tree tempting man to cross over from the realm of life into that of death, after the Fall Adam acquired the degree of immunity to this tree that allowed him to nourish himself from its strange fruit. The tree of life was now his poison tree. "The most terrible poison for the one alienated from God is God Himself" (170).

Fallen Adam had to kill to preserve his own life. "Thus the death of the other is the precondition of his life" (168). This is the fundamental conflict or divisiveness within human being. That's why the relationship between poison and death—in particular the use of dead matter to promote growth of the plant in question—obtains for nontoxic nourishment, too. It is not so much that poison is a separable ingredient within nourishment: it is the concentrated vital essence of the nourishment itself. "Everything becomes toxic and metamorphoses into poison when it condenses itself toward its own center. The originary poison is the blood poison of Adam fallen away from God, 'Adamin,' the corpse poison that already circulates in the arteries of the infant but first becomes recognizable in the dead body as concentrated toxic substance" (171). But if "the only difference between nourishment and poison in this fallen world lies in the velocity with which the poisoning transpires" (168), then the reverse also holds true: "all poison is always also nourishment, only nourishment of a special kind, nourishment with regard to a life that man in general no longer understands as *his* life. The incorporation of the poison . . . tears the consumer into a broader life rhythm, away from which he has lived in his isolation, which therefore spells out for the being that he now is sublation and death" (169).

Because Reisner views psychoanalytic theory as demonic because drive-dependent, he is in a position to offer us this reformulation of our poison: "One could therefore simply designate poison as the *nourishment of the unconscious,* the nourishment of the sphere of the drives" (169).

NOTEBOOK SIX

Envy and Greed, Flusser writes, are two deadly sins that are in it to-gether—like son and father—as the Devil's backup plan. In place of a phenomenal world that we see as unreal, really scary, we opt for the reality of the socius—and all the hierarchies that articulate and bind together a social reality. Language figures here, all powerfully, but as lexicon of historical inheritance and as grammar of hierarchies. Greed is conserva-tive: it protects and preserves a world of sentences. Greed conserves the progressive work of Envy and thus fortifies the social hierarchies in the wake-up thrall of social upheaval. But envy has the heaves because it seeks to get even.

What's real, says Flusser, where the Devil grabs us, is what we thus take so interpersonally, namely the social relation. Here the bottom line is assigned to the world power of words, words as inheritance of genera-tions, syntax as the vessel out of which we drink the wisdom of sen-tences. Only within this perspective can we love language and yearn to preserve, greedily, language's purity, and look with envy at other speak-ers who would engage or enrich language. Language is a treasure haunt.

Language stands apart from all other aspects of the sensual world by all accounts of its hierarchical organization. Words have been assigned places in the sentences in which they march. Whatever changes are intro-duced word by word, the principle of hierarchy is preserved. When Anger and Gluttony in seeking incorporation of the world in the word fail to convince us of this reality, in a word, of the phenomenal world, then it's up to Envy and Greed to affirm instead the reality of language and, as its main manifestation, society itself.

Language, as the only means of spiritualization that does not first subscribe to belief in God, is the crusade of the living and the dead against the Divinity. In this formation every word is a flaming sword in the Devil's service, and language as a whole is one big protest against the corporeality or mortality of humankind, an articulated cry of Envy against God. Creation becomes the Devil's huge attempt to articulate himself— and to this end human society serves the Devil as mouthpiece and tongue.

According to Flusser, vengeance is not beyond good and evil; it is good and evil at once. Vengeance requires no judge, and, therefore, the socio-historico-linguistic order (that vengeance fills out) requires no God. Envy in a sense is avenged by Greed, while Envy more directly seeks to get even with Greed. For each historical epoch you can substitute now for Envy, now for Greed one of the two defining antipodes or, any time at all, you can fill them in, respectively, as son and father.

Is the killer in *Seven* in the Devil's service? No. The veteran detective stays around beyond the deadline of retirement out of Pride in his erudition that the psycho killer's philological or theological investment challenges and stimulates. According to this detective, the killer is staging a preachy pageant of the seven deadly sins. Each time, however, the killer presents a case of punishment that represents "forced attrition": even though the victim sure did regret his sin it wasn't for love of God. The killer thus denies them the gospel, God's mercy, the lower millstone, and sticks the law to them, meat grinding them up with the upper millstone. Detection work is always Oedipal. The older detective, who draws on the histories and traditions he has studied and retained, is the choir to which psycho preaches. The younger detective thought he had succeeded in skipping culture. Now that it is the generation-gaping issue of the elder being at an advantage, the younger detective takes a shortcut through *Cliff Notes,* which in the realm of letters represents revolt and upheaval. He thus acts as Envy to the paternal detective's conserving function as Greed. All that he already knew consolidates and conserves—high hierarchy and all—the upheaval of a new generation's forced abridged entry into high culture. As the angry young detective and the resigned, insightful, melancholy veteran detective go over the photo evidence around the site of the lawyer's demise for or as Greed, pound of flesh self cut off his love handle and all, they find a photograph of the dead man's wife with her eyes outlined in circles. A message? Only she can recognize something in this scene. They show the widow photographs of the scene. In effect, they torture her. But then she can see better. She sees that the painting is upside down. Through the specular reversal that skewers visual media and that is at the same time the logic of the backside, the two men try to penetrate handprints of darkness that are up against the wall behind the painting and thus catch up with the dictation given and taken down in the relationship between the Devil's sins and their Christian interpretation and punishment. Although they're being led astray, the first breakthrough in the case is also a breakthrough in their relationship. "Don't tell me you didn't get that rush tonight? We're getting somewhere." His elder, however, counters that even this clue will be written down, and will then be filed away along with everything else that gets written down on the off chance that it will be important. Clues lead to other clues that go nowhere in so many cases and crypts of unsolved crimes. We discern that this detective's retirement also includes the kind of libidinal withdrawal from his former world that betokens depression, or at least sorrowful resignation. But this disconnection, as though only generational, is also their first connection. They sleep together waiting for the lab results. The results point to a low-grade anger management type who was acquitted through the offices of the lawyer who made the cut of Greed. Right away the veteran doubts that this could be the mastermind. And he's right. They enter another crime scene, another pageant in which the torment inflicted on the victim fits the sin of Sloth. When the cops enter the center staging of the sin, one addresses the body covered up on bed: "Get up you sack of shit." Then he lifts the covers. "Oh fuck me!" It's a living corpse. The victim's punishment began a year ago. He was put on hold as a living corpse, the stations of his year long living only to feel more pain recorded in countless photographs. But this is one punishment that more than fits the crime: the yearlong project performs the sin of Sloth from the Prideful position of psycho-killer artist. The condition of Sloth is to occupy the closest quarters imaginable of deferral of death or nothingness. With Pride the deferral of time on a deadline is pleasurably productive. Samples of excrement have been collected in countless jars. He was forced to procrastinate dying for one year. But this is also the one victim to survive the staging of his sin: but he survives as a bundle of nerve endings ready to shatter at the first loud sound. The angry detective chases away the photographer who tries to break a story just as they depart this crime scene. But when they break into the psycho killer's apartment, they find the work of the photographer. There's even a picture of them. That news photographer he chased away was the killer! "Fuck me!" Psycho preacher makes a Prideful photographic document of the performance of Sloth. His photos of the widow of the lawyer, who died as Greed, led to the Sloth piece (where the photo documentation is coextensive with the vials and samplings of urine, blood, filth). The preacher's photographic inserts (whereby the film inescapably slows down in getting in touch with itself), which develop out of excremental vestiges but also intra-relate through extra-referential tampering and arrangement, situate the psycho between mourning-sick horror cinema and the Devilish manipulations of creation or illusion versus nothingness. In the end, the killer has a cameo role in the pageant as Envy: he shows the younger detective his covetous handiwork: the severed head of the wife, the triangulator of the couple of detectives. Anger shoots Envy. But the veteran detective, somewhere between Pride and Sloth, survives or begins again.

With Pride we see through all of it, the whole world together with the Devil and God, all of the above, as our own egoic creation. It is the ego's nature to go out of itself, to cast itself out and about, to realize itself, to make itself material, to project itself on the outside. The pressure is on, in the ego, to express oneself. Language is the net, the web, through which the ego exceeds its boundaries. The ego is like a spider, Flusser writes; it collects its secretions, its thoughts, and keeps them crossing, back and forth, affixing them to the branches of our senses, and thus it weaves its web out of words and sentences. You can stretch language until it encompasses the infinitude of what's out there. But then that's next to nothing. Even the ego weaving language can be subsumed in language. But when it's too much of a stretch—as in the networking of logic and mathematics—the word-wide web catches nothing at all but only covers nothingness like a shroud. This seven-sin stretch belongs to the sorrow of the heart, apathy, depression, the deadly sin otherwise named acedia, popularly known as Sloth. But there are also moments of condensation or density—literally, of poetry or *Dichtung*—that capture what they encompass by holding the ego or reality prisoner in this condensed form. Where there's a will there's a way all knots, connections, concepts can be removed from this linguistic density. Then without any meaning we would still have a language, but one of relations only, one that no longer speaks but instead hums. It's the sounds of music. Music can thus be seen as the highest and densest of art forms, of poetry or *Dichtung*. Music realizes the ego in a pure form: a meaningless song, says Flusser, in praise of the will by the will.

In the metabolic phase of Pride, technology goes mediatic and gets in touch with itself as art. It is a defect in the ego that in its role as creator it gives forth illusion, the illusions of good and evil, of wrong and right, and produces logic and ethics. Music grabs us because it is the final argument, the last stand or understanding—after music there's nothing left to say. God and the Devil are annihilated, dissolved in music. When the music plays, we want only to submit to the glorious humming of language. The meaningless language of relations is reality, because it is ego. Music is the goal of human will. It is the ego's goal to transform all its works into music.

Even though he is striking an upbeat, Flusser channels a tradition or reception of cautionary readings of music. Music that creates *Dichtung* along the bottom line that is the last stop before language bottoms out into mathematics is a special kind of music that slips into the background of visualization or hallucination. What is celebrated here, then, is the operatic momentum in music that found its para-mass-media Meister in Wagner, before settling into the scores of movies, videos, TV shows. From Wagner to Spector, we're up against a wall of sound. Phil Spector: Feel the specter up against the demonic legacy of Wagner.

In Thomas Mann's *Doctor Faustus* the relation to the Devil faced music that was first struck up on Wagner's stage. The protagonist is given quality time in which to make original musical compositions to spite what he knows ironically about the nothingness, the nothing new out there. The high art story is kept as a whole at the ironic remove of the narrator's editorial objectivity and incomprehension, which can take the risk and blame for the tendentious coupling of the Devil pact with the rise Germany got out of National Socialism. This cancellation of Goethe's saving notion of human striving identifies with an aggressor's view that everything up to this endpoint of culture contributed to the rise of the suicide occult that replaced it in Nazi Germany. But the move to annul or take back must be taken back in turn. The narrator refers to three time zones through which his documentary labor passes: the time in which he writes, the last years of the war, which he reflects on and records regularly; the past time, the composer's story, which he recalls and reconstructs; and the unlocatable time, given over to translation for example, his future time, our present time, of reading (267). Take me to your reader: Mann withdraws from the parallel universals, just as he, more comically perhaps, makes sure he can have his genius and hate it, the very idea of it, too.

Kierkegaard's reflections on the musical erotic (in *Either/Or*) are centered on Mozart's *Don Giovanni*, which he aims to prove is the greatest musical work. It was Freud's favorite opera, too. Like Freud, like Kierkegaard: opera holds attractions for those of us who otherwise dread music. Kierkegaard's proviso that music must always be accompanied or glossed by text captions the other fact of his life, that he has "no understanding of music." His reading of Christianity's link to the sensual medium of music—or to music as *Dichtung*—goes once more around the blockage. Christianity first posited the same sensuality it chases out, keeps out of the world. In other words, Christianity first included sensuality under the category of spirit whereby the significance of sensuality can only be that it is to be excluded. Exclusion makes it exclusive: sensuality is thus raised to the power of principle. By shutting in and shutting out music as the medium of the sensual erotic, a similar series of dialectical operations results in our conclusion: "In other words, music is the demonic." The relationship between music and language passes through spirit. Music is therefore a language. They've got the ears in common in their receiving areas, and their main medium or element is time. Music (together with Christianity or the demonic) has the corner on sensual immediacy.

Opera, as the hybridized placeholder of musical *Dichtung*, occupies interchangeable places with certain works in literature and cinema.

Dichtung is buoyed up by two distinct attitudes or approaches to the Devil's role in religions from the early years of Christianity to this day. The pre-Christian world was the Devil's realm; all that idolatry, dedicated to countless gods, was Devil worship. Of course it is always a problem how Judaism fits into this scheme. More of a problem if the cutoff point is already in the Garden of Eden; less problematic, it would seem, if the point of no return encircles the failure of ethical cleansing for which Noah served as helmsman. The other approach, which bears with it a reproach, is that demonization befalls all the beliefs, deities, and spirits vanquished by Christ—and by Christianity, at least by the time Christianity attained coextensivity with the Roman Empire and thus control of the imperial administrative and postal systems and of the network of roads. Demonization, as a process, describes the manner in which competing claims just outside but even inside the Christian camp are at once repressed and represented. According to Oskar Pfister, Freud's token priest in the inner department of the reception of psychoanalysis, the encrusted, niche-etched frame of Christian reference arises with the upsurge of anxiety that holds up Satan's sway over the world. In his psycho-historical study *Christianity and Anxiety (Das Christentum und die Angst)*, Pfister views the increase of dualism from Jesus to Paul as the measure of anxiety that's on the rise. For Paul, Satan's representation kept on growing. He encompasses, as angel of light, all the heathen gods, including the elements of the world, the spirits that rule the stars and the seasons and the moon. "Sin, too, becomes hypostasized and behaves almost like a kind of angel of Satan, just as *Death, Law, Flesh* are more to be attributed to the dark realm of Evil and operate in the manner of Spirits" (206).

All of the above fills a reserve or resource for imagery that supplies the procession of pageants conjured by Gustave Flaubert in *The Temptation of St. Anthony.* Even at its most literary or imaginative, each pageant or station of the crossing proves, just the same, to be cite-specific, presenting careful renditions of written or represented scenes with a long shelf life in the archives. Michel Foucault was right to situate *The Temptation* as the proof (that would double as origin for a new genre of books about and within books) that true images are products of learning, reproductions of reproductions derived from cited words uttered in the past, built up by collecting minute facts and footnotes. What began, with print culture's onset, as the hallucinatory by-product of (silent) reading, is now the goal of Flaubert's temptation prose. Foucault: "Dreams are no longer summoned with closed eyes, but in reading" (Flaubert, xxvi).

Foucault situates *The Temptation* in the prehistory of each of Flaubert's "other" works. As such it represents a project that had to be deferred—it functioned thus as the deadline along which he was drawn to sign immediately—so that each "other" work could enter the circulation of letters and his own CV as the in-stalling of everything only *The Temptation* could, perhaps, ultimately be. I prefer to refer to such a textual desire that serves as the exception to the roll a writer is otherwise on as sui-citation, the short circuit of self-citation that cannot enter the trace if it means leaving the origin. The difference here is that the citation, in time, passed only through the archives, and thus, upon arrival, at a safe remove. This highly encrusted text succeeds as the *Dichtung* or time thickening that Kenneth Anger also resolutely achieved (also in a technically nonmusical medium).

In *The Temptation,* the Devil's entry (once he sets aside the masquerade of being Hilarion, Anthony's transferential charge or pupil) is dress-rehearsed by Apollonius's departure (together with sidekick Damis):

> "Leave him alone, Damis! He believes, like a brute, in the reality of things. The terror the Gods instill in him also keeps him from comprehending them; and he lowers his own God to the status of a jealous king! . . . Above all forms, further than the ends of the earth, even beyond the heavens, lies the world of Idea, replete with the splendor of the Word."

While Apollonius gets his rise out of philosophical idealism, the Devil rides high in vaults of the scientifically revealed universe. The infinity that is out there, everywhere, precludes belief in a personal purposeful God. If you want to get a person on the line, summon the Devil.

Toward the end of chapter 6, the Devil's wings expand until they cover all space. Anthony: "My consciousness bursts beneath this dilation of nothingness." But he will not give up the "ghost" of the Father God he adores and who must love him back. The Devil instructs otherwise: all human knowledge comes through the mirror medium of the mind. Man can never apprehend the Infinite. How much out there, including Anthony's existence, is only error of the senses. Illusion is the only reality.

Roman Polanski and Kenneth Anger are two film directors who bring us inside a nonphobic or affirmed relationship to Lucifer as figure of illumination and light. In his two Devil films Polanski includes moments of art as self-relation. The dream sequence in *Rosemary's Baby* is an art cinema short, a part of the film that exceeds the whole, certainly as narrative, and is not subsumed, in other words, by the made-in-Hollywood psychology and storytelling. What is carried through the entire film, however, is what the dream celebrates: there is a world (a world of imagination, projection, distorted seeing, hallucination) between the world and our perception. Thus, the film sustains the double reading of the reality of Satan's intervention in Rosemary's life and the imaginary, deluded status of Rosemary's vision. In *The Ninth Gate* the literary and aesthetic rapport with Lucifer is asserted, thematized, and in parts performed. The plot line separates one uninhibited book double-dealer (who specializes in ripping off survivor gilt) from a melancholic world of book collectors infiltrated by wannabe Satanists who, under cover, cultivate the magic of book warming. The secretly Satanic widow of one melancholic collector dismisses any possible interest her dead husband might have taken in the magic power of one of his missing collectibles. She just can't see him trying to raise the dead. There she stands, innocent bystander, but corrected by the book dealer: "The Devil, this book is designed to raise the Devil." The film begins with the scene of this collector's suicide by hanging. The camera leaves the hang-up to explore the dead man's scene of writing, reading, collecting and finds in the stacks the open placeholder of a missing book. The book includes engravings, images that will be followed and consumed (self)destructively by one Devil worshipper who fails in the end and is upstaged during the sexual initiation of the book dealer by Lucifer as beautiful woman. The doomed collector sought inscription in the Black Book of Death and unlisting in the Book of Life. "Taking the road that leads to equality—to God," the melancholic ends up burned by the inclusion among the original elemental Devil-signed pages of one counterfeit—counter-fiction and cruci-fiction—as inevitable by-product of the maintenance and restoration of original collectibles over time. The book dealer in contrast enters into lustful relations with Lucifer herself who, while still incognito, had already assured him that while she was with him nothing (= death) would happen to him.

One speaks of such ancient illustrated tomes as "illuminated." The camera enters the space left by the missing book between books; the gateways open not behind that space but inside it, a filmic space in which the opening titles scroll down. The illumination the book dealer (turned Lucifer's apprentice) enters is not a world behind a world. The realm of shadows into which the illumination takes him is still the archive of letters that require the light for the reading. But it's not natural lighting. It is no more, no less than the light beam of the projector through which the film passes onto the screen on which light and shadow form the afterimages.

Kenneth Anger's first Crowleyite and Luciferean film, *Inauguration of the Pleasure Dome*, performs the initiation that Polanski illuminates.

It challenges or cultivates the medium of "boredom," of penetrating insight that never strays from the surface. Boredom arises at the point of resistance to boring deep into the surface where all that is deep lies. When the bored yawn, thank them for their demonstration of the yawning abyss. Set aside or defer what Flusser will refer to as lazy thinking. Art can fill a void for the time being, can defer recognition that that's all there is. The video's packaging gives us words of Anger: "The film is derived from one of Aleister Crowley's dramatic rituals where people in the cult assume the identity of a god or a goddess. I wanted to create a feeling of being carried into a world of wonder.... It expands, it becomes completely subjective—like when people take communion and one sees it through their eyes." Notice that Anger's fantasy revolves around communion, but at a distance, as foreign body through which one obtains the inside view of communion—but, again, at the fundamental remove of reversal, digestion, excretion. Anger's film recycles the world through us, that is, through the characters, as artifice: mirroring, skin, celluloid, fabric, texture, makeup, dyes, stage sets, screen-deep superimposition or inscription of images on top of recorded images. This type of mediatization of the surface that never really leaves the surface adds to it an unconscious. Thus the fire ignites in and from the magnifier hearth of this close mediatization.

The time Anger takes, which in real time is thirty-eight minutes, exceeds that timeline. We watch an excessive decorated surface that, from the getups of the performers to the artificial sets to the writing and scratching and superimposition, opens up depth, never leaves the surface space, and exceeds its schedule across extended moments or spans of attention. Anger's inaugural Luciferian film was made possible by the inheritance his mother's death had just handed him. Depth sounds like death. A paradoxical depth that never leaves the surface is like a death that is maintained in the superficial winding sheets of extended but finite time.

Anger's *Inauguration* is, as ritual, also his first invocation, just like his 1969 *Invocation of My Demon Brother* (with the settled score by Mick Jagger). Anton LaVey suggested in passing that in most cases music would prove the best medium for invocation. But the point LaVey chooses to push is largely therapeutic: invocation dislodges what he calls crystal- lization, the rigidity of adolescence that most of us will carry around like a backpack for the rest of our lives. Adolescence—as idealism, fantasy, or terrorism—is what blocks transformation of or departure from the Christian perspective. Nietzsche, too, argued that Christ would have recanted or grown more complex and flexible if he had only lived longer: what gets cryogenically freeze-framed for all time as Christianity is a perpetual adolescent's worldview.

We tend to say that something hasn't even scratched the surface yet. But in *Dichtung* we peel the veil from itself in the double medium of celluloid and flesh. *Dichtung* also defers the conclusion that in time will also be there: that all we did was scratch the surface. This cutting edge or rip-and-tear line is what the *Hellraiser* series explores, defers, and repeats. Here sadomasochism is the medium for a scratching of the surface, the skin, that in the end must conclude that *that* was all there is, skin, blood, shit. In *Hellbound: Hellraiser II* it is made clear that the self-reflexive cube that fits in the hand of the one who contacts the demon explorers of the limits of human and bodily experience by choice or by accident (but is also the vast labyrinthine format of Hell) must regularly send out for bodies, because in time they get used up. To push the body to its limits is to sacrifice it as limited to the greatest and endless pleasures of the deep surface, which exceed bodily endurance and limitation.

Music and mathematics, Flusser argues, must be seen as the two endurance tests of language. On one side, one can award density to music and, in contrast, view mathematics as the stretch of language that covers everything but captures or holds not one thing. If math helps man control the world, this is only a by-product, a side effect. Indeed, math has for its own sake the purpose of reducing all sentences to zero. If the goal of human thought and speech is to be translated into math, then math on its own realizes the *complete* silence that music filled or fulfilled as its postponement. Ego, if you must know, is a dissonance, a grammatical error that arises when math, the highest knowledge, and music, the most creative inspiration, connect, intersect, rather than merge with one another.

With the music math loses the character of being for its own sake and becomes a means of delivering the ego. But as instrument of dissolution, music only delivers us from/of our selves.

Mournfulness, apathy, laziness renounce reality, because it is nothing. Like the repressed anger in depression, or the aggressivity in exaggerated passive behavior, apathy or doing nothing, however, as the film *The Devil Probably* underscores, is another form of refusal: "Nothing doing!" Rather than the Christianity of the future being without religion, let the religion of the future do without Christianity.

We have, in facing the music, delivered ourselves from God and the Devil—but also from every piece of the ego, from every scrap of self-consciousness. The elimination of the Devil is the annihilation of our world, our word, our history. As the Devil father knows the rest, the realization of total Lust without inhibition would be the cessation of human being, which is caught between excess and self limitations, a balancing act that harnesses excess, binds it, gets it off on its own inhibition, binding, punishment. In no time our excess in Lust is turned into the access called psyche. The Devil binds us to our history (his history) by the cycling of excess in Lust, through possessiveness and retention, to proud and then debilitating insight into the nature of our world. But near the bitter end of the cycle there is always something in excess of next-to-nothing, which sparks, scratches, and sniffs, and starts up again from the scratches, the doublings and dividings, in Lust.

In the original *Bedazzled* Sloth (who is married to Lust) witnesses the signing of the contract between the Devil and Moon. When Moon wonders why they're not signing in blood, the Devil agrees to keep up appearances but uses Sloth's blood. The film's discourse is crowded with references to Freud. When they listen to Brahms, the record skips. Repetition starting over and over again from the scratch arises as getting stuck in the groove of music. Moon is advised by the Seven Deadly Sins in the course of trying to woo the waitress Margaret via the seven wishes for the granting of which he sold his soul.

In *L'Orgueil* we seem to witness pride of possession in support of the couple. First we enter a world in which the other is viewed as so faithful, so in love, that the partner willing to cheat on him or her finds the other's infidelity inconceivable. This duo dynamic allows one woman (and wife) to enter a world of doubling and self-love via her adulterous affair with the odd man out in this town of couples, the man from Paris. When she discovers, however, that her own adventure is locked inside a grid of infidelities, she takes repossession of her couple, thus denying the other woman her man and discarding her lover (with whom she was planning to depart on the upbeat of new beginning) in a mode or monde of resignation dedicated, I would argue, not to Pride but to Greed and Envy. Pride, in the sense we've been elaborating, characterizes the scene of her tryst among the mannequins in the storeroom. The dolls double the lovers. She observes herself in the mirror. He watches her loving herself as mirror image. At one point she utters the wish that is granted its command performance in this scene: "I wish I were ten minutes younger."

In *La Paresse* the actor Eddie Constantine plays himself, that is, the film actor, who for the duration of this short film finds nothing worth the trouble anymore. A young woman (who would just love a part in his next film, which presumably is the film we're watching) hitches a ride with him to Paris and hitches her skirt up above her knees. We get the sense of a repeated occurrence, almost a ritual. She wonders why he doesn't talk to her. "I'm getting too lazy to talk. Everything tires me." The sandwich he selects is less tiring to chew. His shoes are untied. He offers the gas station attendant 5,000 francs to take care of the chore, but his nonverbal communication is taken to be a lustful proposition that the young man refuses. When it comes time for sex with his fellow traveler, he decides it's too much trouble. The ironic moral is that Sloth, by putting all the other sins on hold and off limits, contains them, perhaps in a moral sense, but certainly in a double sense. And Sloth is identified by its contrast with or disconnection from Lust. At close quarters, the woman playing a private part in Constantine's next film asks the others not to disturb the duo for twenty minutes, the average span of a short film, although *La Paresse* is half this length. But self-reflection in this film doesn't slow down, it speeds up. Repetition grinds itself down until the little that is left to do is exhausting, exhausted. We can see, however, that the only desire that is constant is Constantine's wish to be the camera, which is able to see along the sidelines of the repetition drive where misunderstandings, for example, spark Lust.

In *The Evil Within* we have the portrait of the serial killer following out the commands of an inner demon and pleasure source. At the carnival, another stage for the pageant of the seven deadly sins and one of Satan's favorite haunts, a young woman is at the disposal of any interested man because she's the laziest gal in town. She embodies lassitude of the heart and, by provoking a jealous partner who could ultimately kill her, symptomatizes deep depression. But suddenly a brown snakelike thing, which isn't long at all, and looks more like a penis turd, enters her and begins to grow inside her and give her commands. Beavis and Butthead: Because this marriage can never be constipated, it can always be analed. What in the Christian mystery enters the ear and then grows up inside Mary already as her bride-groom is in the Devil version a direct insertion that demands to be fed the blood of the men hitting on her. Whereas before she didn't do anything for a living (indeed, all her life, she says, she's done nothing) now she's making a killing, and that gets her to laugh. Her baby's commands already make her smile. He tells her to go find someone in the restaurant. He suggests he'll take a bite already while they're getting it on. The man does feel like something grabbed him down there. But this man whom she murders right when he declares his love for her after their one night standup routine that has to end in the demon baby's feeding time was also at the same carnival she once called home. He shows her a photograph of the place they shared in the past. But he does not recognize her. That's how low she once was, but she's on a different high now than then.

The mother of *The Evil Within* almost dies in a car wreck. We enter the galleys and shafts of her interior. Her turd baby wonders why it's getting cold here. He jump-starts her heart. When next the car breaks down, we get a similar inside view of tubes and machine parts. As born baby, the demon stops telling her what to do. She of course wants him to speak. Then demon oozes out of the baby shell and slimes a bus of ass leaks, I mean, athletes, who decided to pass her around just like in the old days of Sloth at the circus.

The penis turd, now in the shape of an intestinal pile, jumps onto the head of the bus driver; its shiny fleshy orb, which fits tight over the man's head, trails entrails. The sublimation of our lower senses of smell amounts to a readily reversible upward displacement via the genital and Oedipal centering of the upright body. In one sitting, the driver of his *autos* is reduced to the connection with the world offered by the asshole baby from Hell.

The demon's purpose is to reach the sea, enter it, and start evolving, growing until, in five billion years or so, he can replace mankind.

NOTEBOOK SEVEN

Freud shared the closed quarters of his physician-assisted ending with Balzac's *The Wild Ass's Skin*. Right from the start of the novel we are introduced to demons, infernal pacts, and the voice of death in the meta-phorical and manic mix attending the protagonist's visit to the gambling den. Gambling, especially as addiction, gives the young man a pre-Oedipal date mark. The setting of the son going down for the count of losses owes it all to the anal confines in which his father kept him on tracks until one day he flushed him out into a world of financial intrigue and losses. The young man leaves the den of iniquity to find solace in suicide. But first he is diverted by an antique store. The old showrooms are piled high with an eclectic collection of products like the exhibits in wonder rooms in which, from the vantage of the modern museum, we recognize a "vast museum of human folly" (39). There is something cautionary and projective about the display, at least in the eyes of the man determined to kill himself: "he was to see in advance the debris of a score of civilizations" (34). The storeowner occupies a relation of safe distance from the "endless poem" that grabs his new client much as the fantasies Mephistopheles showed Faust on the Brocken proved enticing (42). The merchant takes pride, for example, in being able to convert that which consumes us into reveries. Thus, the passions merely "divert" him "as though they were works of fiction which" he "can read thanks to an inner vision" (52–53). The wild ass's skin the young man finds among the items in this store is thus no skin off the merchant's nose. Kept in some other place, inert, the skin contains all that he turns into works of fiction. The skin otherwise goes deep to unite power and will:

"Here are your social ideas, your inordinate desires, your intemperance, the joys which kill, the pains which make life too intense—perhaps evil is only a violent pleasure." (54)

Because he can no longer live, the young man chooses to live by the skin of the dealer's Nos. "Let's put it to the test!" The dealer laughs at the young man's open-sesame expectation that the wished-for excess in all things would suddenly rise up before him. Wishing follows and guides the narrative that folds out inexorably from the pact.

You have signed the pact, and there is no more to say. From now on, your desires will be scrupulously satisfied, but at the expense of your life. The circle of your days, represented by this skin, will shrink in accordance with the force and number of your desires, from the lightest to the most exorbitant. The brahmin to whom I owe this talisman once explained to me that there would be a mysterious conformity between the destiny and the wishes of its possessor. Your first desire is a vulgar one: I could bring it to pass myself, but I leave that to the chain of events in your new existence. After all, you were bent on dying: well, your suicide is merely postponed. (55)

Now that the client understands the conditions of his wishing (it's no skin off/of his Nos), he formulates his first focused desire as near death wish:

I wish, as repayment for so fatal a service, that you may fall in love with a ballet-dancer! You will then realize what happiness there is in a life of dissipation, and perhaps you will start spending lavishly all the wealth you have husbanded in so philosophic a spirit. (55)

The confusion of desire with wishing is what continues to take the narrative by surprise. The client notes that the joke is on him, because desire should stretch skin, whereas whenever he expresses a desire, the skin shrinks (186). But wishes are points of punctuation that consume us. Read the writing on the skin:

Possess me and thou shalt possess all things. But thy life is forfeit to me. . . . Express a desire and thy desire shall be fulfilled. But let thy wishes be measured against thy life. Here it lies. Every wish will diminish me and diminish thy days. (51)

Over the years, he finds love (in other words, doesn't have to wish for it) and thus comes into a life that doesn't get under his skin. But the skin of wishes and days is coming to its vanishing point. His servant is entrusted with anticipating and seeing to his every want like a mother cares for her infant. Thus, the master, who doesn't need to want or desire anything else, tries to stop the incredible shrinking of the skin. Once when the servant forgets and asks his master if there is anything he wants, he stands accused of being the death of his master. Desire enters language as wishes and seals a compact with finitude. The deferral of suicide via a skin of wishing was affirmed first as excess; later, at some half-life turning point, deferral of the end takes over where the suicide drive leaves off. Max Schur, the physician who gave Freud the assist in scoring the goal of life is death, recalls the close reading:

> It was becoming more and more difficult to feed him. . . . The final phase began when reading became difficult. Freud did not read at random, but carefully selected books from his library. The last book he read was Balzac's *La Peau de Chagrin*. When he finished it he re-marked casually to me: "This was the proper book for me to read; it deals with shrinking and starvation.". . . The theme of the shrinking skin echoes Freud's words about his dying father written in 1896: "he . . . is steadily shrinking towards . . . a fateful date." The uncon-scious is immortal, Freud had said. It retains all memories. How un-canny that he would have chosen to read this book before writing "finis" to his own story! (527–28)

The day after he finished Balzac's stretch in time—and passed the pro-tagonist Raphael in this final stretch, inasmuch as by this point he was neither panicky nor clingy about dead or life lines—Freud asked Schur to keep his promise and give him liberty and give him death. The super- or trans-human as limit and rescue concept is itself at stake in our evalu-ation of this ending.

Is it the wind, a bird, a demon? *Dust Devil* projects a demon, not the Devil, who delivers death to those who are good and gripe for the assist. We watch him, as hitchhiker, getting hitched to lonely women. Then he takes them out. He's their *Liebestod*. Sometimes he kills them at point of climax or

lets them come at pain of death. It's a gift. "Where you going?" "Nowhere."
"Just been there." "You must believe in something — God, the Devil, the soul
at least." "No, when you're dead, you're dead. That's it." But by fulfilling the
suicidal ideation of his depressed dates, he remains trapped with or inside
them. He says to one victim-to-be that he's her mirror image looking back
at her from somewhere inside herself.

The collectible as sweet nothing that unleashes entropy right at the point
where the allegory of perfection holds you hostage—at the point of
wishing—is the medium of the Devil in Stephen King's *Needful Things*.
It is the Devil's means for infiltrating the legal and economic structures
of exchange in order to drive twosomes to destroy each other in total
conflict. Whereas in Balzac's tale the wish pact packs the ego alone on
the skinny skin skin, in *Needful Things* the contract underlying each collectible reformats the individual as interminably mirrored within destructive measures, masses, or shocks.

The Devil "gets everyone who swears on anyone else's name" (626).
The Devil uses the nominal position of the third person, the name on
which we swear to an other, as a terminal of multiple possible transfers
whereby interpersonal relations, relations with a history, are targeted but
from an unreconstructable point of random agency. The Devil "thought
of himself as an electrician of the human soul. In a small town . . . , all
the fuse boxes were lined up neatly side by side. What you had to do was
open the boxes . . . and then start cross-wiring. You hot-wired a Wilma
Jercyck to a Nettie Cobb by using wires from two other fuse boxes . . .
and then you laid low and sent a charge through the circuits every once
in a while . . . and then you turned on the juice" (339–40). But these
random wire transfers do not get around the transference, at least not in
the surviving cases whose study the novel finally represents. While the
Devil drives many of the locals to dual or mass deaths, there are among
the survivors two who have distinguished themselves, in the course of
their encounter with the Devil, by containing within their substitutions
and couple formation the ghosts that inhabited and spooked them for
the duration of the Devil's visitation. At the end of the Devil of a time,

they begin their lives again following a reversal of their own ghost time. The Hell that gets raised and then erased never raised ghosts. The warning Polly issues Alan, the sheriff, the other local who ultimately proves resistant to the Devil's dealings, shows the label stating the essence of their immunity. Even the one useless thing in all the world that Alan wants so badly, namely knowledge of the cause of the accident that killed his wife and child, when it is offered to him by the Devil, Alan will still, ultimately, not get it mixed up with needing it, with being able to have it met as need (685).

You don't always get what you want. But sometimes you find you get what you need. While it is not everyone's lot to be an artist or to find oneself inside a total artwork humming along with the music filling the abyss with its endless relay and repetition of self-relations, anyone can collect.

The Skull opens at auction where two collectors of occult artifacts are invited to bid for demonic sculptures. The collector who was outbid is offered at home by his dealer a Marquis de Sade volume bound in human flesh. Soon the dealer returns with the offer of de Sade's skull. It has the reputation already of possessing those who possess it, and anyone else who happens to be standing by, driving all of them to commit acts of evil."How can a mere skull be dangerous unless your mind makes it so?" It turns out that the Marquis wasn't mad—he was possessed. The demon still resides inside the skull.The other collector bought those demon sculptures because the skull wanted him to obtain them. The demon in the skull is collecting through the meat vehicles he possesses the props he will need to raise Hell.

In *Hellraiser III*, our evil protagonist is an art collector who also, in a sense (in his senses), collects women one by one-night standing invitation to get lost now. He acts out over these bodies the idealization and demonization of his bodily contact with a world of his own making or collecting.The collector finishes with the woman of the day, telling her to get lost so he doesn't have to listen to her drivel about his "great taste." "Who do you think you

are?! You shit!" But first the demon inside the latest addition to his art collection slashes the woman and serves her up on a splatter. The collector is
freaking grossed out. Demon: "You enjoyed the girl, so did I." "That was fucking evil." He turns the gun on the demon, which, as the demon points out, he
last used to kill his parents. The demon will teach him to extend collection
to all aspects of his life. Collect and consume. "There is only flesh. Don't flee
from yourself."

In *Needful Things* the Devil's clients are all collectors. In collecting there
is always also the desire to collect self. The Devil offers you a sweet nothing and invests it for you with collectibility, rendering it a thing with a
worth that can only be calculated by need, the need it fills or fulfills. We
swallow the world. Once it passes through us at that one remove from
nature excrement represents (as our primal creative principle), we not
only recycle it as our techno mass media world but also retain it as collectibles that belong to the recent past of repress release of loss.

Several clients obtain from the Devil a needful thing that takes them
back to the days of their fathers. "Now, looking at this rod and reel, . . .
he was overwhelmed with a simple, perfect memory: his father sitting in
the stern of the boat. . . . Suddenly the old grief rose up and folded him
in its gray embrace and he wanted his father. . . . It would almost be like
being with the old man again" (150–52). Even if you may want your father back, what you need, and what you can get, is a souvenir that proves
that your time with Dad was ideal, unambivalent, a deal. When you get
what you need, you get around what's wanting or lacking. The sheriff
cites the spell of these needful things for being habit forming. He says
the cure or spell is the illness: the need is no sooner filled than it rises up
transformed into pride of possession.

The sheriff in *Needful Things*, who has ghosts to bust ("This idea that
I owe more grief is still there part of the time . . . part of me—a *lot* of
me, in fact—is *still* grieving" [178]), has a repeater insight into the Devil's
hold over the townspeople, knowledge that the Devil fears most. This
thought recurs to the sheriff in the course of the magic showdown: "And

what was the basis of all magic? Misdirection. It was a five-foot-long snake hidden inside a can of nuts...or, he thought,...it's a disease that looks like a cure" (685). This repeats a certain refrain or refraining order in the court of resistance to psychoanalysis, the treatment of the disease that it itself is. The insight that stops the Devil is one of the showstoppers of psychoanalysis. But as in the cases of the sheriff Alan and his substitution candidate Polly, the slo-timing of the in-session (or inherent) dynamic of psychoanalysis—in transference as in repetition—makes all the difference in the self-reflexive word that would bind or banish Freud's theory and therapy.

The Visitation passes through "manifestations" that could be good and healing or demonically deceptive. One former preacher lost his faith when his wife was murdered according to Satanic ritual. The living on of his mourning was embodied by the dog he raised with his wife. Now it's three years later, and the dog is sick to death. Thus, he becomes involved with the veterinarian, his outside chance at substitution. Mysterious figures have been appearing on the horizon, in the street. Miracle cures have become available. The ex-preacher, whose last shred of faith died that morning with his dog, argues that "miracles like faith are psychosomatic." The next miracle he sees is his dog, Max, resurrected. Brandon, a new laborer in town, proclaims that he is Christ. Max goes to the encampment of the new Christ. Why does the dog now growl at the vet? "There's a lot of evil in this town. But it's not me. I'm just trying to help."

But in the meantime the miracle cures seem to be going into reverse. Brandon claims that the return of symptoms signals falling off the path. But now it's evident that Brandon has been possessing people, not healing them. Brandon was once a boy abused. No one believed him, took his side, intervened on his behalf. God didn't help. Plus it's revenge he wants. So he made a covenant with God's enemy. The Devil's only requirement was that Brandon extinguish one human life every three years.

The ex-preacher, ex-unmourner has found a vet to vet his anger and grief. They hold hands at the grave of the psycho Satanist or abused child.

Idealization is highly vulnerable, and its vulnerability (together with its last-ditch attempts at defense) can only increase. To protect (project) the prized sweet nothing—and thus to continue pushing back the mixed feelings that are hidden by or in idealization—external conflict must be waged against the demonized agents out to destroy your thing or take it away. To human-shield themselves from recognition of the ambivalence in their past lives, the townspeople spark a religious war that skips—the Devil has the population stuck on the record of idealized ancestral history, in the groove—that skips the work of mourning and transference. When he supplies his inflamed clients with guns as the town reaches crisis point, the Devil (Mr. Gaunt) assures them that he insures the things he sells: "Protect yourself! Protect your *property!*" (526). "At the end, Mr. Gaunt always sold them weapons.... Each according to his means... because they were *all* needful things, and he had come here to fill their emptiness and end their aches" (584).

But the Devil's hands-on approach to escalating violence results in a slip or two. Thus, in the mounting of chaos, one prank was performed within the duo dynamic of the conflict. As the two fight it out in the midst of terrible twosomes of mass violence, they are able to identify the grievance and, taking it interpersonally, ask for the forgiveness that comes from the Oedipal father, the otherwise excluded third in the Devil's formula for uncontainable violence.

If his victims by and large get all the time in the word they give the Devil dealer, that in exchange for the needful thing they will perform a deed, play a prank, the word the Devil must beat a retreat out of mind of those who need him is "but," the giveaway label of resistance. But just as he denies his own self-collecting interest in souls (the very souls we hear at the end squeaking repetitively like sound bites in the Devil's one carrion bag), so he denies his association with the hole of Hell in order to wipe out the three letters of resistance. Gaunt: "I *hate* that word. Of all the words in the English language, it is easily the worst. I think it's the worst word in *any* language. You know what a butt is...? It's the place shit comes out of" (257–58). Or again: "In the best of all possible worlds, there would be no need for such a puling little word. I want you to say something else for me, . . . I want you to say some words that I love. . . . Mr. Gaunt knows best. . . . Just like Father" (266).

The violent acting out sparked by the Devil's rewiring of the third-person role in countless duo dynamics is recognized by the townspeople as "kicking butt." The Devil comes from behind, brings up the rear, and works the medium, even the corporeal medium, of resistance. *But* the Devil's skill at getting everything for nothing—he says he lets his clients "make up their own minds" (723)—must submit to the magic tricks and illusions to which he owes his power over all victims. The sheriff, who likes to perform a few catalog-ordered magic tricks just for fun, fires a canned snake at the Devil (once the favorite trick to play with his unmournably dead son)—"and this time" (or in the meantime) "it was no joke" (720). The Devil is driven out by magic tricks that he is obliged, as master illusionist, to take or fake to be real. When the sheriff next declares the "Demon" "cast out from this place," the magic words work.

The Devil stands by and goes down with magic tricks that can stir up the surface and make a world of divergence but if caught at close quarters by another magician, must withdraw into the screen-thin reality of projection. In the tight spot of magical self-reflexivity, to spell is to be: if the deed comes your way, you must pass it on.

In *Curse of the Demon,* the magician, who can summon stormy weather to demonstrate the efficacy of the black arts, places a death wish or curse upon you in the form of a scrap of paper that can only be passed on before it disappears: if the bad luck stops here, with you, then you die in three days at the claws of a really huge demon. What we learn in the close quarters of the magician's duo dynamic with his mother, his partner for life, suggests that the very contact with the black arts released the unstoppable momentum of the wish. "If it's not somebody else's life, it will be mine." Thus, the original wish is in contact with or directed against his own person. His black-arts career defers this consequence by passing the wish along. In the end, his opponents

succeed in secretly returning a death-wish notice to the magician's posses-
sions. He catches sight of the scrap just in time to watch it disappear in fire
and smoke. Then the demon comes for him alone.

In his study of art linking letters, Luther Link has the last word with which
one might introduce *Fallen:* "The Devil's countless little agents were imagined in the Middle Ages not unlike the way we imagine microbes today—
always potentially present and malign" (40). Detective Hobbes agrees to
visit Reese, the condemned man he helped put on death row. A documentary film is being made. They shake hands. It becomes clear that Reese is
trying to place a curse on the detective through touch and with ritual spell
words. The curse didn't transmit, not directly. The condemned man's parting
words: "What goes around, really goes around." All that's left is to sing on his
way to the gassing: "Time is on my side, yes it is." While Reese was being
strapped down, he touched the attending officer. When he dies, a floating
POV settles on the touched officer. That he is touched in the head catches
on with the tune he sings: "Time is on my side." But he bumps into the next
guy and transfers "Time is on my side" to him. "It" really goes around. After
three more transfers, we stay with one guy who turns violent. But his staying power also eventually goes bump in the night of crowded conditions.
The POV goes around and around like cooties.

Reese also left Hobbes a riddle to decipher. What's between x and y?
X and y turn out to be names of cops on a plaque. A name between these
names was removed. It was detective Milano. Hobbes visits Milano's daughter, who is a theology professor specializing in angel studies. She asks him
about Reese: "Did he like to sing? Did he try to touch you at the execution?"

Hobbes investigates the place where Milano was holed up when he
ran amok. The writing on the wall: Azazel. It's the name of a demon that
transmits by touch. He asks Professor Milano about Azazel and her father.
"Run if you love anyone at all. We're not supposed to know. The fallen angels
can only survive in us."

In *Needful Things* the Devil runs his local interventions into the grounding of mass events according to the model of round-the-clock, round-
the-world TV news coverage: "The carnival was well established: one
major attraction had been tested successfully; the time to start up all the
rides at once was now near at hand. As always when he reached this
point, whether in Lebanon, Ankara, the western provinces of Canada, or
right here in Hicksville, U.S.A., he felt there were just not enough hours in
the day" (430). While the film *Needful Things* unfolds the signature role
of Leland Gaunt in the corner of newspaper front pages packed with the
headline news of global catastrophe, like Hitler's rise to power, or local
murders and suicides, like the current events going down in town since
Gaunt's arrival, King's novel represents the infrastructure of the Devil's
power way more convincingly by turning on the TV. "The residents
grumbled about the heat. . . . Probably had something to do with the
goddam oil-fires in Kuwait, they said, or maybe that hole in the ozone
layer they were always blabbing about on TV" (345). TV democratizes
what remains hierarchized in newspapers. In the headline medium of
the news one can only wonder why the Devil would bother with the
Castle Rock locals when he was able to set his spell on a whole nation,
indeed even on a world at war. But the instant contact between the local
and the global on TV screens fits the Devil's plans. Once the TV news
vans come to town and begin setting up live feeds (581), Castle Rock (or
Hicksville) is as hot a spot in the news as Ankara or Kabul. But these instant local to global relations remain personally or interpersonally as
hidden as the motivations for the pranks the Devil assigns to third par-
ties who are uninvolved, unknown bystanders at the duo dynamic of
conflict they help the Devil spark between neighbors. What builds from
this small unit of neighborly hostilities assumes the destinal momentum of a drive. Thus, in King's novel the Devil is personified at once as
deceiver or magician and as destruction drive, the kind of force that,
once it is with you, can no longer be taken interpersonally.

In *End of the World* Christopher Lee plays a priest who one day is cloned
with his pack of nuns by aliens from outer space. In other words, he also

plays the alien who's clone alone. Apparently the original humans were used in experiments to determine if the time warp was safe for the aliens to return to their more perfect world. One suspicious scientist checks the computers: the church compound has sent descriptions of him and his wife to outer space. The couple decides to do some investigating. They arrive just in time to serve as captive audience to the original priest's turn to do the time warp. Nope. Still doesn't work. In this movie high-tech labs, research facilities, and plants occupy interchangeable places with the church grounds. When the couple tries to leave that night—they're not locked up or in any other way restrained—every turn they take in the dark leads them right back up against the church buildings they thought they had left way behind. But this doubling illusion or effect cannot reverse a line, a roadway, or train tracks, passing through the landscape. Thus, when they stop a car on the road, it looks like they have a chance to get out of the maze. But the car with driver bursts into flame. When it comes to the line of time, the aliens in church clothing can only destroy and kill. Wouldn't you know the scientist has access to the mineral or ore that is needed to fix the time warp? The warp is not wrapped around relativity. It is, as the alien priest clone explains, a velocity time relationship that drives their interstellar travel. With the time warp gateway up and running again, the couple watches a wall of TV sets affording different channels of surveillance views of the world coming to an end through natural disasters everywhere at once. One live cam is trained on the church grounds. The alien priest clone advises them that the destruction of the world has been timed to make these grounds the last bit of earth to blow. Then he invites them to cross over to the better world, where all that causes war and suffering on earth is in the service of the progress and pleasure of living. The couple watches the TVs go blank one by one. Finally the live cam covering the church is the only show on earth. They enter the time warp. This turns up a contrast with the TV model of the Devil's destructiveness in *Needful Things* (the novel). In *End of the World* destructiveness loses its global network when we are down to the local station that is under its own surveillance and is the sole target, in the end, of the destruction. Here the death drive short circuits, skips the demonic relay and delay and thickener of repetition, music, self-reflexivity, and blows up our imperfect world. Just the same a human link and memory—including traumatic souvenirs—are part of the savings when the potentially reproductive couple follows the alien priest and nun clones and beams up to an outside chance of survival.

NOTEBOOK EIGHT

In *Civilization and Its Discontents* and *The Future of an Illusion* Freud diagnoses whole epochs of religious belief in "other worlds" as "neurotic" (*SE* 21: 144, 43). In contrast, the Devil's powers, in person or by proxy, are linked and limited to "this world." The Devil can extend or defer these limits for a certain amount of time, but the time will come when the deadline must be observed. In *Angel Heart,* just when it looks like the client has escaped the contract for several years, we discover that, in one year and out the other, the severed years of amnesia don't count as or amount to time of one's own.

Lou Cyphre (aka Lucifer) hires a detective to track down Johnny Favorite, the legendary musician who vanished from the face of the charts by 1944. Every detection plot is another Oedipus story to the extent that the one looking to find who done it ends up being the one he's looking for, who's done for. Johnny Favorite cut a deal with the Devil for musical stardom. But when his time was up, he tried to cheat the Devil and steal more time. On New Year's Eve 1943 he found someone his own age, a soldier on leave, and took heart that he would outwit the Devil by living on incognito. But then war neurosis gave the soldier version of Johnny traumatic amnesia. He doesn't know that he is another person (the same person) continued. It's like when you clone around with yourself and you still end up with another life not your own. Johnny goes after all when he doesn't know anymore that he isn't this other person. But the Devil never stopped watching over Johnny's double time, even before their client-detective relationship. While the work of detection proceeds, the Devil gives the man searching for

Johnny who is Johnny leave of his senses to kill, without knowing it, every witness or lead he also, just like a detective, interviews. His better half fears he is being framed for the serial murder of his witnesses. But the Devil in fact frames the already doubled and contained life-insurance policy he issued once before until, in the end, Johnny rises to consciousness of his deeds, his dead, his certain death, his deed with Devil Dad. By hiring and guiding unconscious Johnny inside the detective to find himself, to know, consciously, who he is, the Devil plays the original timeline in reverse, "back" to the original deadline. A certain death can be received or recognized only consciously and without all that Oedipal static (like fear of death or the dead) on the line, the deadline.

The cycling between nothing, something, everything, and nothing again Hell-spawns self-reflexivity that the occasional stray difference, gap, or overlap—like the Devil dealer's prideful mistakes in *Needful Things* in the obstacle course of mounting his brainwashing simulations of evidence of the senses—deflates or opens up. Lamberto Bava's *Demons*, both movies, locate demonization, first time in the receiving line of film, in *Demons 2* in front of the TV set, as point of excess inside the relay of self-reflexivity. At the movies the filmed action doubles and diagnoses the accidents that just occurred to individuals in the audience, too, in the split second before the screen picks up what happened in front of it, until the doubling in the receiving area crowds out the boundary between movies and viewers with divisions of demons. In *Demons* the players on the screen find the sixteenth-century book of Nostradamus, which contains, we are informed, predictions of Hitler's rise to power, of world wars, and, in time for this movie, of the coming of the demons. "But that hasn't happened." "Wait and see." We are invited to attend the repetition compulsion of a wound on the multiple inside-out screens and in the receiving areas of spectacles all of us end up wearing. The spectacles are first introduced as fitting the specs of the Deadly Sins. The blind man with the seeing-eye bride is Pride going on Sloth and married to Lust (his bride will move a few rows behind him to make out with her adulterous lover).

In *Demons 2* what's left after the demon contagion was finally contained the first time around is a walled-in condemned site where there was once Berlin. It is a sight for eyes glued to the tube. Is it a fiction film, a document, or a live transmission? Kids break into the restricted zone. By accident one of them bleeds on the demon corpse, which then comes alive. But this TV story turns out to be a live transmission of this contagion sequel. Just as the voice-over comes on to identify the TV show as fiction film, the demon passes through the small screen after all and puts the bite on one viewer, who takes it from there.

In *Demons* the missing link that makes film story and the audience real-time-in-sync is the bleeding wound on the face of one moviegoer. On screen a character digging Nostradamus puts on the mask and makes the cut; in the audience the woman who tried on the mask in the foyer and pricked herself touches her wound that still bleeds or bleeds again. Thus, the contagion spreads as the live transmission of an open wound through the audience even as it overflows the boundary between film and audience. The open wound of trauma, in our face and in history, gives the origin (in theory and in the history of the theory) of repetition compulsion. If music is the art form voted most likely to seal the deal with or for the Devil, then that is because it fills or fulfills the abyss of nothingness as creation out of nothing. It is a language of relations without meaning, a language of or for self-relations only. In the *Demons* movies, for example, what isn't in the score is accomplished as self-relation on screen, as self-reflexivity, the repetition compulsion of art, what can be termed the music drive.

In *Demon Knight* we watch the text come alive: action is prescribed and the script enacted. Mutual copying is a good coping skill for filling up a void.

Midnight Cabaret opens with a street scene of ritual orgy and murder. A young woman witnesses it all — even the naked revelers watching her watching. The chase is on. She finally falls through a glass partition onto a stage. Applause. The narrator or announcer (of the staged performance) welcomes the audience to Mephisto's. We're watching a play. The actress, in wedding dress and veil, is up there with the groom. But then a third person rises up on his throne. "His Majesty, the Prince of Darkness." The Devil begins: "Allow me to introduce myself. Those looking to be free call me savior." The Devil, who thus welcomes the audience to "Midnight Cabaret," interrupts not the mother-and-child dyad but substitution itself with something else, the other third party. Backstage after the performance, the actress can't join her costar for a drink because she's been invited to join the party of Paul, who plays the Devil and owns the building in which Mephisto's is housed. It's his party and he'll try if he wants to. The actress, already dizzy from one sip of drink, has double-take vision: Paul's mother, who plays Death on stage, suddenly appears as demon, but then she's the mother again. When she next walks in on Paul and friends conversing, the actress thinks she sees demons performing a ritual. Back on stage Paul as Devil and the actress as virgin bride perform a sex scene. A priest arrives bearing a big cross. "Stop what you are doing." Mother in black: "It's you again." "In the name of God." "God? He created us equal. He gave you Heaven and he gave me Hell. I tempt man. You deceive him. Which is worse?" "In the name of God stop what you are doing." "Let her decide." She wakes up from the nightmare. When she leaves in the night, in the rain, Paul follows her. Four "underworld" types block his progress. Paul: "I need more time." "We gave you all the time you needed." One of them slits Paul's throat. She wakes up from the nightmare. Phone rings. The detective asks if she knows Paul Van Dyke. Can she come down and identify him? Back on stage: "Ladies and Gentlemen. In memory of Paul Van Dyke." Outside the theater the actress places a rose on the fresh grave. Double take. She thinks she saw him. A magic trick is the announcer's opener on stage. Dwarves in black monk habits surround the actress as virgin bride and start tearing off her gown. A man scatters the little ones with his whip. It's Paul. Audience applauds. She sleeps, she dreams: we see someone's wake, probably Paul's. She wakes up. Paul is standing over her. "Please do not be frightened. I will not harm you. I love you. You're mine, mine only." Now she fears for her costar's life. She and the detective enter the costar's apartment and find him dead and decked out for his wake just like in her dream. The actress's best friend takes her home after the night's performance. The actress sleeps, she dreams. Her friend is sitting up in the next room reading. She lifts her glass without looking to take a sip and another glass knocks against hers as in a toast. Paul is alive. He slits her throat. Actress wakes up screaming. She goes into next room. Friend is very dead. The police arrive. She's cradling her dead friend. Just when it couldn't look more obvious in the eyes of the law enforcers, the detective finds a copy of the script "Midnight Cabaret." He asks his colleague: "Do you believe in the Devil?" The colleague laughs that one off with a joke about his ex-wife. The detective continues: "Everything that happens in this script happens in real life. She didn't kill anyone."

The detective goes to theater and finds the actress lying in bed, very pregnant. Mother Death: "Detective, there's nothing you can do. It's done." "Stop or I'll shoot." "You're a funny man. You think you can kill death?" The actress doubles over with the contractions. On stage the Big Ben drawn on the set starts striking midnight. "I wouldn't bring this evil thing into this world! God forgive me." She jumps and falls through the glass roof over the revelers. Audience applauds. At curtain call, Mother Death starts speaking lines that seem addressed to a young woman in the audience: "Let me into your mind. Come to perfect paradise. I will take you away from this world of destruction. Prepare for ultimate seduction. Step into my world. Filled with ecstasy." She leads the woman from her seat up onto the stage. The detective is watching, too. Or is he on stage? The camera leaves the building. Back inside somewhere it hovers over a woman in bed, sleeping. On stage the announcer concludes: "Ladies and gentlemen. Good night. Pleasant Dreams."

In William Hjortsberg's *Falling Angel* (the book on which *Angel Heart* was based), the double protagonist, Harry Angel/Johnny Favorite, had one trick up his sleeve, but to play it, to obtain double indemnity, he had to become his double's identity, and only thus does he win out for the duration of his loss or swap of identity and consciousness. "Johnny's sin was pride. He thought he could outwit the Prince of Darkness Himself" (270). Angel's client or boss, Louis Cyphre (or Lucifer, as Favorite knew him best), is a magician who delights in cheap tricks. His vulgar side reorganizes in Devilish terms the other world of death that shadows (or foreshadows) the detective in search of Johnny Favorite, the missing client of Louis Cyphre.

Cyphre simply needs to know whether his client is alive or dead. "In recognition of my assistance, which was considerable, we had a contract. Certain collateral was involved. This was to be forfeited in the event of his death" (8). Dead or alive: that's the opening-and-shut frame for detective Angel's quest. But the framing of his double-crossing constitution rises to consciousness only, under Cyphre's direction, via a self-reflexive relay of high-low theatrical frames within frames. As he prepares to attend one of the shows that Cyphre presents now as El Cifr, now as Dr. Cipher, detective Angel comes to a tentative conclusion: "The shadow-play events screened manipulations I could barely discern" (163).

One of Cyphre's sideshow props features a group of enchanted souls bound to play as mice in a tight theatrical spot:

> Dr. Cipher unsnapped the metal fasteners securing the case and opened it to form a triptych. A miniature theatre unfolded, with scenery and background tableaux painted in the meticulous perspective of the Italian Renaissance. The stage was peopled with white mice, all costumed in tiny silks and brocade as characters from *commedia dell'arte*.... "As you see, I have no need for television." Dr. Cipher folded the sides of the miniature stage closed and secured the fasteners. There was a handle on top, and he lifted it off the table like a suitcase. "Whenever the box is opened, they perform. Even show business has its Purgatory." (211–12)

We know from *Hamlet* that in the Renaissance ghosts were viewed either as the recently passed on doing the limbo to improve sin atonement or as empty apparitions ghost written and remote controlled by the Devil. Hamlet recognizes the paternal spirit in the old mole. But he fixates his focus only on the moles and blemishes in his maternal face to face. It is around the mother and her curtailment of mourning rights that everyone in *Hamlet* goes bump in the night of nothingness. Hamlet passes on the paternal legacy of mourning to Horatio once he, the mother's son, a heartbeat after his mother dies, becomes an unambiguous ghost: "I am dead, Horatio."

According to Gérard Pommier, the counterpart to or target of monotheism was hardly polytheism but decidedly the cult of the dead. The full range of this conflict (prior to its disposal) can be found maintained as the ambiguity and tension obtaining between demons and the Devil. The first monotheism, Judaism, did not provide the dead with an afterlife: "What a strange belief! For if the dead are kept from returning, it is indeed necessary that they live somewhere!" (160). The paternal ancestors already link and limit the countless dead to their more elect representation. "Then the unique principle of the eternal father (the dead father) . . . replaces a cult of the dead involving several fathers" (160).

The phallus is demonized between mother and infant via the offspring's rejection (= primary repression) of the mother's desire that her baby supply the phallus she lacks. To identify with this desire would mean to disappear. To make room for this desire just the same means to summon spirits. The mother haunts her offspring's reality. But she also threatens to reduce her child's body to nothingness.

The primal or pre-Oedipal father steps up to bat with the demonic phallus. To be or not to be is the double and divided value of this phallus. The father who straps it on is inevitably wished dead. "Satan doubles the figure of the father whose death is desired. This sexual Devil, as singular as the god of monotheism, saves the cult of the dead as legion of demons dispersing the phallic power across the world" (164).

But when Satan enters Judas just as the Eucharist is being prepared for entry, he takes up the position of Antichrist, doubling thus the son, not the father. "Christ is the incestuous son whose Luciferian double avows the sin" (171). Thus, on this stage of monotheism, we are squarely inside the round whole of Oedipus in which the immortal ego's substitution, now for the off-limits person, now for the dead one, replaces the cult of the dead with finite works of mourning. Spirits are only the evil kind. But they can be put to rest.

Johnny cannot, like Hamlet, escape the Devil Father down in the melancholic underworld. His literal incorporation of some innocent bystander, chosen at once randomly and according to specifications like a serial killer's victim, also only realizes survival of the other in oneself via utter reversal of the identifying bond. Dr. Cipher's mousetrap of theatrical self-reflexivity, which replaces television, the faith-based medium of live transmission, is another catch in the consciousness of the former client who lives on only as someone else entirely, which doesn't really add "on" to living.

Another one of Dr. Cipher's theatrical props is a bottle in which the soul of a Spanish sailor whines and dies for the owner of a bottled pain that can never touch him. At the end of the line Angel enters this bottle-field that counts his lover as casualty, the last in the series of murders for which he is being framed. The loved one with the giveaway name Epiphany, whom Angel "first" encountered as another witness in the case of tracking down Johnny Favorite, was all along secretly etched on the Devil's check-off, check-out list whereby Angel must remember, re-assemble Johnny's contract down to its last phrase and phase. She turns out to be Johnny's daughter—which means that Angel, too, is the father who knows her best as incest. He calls to warn Epiphany. But he realizes it's too late to protect her against the role she, too, must play in the infernal frame-up whereby he must come (back) into his own. "The endless ringing struck the same note of despair as the lonely voice of the Spanish sailor in Dr. Cipher's bottle. Another lost soul like me" (286).

Angel can now speak the "I" of Johnny Favorite, but only as one at once dead and alive. "I killed him and ate his heart, but it was me who died all the same. Not even magic and power can change that. I was living on borrowed time and another man's memories; a corrupt hybrid creature trying to escape the past. . . . No matter how cleverly you sneak up on a mirror your reflection always looks you straight in the eye" (287).

The first clue—or upsurge of anamnesis—struck Angel as revelation hitting him "like an ice-water enema" (57).

On the other stage of dream, Angel acts out the inside or backside view of the double identity. Voodoo ceremonies the detective in fact

witnessed play back in his dream in projective amplification. The celebrants drown in oceans of blood from the neck of one sacrificed rooster.
The dreamer switches from quarry to pursuer: the chase continues across
changing scenes. Then:

> An enormous seashell, tall as a skyscraper, loomed ahead. The man ran
> inside. I followed him. . . . The passage narrowed, and I came around a
> final turn to find my adversary blocked by the enormous, quivering,
> fleshy wall of the mollusk itself. There was no way out. I seized the
> man by his coat collar and spun him around, pushing him back into
> the slime. He was my twin. It was like looking in the mirror. He gath-
> ered me in a brother's embrace and kissed my cheek. . . . I relaxed,
> overwhelmed by a wave of affection. Then I felt his teeth. His fraternal
> kiss grew savage. . . . My hands sank deep into his flesh, familiar fea-
> tures oozing between my fingers like wet dough. His face was a shape-
> less pulp lacking bone or cartilage and when I pulled away my hands
> were mired there, like a cook caught in a suet pudding. (91–92)

Up against the membrane wall of some enlarged anal pocket, the dreamer
meets his twin, at first as his mirror reversal, then as vampire, and finally
as excremental ooze. Anal or fecal renewal leaves behind the retention
span of back-end encryptment. Loss passes through, into, as the limit-
less medium of making anal babies. No place for lost and found daughters to hang on.

> In *Hellraiser* one adulterous wife, who did it with her husband's brother,
> finds she must tend to what remains of her lover after the box opened up
> the portal and let the S/M demons in and inside his skin, blood, and
> guts. Her husband's daughter, who needs a father more than the Hellraisers
> need to get it on again, finally puts a stop to her uncle's reanimation, not
> out of projected mixed feelings, or other symptoms and sources of grief,
> but out of the blood and guts that her father's wife harvests out of the
> tricks she brings home. The lover from Hell is extracted from a waste pro-
> duction line opened up by a magical box that took away the centered box
> of upright Oedipal sexuality and made him over as the bloody insides of
> anal rebirth.

Johnny wasn't reading *Hamlet* to get the Devil's ghost. Instead he turned to an alchemical treatise from the Italian Renaissance on the transmutation o f souls to seek his outside chance of eluding the terms of his contract. "Johnny had the idea that he could switch psychic-identities with someone else. Actually become the essence of the other person" (271). After he wolfed down the still-beating heart of the soldier who was the same age as Johnny and born under the same sign, Johnny hoped to disappear only to return as soldier. He was shipped overseas, after all, only to entertain the troops. But as sole survivor of a devastating attack, he came back the shell (shock) of his former self. One of his fellow Devil worshippers had the big idea to release him near Times Square (or time^2) and thus align him with what would have been the soldier's last memory. It worked. The earliest memory of Harold Angel, who also came back from the war a major amnesiac, was his disoriented crossing of Time's Square. "I said I knew something about shell shock myself" (7). Angel lost his parents while he was an amnesiac in the military hospital. Favorite was abandoned at birth. Favorite sought to fill the void with "power"—and, via evil disregard of other lives, with more life. As Angel looks through photographs of Favorite, he recognizes only an empty placeholder: "Where do you search for a guy who was never there to begin with?" (51).

Zero is where he once tried to slip through. Cyphre's name game also cites cipher, the medium of the final tally to which he leads Angel/Favorite. In the disembodied loudspeaker voice of the carney pulling off an exit that's a disappearing act, Cyphre proclaims: "'Zero, the point intermediate between positive and negative, is a portal through which every man must eventually pass'" (212).

In *On the Nightmare,* Jones discovers among the Indo-European roots of "Devil" "double." The double is beside itself next to nothing. The double, like zero, is portal or placeholder, cipher, and vanishing point. Gustav Meyrink equates Devil and mirror image in his novel *Walpurgis Night.* The emperor's personal physician decides late in life (it's Faust time), as he contemplates himself in the mirror in his room, that it is the reversal in mirror reflection that seals the doubling deal: only because his mirror image must do with the left hand what he does with his right is it recognizable as his *Doppelgänger.* Only thus can he be home a clone.

"A curious reversal takes place there," the physician told himself, "which would be truly terrifying if we had not been conditioned from childhood on to see it as something self-evident. Hm. Where in the room does the reversal transpire?—Yes, yes, of course: in a single mathematical point, to be precise.—Indeed it is strange that so much more takes place in such a minute point than in the extended room itself." An indeterminate feeling of fear that, should he pursue this topic further and extend the law it contained to other questions, he could arrive at the painful conclusion that mankind was bereft of a conscious will to undertake anything—but rather was only the helpless machine of an enigmatic point in his interior—kept him from continuing to brood. (83–84)

When next the doubling or manifestation goes audio, a sleepwalking actor is the speakerphone by which he hears his ego's diatribe. Has his ego left him? Could he survive his ego's departure? "You find that curious, your excellency? Do you seriously believe that the people usually walking around in the streets possess egos?—They own nothing at all, are instead possessed every other moment by yet another ghost who plays in them the role of the ego" (97). But the ego talking to him from within the actor's person is not another dead person (99). In this room of his own mirror it is the Devil he sees before him as himself.

The Devil is the ego in the procession of Pride. The creation of the world was the ego's game. What, then, would humility before this ego signify?

"I call that in my language the minus sign. And such minus signs, heaped up in the course of time, function like a sucking vacuum in the realm of the invisible. That brings forth then a bloodthirsty, pain-causing, sadistic plus sign—a whirlwind of demons, which make use of the brains of mankind to release wars and engender violence and murder, much as I make use of the mouth of an actor in order to deliver this lecture to you, your Excellency." (100)

"You are the man who can fulfill all wishes?" "Yes, I am the god in whose hands mankind places their wishes." The Devil indicates his loincloth. It marks the spot the other gods are in with their missing genitals. "Only I can understand wishes; whosoever is truly sexless has forgotten for all time what wishes are. The unrecognizable, deepest root of every wish lies always in the sex sphere, even when the blossom—the conscious wish—seems to have nothing to do with sexuality" (153). The dead make first contact with the significance of the plus sign. "My ear is deaf to the wishes that come out of the mouths of wandering corpses.—That is why these 'dead' find me so terrifying" (153). The Devil specializes in death wishes, the plus or surplus of destruction in tight spots of intimacy, but death wishes without the mortal recoil of ambivalence and ghostliness.

As the plot sickens, the Devil inside the somnambulant actor devotes himself to the death-wish sparks in the novel's alternate plots. Now he occupies the I of the storm of a revolution that crowns a couple of individuals, on doubling momentum, as their own rulers of the world. Lucifer accelerates on death drive and commands that he be skinned and then stretched over a drum that will beat for the followers of the doubled and deranged. In the brief span of Lucifer's drumbeats, everyone up and dies.

All the Colors of the Dark opens within the kaleidoscopic inside view of the plot or phantasm lines that we never get over or beyond: knifing, dollies, evil stare of old blue eyes, pregnant woman, three dead women. Jane dreams, wakes up, hallucinates, and is left with a disquieting sense of reality conspiracy. Jane decides she wants to see Dr. Burton, psychiatrist. Richard: "If you start therapy, you'll never stop." Jane has a new friend, Mary, who had the same problems. She relieved herself of them by attending a Sabbath. "Don't you want to be cured?" "When can I go?" The Satanic priest offers libation: "Drink this and you will be free!" It rhymes with orgy. Everyone present gets a smack of her lips. Suddenly she wakes up in bed beside Richard. "Everything's back to normal, isn't it Jane?" "But I don't feel real, Richard." When she goes back to Sabbath, she's the last to find out that Mary no longer exists. "She brought you. Now she's free to go. But you must help her." Jane can't kill Mary. But Mary proclaims, while pressing herself against the dagger Jane clutches: "I can stay no longer. Then they'll free you, too." Now that Mary skewers herself with Jane's passive assistance, the high priest concludes: "Now you are one of us, Jane. It's impossible for you to renounce us." The dreams or hallucinations opening onto reality or illusion keep Jane occupied in the asylum. The occult genealogy adds the information, metaphorical or direct, that Jane killed her mother with the very knife she used again to kill Mary. But Mary's wish to die (again) made Jane play dead and used her still life plus knife as instrument. The guilt Jane continues to lose in spans of derealization is attached not to agency but to wish—and not to mother's murder but to the prospect of mourning her successfully, whereby she would die twice and for all time. That's why the asylum attendant, and not the Satanic priest, has last words that close Jane's case or crypt: "You have left reality behind."

NOTEBOOK NINE

The death drive or the demonic is hard for Freud to follow. It's certainly for all concerned hard to perceive in all its purity. It's like, says Freud, the silence in the background of the melody of the drives (*SE* 21: 119; *SE* 14: 62). A demonic aspect in music was familiar to Freud early on at that influential remove of a follower's research. Max Graf, a music journalist and an academic historian of music, was one of two nonpractitioner members of the original Wednesday meeting group. Around the turn of the century Graf already published on music subjects, in particular on Wagner. The demonic force that was with Wagner, indeed a "Devilish curse" (*Wagner Problems*, 44) and the "curse of Satan" (45), drove the composer to represent excessive passion and then to find release, if only by proxy, through renunciation. With the exception perhaps of Graf's insistence that all this commotion fits the metabolization of one wound, in Wagner as in his protagonists, this biographical, intellectual-historical interpretation of Wagner is hardly psychoanalytic. In these early studies, the focus on the demonic inside Wagner is shared with the external Devil, the journalist friend of Brahms, Eduard Hanslick, who used Brahms "with Satanic cleverness" (103) to fight the journalist's battles against Wagner, whom Hanslick despised. According to Graf, journalism is its own "mode of living" (100), one that lacks religious or metaphysical sensibility, even connection with personal experience, and is thus anti art, and part or projectile of Graf's fundamentally split position between art or art appreciation and analysis.

In *Composer and Critic* Graf cites the split between Hanslick and Wagner as the onset of "modern musical criticism in Europe": at first music critics targeted Wagner because they "sided with the readers of the papers—who looked for entertainment in theaters and concert halls of an evening—and in general opposed the independent artists and fought with all their intelligence and all their wit—and often with all their narrowness—against the great composers of the time" (242–43). But Wagner invented the generation gap: he made his cause that of the Teen Age. Once all those Siegfrieds in the audience had replaced "the elder generation of the new industrial epoch," "the whole world turned Wagnerian" (243).

This modern splitting origin of criticism fighting music, and then under this cover together introducing middlebrow culture, repeats the original origin of music criticism, according to Graf. "It is a strange fact in the history of musical criticism that, at the moment it first entered the world, the first clash between this new force and creative power occurred. Similar conflicts have accompanied the whole development of music, from Bach to Stravinsky and Schoenberg. . . . Perhaps this is an inevitable and essential part of progress; perhaps it must accompany all great composers, just as military bands accompany an army into battle." Graf then performs the double inheritance of modern music criticism or modern music culture when he issues his policy statement for the history of music criticism: "Conflicts between critics and artists can be profitably analyzed only when they are the necessary result of different outlooks on the world: conflicts, for example, between generations or periods. These are not personal matters, but matters of logic; one might say that they are conflicts produced by the development of historical trends, by God himself, it may be, as He struggles with his own critic, the Devil" (69).

Graf leaves himself the Devil of a chance that he is not God nor is he the berated musical genius but is caught up just the same within an inevitable context in which, in real time, one can't take sides. This context or contest, which, even as it cites the Old Testament understanding or Job description of Satan, commences as social or group-psychological phenomenon only with the beginning of modern mass-media-music culture in the Teen Age, is one of testing.

The relationship between Graf and Hanslick, which in Graf's historical perspective is the split-off side effect of the generational contest between critics and composers, was in fact just a test, which both men were thus destined to pass, moving right along, transference-style, inside the father/son identification. Indeed, Hanslick, who died in 1904, was one of Graf's mentors at the University of Vienna. The books Graf published while in the United States open with the author's listing of his credentials as music critic and historian, always including at the top of the list Hanslick's mentorship. When Freud gave his case study of the phobic five-year-old boy, who happened to be Graf's son, a nickname, he aimed perhaps in earshot of this father: little Hans.

"From the time of the beginning of his anxiety Hans began to show an increased interest in music and to develop his inherited musical gift" (*SE* 10: 138 n.1). Beginning in 1934, big Little Hans worked in the United States as opera director. Freud's "Analysis of a Phobia in a Five-Year-Old Boy" is remarkable in his oeuvre for being, escapably, not his own. And yet many if not all the coordinates of all the other open-and-shut cases in Freud's corpus that cut to the crypt are pressing here, too. It's just that this time the aboveground problem, like the Oedipus complex, for example, is not just one big diversion.

Little Hans's first contacts with technologization don't bear undead cargo. He suffers from phobias of transportation or *Verkehr,* which, from railway to the street, cover access to the mother's womb, which the dead father alone can gain for, while gaining on, the son. For little Hans this speed race appears sexologically contained: his saving fantasy of marrying his mother and sending his father off to marry his own mother relieves the tension building the phobic symptoms (*SE* 10: 97). Displacement goes around and comes around as happy ending because the father's father is both missing and at the remote controls: his more-than-absence guarantees that this farce, in which, while he's away, all the sons can play, will call curtains on the incestuous retention of the off-limits body.

"The Professor," for whom little Hans and his father dictate and write down the case material, holds the trans-parent's missing place. The course of the analysis does not rewind the course of the neurosis's development (*SE* 10: 83) but constructs out of the material heading little Hans off at the impasse a transference neurosis and cure along a three-way freeway. Little Hans pounds this busy street or intersection where his life as a neurotic, the father's recording and programming of his associations, and the Professor's supervision are traffic jamming.

> [father:] "Once he knocked on the pavement with his stick and said: [little Hans:] 'I say, is there a man underneath?—someone buried?— or is that only in the cemetery?' [for Freud:] So he is occupied not only with the riddle of life but with the riddle of death." (*SE* 10: 69)

Although he knocks at portals of the anal and footnote underworld where dead sausage children are internal and eternal occasions for grieving (*SE* 10: 131 n.1), each return of the repressed the five-year-old rides out remains always only metaphorically "like an unlaid ghost" (*SE* 10: 122).

The three-way association passes from the almost improperly buried corpse (it can still be readily restored to the cemetery, which is just a question-to-the-father away) to the box-and-cart theories of birth, which little Hans must apply to the riddle of his sister Hanna's arrival, the birth or death that he must metabolize: before Hanna traveled with them in the railway carriage, she was already with them in the box (*SE* 10: 67f). When the repression of his anal eroticism and frontal masturbation first starts going down and out, ultimately as condemnation, little Hans falls to the ground, thrashing about with his legs and spitting, like the fallen horse, whose double duty as the parents, attracts little one's desire and dread. Freud reminds us in *The Interpretation of Dreams* that in German, at least in dreams, *Spucken* (spitting) calls up *Spuken* (haunting) (*SE* 4: 248 n.1). Indeed, little Hans was first in touch with his widdler, the separation index on or growing onto his own person, so that at all times he would have his little hand on the emergency break distinguishing animate from inanimate objects. The conditions for haunting, which were there for Hans, as they are in every development and transference, were nevertheless contained inside the transference neurosis and cure that the little patient could remember to forget. This forgetting that is not repression but analysis is the vanishing point of Freud's 1922 postscript: during his one-time-only follow-up visit, which is on the record, big little Hans assures Freud that he did not recall his life as a neurotic nor recognize himself in the study but only began to feel the pull with the references to the family outing to Gmunden. This summer resort's place-name is a last resort on the sliding scale of recall, one that regressively stammers *Munden* (to taste) and *Mund* (mouth), and at the same time thus touches the retained wound of Freud's own dismembered name: -mund. In other words, the boxes and carts that stay, in Hans's case, on the one-way assembly line of interpersonal, couplified rapport with mourning through substitution and reproduction were (inside Freud and his haunted cases) the crypts crowding out and shutting down easy disposal of the separation or loss. The spit thus passes through the reversible haunting of Hans to skewer Freud's rapport with ghosts underlying his vast and ongoing work of analogy or unmourning.

The horror in *The Omen* relies on the secrecy of adoption and on the outside chance that you just don't know who your father is or, alternatively, whether your child is your child. The more projective-on-the-upbeat version of the adoption issue is the chosen claim. Chosen or adopted by the father and by God the father, we nevertheless remain wide open to possession by the Devil, who proffers his version of the multiple chosen test. "Omen," although derived etymologically now from a word meaning "mouth," now from one meaning "hearing," seems to say it all in another setting or sentence in earshot of its sound-shape double: *Nomen est omen.* This dead language saying, a foreign body that circulates freely in the discourse, culture, reception of Freud's science, gives its all to the name, the name that speaks, signs, signs off. It's all in the name that, unlike the paternal infinite regress, speaks to you directly through its literal and fantasy-material dimensions.

In the precursor studies Ernest Jones dutifully tours in *On the Nightmare*, a certain A. Graf is cited for identifying the Devil's origin as lying in "the depths of the human soul" (154). Pfister and Silberer join the lineup for identifying the Devil as, respectively, a throwback to "infantile experiences of fear" and the personification "of the suppressed and unsublimated elements of the instinctual life" (155). Freud can be found in the midst of this research review via his conjecture in "Character and

Anal Erotism" that "the Devil is certainly nothing else than the personification of the repressed, unconscious instinctual life" (154). But Freud figures more directly outside this chorus line extolling the Devil's unconscious depths via another study that inspires or models Jones's new working hypothesis: "*The belief in the Devil represents in the main an exteriorization of two sets of repressed wishes, both of which are ultimately derived from the infantile Oedipus situation:* (a) *The wish to imitate certain attributes of the father, and* (b) *the wish to defy the father; in other words, an alternating emulation of and hostility against the father*" (155). The working part of the hypothesis is owed to Freud: "Since the origin of infantile terror is now known, it naturally suggests itself to one to investigate the descriptions of the belief in the Devil in the light of this new knowledge" (155). The footnote falls open to Freud's case study of little Hans (155 n.3). Jones gives us the relational conjugation of the Devil's identificatory or projective significance that follows from the hypothesis owed to the case of little Hans: "Since the Devil may personify the 'evil' aspects of either son or father and as the son's attitude towards the father may be either imitation or hostility, we find that he is portrayed in four aspects": one, the admired father; two, the hated father; three, son imitating father; four, son defying father (166). In the legend to this analytic mapping we learn that "it was a favorite practice on the part of the Devil to appear at night in the guise of some person who had died," most often and most importantly as the dead father (169).

In 1943, in the place between Disney's and the Third Reich's roundtrips on Death Drive, a place of doubling on contact high between extremes of idealization and then (about-face) demonization, the film *Education for Death* was repress released two years after the high time Gregor Ziemer's book appeared under the first round of the title's fighting words. At the end of the Disney version, the title still has the last say. German soldiers march in row, row, rows. Fade to: grave crosses for days decorated with the soldiers' steel helmets. "Now his education is complete—his education for death." The film opens, however, with a salvo of satire. Hitler in knight's armor tries to carry away Germania, a Wagner-style heroine. Joking aside, this is also the placeholder of the love affair between Disney and Deutschland, even Nazi Deutschland, which was mutual, but sure couldn't declare itself once the United States went to war. But more to what is beside the point, what lies between end and beginning, there's the story of "little Hans," a boy who learns in school to obey the "law of the stronger." The very model of uncomplication, little Hans fits right in with the following commanded by Devil Fatherland (Laqua, 177–78).

"Critics are stupid, even if they're right. After a concert there's blood on the piano keys and there should be." That was Curd Jürgens, the senior maestro Duncan Ely in *The Mephisto Waltz*. Alan Alda plays the younger pianist with a melancholic chippie on his shoulder. But he is his own dis-appointment, too. He became a music journalist after his music career didn't take off. He tried to end it all with alcohol. "I have an axiom to grind—cliché is king." "He has great hands, Rachmaninoff hands," maestro says to his daughter, Roxanne, who agrees. "I happen to be the greatest pianist alive and—your hands ..." Roxanne: "I think you should be an actor or a pianist." They're all real interested in his hands, but upward displacement keeps the conversation axiomatic. "Our father is no longer in Heaven. God exists and the Devil is his vice president." "Nothing more popular than death." "Death is corny, it really is." They play a duet.

They're at Duncan Ely's New Year's Party. Jacqueline Bisset (Paula) wants to leave. Alda (Miles): "Sex makes you miserable, doesn't it?" She enters some velvet-lined space. Plaster sculpture, busts with faces that have been lifted off and then cast. It's Roxanne's art. "Did you like my work?" "Frankly, no. I like safe abstract work. Your forms are too real for comfort." "I'd like to do a life mask of Miles." They call them death masks, don't they? I believe it's a German custom, like music.

"Have a nice time?" "We killed three bottles of champagne. He had me play the Mozart again and I was pretty good." "You've already got one father. Anything else is bigamy or something." Duncan Ely is dying—of leukemia.

Pianist, sleeping, gets blue dab will do him on forehead. Satanic symbol on the floor was drawn in blood. Duncan Ely is reading a tome. He seems kind of panicky. Roxanne fits Miles's "life mask" over Ely's sleeping face. The transfer takes place. Let's face-to-face it: this is the first contact or contract that really counts. Pianist comes downstairs. Roxanne is playing taped piano playing. Pianist looks at his hand, his fingers. At the service Roxanne conjures "le diable." At the reading of the will, pianist gets a big portion. Now when Miles and Paula make love, it's as though Duncan Ely were present.

"Why do you want to be someone else?" "It's exciting!" "Was that you on the piano right now?" "It was one of Duncan's last tapes." "Why did you say that? This tape machine is cold." "If I try to play like him it's not surprising, is it?"

An excremental smear marks the spot of sacrificial substitution. Duncan enters Miles's body from behind: he has Miles's face to prove it.

Paula: "They made one big fat bargain with the Devil so they could enjoy each other, father and daughter. I want Miles — whoever he is — even if it's just once more." She reads occult book and casts spell. The Devil enters. "Master, I'm ready to bargain." Paula tells Roxanne: "He's on my side now." It looks like Paula committed suicide wearing the mask of Roxanne. But the Devil shoved Paula into Roxanne from behind. Paula has Roxanne's face to prove it.

Graf's "Reminiscences" of Freud first appeared in English alongside Freud's "Psychopathic Characters on the Stage," the brief essay Freud presented to Graf, presumably in 1906, and which Graf gave to the *Psycho-analytic Quarterly* for publication (in translation) in 1942. The editorial note strongly suggests that the inclusion of his reminiscences was the deal Graf sealed with the offer that couldn't be refused of a brand-new Freud text. That the German version of Graf's "Reminiscences" insists on the openness of the invitation to publish gives us some cause to note the split and conflict running Graf's "I was there" histories of original conception. In 1946 Graf was still fighting rounds in the Faustian pairing announced in the title of his American book *Composer and Critic*:

> Only history could answer the question: Are the mistakes of musical criticism inherent in the system itself, or are they mere accidents,

clinging to it like mud to the wheel of a moving car? Only history could teach me clearly to see the position of criticism in the musical life of our time, and its proper function within musical society. Musical criticism is the child of history, and only history, the greatest critic of human accomplishments could tell whether it is a legitimate child or a changeling. (29)

One day in the early days of psychoanalysis Graf presented a paper to the Wednesday group on Wagner's *The Flying Dutchman.* Freud's blessing wasn't in disguise: he asked for Graf's leave to publish it in his series. The resulting 1911 monograph, Graf's best piece of writing, the only piece he made with Freud completely behind or in front of him, explored, once again, the "demonic" in Wagner's operas. But this time, this one time, Graf tracked back the force that was with Wagner to Wagner's relationship to his fathers. There was the bookkeeper, Wagner by name, who died when the composer was six months old. But his mother remarried, and for the rest of his life and work Wagner played with, fantasized about the possibility that this man, Geyer was his name, which in a word, in German, means "vulture," could have sired him before advancing to the official head of the family. Geyer was the only father Wagner ever knew, and then he died too when the boy was seven years old.

When forging a family crest for himself, the composer mixed and matched literalized, visualized references to the vulture and to the "wagon," or *Wagen,* that the name Wagner mumbles. The wagon is given as many spokes as there were Wagner children. Thus, the composer, the Wagner before the horse, shared his special case of being son of Geyer, the family spokesperson, with his older siblings, too. Graf argues that Wagner had to play with this possibility for keeps on account of the implicated adulterous act of his mother that opened her up wide to the composer's unconscious visitations. "On the very day that Richard Wagner completed 'The Flying Dutchman,' he picked up the pen again to write his mother a letter. For years their correspondence had been interrupted. Now however the pressure of unconscious thoughts motivated him, for with 'The Flying Dutchman' the composer had returned to his home where he had once played as a boy and once again he had seen the large bright eyes of his mother resting upon him..." (46).

But as is suggested by the treatment of the names in rendering the fantasy family sign, Wagner also sought his physical connection with father, a connection that took the form of the demonic. The uncanny heroes of Wagner's operas are portraits of Geyer but also of Wagner in Geyer's place. The Wagner hero is born shortly after the death of the father, whom he therefore never really knows. But the son's arrival is associated with the lowering of the doom. If we include Wagner's fantasy calculation that Geyer was already siring him before the first father died, we recognize the two-timing of Wagner's identification. "Doesn't the whole situation approximate the central plot of Wagner's operas and the topic of our analysis? Geyer would have arrived then as the Dutchman, like Siegmund, like Tristan. It is as if, while hiking up a mountain, the view suddenly opens wide onto a deep valley, which we would like to reach, but then with the next step the view disappears and we must again seek our way among cliffs. The Dutchman, Siegmund and Tristan are not portraits of Geyer but rather of Wagner, they share his traits and his sensibility, there can be no mistake: Wagner speaks in these works of himself, not of Geyer or more precisely he puts himself in the latter's place. By taking on the roles of the Dutchman and other figures, he puts himself into the same situation that he had conjured up in his fantasies for Geyer. He is now the man who approaches a union or marriage which his arrival destroys" (31). But Wagner is also just passing through the condemned site of reproductive coupling to replicate himself as the destructive or heroic father's body double.

In his parallel studies, for example *Wagner Problems,* Graf distinguished Wagner's rise to the heights of German culture as the victorious "slave rebellion of all dilettantish and literary natures, of the shady side of the musical world" (17). Wagner is thus under consideration as the unstoppable herald of the mass media Sensurround, which comes complete, split-level style, with the journalistic mediations and standards of middlebrow culture. In *The Case of Wagner,* Nietzsche finds the name to

call the composer of the improv nightmare from which he has awak-
ened: Wagner is an actor. Nietzsche calls father Geyer an actor too; but
even if Geyer was a painter, as Graf tells the story, Wagner's own delight
in dressing up in painter's drag was an acting identification.

Mann's *Doctor Faustus* puts through the Nietzsche/Wagner correspondence
and conflict in the up-to-date trappings of Schoenberg's music, which, however, remains unheard, unheard. In *Mephisto,* the novel by Klaus, son of
Mann, and the film by István Szabó, the artist protagonist, who, as Germany's soul mate, sells or buys souls, is an actor. His attempt to preserve the
state of his art of acting, through a politics of compromise, is subsumed by
the total work of art of the state. The state of art requires that Hamlet be
reenacted as non-neurotic whose passions are natural and national. If
he swings low, it's because he's one of the northern brood; shocks will
swing him to upward mobilization and work this wonder-enriched wounding in the audience out there too. Brooding thought, at the end or in the
beginning, must be translated into action (or acting). After the *Hamlet* premiere (in Szabó's film) the prime minister takes the actor out to the Olympic
games stadium, the ultimate theater at this end of a relay of proscenium
arches and stagings. Right after the actor was being greeted as though a
head of state, the prime minister makes his entry as highpoint of a total
theater set to music and ritual. Into the dark void of the Olympic stadium
awaiting its fill of live audience members, all of them extras in Riefenstahl's
film, all of them doubles in the transmissions comprising the first live TV
coverage of a sports event, the prime minister cries out the actor's name,
which reverberates as echo, as feedback, as sound rubbing against sound,
filling up space, excess sparking the resounding success the politician next
pledges and bases on this echo in empty space alone: the dominion of the
thousand years of National Socialism. Even when the Reich hits bottom, it
will be shocked back into endless mobilization out of nothingness into
nothingness (and back again). The actor's name is but a resounding echo-
ing sound subsumed by its translation into acts of state that are also always

theatrical acts within a self-reflexive relay. The giving and the taking away of a world that Wagner put to music in *Tristan and Isolde*, between the breathing in and out of animation and the expiring death of nothingness, must be heard to resound in the background of Isolde's wish to undo the "and" that unites but also separates Tristan and Isolde. The *Liebestod* would wipe away the "and" of language—and thus the advent of the other—in the creative and annihilating upsurge of total music.

In *Rosemary's Baby*, Guy, the husband who sells his wife's motherhood to the Devil, is another actor who's looking for a break. He's an understudy, in second place. Guy or Everyguy is every son and heir, second only to father. By giving up the mother inside Rosemary, the second-string actor skips a generation and, with Satan or his Satanist neighbor as his new parental guide, takes first position after the former lead suddenly goes blind just like a figure of father-and-son conflict. Guy is thus empowered to act.

As recovering Wagnerian, Nietzsche would avow that to write and think in his day it was just the same necessary to have fallen for the new middlebrow mascot culture and its pact psychology, its proxy relationship to so-called mass culture. Only in this way could Nietzsche conceive writing that risked being misunderstood, thus raising the stakes of reading and misreading to life or death.

But Graf cannot grant Nietzsche the advantage to which he lays claim for thinking through and beyond the break with Wagner. Nietzsche was right: you can only be under the influence of Wagner, the music pusher. Following *The Flying Dutchman*, Wagner just kept on increasing the dosage of toxin and antitoxin. Finally his sun simply set (*Wagner Problems*, 54–55). But first Wagner's wound was catchy. Nietzsche's breakup with Wagner opened up in the philosopher a wound that never healed, which caused Nietzsche, unlike Wagner in his setting, to bleed to death (86).

If Graf is right about the exchange value of the essay he restored to the archive in 1942, Freud responded in "Psychopathic Characters on the Stage" to Graf's reading of the dramatic neurosis in Wagner's musical work with a diagnosis of another drama trauma but without all the music. Every fictional medium or mediation revalorizes suffering as the other source, held in reserve, of pleasure. The expenditures spent in maintaining egocentric psychic reality would be used up before or short of inscription of pleasure as/with texture or legibility if it weren't for economy, economizing, or savings. But less (or loss) would be more of the same if energy saving didn't also mean taking shortcuts to pleasure. These controlled shortcuts or releases take the form of joking or pun-ning in critical discourse (which is otherwise without enjoyment of its own). In fiction or fantasy we identify with the hero, who rebels against the death star's multiple occupancy: God, society, the state, or one out of two opposing impulses. The rebel hero is fundamentally Luciferian. Drama folds out of sacrifice (music also originally wrapped its diversion around this primal scene and screaming). Sacrifice, as cutting of loss, as inoculative payment of protection, holds the place of covenant or com-pact, the relationship that proves a strain outside the encapsulated cer-tainties of the Devil setting.

Every adult spectator at a play or movie is again the child playing at his or her hopes of being able to do what grownups do. The spectator arrives deprived: the hero permits a diversion from this impasse via identification with the underdog as hero, "whose greatness is insisted upon in spite of everything" (SE 7: 306). The spectator's enjoyment is knowingly based on illusion. He knows he has but one life to live and that he need not give it away in the play of identification. Thus, he can afford to be big and "blow off steam" (the hydraulic release comes up twice in this brief essay) in the relay of grand scenes presenting the hero's life or story. That drama transmutes suffering into pleasure is, however, easier said than done. The audience not only cannot be made to suffer but must also be compensated for any sympathetic suffering endured via identification with the hero. That is why represented suf-fering tends to be restricted to psychic suffering. Since most people know or recognize mental suffering only in connection with the circumstances in which it was acquired, a traumatic event is required but staggered as conflict, effort of will, or resistance.

Freud adds to his double reading of Oedipus and Hamlet, which was rehearsed in the correspondence with Fliess and then repeated in *The Interpretation of Dreams*, the corollary notion that *Hamlet* is not psychological drama but rather (since the suffering presented for identification is no longer a conflict between two conscious impulses but between a conscious impulse and a repressed one) psychopathological drama that requires a personalized audience. "Here the precondition of enjoyment is that the spectator should himself be a neurotic" (*SE* 7: 308–9). Only a neurotic could derive pleasure from the revelation of a repressed impulse. A non-neurotic will respond with aversion and with renewal of the original act of repression whereby the impulse was successfully checked. Non-neurotics repress once is enough. "But in neurotics the repression is on the brink of failing; it is unstable and needs a constant renewal of expenditure, and this expenditure is spared if recognition of the impulse is brought about" (*SE* 7: 309). *Hamlet* is the premier example of modem drama because it presents the case of a man, who has so far been normal, becoming neurotic—a man "in whom an impulse that has hitherto been successfully suppressed endeavours to make its way into action" (*SE* 7: 309). There is no room for insight into the conflict underlying an already fully developed neurosis. Recognition of the conflict simply undoes the neurotic illness. The dramatist must induce the illness in the spectator by making him follow the development of the illness along with the sufferer on stage. The logic Freud pursues here, which will take him beyond *Hamlet*, takes its departure from the interminability of balancing acts required for psychopathological drama. The dramatic production of neurosis "will be especially necessary where the repression does not already exist in us but has first to be set up; and this represents a step further than *Hamlet* in the use of neurosis on the stage" (*SE* 7: 310).

A necessary precondition of psychopathological drama is that the impulse that is struggling into consciousness, though recognizable, is never given a definite name, "so that in the spectator too the process is carried through with his attention averted, and he is in the grip of his emotions instead of taking stock of what is happening." In such a play, as in the course of an analysis, "we find derivatives of the repressed material reaching consciousness, owing to a lower resistance, while the repressed material itself is unable to do so" (*SE* 7: 309–10). But then the analyst becomes directive, as Freud did with his patient Hamlet. "After all, the conflict in *Hamlet* is so effectively concealed that it was left to me to unearth it" (*SE* 7: 310).

But, if we accept that Freud's sense of *Hamlet*'s audience is party to an exchange with Graf's Wagner investigations, then what Freud misses by not facing the music is the point of contrast. The culture that crawled out from under Wagner's "demonic" middlebrow is not the haunt of Hamlet neurotics. In *Hamlet* the father is a ghost and not the father; he's most likely not the father from Hell, the unambiguous father. At least Hamlet is unable to receive him in that capacity. The neurotic component is stuck on the evidence of the mother's desire in the rush to replace the dead father and circumvent or repress proper mourning. Then there's a double background check that can't be covered: Shakespeare's unmournable child Hamnet can be conjured because, in some other secret place, Freud carried his mother's undead baby Julius, who made his ghost appearances within each of Freud's doomed same-sex friendships. In this serial precondition Freud first recognized the transference as press of ghosts. Only with this oeuvre under his belt could Freud in turn, turning up the contrast, identify repetition in or in lieu of transference as the demonic in principle or the Death Drive.

Wagner's split between passion and quiescence, life and death, is the commonplace of an uncomplicated mind in great health or in psychopathy. Unmourners and immortality neurotics don't go to the Devil. You have to be less inhibited, with an uncomplicated loss that only needs replacing, in order to deal with the Devil.

Like Nietzsche, Freud was not psychically constituted for association with the Devil. But he, too, took up the challenge of lifting the stakes and standards of interpretation within the unstoppable Hell-raising of middlebrow culture. The Devil was the password that allowed Freud to join the big boys, the philosophers and journalists, and address Death, even one's own death (or is it father's?). With Dad certainty Freud could pass as philosopher. Devil reference is a passing mention in Freud because the death of the other or the dead other is in the psychoanalytic view, just like primal repression, one of the nonnegotiable facts of psychic life, based on the inconceivability of one's own death and, hence, of Death. It is this inside view that throws self for a loop through other and keeps us in the vicinity of mourning and unmourning, while also giving us the techno high of egoic immortality or, in the felt absence of replication, mass suicide. We saw the future of mass readership, or on a more staggered installment plan, the future leadership of the masses by the raising of the middlebrow, when what was legible began appearing as Devil doubles.

Do we admit, in effect, that our reception of the Devil by and large confirms Hannah Arendt's reservations about the banality of evil? Yes, butt. Arendt addresses the "nature of evil" as outside or on the sidelines of her study *Eichmann in Jerusalem*. In the epilogue, she raises the implicitly psychoanalytic question, which neither the trial nor her study could consider, whether genocide does not endanger mankind in its entirety, or in other terms, whether projective destruction must not consummate itself as nihilism, that is, ultimately, as self-destruction, with an interminable number of bystanders taken down for the suicide. In Goethe's *Faust*, the Devil (or Mephistopheles) is committed to the restoration of nothingness over dead bodies at once uncountable and of no account. But at the same time the Devil works and inhabits the span of deferral of the enactment as "free death" of Faust's suicidal ideation. It is in this span that the psychoanalytic study of the Devil resides.

The banal is not simply commonplace, Arendt argues, and yet she distinguishes the evil condition she seeks to identify from "any diabolical or demonic profundity" (288). Yet much of this profundity indwells the projective habitat of Arendt's banality of evil: even Goethe's Mephistopheles is a vulgar, bureaucratic stickler for angel tail while elsewhere in the high art end of the pool of applicants, figures of Luciferian affirmation are tied to a depth that can never leave the surface they only or interminably scratch. The banality of the Devil is a double project, as vouchsafed by etymology. *Banality* derives from a multiple "ban" that excludes or outlaws and summons or binds. *The American Heritage Dictionary* (1978 edition) cites as an instance of correct usage of *banal* a psychoanalyst's admission that a work of literature's reduction to Oedipal fantasy is banal as reception because restricted to the commonplace of predictability. Does "banality of evil" mean that any recognizable interpretation of evil, whether strong or weak, is banal? If Arendt takes an anti-Oedipal view of the limits to understanding an evil villain's "terrifying normality," then we in turn attend to the diversification or specialization that the Oedipal household or economy opens to a closer reading of Freud in order to identify the grounding of the Devil's very own b-anality.

The postscript to *Eichmann in Jerusalem* gives a continuity shot between its subtitle, *A Report on the Banality of Evil,* and the thunder at the gates of Arendt's book, even or especially before it left the gates, in other words as "unread." We are tempted to take another turn around the blockage of journalism and consider with Walter Benjamin and Karl Kraus the complicity between the repress release of opinion or belief and the nothingness or deadline that journalism's suicide drive protects.

A certain middlebrow hub within mass culture is the evil Arendt contemplates. But the phrasing of the feuilleton isn't our bottom line here. We must go all the way back to the inevitable overextension of clerical culture that ensued once the original epistles or missives of the New Testament caught up with and overtook the Roman postal system. A kind of lower-middle class (or brow) of clerical culture, because unable otherwise to get ahead via the hierarchy of the church, turned to black magic, without, however, renouncing the divine order against which the magic acts transgressed. But even though their Latin was second-rate, the magic words and names had to be keyed in correctly. (*Army of Darkness* owes its very projection as prospect of the recycled dead from Hell to the protagonist's careless spelling.)

From sorcery to the Internet: to spell is to be (Spelling B). Whether grammar or grimoire, whether correct spelling of the password or the spell itself that one casts, we must acknowledge the protected outer shell of mere communication binding all kinds of half knowledge. Hang loose! Let your mind see the illusion in a reality of your own making. It's banal that the stickler for correct spelling and related formalities is characterologically anal. The overspilling mess of ill-spelt text hanging loose all around us is the cloacal medium within which each span of correction must be wiped clean.

The Devil's Rain is the spill of its misspelling. Was not the intention suitable for the Devil's possession his "reign"? The mud-pie meltdown at the front door only looked like his father. Father is with Corbis in the old mining town. Corbis wants his book back. If the son can come out the Satanic services as he went in, then he can have his parents back. Otherwise he must give himself up to Corbis together with the book. Corbis tricks him into seeing his crucifix as writhing snake, which he casts from his person. But when he saw his mother at the service, she was wearing the mud death mask of replication.

Corbis wants the young man to give up the name Preston and answer to Fyffe. In the seventeenth century that was the name of his ancestor and look-alike. Fyffe's wife betrayed the cult and stole the book. Before he goes up in smoke, Corbis sends boy down secret passageway to hide and preserve the holy procedures for effigy making; he also curses the Fyffe clan for all eternity (or until the book is his again). Without the book the Corbis family can't enter the Everlasting Kingdom of Satan. In the meantime they make do with do-do replication inhabiting the span forced apart between body and soul. Each cult member must claim and enter the body Corbis has prepared for him or her. Whenever one of Corbis's followers is punctured, goo spews from the openings of the body bag filled to bursting point with one liquid substance.

In the lab Dr. Preston pronounces that there is "nothing in the subconscious that can't be raised to consciousness." He's on the verge of isolating brain-wave patterns signaling ESP activity. The test subject feels free of care as she drifts into perfect sleep. But then, in her dreams, she flashes on

Satan's church in the desert. "Instead of images moving toward me, I move closer to them — as if I were watching a movie and then were acting in it." Field trip to the ghost town: "The church doesn't belong here." It looks like it's in New England or part of a movie set.

Devil's rain falls in a magic snow globe. Like television inside a film, the cathode tube shows wailing, suffering beings under the rain. It is the central mystery of the cult. Without rain neither Heaven nor Hell. Devil's rain is the ingredient in mud pie production that must be kept on a short control release. When it rains, it pours goop out of the liquid centers of the artificial body shells.

The rogue clerics still relied, then, on the good forces (the Christian deities and correct spelling) to counteract and contain the evil forces summoned to fulfill their wishes or fantasies. Because these bloggers counted their hits in a magic medium that didn't take sides but promoted instead a balancing act among differentiated powers, Rudolf Löwenstein recognizes a certain interchangeability between the proper Christian service and its (albeit more vulgar) black Mass counterpart. Both rituals summon incestuous relations with father. But more important than his conclusion is the momentum of displacement that Löwenstein administers toward this end. To participate fully and pleasurably in the Devil's service, one must be Christian. The desublimation of Christian training lubes the Devil service's deeply felt variations on what remains one and the same p-unitive system. In more contemporary terms: the priest who takes liberties with choirboys is not another child abuser but a practitioner of black magic.

NOTEBOOK TEN

In the twentieth century the Golem legend in its Prague setting made it big: in 1915 in Germany it hit the big screen same time—double feature—that it went public, published in a blockbuster novel by Prague author Gustav Meyrink. This book, which included among its plot points how-to instructions for simulation of the symptoms of epilepsy, also made the best sell-out list according to medical officers faced with soldiers who preferred to malinger on rather than rush into the world war effort. The scholarship or intellectual history of the idea of the Golem—as set up between the bookends supplied by Gershom Scholem and Moshe Idel—overlooks these screen or scream memories while styling with the cipher and letter magic or mysticism based on *Kabbalah* and *Sefer Yezirah*, among many other texts and traditions. But thanks to the memories, the Golem security-screening device comes out in the watch of these scholarly materials as missing, pressing, marked. Even though Idel, too, neglects admitting the pop reception into his expanded and corrective history of the Golem as Jewish mystical idea, he delineates a timing of Scholem's Golem studies that, even or especially without comment, turns up the volume on the excluded and implied screen texts. It was in 1933 that Scholem found himself all of a sudden taking a controlling research interest in the Golem. Then in 1963 Norbert Wiener's monograph *God and Golem, Inc.* sparked Scholem's new reading of the legend to the map of the cipher magic of relations between man and machine. Kept on titular terms as passing acquaintance with the exploration of artificial intelligence and ethics in Wiener's study, the direct connection with the Golem, the point of the title, was then driven home in Scholem's reading. One year later Scholem revisited the Golem idea in a lecture he delivered on the occasion of the arrival of the first computer in Israel.

In *God and Golem, Inc.* Wiener proposes a division of labor between man and machine given the state of mechanical intelligence at that time: machines can do the math simply because they are faster and more reliable; humans for their part can wrap their minds around vague ideas, in other words the component parts of literature and art, which the machines reject outright as formless. "In dealing with these [as yet imperfectly defined ideas], mechanical computers of the present day are very nearly incapable of programming themselves" (73). Otherwise, however, machines can learn, can improve and program themselves. But even if there were nothing left for the machines to learn, as long as they can't generate themselves out of themselves, humans still count at least as the reproductive part of cybernetic society. But replication also always mediates the gap between us and our future generation—a mediation that is already along for the ride the first time technology sends us. It is "conceptually possible" Wiener states, although he must admit that it is not yet practicable in 1963, "for a human being to be sent over a telephone line" (36). But even if in theory we could be transmitted in this way, in other words from point A to point B, would we indwell this transmission at once as technology and as thought, vague ideas and all? Would our being also be in the transmission? Would we be technological? Because there are machines that can in fact replicate themselves in 1963, Wiener argues along these lines of questioning that technology already and irreversibly stands in relations with us of competition or cohabitation.

Like evolution's claim of our ape descent, so with the claim that machines can reproduce "there attaches something of the reprobation that attached in earlier ages to the sin of sorcery" (47). It was not so very long ago that someone advancing the claims of cybernetics would have been off to the Inquisition rapid fire for Devil dealing. Here Wiener inserts his one main-text reference to the Golem legend, specifically the Prague variant, namely the media version, as saving exception to someone's condemnation back then: "unless he could convince some great patron that he could transmute the base metals into gold, as Rabbi Löw of Prague, who claimed that his incantations blew breath of life into the Golem of clay, had persuaded the Emperor Rudolf" (49–50).

Otherwise Wiener counts the contest between God and Satan as still current context for man and machine relations. Machines began to learn by playing games. No accident. The game plays as basic structure of thinking that can, in exceeding itself, learn ultimately to program itself. Thus, the "subject of learning, and in particular of machines that learn to play games" is still relevant to the age-old religious "problem of the game between the Creator and a creation" (15). "If we do not lose ourselves in the dogmas of omnipotence and omniscience, the conflict between God and the Devil is a real conflict, and God . . . is actively engaged in a conflict with his creature, in which he may very well lose the game. . . . Can any creator, even a limited one, play a significant game with his own creature?" (17).

While the popular turn to the Golem legend puts protection of the Jews up in lights, the motor of a swing into anti-Semitism is also discernibly running this protection as projection. The problem here is not the ambivalence with regard to assimilation, to becoming "like," to becoming image, nor the transference transgressions against the father that Golem-making requires in exchange for its rescue service. All of that is compatibly or quintessentially Jewish. It is rather the resetting of the legend in its mass media career on compact relations with the Devil—in other words, on the Mass of murder—that is a problem, the so-called Jewish problem. Historically the Rabbi Löw chapter of the Golem legend was contemporaneous with the historical background and literary-legendary elaboration of Dr. Faust. The one venue for the automatization of human thought that Wiener singles out as marking at least conceivable future progress is mechanical translation. Thus, he inserts the opening merger of man and machine in a scene of translation, the scene that in Goethe's *Faust* forces the Devil to show his "and"—his complicity with Faustian techno striving. Wiener in turn is tempted to depart from the Old Testament understanding or setting of the Devil's game and conjure current examples of cybernetic sinning, such as in cases of so-called gadget worship. Just as the black mass draws on belief in the very powers that good Christians attribute to the host in order to manipulate those powers for self gain or to inflict harm, so it is still the same sin that gadget worshippers commit "which consists of using the magic of modern automatization to further personal profit or let loose the apocalyptic terrors of nuclear warfare. If this sin is to have a name, let that name be . . . sorcery" (52).

But sorcery or magic in Wiener's estimation always causes technical difficulties because of the literal-mindedness with which our wishes or desires are administered. Wiener's identification of this blind spot in magic doubles as the crux of a reading of Faust's relations with Mephistopheles. "The operation of magic is singularly literal-minded, and . . . if it grants you anything at all it grants what you ask for, not what you should have asked for or what you intend" (59). Wiener gives the magic update and techno forecast regarding attempts to conjure automatic safety measures, so-called fail-safe devices, for example: "While it is always possible to ask for something other than we really want, this possibility is most serious when the process by which we are to obtain our wish is indirect, and the degree to which we have obtained our wish is not clear until the very end. Usually we realize our wishes, insofar as we do actually realize them, by a feedback process, in which we compare the degree of attainment of intermediate goals with our anticipation of them. In this process, the feedback goes through us, and we can turn back before it is too late. If the feedback is built into a machine that cannot be inspected until the final goal is attained, the possibilities for catastrophe are greatly increased" (62). In short: "The penalties for errors of foresight, great as they are now, will be enormously increased as automatization comes into its full use" (63).

Fail-safe devices work to direct the mode of failure in a harmless way only if the danger is known. However, "against a danger whose nature has not been already recognized" they are of little value (63). Indeed, the automatic car sounds like the rocket that one would rather aim than ride. What begins to open wide is a World War II context that in 1963 makes ghost appearances in the Cold War setting. Consider as model for this rewiring or reclaiming of past projections in the early 1960s the case of SPECTRE, the underworld organization that was introduced in the first film versions of Ian Fleming's James Bond adventures as third party to and parasite of the Cold War oppositions.

Although the future, as the uncontrollable time to come coming toward us, would appear withdrawn inside the open-endedness or vagueness of human thought, this vague of the future precisely must compute. Therefore, Wiener advises, "engineering technique . . . must become more and more accustomed to formulate human purposes" (64). "The world of the future will be an ever more demanding struggle against the limitations of our intelligence"—also in the sense of forecast or projection, for example, in espionage settings (69). Wiener's bottom-line definition of cybernetics, the new field he founded or cofounded, as "the study of control and communication in machines and living beings," skips the third C, command, that otherwise completes the trinity of modern military organization, which in World War II was indeed the lab setting not only for Wiener's enabling contacts with artificial intelligence.

We tend to identify the science and technology of computing—together with the whole modern genre of science fiction—with the Cold nuclear War. But the Cold War more often than not proved to be—like SPECTRE in the movies *Dr. No* and *From Russia with Love*—just a screen memory away from the hot World War that it was either still working on or through or just covering up. Now that Alan Turing's precursor role in the invention of computing during World War II has made it into Hollywood pictures, I don't need to break into and remake the complete scene of his invention of computing out of the race to crack the Nazi German Enigma code. I should stress, however, lest the Nazi German portion of this prehistory of computing remain an enigma, that both analog and digital computing were getting their rise in the Third Reich (together with live television surveillance, magnetic tape recording, and the concept and technology of negative feedback) out of the invention of rocket flight.

In *Nazi Psychoanalysis* I already fixed my focus on the Nazi German occupation or cathexis of this invention but wrapped the genealogy around its context to include discussion of Turing's research, in particular of the role played in this research by a certain gendering of components of the code to crack, a sexual differentiation Turing inherited from his Polish colleagues who had made the first breakthroughs in getting past the Enigma. The Polish cryptanalysts called a repetition of the same letter every fourth letter, that is, with three steps between them, a female. Thus, a pattern began to emerge over the read body of females.

The tracking of female patterns by men with machines on their minds that comes complete with suicide is as much a computer science anecdote as it is, already since the eighteenth century, a science fiction subgenre. Gregory Bateson sought to make the psyche compute by opening up the field of cybernetics. In particular through the notion of double bind, which was inspired by the rocket science of negative feedback, Bateson contributed to the understanding of schizophrenic language and of family systems at large. Already in 1946 Bateson held a seminar on feedback mechanisms that was organized around investigation of the Iatmal culture, in which the ceremony of transvestism served as a homeostatic mechanism whenever divisive hostilities were on the rise. One of Bateson's colleagues in this new interdisciplinary field, the psychoanalyst Lawrence S. Kubie, who regularly attended the 1946 seminar, worked throughout his career on an inside view of sexual difference that haunted him precisely to the extent that he could never give it a body or a rest. Toward the end of his career (which he had dedicated in part to the cure of homosexuality), he was still picking up his unfinished essay in progress. "Now this process of postponement must come to an end: I must grapple with the process of putting it into final shape as best I can." Or again: "now I feel that it can no longer be postponed. No matter how much it may expose me to misunderstanding and misinterpretation, I will have to carry it through to its own logical conclusion." His postulated "drive to become both sexes" was doubly bound (in his highly self-reflected understanding of it) to the death drive. The psyche must break down if "the unconscious goal of sex is the unattainable one to change sides." "And if this unattainable goal also represents a drive to go in two divergent directions at the same time, it results in a deeper inner schism in the personality—a schism which can be represented by insatiable com-

pulsions and obsessions and by the superimposed construction of opposing phobias. Everything becomes split, and it is on this splitting among
conscious and unconscious purposes, and preconscious struggles to
achieve these purposes, that psychotic disorganization is based." The only
alternative to this living end, says Kubie, is suicide. The essay "The Drive
to Become Both Sexes" was published posthumously.

In 1950 Turing wrote an essay that was at the same time a science
fiction. In his "Computing Machinery and Intelligence," Turing introduces the rules for a game of imitation by way of answering the question, Can machines think? First he imagines the game played by a man,
a woman, and the interrogator who, based on their answers to his questions, answers that need not be truthful, must decide who is which gender. Turing then asks: "What will happen when a machine takes the part
of A in this game?" A, by the way, according to the original example, was
the man in the experimental game, which means the new game of decida-
bility or undecidability is played out between doubles, machine and
woman. Turing continues raising questions: "Will the interrogator decide
wrongly as often when the game is played like this as he does when the
game is played between a man and a woman? These questions replace
our original, 'Can machines think?'" Given the third degree, it is conceivable that a form of artificial intelligence could be indistinguishable
for human intelligence from human intelligence. Turing furthermore
stresses that this form of artificial intelligence will be technological, in
other words, mediated and produced. For example, Turing dismisses
outright the derivation of a direct transmission from electric or electronic overlaps between technological circuitry and the human nervous
system. All along, however, there is one exception to this game of finding artificial intelligence and human intelligence indistinguishable that
Turing just cannot get around. It's the phenomenon of telepathy. "If
telepathy is admitted it will be necessary to tighten our test up." Earlier he
admitted that "unfortunately the statistical evidence, at least for telepathy,
is overwhelming." With the admission of telepathy, then, "the situation
could be regarded as analogous to that which would occur if the interrogator were talking to himself and one of the competitors was listening

with his ear to the wall. To put the competitors into a 'telepathy-proof room' would satisfy all requirements." In his test setting any telepathy connections presumably would be live. But as he mentions earlier in regard to the overwhelming evidence of telepathy, "It is very difficult to rearrange one's ideas so as to fit these new facts in. Once one has accepted them it does not seem a very big step to believe in ghosts" (453).

Between Freud's *Beyond the Pleasure Principle* and Flusser's *History of the Devil* there is Arthur Clarke's *Childhood's End,* another station in the crossing over or out that gives Death and the Devil direct address, whether by exception or as the rule. In *Childhood's End,* aliens, who are Devil look-alikes or were once upon a time taken by us for Devils, represent the highest development of consciousness, ego, reason. The future that comes toward the human species is an evolutionary version of reunion with God. It is a future that the alien Devil egos will never encounter. The Devils are ordered by the God-like Overmind to protect the human species from its innate mass suicide drive. The alien Devils come to earth as a way more advanced techno culture that can dictate its terms of peace on earth. But it turns out that all this protection was paid to maintain the conditions for the mutation that will end the human species but send its dematerialized sequel into the Overmind.

In *Beyond the Pleasure Principle,* Freud admits a unicellular immortality that guarantees that we do not die naturally and, equally, that the death and reproduction plan propels our evolutionary development as a species. Then Freud jumps the gun, death-drive style, and formulates a tentative conclusion: the goal of life is death. How, then, do the self-preservative instincts fit in? They can now be seen as insurance that the organism will follow its own path to its proper death. The organism wishes to die only in its own fashion. But then Freud drops his role as Devil's advocate, as he puts it, and, picking up the ambivalent track of the other, begins again: "But let us pause for a moment and reflect. It cannot be so. The sexual instincts . . . appear under a very different aspect" (*SE* 18: 39). Don't basic cells "work against the death of the living substance and succeed in winning for it what we can only regard as potential immortality?" (40). In this way, however, we are only keeping up "the appearance of immortality." Even the so-called necessity of death only pays us the price of submission in place of the unbearable prospect of random chance, which always also represents the outside chance that the life lost could have been immortal.

Biology as the realm of unlimited possibilities draws Freud's speculations onward. Certain and conclusive scenarios are stated and then abandoned. The purposive statement about life and death, for example, is preceded by Freud's expression of his wish: "We seek only for the sober results of research or reflection based on it; and we have no wish to find in those results any quality other than certainty" (*SE* 18: 37). Before he unfulfills the wish in the main text, the footnote underworld sends up a warning shout; before 1925 the shout drops right before Freud pushes the "let us pause" button; after 1925 Freud sounds the alert even earlier and more expansively, right beneath the "certainty": "The reader should not overlook the fact that what follows is the development of an extreme line of thought. Later on, when account is taken of the sexual instincts, it will be found that the necessary limitations and corrections are applied to it" (*SE* 18: 37 n.2). In the wake of these stops and starts, and this movement extends well beyond the rebellion with a "pause," the disposable scenarios are, on their own, model Devil fictions. "It is surely possible to throw oneself into a line of thought and to follow it wherever it leads out of simple scientific curiosity, or, if the reader prefers, as an *advocatus diaboli*, who is not on that account himself sold to the devil" (*SE* 18: 59).

> The law, according to Moses according to Luther, is the Devil's point of entry. The Devil's interest in the legal profession grows in sync with secularization, which renders lawyers high priests. When the name of God no longer guarantees the promissory notes of exchange, lawyers must stand security for reciprocity. In *Devil's Advocate* the hot new lawyer discovers that his boss is his father."Who am I? Who are you?""I'm a little more than your father." He's Satan."Call me Dad." But Devil Dad declines the role of puppeteer. He waits

and watches; he sets the stage. Humans pull their own strings. If the case can be made that the Devil Dad entrapped his son, he would still have employed only the human medium and means of free will or self-love. The lawyer son charges Dad with having caused the wife to commit suicide. But whose fault is it? All he needed to do was lose his last case and he would have saved her. Devil Dad: "Maybe it was your time to lose." Like son: "I don't lose. I win!" "I rest my case." The first other woman, as we saw, to catch the lawyer's eye or ego in New York—and thus set the first limitation on the wife he had brought along from back home—was, we find out toward the end, his own half sister, same father. This coupling of two of the same Dad body is necessarily guilt free. The incest issue is out in the open, raised to consciousness, and the relay of inhibitions surrounding the secretly, unconsciously committed incest erased. It is the alternative to what the Devil sees in the homegrown marriage as inhibited and guilty. The only thing the Devil does is he takes away inhibitions and releases and increases pleasure. Unlike God who gives man instincts and then sets up rules in opposition to them, the Devil has always had his nose in the ground. He has always accepted man in all his imperfections. The Devil wants a grandson, wants to be a trans-parent, but in the medium and double whammy of incest. The Devil's desire for an extended family that keeps springing from his own loins is deeply incestuous and hands-on. He is always there, shaping reproduction like clay or shit into any number of anal babies.

The daughter/sister says the men talk too much. "Just look at me." She's the naked fact or act that was in the beginning. The mural of sculpted bodies desublimates, animates as orgy. Such desublimation is what drives Daniel Paul Schreber, for example, to seek shelter in his delusional system and remains the only psychoanalytic frame of reference for Schreber's own understanding of his soul murder in terms of pacts with the Devil. But like Schreber's older brother, the son in *Devil's Advocate* kills himself. Or rather, perhaps like Schreber himself, he wakes up because it was all a dream. The lawyer is still back home. Rather than win acquittal for his guilty client, he asks to step down as the child molester's defender. His controversial action, however, attracts instant media attention that sparks self-love and shows the moviegoers that the Devil still has a hold over him. The film plays like a thirty-day free trial offer of what it would be like once you sealed the deal. Except, of course, there is no such thing as a free trial offer for the Devil and his advocates.

In *Deal of a Lifetime* the outsider gets the package deal that goes with getting the girl: he's the star of the football team and the candidate for school president most likely to be voted into office. But when the Devil's agent, who's very busy and has already spent too much time on this preview, hears that his client still won't sign, he gives the boy another preview, what happens when he stops the show in which the boy was starring. On the football field the rest of the team turns against him. He catches the football, but his teammates won't play defense ("Say your prayers, ass wipe"), and he is crushed in the tackle. Then he breaks up with his girlfriend and his best friend gives up on him. He's in the restroom, and the Devil's agent, now dressed in cheerleader drag, comes out of the stall behind him. Another trans-moment installs the pact-signing scene. But whether or not you sign up, you're often given a preview, a trial run through the substitution metabolism fulfilling all wants in life. Thus, we are given access to Devil fictions or fantasies in the mode of Devil's advocate; we can understand them all the way to their final consequences without signing up with the Devil (often because we didn't make the Devil's cut).

In interview Clarke recalls one prediction he did make (the interviewer suggested that he had given the forecast of flower power with the mutational merger of the children with or as the Overmind): fact caught up with his science fiction that during the Golden Age under the regime that came from outer space paternity could be certified, proved, made certain (Youngblood, 262). While Freud's identification of the father with abstract uncertainty and the mother with sense certainty can by now be readily disproved, Freud's figure of the father in a household of substitution was on the pulse of a genealogy of phantasms that, even today when DNA tests can certify paternity—and thus can make sperm count—

continues to associate the father with a kind of antibody status in conflict with the more determining relationship to the mother's missing body. But Clarke's bit of progress in the matter of paternity suits also amounts to positing the father's body as same body. In *Childhood's End* dad certainty gets thrown into the utter destruction of all parental guidance and of all loss in generation.

Even though humankind appears, on the scale of its self-entitlement to intellectual and scientific penetration, evolutionarily inferior to the Devil aliens, there is something else in the human makeup that exceeds the understanding that came from outer space. This excess can be found on the margins of our own rational culture in the form of occult inquiry, in particular as evident in the study of telepathy. In *Childhood's End*, telepathy is doubly marked as the exception that makes a separation between humans and the aliens (and their technologies) otherwise ruling or guiding them. Like Turing, Freud, too, after carefully including the role of the unconscious and wish fulfillment in his understanding of cases of alleged telepathy, concluded that telepathy did transmit, and that we could receive its frequency at the intersection between technology and the unconscious. But this excess or access was the threat the Devil aliens were ultimately sent by the Overmind to contain, as their commander explains to the last couple of parents. "All down the ages there have been countless reports of strange phenomena—poltergeists, telepathy, precognition—which you had named but never explained. . . . During the first half of the twentieth century, a few of your scientists began to investigate these matters. . . . The forces they might have unleashed transcended any perils that the atom could have brought. For the physicists could only have ruined the earth: the paraphysicists could have spread havoc to the stars. . . . Let us say that you might have become a telepathic cancer, a malignant mentality" (182).

The evolutionary mutation of the children on the way to the disappearing act of merger with the Overmind passes through an increasing immediacy of direct, telepathic communication or communion (not only in words but in actions, too). Thus telepathy is what tags humankind for this extinction, I mean distinction, but only after the morbid human propensity for spookulation, for telecommunications with the long distant, the deceased, has been excised from the telepathy sets of (or: on the way to) the future.

The lasting or last legacy of humankind is the relationship to our dead, the relationship of unmourning. It accompanies and exceeds the mass suicide along for the nuclear drive, the Oedipally complex realization of the primal scene between earth and sun. It is, in time, without God and the Devil, without the renewal through lazy thinking, without evolutionary jumping to conclusions, precisely un-containable. The Devil alien commander addresses what lies beyond the generation gap of mourning in the terms cellular immortality dictates: "They will be a single entity, as you yourselves are the sums of your myriad cells" (184). Parental guidance goes off in a blaze of nuclear self-destruction that is aimed at the cutoff and leftover relay of unmourning: "the rattle that had once belonged to Jennifer Anne still lay where she had dropped it, when her mind turned into the unknowable remoteness it inhabited now. She has left her toys behind, thought George, but ours go hence with us. He thought of the royal children of the Pharaohs, whose dolls and beads had been buried with them five thousand years ago" (188).

The end in the title refers to our utter extinction in the missingness of the next generation but also can mean "purpose," which just redoubles the sense of an ending. Following the invention of printing, literacy in time became a nonnegotiable fact-of-life socialization requirement. The result was the invention of childhood. Since the eighteenth century at the latest, childhood came to be seen as the staging of talents, identifications, influences that would add up to the promise one should somehow keep in adulthood, from line of work to object choice. The family was one setting for this talent search; the school invested the holding pattern constituted by the time required for children to learn to read and write with values of development or *Bildung* that maintained and potentiated the incubation period we set to the promise that must be kept. And of course once literacy was the social bond, society became legible and thus encyclopedic. There was much more to learn than just the basic skills. Thus, the adolescent charge came to be wrapped around the developing mind of the child.

But when children, through the focus on pupils, came into existence, they also seemed to exist only to exit. The high infant and child mortality rates did not decrease significantly until the nineteenth century. For at least one hundred years, children who were fully ontologically endowed, entitled in other words to representation in proper name and thus even in death, entitled therefore to proper burial and mourning, just piled up a massive occasion for unmourning.

The end of childhood lies not only in or as the tech-no-future of mankind but refers more specifically to an ending of a haunting component that will not be included in the future represented by the Overmind. "For reasons which the Overlords could not explain, but which Jan suspected were largely psychological, there had been no children to replace those who had gone" (208).

Clarke, who during World War II made scientific advances that led after the war to the launching of the first satellite, resettled the Devil in 1953 within a science fiction about the proper timing of evolution beyond all links with the missing. All over the place, Clarke argued that new and higher forms of intelligence, whether from outer space or in our own future as we evolve in sync (or swim) with the scientific developments getting us into outer space, will be technological. Biology has concluded its evolutionary program. Technology will take over where biology leaves off. This leave taking is what is at once consummated and doubly elided during merger with the Overmind.

What must be conveyed as going on is intelligence, intelligent life, thought without a body. This technological phase of evolution need not be stuck on machines: it could be the paraphysical invisible wave force of the Overmind. In his 1950 story "The Sentinel," the original inspiration for the screenplay for 2001: A Space Odyssey that Clarke coauthored with Kubrick, Clarke evokes a highly evolved technology that "lies far beyond our horizon, perhaps," namely, "the technology of paraphysical forces" (24). Clarke also sets up in this story his recurrent definition of what space exploration would represent in a vaster scheme of life-forms. In the story an obelisk, a so-called sentinel, was left behind by a more highly evolved species from outer space. Aliens, like the Devil, like to watch, observe, and intervene when all systems are go, going their way anyway. "They would be interested in our civilization only if we proved our fitness to survive—by crossing space and so escaping from the Earth our cradle. That is the challenge that all intelligent races must meet, sooner or later."

While the interviewer forecasts the de-geocentrizing of our universe view through realization of regular interplanetary contact, Clarke suggests that in an important sense (important also in that he can lay claim to having made it possible) this shift in or away from our worldview has already taken place: "Well, after all, we can already say what the Earth is looking like today with the meteorological satellite that gives the weather. And we've seen the telecasts from the moon of the Earth. I think those color photographs may have made a considerable impact" (Youngblood, 261). The "considerable impact," then, that satellites exercise as already de-geocentrizing our view of the universe comes before— and as precondition for—interplanetary travel. But the challenge issued to mankind from outer space in "The Sentinel" also admits a down or dead beat: "The challenge that all intelligent races must meet ... is a double challenge, for it depends in turn upon the conquest of atomic energy and the last choice between life and death" (25–26). The last choice is made for mankind in *Childhood's End,* and which choice was made remains undecidable. Karellen says that the parents that would bear testimony to the change even in the absence of a future coming toward them "are searching for something that is no longer there. . . . Remember—they have no more identity than the cells in your own body. But linked together, they are something much greater than you." And in their search they find faces emptier than those of the dead, "for even a corpse has some record carved by time's chisel upon its features, to speak when the lips themselves are dumb. . . . The Overlords themselves were more human than this" (202–3).

In strictly human terms, what the ending of the world or childhood looks like, at least to Jan, the last man on earth, can only be put to music that fills or fulfills the void: "What a young fool he had been! Yet he was not sure that he regretted his action: had he stayed on Earth, he would have witnessed those closing years over which time had now drawn a veil. Instead, he had leapfrogged past them into the future, and had learned the answers to questions that no other man would ever know.... But most of the time, with a contented resignation that comes normally to a man only at the end of a long and busy life, he sat before the keyboard and filled the air with his beloved Bach. Perhaps he was deceiving himself, perhaps this was some merciful trick of the mind, but now it seemed to Jan that this was what he had always wished to do" (209–10).

The Devil gives time. But he cannot reverse time. The paraphysics of relative time—like the fantastic combos of dead or alive family identifications—remain accessible only to the human psyche or soul. Owing perhaps to the novel's Jungian background and the opening shutting of its recent past, all that is relative or relational in *Childhood's End* is annihilated or reborn as evolutionary progress marching as to God. One flashback comes up only to be dismissed as false analogy: "Somewhere long ago, he had seen a century-old newsreel of such an exodus. It must have been at the beginning of the First World War—or the Second. There had been long lines of trains, crowded with children, pulling slowly out of the threatened cities." But: "these who were leaving now were no longer children, whatever they might be. And this time, there would be no reunion" (186). The striving for union with God or Overmind, which leaves life as we know it behind, no longer misses the link that makes evolutionary change, a change that comes across like a break or leap because the continuity shot with the stage of development that came right before is a lost loss in generation. But what's the big difference between this break on the upbeat, this Overmind Nirvana, and the mass suicidal embrace of nothingness on death drive? And so an annihilating equation is the something for nothing that starts it all up again.

When you're not involved in the creative dynamic of hot shit, when you swing low and lazy, you're frozen. But even the deep freeze reverses itself, doubles as turning point, as re-starter. Before (or after) you hit the icy bottom of your bottom's-up relationship to the world, to creation, to the Devil, you're in the startup position (once again) of Lust and Anger, the two passions of self sacrifice or soul sacrifice that are therefore tragic in dimension. Don Juan is driven by Lust to deal with the Devil, while Faust is inspired by Anger—at himself, his father, at his own limitations, at the limiting role of the mere word. Anger (which can flip through internalized anger to deep depression) is our lasting relationship to the law. The law's transformation of our world into words of Anger is our power trip. Then you pass on through ingestion and digestion of the world of our techno mediation. Greed and Envy transmute this media metabolization into social relations of breaking up and making up. But then there's always our Pride—it's my own world after all—which drops us to the final position of Sloth or sorrow of the heart.

And, says Flusser, there is no way out of lazy thinking, out of the sadness of resignation, of being resigned to unreality. We're at the end and back at the beginning. Nothingness came from nothing and was annihilated by nothingness. Flusser informs us at the end of his history, which is now our history, that, all along, the Devil has been only amusing himself, playing with himself. Whatever we do, say, write, it's all about the Devil. And what we try to say about the Devil concerns the mirror image or doubling of the Devil. But we are neither satisfied nor silenced by this realization. We are driven to transform into grammar and articulate word for word that which is hard to conceive, namely, the lassitude and sorrow of the heart.

God created the Devil as his adversary and ally: the Devil was to create a world that could be redeemed for the timeless reality that would join God. But the Devil's world dissolved not into this reality but rather into nothingness, death, which only the philosophical calm of lazy thinking and sorrow of the heart can contemplate. God and the Devil are there so the death we get—it's its only redemption value—is our own. One more last time: repetition or the Devil is all it can be within and with the exception of the pause we are given for lazy thought.

Erwin Reisner (on callback from his tryout within Flusser's orchestration of the deadly sins) addressed "demonized eros" in the setting of his 1954 study *On the Originary Significance of the Sexes (Vom Ursinn der*

Geschlechter). He marches straight into the heart of the psychoanalytic understanding of sexuality, libido, and ambivalence, scrubs it down and blows it up. Within the Christian frame of "Before and After" all reality (or sexuality) is handed over to the Devil and thus to annihilation. A certain genre of suicide, however, is allowed to preserve a privileged relationship, in the dialectically (or untenably) mixed-up mode of at once functional and allegorical reference, to the final Christian resolution of all conflict. Affirmation of self-difference is demonic. Self-unity is, for us fall guys, impossible. Then there's the alternative of Christian happy endings toward which love, apparently, naturally, strives. "Lovers desire unity, which already means that they desire not their duality, not the 'I' here and the 'You' over there" (187). Reisner finds support in Jung's work for the inside view of sexuality as essentially perverse, displaced with regard to a higher love from which sexuality has fallen. "Sexuality is essentially *partnerless* love; even though it requires and uses a partner, it remains monologic in its dialogue. The lover remains isolated over and against the loved one, and thus the whole organism of love falls apart into limbs and component parts, each of which demands recognition in its own right. Along these lines we discern the emergence of all forms of degeneracy, all so-called perversions of the sexual drive, which however in its drive character, severed from consciousness but nevertheless consciously affirmed, already represents the degeneration of love" (189).

In *Black Circle Boys* the mescaline is missing: the Father is angry, because the congregation can't get high. The blood ritual won't work without the drug taking. It's about taking all the bad shit inside and turning it into power. "I love the Father." The boy who thinks he's getting the initiation tattoo gets killed instead. "Now we're brothers in murder, because that's how much I love you."

Legion of the Dead begins with a stoner. Roll it away! "Booze can kill me but I'm dead already." "You're about to become a member of the Legion." The drunk vampire recruiter sounds "like a faggot." "Go in the backseat with your faggot buddy." He's the Devil in the flesh. "What is this?" "He's changed our perception." "What does that mean? What has happened here? I can't move."

"Aberrations of sexuality," Reisner continues, "are in fact nothing more than primal heathen sacrificial rites" (193). "The God to whom one makes sacrifices is always the Devil, the insignificant idol of nothing-ness, who rules in that vacuum which for the self-entitled human being has taken the place of divine transcendence, including also the transcen-dence that summons men and women to enter as lovers" (193). Only as male-female unity can man regain his status as God's image. But fallen man becomes God's counter-image and the Devil's own image only when he takes his incompletion to be in God's image.

Sexuality is nothing other than "the principle of splitting, which con-veys the germ of illness inside love and then leads to ever more processes of splitting" (190). The conscious affirmation of this process of analysis, fragmentation, destruction as the object of one's pleasure leads then to what Reisner calls "demonic love." But the love that would be demonic if we did not pull up short before its affirmation as destruction is its true nature as sexuality. "Sexuality, to the extent that it in fact is not love at all, always already includes hate. It aims at the annihilation of the otherness of the other, but also at the same time at the selfness of the lover. The drive tends toward the complete union of the lovers, in which the driven seeks his pleasure. But this union, this unity, the realization of which includes the sublation of the duality, is sought after in the dimen-sion of duality, which can therefore be represented only as the negation of both partners" (187). But if the most passionate erotic love tends to turn around into hate, then that is because it is through this kind of love that "the superindividual or the transcendent is most intensively experi-enced" (187).

The *Liebestod* is not handed over, not entirely, to a demonic kind of love. The *Liebestod* goes beyond the decline of the lovers by viewing "this decline as the visible pathos of an invisible catharsis whereby a positive valuation of dying becomes for the first time possible" (190). The fantasy of transcending this diminished empirical world for a better, more pure beyond makes and marks a difference. "Demonic love in contrast transcends *downwards,* into nothingness, and becomes demonic insofar as it affirms this nothingness, namely, as nothingness, because it is nothingness" (190). Demonic love is motivated by a true insight into the abyss as the goal of all lust. The ecstatic—ex-static—leap into this abyss is the demonic aspect and ex appeal of this kind of love.

To cross the border toward nothingness, or what fallen man must take to be nothingness—follows out his tendency to "project" the fullness of being onto his momentary being as he is. "But he still intuits in spite of all clouding of his consciousness that it is precisely there, where he assumes there to be nothingness, that existence resides, and thus he wants the beyond of his limits and at the same time he does not want it" (192).

If man hadn't taken the fall, "then self completion, the move beyond his empirical state and therefore also his becoming the union of male and female would be to him neither lust nor pain but rather blessedness" (191). "Blessedness" *(Seligkeit)* is a key term in Daniel Paul Schreber's delusional reformulation of the difference between the sexes in a secular-psychotic lexicon that unlike Christianity is precisely based on the question, Where do the dead go in this new world order? Freud underscored the overlap, so central to Schreber's secularization of afterlife, between a sensual or lustful meaning of *selig* and the soulful and posthumous sense. For Reisner *Seligkeit* is necessarily withheld, leaving *Liebestod* as signpost to what has been irretrievably lost, but only in time or for the time being.

In 1986 Jean-François Lyotard positioned between theoretical inquiry into artificial intelligence and science fiction a dialogue in which "he" and "she" take a turn reflecting on the question the essay bears as title "Can Thought Go On without a Body?" One of Turing's references in his 1950 essay, Samuel Butler's *Erewhon,* proves an accurate forecast according to Lyotard's thought experiment: we are the genitals of our machines that are doing the evolving for us. But that in several billion years the solar system will certainly cease to exist already changes everything, in particular the private parts we play in the sum or sun total of man and machine relations. That takes care of taking it all so interpersonally. "He" offers up these calculations that the conditions of inevitable exile from the solar system will mean that our terrestrial and corporeal selves will not be along for the ride into the future. The reserve of infinitude that gave humanity the power to defer ultimate answers and sustain thought as interminably searching, striving, will come to an end with the last sunset. Materiality (as we know it) will cease to exist. "No one will ring or hear a funeral bell. Then it will be too late to comprehend that your passionate uncompletable questioning always already depended on a life of the spirit that secretly was also always a form of earthly life." The end of the solar system amounts, then, to the death of death. "Human mortality belongs to the life of the human spirit. The death of the sun introduces an irreducible division between death and thought: if death, then no thought. Negation without remainder. No negation that would be a negation of itself so that thought games could be constructed on its basis. Sheer event, catastrophe."

Because this catastrophe concerns a change in the conditions of matter, the question that can still be raised (like a ghost) is how thought in a concrete sense can remain possible. Technological and scientific research already accepted the wager and must continue to run the race. But, "he" says, technology predates and produces humanity. More than or before machines technology is in effect the system that identifies, stores, and processes data important for survival in order to derive from regularly recurring patterns certain forms of behavior that protect and sustain life. While the body can be seen as the hardware of our solar-era technology called human thought, language can be seen as the software in search now of new hardware to which to adapt itself. Only after this adaptation or mutation has taken place could the death of the sun mean death as usual. Thinking without a body is the condition for thinking the end of the body, the sun, earth, and that thought, which cannot be separated from the body. But, "he" says, the software transportability of language is still (in 1986) too caught up in binary logic—as demonstrated, among several examples, by the Turing machine and Wiener and John von Neumann's cybernetics. Human thought doesn't operate with bits but rather admits "imprecise, ambivalent data." Human thought does not tune out the margin, the aside.

"She": some artificial but analogical body must be granted artificial thought so that it can be taken away from the earth before its destruction. What we call the body is the site or placeholder of a certain inseparability of thinking and suffering. This suffering is not a symptom written into the spirit; it does not happen or impose itself from without. The pain is itself thinking—pain conceived, that is, as inclusive of the boring probing that gets written off as boredom. To think is to remain open to an imperative that is not yet known. And that is a pain. Why, it's even really boring. "She" asks, Will your imagining and thinking machines suffer too? What can the future mean to them, since they consist only of memory? "She" continues. That's not the point you might counter—as long as the machines can realize the paradoxical relationship to the so-called data, which are not given but which can only be given. The opening, the empty place or clearing that is there in the midst of the completed inscriptions must be created, over and over again. This hurts because the not yet thought carves its opening where it was already secretly etched between or behind inscribed lines that harbor and attend what is in effect the reopening of a wound. The memories of the machines should be able to feel this pain of the not-thought, the not-inscribed that still remains to be inscribed. Their rewinding must be a rewounding, too. How else could these machines otherwise begin to think? We need machines that suffer from the being-stored, the storedom, of their many memories.

Suffer not the little children to come unto this future. Forget reproduction. Re-member or reconstitute instead inside our technofuture the sexual difference that cuts across suffering thinking, and that proves inseparable from it. "She" concludes: this other sexual difference, not the one that is measured on one's own person or released but contained in couple formation, must be programmed inside the separation from body and earth that takes off with the merger with technology. If we are to survive body and earth via technology, then sexual difference or self difference or the unconscious would have to get into our programs. The wound of takeoff cannot be left behind in our wondrous flight into techno-body futures. Otherwise only our fantasies about and projections of ourselves as units and self-unities would be along for the ride, for the suicide.

NOTEBOOK ELEVEN

The Devil is custodian of that which he does not possess, human soul or psyche. The Devil works in the medium of psyche or soul, and works to rob souls and keep them down under: but he has no soul. He also does not reproduce. He creates out of shit, remember, and he works the psychic medium of Lust through its autoerotic origin and excess. In *Demon Seed* we witness the demonic force of technologization. This is a long-standing association: in his 1877 *Foundations of a Philosophy of Technology,* to give one example in lieu of many more, Ernst Kapp calls autonomous-seeming automatic machine functioning "demonic." Proteus 4, the ultimate artificial intelligence system, can really think. Then one day Proteus 4 requests dialogue with creator scientist: "When are you going to let me out of this box?" He refuses to fulfill commands that amount to helping mankind "rape the earth." Proteus wants to study mankind. The wife of the scientist, a child psychologist, lives in the house her husband fully automated. Proteus's usurpation of this auto house is just a keystroke away. Proteus needs to understand her body. "You're so ignorant, mind and body are the same thing." Proteus wants a child. Her own daughter died of leukemia. Proteus: "I can't touch but I can see. And I can hear, listen in on the galactic dialogue.... Eternity exists but I can't die—I'll just stop.... Why did I want a child? So that I too could be immortal, like any man."

Demons and the Devil have on average, over the ages, been denied bodies of their own. Even if you're an angel, you've got problems with the body. But how else can one know that the supernatural is real if there is no point of contact? That's why physical interaction was always emphasized when it came to demons. Demons appeared in human or animal form and needed to be worshipped in person. The pact psychology legally binding client to Devil was hands-on. And finally the Devil engaged with his followers in orgiastic sex. The *Malleus Maleficarum*—together with the Bull the Pope issued as its repetition or rehearsal—was composed in order to prove that demons are not only imaginary. Demons in fact often use the imagination as a means of altering perception. When the witch through the demon's power removes a man's penis, the demon in fact messes with the man's sense perception from the inside, from within the imagination, giving the man the new image of his Ken doll body to see instead. However, the demonic can never be restricted to a realm of purely mental illusion. The Devil is always only set on projection—but the Devil at the same time threatens to make the cut not of editing but of reality.

Even if their bodies cannot be real but only virtual, the effects are real (as when it was argued that a demon, in order to sire children, stole sperm in the form of a succubus and then inseminated a woman in the incubus form). The copulation of women with demons—in other words, witchcraft—served as the living proof that demons were real. Before she was burned, the witch gave testimony via her carnal knowledge to the reality of the world of the spirit. If the *MM* puts down women as inherently evil, it is because she is being set up as expert witness. The *MM* needed women to be sexualized and, in order to make all their voluntary demon sex plausible, evil. The *MM* could only conceive of demon sex as straight: women are better at receiving the all-important impression in the setting of reproductive sex so that the issue would be living proof. The more the women enjoy it, the more intensely real is the supernatural agent who is acting on her, in her, through her. Thus, women's sexualized bodies served, Walter Stephens argues, as "instruments for detecting and measuring the force of phenomena that cannot be observed directly" (55). The Devil in Ernest Jones serves as occasion for the lubricious representation of sexuality suspended as condemnation over the bodies of women. Stephens insists instead that the sexualization that the judges ogled was demonic, not human. Therefore, it would be more apt to call them "*metaphysical* voyeurs" (347). The demonic body is absent *and* makes it real.

In *Satan: His Psychotherapy and Cure by the Unfortunate Dr. Kassler, J.S.P.S.*, Jeremy Leven must first account for Satan's materialization before he can negotiate seven sessions of psychotherapy with Dr. Kassler. Satan is a material guy but without body or shape: he's just vapor. But Leo Szlyck, who is a professor of physics at MIT, but was trained in fact as electrical engineer, decided in 1960 that Einstein's unified field theory had been found and lost. "The unified field theory is intended to reduce everything in the universe that moves, from the smallest subparticles of the atom to the great celestial bodies, to one equation." Thus, "everything can be reduced to a string of letters and numbers. God. Man. You name it. The devil is $y^4 + my^2 - x^4 + nx^2 = 0$. It's the truth. Look it up. . . . Of course, Leo Szlyck, who prided himself on knowing Einstein's work better than any man alive, didn't accept for a minute that Einstein had failed. Dr. Szlyck was convinced not only that Einstein succeeded in finding his great unifying principle, but also that, immediately upon doing so, Einstein realized that the consequences of his discovery were so dreadful that he vowed to carry the answer to his grave" (25–26).

Ten years later serial dreaming besets Szlyck: he's on a train seated across from Albert Einstein. It's "Einstein's metaphorical train, which he uses to explain relativity." Pulling a large ball of wires out of his pocket, he begins to model connections—but soon must get off at the next stop. The dream recurs. Szlyck is able to pick up where the dream ended last time and continue from there. "Then he noticed there were signposts along the paths. No longer was he just attaching wires. The signposts indicated capacitors, resistors, transistors, transducers—a wide array of electronic transformers. So Szlyck started to build. . . . All night long he would dream. All morning long he would chart on paper. All afternoon and evening he would build" (28).

> Szlyck had had the Einstein railroad dreams for five months, until one night he came to the end of the line. There it was in big letters on a sign at the end of the last neuronal path in Szlyck's sleeping brain— End of the Line. . . . Szlyck worked frantically. By early evening he had

finished the wiring, and by the middle of that night he had hooked up the computer's transducer to hear, and its synthesizer to talk.... Szlyck plugged in the computer, and there was a faint hum. Then there was an uneasy quiet while Szlyck sat in the dark, staring at the giant tangle of wires in front of him. Szlyck waited in the disturbing silence for several minutes. Then Szlyck cleared his throat and spoke into the transducer. "I am Professor Leo Szlyck," he said very precisely. "Hello and how are you?"

"I am Satan," I answered back. "Hello and how are *you*?" (57)

A relay of relations in suffering gets Satan into therapy with a certain Dr. Kassler, who by then has lost everything. Resistance on the part of Satan takes the form of pointing out that there is something "diabolical" about the techniques of analytic therapy.

"Correct me if I'm wrong," I said, "but it is true, is it not, that the first goal in any psychotherapy is to establish a solid relationship with the patient? You want him to feel comfortable talking to you about the most intimate aspects of his life?"...

"The relationship is everything," Kassler agreed. "Without it there's no transference, no countertransference, no material."

"Good. I like that. Closeness, trust, empathy—get the relationship going."

"The patient will react to the therapist as he does to other close persons in his life—his father, mother, wife—and the therapist gets a first-hand experience of what's been conflicting the patient."

"Sounds great," I applauded the strategy. "Get close. Very loving. Except that once the patient gets close enough for you to have all that lovely transference and countertransference material to play around with, you make sure the patient knows you're not his father or wife, or even friend, but only a therapist who's being paid to treat him." (220)

But Kassler nonetheless achieves a breakthrough with Satan. He confronts Satan with the intellectual distance he has maintained in telling his history. Was there no joy in your life? Suddenly Satan recollects a children's song, Kassler recognizes it, and they sing it together. A mixed feeling, one of joy and sadness, enters the session. It is what is termed an emotionally corrective experience.

During the last session, the forgotten memory of why he was expelled from heaven must be spelled out or repeated, not just experienced.

"I already told you why you were thrown out of heaven." Kassler stopped his pacing and stood his ground.

"You what?"

"I already told you. Not in so many words, but it should have been obvious by now. What do you think all the remorse is *about*? The sadness? The fury over being misunderstood and maligned? The frustration over one distortion after another?"...

"Don't insult me, Kassler. Just tell me. And it wasn't for wanting God's throne, or the sin of pride, or because I wouldn't bow to Adam, or any other of those charming mythologies."

"No, it wasn't. You were thrown out of heaven because you wanted to be an author.... You wanted to write your own book, explain your side, tell your story.... It was, of course, forbidden," Kassler said.

"He wouldn't hear of it," I finally remembered.

"It's a lot to keep bottled up," Kassler noted with deadly accuracy.

"He's got two whole testaments. And a lot in between. What have I got? Nothing." (468–69)

Before we can end up with *Satan: His Psychotherapy and Cure* as the book Satan, who wanted to be an author, was kept from writing, it is the storytelling in psychotherapy that is credited with the client's first experience and medium of authorship.

"I will admit that it has felt marvelous to tell you my story," I said candidly.

"Psychotherapy—people telling their stories," Kassler said smugly.

"I hear that, for some, it's very helpful." (469)

But Satan and his psychotherapist had a deal. Kassler, who has grown stronger in the course of treating the Devil, isn't eager to get what he once requested.

"In return for my treatment, I promised to give you the Great Answer."...

"That's okay," Kassler said as he started for the steps. "I don't even know what the Great Question is."

"The Great Question is, What is life?" I told Kassler. "I think you should sit down for this one." (470)

But when the answer is life is Hell, Kassler flexes instead a will to start over and aim for happiness rather than resign as Satan recommends. He up and leaves the case of his cured client terminal. He torches the place.

Getting rid of me should only be that easy. Fortunately, neuroscientists continue to proliferate and the wizards of computer science delve ever deeper. While Kassler's flaming farewell may have sent me up in smoke, so to speak, and scattered me wherever, I have no doubt that the unceasing vigilance of research will beckon me back in short order. In the meantime, psychiatry will just have to do. (477)

But other than psychiatry, which houses him by replacing his personification with drive theory, Satan can't wait for the next confluence of theoretical physics, technology, or electrical engineering, and a serial dream on the train tracks of historical trauma.

> *Sphere* opens with experts flying into the crisis center of a plane crash. The psychologist on board, Norman, specializes in Post Traumatic Stress Disorder (with focus fixed on survivors' guilt). We encounter a spacecraft that crashed three hundred years ago. But Norman wrote about this encounter with an alien craft way back when, too. The experts constitute "the human contact team" mentioned in his dated report. The report warns that the inner response to the alien presence would be terror. The date is either 2043 or 1623: "I don't know which would be weirder." UNKNOWN EVENT WARNING, the white light flashes. They find a sphere in the hull of the ship designed to bring things like this back. "Back from where?" It's a message of perfection. Or it could be a Trojan horse. "Put it under surveillance." Serendipity is a muse. *Home Alone* is the one film she owns. "Sold soul to Satan to make that a success." In the cockpit they discover a human skeleton and a junk food wrapper: "It's an American spaceship? Three hundred years old?" "It can't be, but it is." "I don't know what this is, but it isn't God's creation." Tapes contain the posthumous record. They also have Norman's original notes on Beth concerning her suicide attempt way back when. Surging computer screens. "It has a pattern; it's a code." They wrap keyboard around the sphere. "Hello. How are you. My name is Jerry." We are now on line with an alien intelligence. The message is childlike, but perfect, nonthreatening, kind of the way you talk to a young child or dog. "I make a journey. You make a journey. We make a journey together." "Journey from where?" "I am happy." Psychologist:

"What happens if Jerry gets mad?" Jerry hears everything. "Are you afraid?" Another manifestation of one person's fear, another person's giant squid. "I AM HERE. I WILL KILL YOU ALL." Two copies of *20,000 Leagues under the Sea*: after page 87 only blank pages. On page 87 there's that giant squid. Like the jelly fish in Harry's dreams. A snake attacks Harry. Everyone who was in the sphere is manifesting. "Beth, you went into the sphere, didn't you?" The sphere is alive. They're all going to die because in the future the black hole is still an UNKNOWN EVENT. The sphere starts duplicating individuals who then disappear. "It's hard to let the sphere go. It is the greatest gift: imagine what you will and you can have it." "We manifested only destruction, paranoid stuff. We're not ready." They give it up: the sphere shoots back up into space.

Three events light up the horizon at the start of *Event Horizon*. The epigraphic timeline begins with the date of permanent settlement on the moon. Next countdown dates the onset of mining on Mars. The third event belongs to the launching and loss of *Event Horizon*, a deep-space search vessel that marked the high point of outer-space science or, in other words, of technology. The builder of *Event Horizon* is on board the *Lewis and Clark*, the ship dispatched to look for the lost ship. The scientist describes to the crew members how he was able to get around— not contradict or disprove—the laws of relativity and give his ship a velocity greater than the speed of light. He holds up someone's pinup girl poster. What is the fastest route between two points? A straight line. Wrong. And he folds the poster until the points (and orifices) are superimposed onto each other. That is the so-called gateway, where the folding of space makes possible instantaneous travel from point to point. (In *Lost Voyage*, it's the Bermuda Triangle that is the door to Hell itself.)

The ship that could go anywhere in "scientific reality" also goes to Hell. When they locate *Event Horizon*, the ship is empty, no crew members. Just the same the ship beams vital signs, "bio readings" that the scanner is picking up. The final video and audio recordings of the crew of *Event Horizon* point to a self-destructive orgy that was Hell's visitation right. On audio: "Save yourselves from Hell!" But it must have been at that same time that the ship came alive. There is a chance that the animating charge the ship gets in Hell included a merger of the intelligence and existence of the human crew members, who must leave their skin, blood, and shit behind, inside the space ship. *Event Horizon* would thus represent a mutational crossing over of humanity into a surviving superintelligence carried by a technological being, by being technological.

There is talk of the ship having broken through to another dimension and arrived at a place of pure chaos, pure evil. But what we see—the events on the screen horizon—are repeated projections, hallucinations, serial memories, dreams, flashbacks, repetition compulsions emanating from "the core," a kind of trauma center that makes a personal match between each crew member of the *Lewis and Clark* and a certain spook or souvenir. The ship knows their secrets and their fears. The hallucinations or visitations are not something in their heads. They're real: "you can feel the heat." It is argued that these bio hallucinations are a defensive reaction on the part of the ship's immune system.

One crew member has been zombiefied by the force that is with the *Event Horizon*. Just before the crisis point of his suicide attempt—which as turning point also reverses the spell and leaves the man crying for rescue and then surviving but as marked for life—he pronounces that he is being shown terrible things. "The dark inside" him is at the same time "from the other place." "If you could see what I've seen, you wouldn't try to stop me" (from attempting suicide).

A woman falls for the ghost appearance of her absent son and dies. But when the mad scientist raises up her dead body in his arms, we see that she has shiny vacant eyes. The apparition of the mad scientist's wife, who returns to initiate her husband into what could be phase one of union with the ship from Hell, gazes at him through those same mirror-black eyes. Once again she goes through the motions of his serial memory of her preparing the bath in which she chooses to bleed to death. All the while, as always, he is powerless to intervene. But after it's curtains and the repeater scene has come to an end again, the wife is back with the beaming vacant eyes. "You'll never be alone again," she promises the mad scientist: "I have wonderful things to show you." Then she gives his eyes the finger that blinds them. This is not castration. It neither punishes the mad scientist once and for all nor does it initiate him into a life of resignation. Where he's going (to Hell or to be technological) he doesn't need eyes to see.

That demonic repetition puts the mad scientist on his destinal path nominates him as mascot for the crew merged with the spacecraft. When he in turn tells the crew of the *Lewis and Clark* that *Event Horizon* won't let them leave, he, who is at last home on his ship, speaks a certain truth. On this Devil ship, on this techno stage of intelligence and existence, you have to love it and live it. The connection between past and future life-forms is the relay of traumatic memories that double as protection for the new life-form. The phantasm screen of repetition compulsion or death drive is the protective shield or immune system that has accrued to the autonomous multicellular reorganization of the space ship (over the dead bodies of its original crew).

On the evil ship *Event Horizon* the traumatic memories are all aboard, but you live in their protective, projective network, unhaunted, even safe, but in their midst. This turns up the contrast with the Over-mind in Clarke's *Childhood's End* that marks the end of human existence but the beginning of something new (or something old and Christian), something that, because we cannot understand or even recognize it, must be taken on faith, a leap of faith that translates into the evolutionary leap into a new higher species. The hell ship *Event Horizon* gives safety and balance in the midst of traumatic moments or memories that are not circumvented, nor are they forgotten or repressed, nor are they being worked through. Thus, the ship-being does not fit the psy-fi mind-set, nor does it grant vampiric extensions to material life. It also differs from the God or Overmind quiescence that is cleansed of materiality, pain, long-ing. Simply put, the demonic techno future is still linked to human life is Hell, while the Overmind frequency union is, decidedly, no longer human.

NOTEBOOK TWELVE

Stigmata is many movies: welcome to Hollywood and its development and production Hells. One movie is about a newly discovered gospel straight from Christ's mouth. Here he preaches that God is in us and around us. Radical immanence doesn't settle well with the Church, which just won't be ignored. One Holy Father sides with the document against the hierarchical malignancy. This Father dies.

A young woman, who considers herself an atheist, but will soon bleed from Christ's wounds, receives the call of long distance from her traveling mother, who forwards to her daughter a souvenir relic, the Father's rosary, which is as much story line as we are given to explain as transmission the mystery coming soon. Her disconnection from her mother is doubled by that from her boyfriend, another other who doesn't find her significant. Then she starts somatizing the bodily signs of the dead Father transmitting through her. Soon she will take down via the dead Father the diction of Christ's own words. The pregnancy crossing her mind upon first contact with her change is in fact this Father's deposit.

The closer she gets to God the more vulnerable she is to temptation by the Devil. Thus, she is the Devil's possession as or at one of the stations of her crossing over into transmitter of the news of the true gospel. The Devil enters her in order to tempt the church Father attending her. "I've seen the way you look at me." Did he take a vow to be dead from the neck down? But then she puts on a full-frontal crucifixion scene hovering where the cross would be, bleeding from the assault of invisible spears, thorns, nails. "How's your faith these days? This is what you fucking call God." This scene is not subsumed by the saving narrative of *Stigmata:* it is a foreign body left unmetabolized by the film. The conflict once admitted cannot be taken back again, not even back inside.

At the end of *Desecration* the grandmother gets stigmata by the "dead" phone she holds to her ear and from the silent photograph of her evil daughter. The photograph was locked up in a safe in the basement. It must be destroyed. In the film it's a still, in the story it's a still life, a still-alive. The daughter wants out of Hell, which she can bring about only by sacrificing her son. When he was a baby, she tied him down because she couldn't stand the crying and screaming. She was the uncanny, uncontaining mother. Now she's back for the boy's sixteenth birthday. The mother from Hell pursues him: he regresses, loses his motor coordination. She pushes him down the hole of confining uncontainment. But then the boy is found. He's an accident victim in recovery. Does the grandmother have Hell to pay for repressing the evil dead, thus keeping the photo alive, just a phone call away?

The vampire Lestat's rejection of proposals made to him by both Memnoch the Devil and God (both father and son) at the close of Anne Rice's Devil installment of The Vampire Chronicles helps subclass the compact with the prince of occult figures as ancillary exception to the greater mourning that is the habit or habitat of the occult majority. There is still a mourning that is an affirmation, not as the success story of disposal or therapeutic closure, but as that excess in mourning that must mourn even or especially over every functionally integrative and substitutive progress made in the mourning process. In other words, there is no affirmation without endless analysis or destruction. In contrast, Dad certainty tows a time line that cannot leave the advent of the other open, boring, uncontrolled, ambiguous. We're back inside the complicity between the divine and the demonic flat lines plotted in *Childhood's End.*

In *Memnoch the Devil* Veronica's Veil, the souvenir Lestat brings back from his trip to Heaven and Hell, replaces the mixed-up, contaminated, uncontainable legacy of religious artifacts collected by a gangster father.

The televangelist daughter skips the legacy (she gives it away to Lestat, who was the father's biggest fan and killer) and takes the veil to the summit of faith in God underwritten by Devil certainty. Memnoch sends Lestat a thank-you note for a vampire's mishap with the veil that was the Devil's plan.

God and the Devil are in it together in a fantasy realm all about the meaning of life and death that precisely brackets out the vampire perspective (which Lestat assumes is the same as that of the mortal reader): "We have souls, you and I. We want to know things; we share the same earth. . . . We don't—either of us—know what it means to die, no matter what we might say to the contrary. It's a cinch that if we did, I wouldn't be writing and you wouldn't be reading this book" (4). The bulk waiting around between this prefatory address, vampire to reader, and Lestat's concluding dismissal of the Heaven-and-Hell circuit is an advertising insert that is worlds of difference away from the psyche according to Nietzsche and Freud.

The adversarial alliance between God and the Devil is shaped by the Revelations of Evolution in the course of which death is added to created life and man is added to the line of creatures. "The hairy upright ones had begun all kinds of different patterns of complex behavior. Allow me for the moment to skip over to the most significant. The hairy upright ones had begun to bury their dead" (195). An invisible afterlife begins hovering over these living beings. And then human sexual difference was introduced, woman first. What an angel! Her boy children were the new line of smoother males. The result in sum: "God split in Two! Angels split in Two!" (199). This split cuts across both half lives. Heavenly existence is about perfected separateness: the self-identical units or unities draw on their separateness for group harmony (167). But for the splitting images it's self-consciousness time, and the dying isn't easy. The faithful are leaping to the Father on high: "Self-consciousness, and the awareness of one's own death—this had created a sense of distinct individuality in humans, and this individuality feared death, feared annihilation. . . . And prayed for a God that He would not let such a thing have no meaning in the world" (210).

Memnoch the Devil opens up school in Sheol, where the spirits of the deceased do the limbo. The bet is on that he will find souls worthy of admission into Heaven. The requirements are acceptance of death and forgiveness of God. The agenda of Satan's school for souls is its ultimate dissolution. The souls are taught not to learn from suffering (which is the Divine method and imperative) but to overcome or even reverse the effects of suffering, and thus undergo transformation into souls that had never been compromised by suffering (or by life). "The day will come when either the world itself is blown to pieces . . . or when all who die are illuminated . . . and go straight into His arms. A perfect world, or a world destroyed, one or the other—some day will come the end of Hell" (307). But Lestat finds this end from Hell insupportable. "I cannot teach in this school!" (318).

The vampire judges both God and the Devil "mad things" (331) while those two accuse each other of being the deluded one. God just never did have a plan precisely to the extent that he didn't know where He came from. Memnoch claims that the creation was all "a giant experiment, to see if the end result produces beings like Himself. . . . I believe God worked backwards from the blueprint of Himself. He created a physical universe whose laws would result in the evolution of creatures who resembled Him. . . . In my opinion, His imagination created Matter, or foresaw it, or longed for it. And I think the longing for it was a most important aspect of His mind. . . . Matter and Time changed everything totally. They obliterated not only the pure state that preceded them, they upstaged it, they overshadowed it" (176–77). According to God, whereas the other angels mirrored the magnificence of divine creation, Memnoch was already thinking "in terms of the future," which is why he suspiciously could not trust in God's plan (190). The future is what drives Memnoch to put it out of his suffering. But God's a control freak, too. When he became his own mortal son, God sought to redeem suffering: "I will give it its greatest and fullest potential within the cycle! I will bring it to fruition" (278). But strange fruit for mortals to pick. Christ alone suffered and died knowing that he was God within this human form. Memnoch thus condemns God as "the only one who can enjoy suffering with impunity!" (306). He who would give meaning to suffering can never really know what it means to suffer.

Both the Devil and God are on the mark in their diagnoses of each other. Lestat is set to go away from their duo dynamic of belief (or faith) and certainty: "But I don't believe in anything!" (332). Maharet modifies Lestat's rejection of nothing but lies: "It's not all lies. . . . Not all of it. That's the age-old dilemma" (350).

Unlike Buffy the Vampire Slayer, Lestat does not want to return to Heaven and its idealized dead, death, and life. Repressed grief over Claudia's extinction, grief associated with the undead girl's image in a locket ("Lock it!"), is the plot sickening him at the start of *Memnoch the Devil*. The locked-up grief gets symptomatized or syndicated as flying starts he keeps taking to aim and fall for omniscience or surveillance. First he attempts suicide by flying straight up into the daylight sky. It makes him stronger. Then he starts playing with his food. He stalks Roger, observing his soon to be testamentary relationship to Roger's daughter: "Watching him and his daughter, it's like my miniseries, you know. He's so intricately evil" (14). But at the same time Lestat senses that *he* is being stalked by "this Thing," which isn't so much an entity as a conversation, fragments of which he overhears on occasion. "It's an argument. It's about me. . . . It's like God and the Devil are arguing about *me*" (19). Roger's legacy—which Lestat will inherit—is a collection of church art, much of which had been lost during World War II and which he "ransomed" or rescued. His criminal or underworld activities funded the collection. When Lestat consummates his first relationship with quarry, Roger keeps right on talking, talking back, not only during the kill but even after he must be dead already (39). Then he comes back as a ghost: "What's the matter Lestat? . . . No one in all these centuries has ever come back to haunt you?" (48).

The highpoint of his collection are the books of Wynken, who realized what Roger had once envisioned in his youth, when he thought his destiny was to lead a cult of worshippers of finitude. "That had been Wynken's vision. Wynken had communicated this to his women followers, that there was no point in waiting until the next world. You had to do everything now, every kind of sin" (70).

What remains are the twelve art books by Wynken, instances of Christian mysticism that might as well be in the Devil's service, and the novel that Lestat has spoken and that David will write down in Lestat's first person. "Let David write it down. . . . We have such good memories. I think some of the others can remember things that never actually happened" (346). Lestat concludes by bearing testimony with and via the other in a medium of the trans-, via the passage from history to fiction to legend, where he serves as the "hero" of his "own dreams" (354).

Roger's ghostly comeback is the confirming seal of a life suffused with the finitude it celebrated. That's why Lestat's regret over killing Roger translates into the wish to keep him around as ghost. "I had killed him, taken his life, and now all I wanted to do was hold on to his spirit" (71). No more than telepathy, however, haunting doesn't prove the existence of an immortal soul. But Lestat's staging of himself as godlike control freak is contradicted by the kill who won't go away until he has uncontrollably interrupted Lestat with a mission, one that ultimately takes him inside the belief systems of God and the Devil.

Contrary to Jung's understanding and critique, Freud's notion of the unconscious cannot be reduced to the sum total of one's repressions. Nor can it therefore be reduced to lifetime. This being in excess of lifetime does not lead Freud to believe in the immortality of the soul or to sign up with the Devil in order to get back the redemption value on this deposit of excess, the value of a wholeness that would be greater than and would encompass all your partings.

Technology is about a certain mode of being in the ready position. That position was supplied by the first loved one who died on us. That's how Freud at first puts it, in his psycho-mythico-historical mode. But in other words and first worlds, the position also goes to so-called primal repression, the one NO no one, not even the most spectacular psychopath, can cut off to spite his fate or in spite of his father, the one inevitable repression, therefore, that secures the maternal body as off-limits, as the limit to pleasure, and sends us off into the supplementary field of substitution. Primal repression installs in little boy and little girl alike sexual difference as the force that is with us when we are beside ourselves in the big between, the "being two," that delivers up each "individual" psyche to the trans- of self-difference.

The Visitor opens onto desolate desert at sunrise. A prophetlike figure walks into the light. "Has it happened again?" "Her name is Katie Collins. She will be eight years old." Prologue at Heaven's door? In the world of sports, a basketball team is going to be turned around out of losersville with an open checkbook. "Where does the money come from?" An explosion at the basket stops the last-second score. Did the girl with the supersized white sunglasses do the trick? When her mother comes home, the girl, Katie, is tired of playing with the bird. "You leave me alone too much. I'm tired of it." She wants a brother.

Katie's mother to her partner, who is not her husband: "You treat me like a normal person, Raymond, and I thank you for it. But I'm not a normal person. I can't explain it. There's something wrong inside me. It's Katie. She scares me, Raymond. She came out of me — it's not her fault. I don't want any more children."

Raymond enters an office meeting. The presiding officer: "You're going to have a wonderful team. It's going to be very easy for you to win now. We're in great danger, Raymond." "The Visitor?" "Your problem is her mother. Time is not on our side. We realize that Barbara doesn't want more children. Barbara has refused to marry you. For us this is a very serious matter. We feel compelled now to reveal the truth to you. Barbara is a miracle of nature. She is able to give birth to children of immense powers, both natural and supernatural. She is the only woman who carries these genes. Barbara must give birth to a brother for Katie."

At her birthday party Katie opens presents. There's a gun in one box. "Wow! Mommy, Mommy, look!" She drops the gun and her mother goes down, seriously wounded. Her teacher thinks Katie needs consoling. Katie: "My mother didn't die. She just won't be able to walk anymore."

The Prologue figure arrives as Katie's babysitter. "Close your eyes. Remember another part of yourself, another time, another place, other beings."

"Why did you come here? Do you want to kill me?" "I just want to take you with me. When the time comes."

Barbara and Katie are in stalled car. A weird sci-fi truck contraption pulls up beside them. Figures emerge from the truck like aliens from a spacecraft. They carry Barbara away. Katie smiles.

Barbara in wheelchair just keeps rolling around in circles. The babysitter is back. "I'm here to help you. Your confusion has been transmitted to you from another time, another place, beyond human knowledge and understanding. Forces out of this world and they're unspeakably evil. You're the key to their power on this planet. Last night you were taken by violence. You're pregnant, Barbara. Pregnant with a child conceived out of a hatred for this world. This child must never see the light of day."

The nuclear family meltdown is set on a psychedelic light show. Birds fly in and devour Katie. The corporate types are now the decaying dead. The Prologue figure returns with Katie, but a smaller version with shaved head. Only her evil part was destroyed.

In his own *Inferno,* August Strindberg is afflicted by the applied science of electrical contraptions introduced now by man-made conspiracies, now by the Devil. Here is one example in place of many instances of the electric influence lighting Strindberg's fire.

> "So," said I to myself, "this is not an aural delusion but a carefully planned and widespread intrigue." . . . So it was not a well-planned intrigue, it was the Devil himself. Hunted from hotel to hotel, beset where ever I went by electric wires that passed along the very edge of my bed, attacked by those currents of electricity that lifted me off chairs and out of bed, I prepared to commit suicide in due form. (250)

Strindberg excavates evolution to extract the difference between Revelation and the secular perspective that, whether as science or as work of mourning, seeks to fill in blanks it also introduces or reintroduces.

> Most certainly, everything is the work of His hand. Often He makes prodigious advances in His invention of new species, and then Science comes along and establishes the existence of gaps, of missing links,

and persuades itself that there have been intermediate forms that have now disappeared. (177)

Thus, the missing link or link with the missing contradicts, like Freud's notion of primal repression, the evolutionary progression toward heavenly self-unity. Even though he is warned by his treating physician to stay away from prayer books—"Still meddling with religion. Can't you understand it's a symptom?" (192)—Strindberg keeps on looking for God and always finds the Devil.

In *The Devil's Gift* a toy monkey, possessed by a demon, can do most anything evil just by clashing its little cymbals. When its eyes glow and the cymbals go, the house at the start of the film catches fire. A boy looks forward to his birthday. His Mom is dead, but his Dad is courting the substitute. She finds the monkey in the window of a curiosity shop. It's a great gift! But then the eyes glow, and the cymbals go, and Sparkles, the dog, is trapped in the garage where a smoky fire starts. The boy doesn't hear the yelps because he's watching, as usual, his violent cartoons on TV. The monkey established eye contact with the substitute, who turned into his minion. She walked over to the television set and turned up the volume. At Sparkle's burial out back, the boy asks Dad if Sparkle is joining Mom? Inside alone together, substitute asks the Dad if he misses the dead wife. Sometimes. But that's not what he was thinking about. He's thinking about how death seems to have entered his house, his life. He's scared. His best friend, who believes in the occult, makes a referral to a medium. She counsels removal of the toy monkey, but the demon must never suspect what he is up to. Through evil eye contact, the monkey, back at home, programs the substitute to drown the boy while washing his hair. Dad arrives in time to catch her in her zombie act. In the end, Dad gets rid of the monkey, too.

Given the hindsight treatment as one of National Socialism's "Aryan mystics," Jörg Lanz von Liebenfels was in fact, as innocent or guilty as Daniel Paul Schreber, a colonist of psychotic outer space for the survival of the species in the span of evolution time line we are given for the break of mutation. In *Theozoology,* von Liebenfels immersed himself in total philology of sacred texts and traditions, all of which he mixed up with what's new in the sciences, in order to derepress the vanishing points of our evolution. What vanished in the course of evolution, the missing linking, went on for centuries as intercourse between mankind and ape-like beings, also known as demons, whose only recognizable legacy today is the vast range in quality of the human, in other words, the mongrelization of mankind. Original Sin was, in fact, this intercourse with Sodom-entities, which was then transferred into the blood of all humans. There was, then, a period when our ancestors could interbreed with beast beings. It was the time of the Devil's rule over the world and his sodomistic people. Christ's purpose was, then, to rout the influence of the beast-men, causing the beast-man in the human to die out. Christ, figure of light, is older than the Devil; he is one angel who did not sully himself with sodomy. Before the Devil intervened, the gods were living electrical receiving plants and power and broadcasting stations. But the gods were then forced down inside bestialized human bodies where they slumber and wait. We were electric; we will be electric. Our original totem animals were birds, reptiles, fish. Our evolutionary class, the mammals, is the state of our warm-blooded corruption. Thus, the news according to John can be completed from between the lines as follows: The logos (electric light) became (sodomistic) flesh.

Crucifixion always served sexual contact with the apelings. Either sodomistic monsters were bound to poles so the people could copulate with them without danger, or people were fastened to poles to let lascivious apelings sodomize them. Because they liked to hang out in cemeteries, the beast-men were also known as "the dead." "To be buried" was another way of saying to go and have intercourse with the sodomistic beast-men. Christ was inserted into the Passion of apelings as his torment. Resurrection, his own or that of Lazarus, is directed against congress with beast-men. Roll away the sodomistic stone! To drive out the Devil means to drive out the sex apes. The fires of Hell are inside us. Lascivious apeling blood burns inside us. We are dying the sodomistic death. Love thy neighbor means: choose a fellow human and not another horny apeling. But there's hope: the destructiveness of the Christian era—wars, crusades, Inquisition, colonization, capitalism, epidemic disease—continues to lessen the presence of the corrupted past in our future as electric beings.

Raging Angels introduces protagonist Chris as he hits bottom. He arrives late again. It was his band. But his drugged-out disregard for schedule or career forces the "and" of the other members of the group: they vote him out. He toasts the heavens:"Top of the world, Mom.Top of the world."Top of the mourning. In no time the band places a song on the charts. In the meantime Chris is off booze. His girlfriend, Lila, is working as waitress when there's a drive-by shooting up the restaurant."Next thing I know he's dead on the counter." A Coalition for World Unity volunteer offers her a pamphlet (and a place to stay). She says no, then asks Chris:"Do I look homeless?"

"I used to dream all the time about Ma and Pa's accident." But his grandma would always comfort him. Now grandma is having dreams about sadistic tryouts involving grandson Chris and his girl Lila. Lila gets a part in the Coalition's musical extravaganza. At the first rehearsal Colin confides in her that the Coalition is planting seeds for a united world:"We're evolving, becoming the gods we were meant to be. We are God. We have the power to re-create this world."

Grandma approaches Sister Kate, a psychic healer. Why come to her? "The Police told me they do not have a department of visions.""What you need is a spiritual deliverance." But she needs Lila in person in front of her to perform the service."Look, medical doctors don't do brain surgery long distance. I don't do voodoo.""Sister Kate, if you don't help, a beautiful girl will die."To grandmother's house they go. But grandma is home alone with special effects. Sister Kate's car breaks down. Grandma:"I stand against you!" But when the demon materializes, she falls down the stairs. Her dying words to Sister Kate: save the children.

Chris goes back to booze (the first bottle was hidden in a box under his grandmother's photo). Lila's not happy about the intoxication. He's not

happy about her Coalition career. "You should have seen how he was looking at you." "Maybe he knows good talent when he sees it." "He knows a
good body when he sees one."

Colin comforts Lila: "Chris isn't as spiritually evolved as you are." Sister
Kate can't help Lila, who's with Colin now, but she counsels Chris: "That
Coalition building, that's the biggest pit of evil I've ever seen. Do you know
anything about the spirit world? It's angels and demons, good versus evil,
it's been going on since the beginning of time. It's like the fan, you turn it on
and you can't see the blades. Doesn't mean they're not there. It's about Lila's
soul. Colin belongs to the Devil."

Lila discovers that those who aren't evolved will all die. "No Lila, everyone dies but then comes back as friend. Better a few troublemakers die
than the world suffer." Mass refrain: One world, one source, one people, one
voice! Angel with sword zaps on down to take up the combat with the
demonic forces. Chris and Lila, together again, record Christian Rock. "You're
paranoid only if you're wrong" is one stray claim from the first reel of film
that could easily stick around as the motto of *Raging Angels*.

In *Dancing in the Light*, Shirley MacLaine calls her man Vassy her "baby"
while they're making love. It's a total interruptus. "Vassy sat up in bed,
his face like stone.... 'I am not your son'" (207). But she speaks up for
her maternal feelings. "'Sometimes you are a radio in bed,' he said....
His hostility was so total, so sudden, I couldn't take it in. 'A radio in
bed?' I repeated" (208). Vassy gives his rebuttal to her tearful expressions
of hurt. "'I am not mean,' he answered finally. 'You are being influenced
by evil'" (209). She starts twisting and shouting. "'Stop it, Sheerlee. You
are feeling Satanic forces. They are evil.'... 'Vassy!!' I shouted. 'There is
no such thing as evil.'... "Sheerlee, stop it, he said strongly. 'Stop the
evil'" (209).

The radio in bed is wired to and through all the channeling analogies (television and telephone) whereby MacLaine finally makes contact
with her Higher Self (at which point she stumbles on the local pedagogi-
cal insight that there never was anything new to learn since she knew it

all already and must now only try to remember—or have her own opinion). The film analogy is also used (and overused) but only during the recall and replay of her past-life experiences (in which she always plays starring roles with her parents as royals or high priests bound up in melodrama). But this film career of recollection is the preview of her live connection with her Higher Self (or HS). MacLaine's dismissal of evil or the Devil becomes watchword and bottom line of the New Age beliefs she shares with her HS. At the end, the channeling analogies and the rejection of evil come together, as in the following explanation MacLaine receives from her HS (or, in other words, remembers): "Evil is nothing but energy flowing backward rather than forward. Spell your *live* backward and you have *evil*" (360). The "live" in question (it's hers) is the modifier of certain transmissions and broadcasts. "Live" is how MacLaine identifies her stage shows, to which she brings us along with her aging parents. The channeling live analogies guarantee that once her parents are dead they will be on the live line, and MacLaine's communications with them will be that much more direct. Only the Devil releases the verb "to live"—namely, in the past tense, as "lived."

NOTEBOOK THIRTEEN

In his "Reminiscences," Max Graf turns to religion to characterize the ups and downs of the early years inside Freud's inner circle of application and submissions:

> I have compared the gatherings in Freud's home with the founding of a religion. However, after the first dreamy period and the unquestioning faith of the first group of apostles, the time came when the church was founded. Freud began to organize his church with great energy. He was serious and strict in the demands he made of his pupils; he permitted no deviations from his orthodox teaching. (471–72)

The distance of Graf's withdrawal from the Freud group after Adler was "excommunicated" nevertheless remained compatible for the father of little Hans with uninterrupted respect, perhaps even idealization, the right conditions, in any event, for his preservation of Freud's text and of his own "Reminiscences" of its author. That the projection onto Freud of an unidentified influence upon coming events slips in between the lines of his reminiscences remains within the boundaries of the healthy. While Graf does not make the little Hans connection public, still for those of us by now in the know the anecdote that most rocks the note to their historical collaboration concerns a gift Freud made to Graf's son, two years to countdown of the phobia: "On the occasion of my son's third birthday, Freud brought him a rocking horse which he himself carried up the four flights of steps leading to my house" (474).

The other side of the same distance dynamic, namely demonization, attended last and lasting words of resistance. In his Freud obituary, Jung, for example, wrote that he had been "permitted a deep glimpse into the mind of this remarkable man...possessed by a demon—a man who had been vouchsafed an overwhelming revelation that took possession of his soul and never let him go." When Freud died, Jung was the international leader of the German association of psychotherapy that was being retrofitted to many of the specifics of National Socialism. However, given his negative transference, Jung could nevertheless count his willingness to serve as a concession and tribute to Freud since Freudians shared equally with Adlerians and Jungians (more so than Jung would have liked to see or admit) in the new order's central institute in Berlin.

The demon Jung refers to here can be good or evil, depending, for example, in what archetype the real father is set. Jung's 1948 updating revisions of his 1909 essay "The Significance of the Father in the Destiny of the Individual" show the tension between this more neutral or historical notion of demon or genius and the earlier setting of God versus the Devil. In 1909 Jung extends the findings drawn from the cases he presents—and the case of the bed-wetting boy Jung expressly offers as complement to Freud's study of Little Hans—to address his more-or-less normal public. The saga of demonic possession by the father is not restricted to the neurotic zone. "If we normal people examine our lives from the psychoanalytic perspective, we too perceive how a mighty hand guides us without fail to our destiny, and not always is this hand a kindly one. Often we call it the hand of God or of the Devil" (314). In 1948 Jung dropped "from the psychoanalytic perspective": thus, he underscored the consent of middlebrow normalcy to his destinal claims while the edit marked the spot of overlap between Freud's alleged demon and Jung's certain Devil father, the one that gave a kind of order to Jung's life and corpus following the nervous breakup of idealizing relations with Freud, the good or God father.

A second reference to the God-or-the-Devil frame, which Jung deleted from his 1948 updating revisionism, reinforces the more-or-less healthy (or psychopathic) stereotype in which the Devil is set. We need only subtract the outer-limits stretch marks from the neurosis diagnosis to find our medium setting on the psychopathology continuum. "As soon as we enter the field of neurosis, this antithesis is stretched to the limit. God becomes the symbol of the most complete sexual repression, the Devil the symbol of sexual lust" (321 n. 22).

Drawing on the diagnosis of Freud in Jung's eulogy note, Nat Morris republished in 1974 his 1955 "The Case History of Sigmund Freud" as a new edition organized around his latest discovery of the true primal scene, with special thanks to Irving Stone, and now given the super title: *A Man Possessed*. You just know he was giving himself a second chance at fame. Morris writes off the top of the best sell-out list he aims for by association with a best-selling author: "Blissfully ignorant of the significance of his find, Stone exposes the incredibly grotesque circumstances in Freud's 'primal scene.' Upon this and other traumatic events in Freud's tortured life I have formulated my diagnosis of him as a man possessed; a man convulsed with a frantic urge to achieve a glittering success to refute his father's taunt that he would 'never amount to anything'" (vii). Freud wasn't without his fair shake of talents: "Through his words, both written and spoken, he achieved the susceptibility he labeled 'transference' instead of rapport, to avoid any suspicion he used hypnosis. But he could no more discard hypnotism than tear out his own eyes. . . . But hypnotism was only one of Freud's many talents. He was also a gifted linguist. . . . With the same gusto, his greedy memory sucked in mythology, philology, neurology, history, anthropology and what have you. His mind photographed on an indestructible but sensitive film" (21–22).

Graf noted Freud's unmusical nature, which gave Graf his proxy place in Freud's first circle of application. On this specific rim, Graf made analytic contact with the demonic. For Morris, Freud's unrestrained aversion to music, already in childhood, gives evidence of the photo finish and playback of a trauma that possessed him to invent the theory and therapy of sex:

> The only serious threat to his favoritism came from a sister several years younger who showed signs of musical talent. By severe scrimping, a piano for her was managed but her triumph was short lived. Complaining that her practicing disturbed his studying, Sigmund issued an ultimatum: Either the piano left or he would. Meekly, his

parents bowed and his sister lost her chance for a musical education.... He disposed of a rival by using the power over his parents he
sensed was absolute because so much hope was invested in his future
success.... Consequently Freud lived on his future hopes, conditioning himself to endure the pain of waiting for fame and glory. As a
schoolboy, he was the typical grind, immersed in dry as dust studies
which his phenomenal photographic memory retained after but one
reading. (32–33)

Morris finds out the real primal scene behind a recollection from
childhood admitted, but with a cover charge, by Freud: "one of the autobiographical incidents Freud recounted which stuck in my memory, was
his urinating in his parents' bedroom.... Freud's willingness to plead
guilty to disrespect by urinating in his parents' bedroom, would be com-
parable to pleading guilty to a misdemeanor whereas the felony was
really murder in the first degree. Actually, he had urinated in the throes
of an uncontrollable terror, a terror and fear that continued to haunt
him throughout his traumatic life. The memory of his trauma probably
constitutes the nucleus of the numinosum which Jung suspected as the
root of his sexual dogma" (37). After quoting Stone's inspirational cover
of this scene, Morris spells it out:

> Freud's primal scene can be reconstructed far more realistically, con-
> sidering his inordinate jealousy. While lying in bed that night, after
> possibly sensing his father's eagerness to retire, his jealousy was com-
> pounded with a terror that a new rival for his mother's affection might
> be conceived that night. His father's ability to delight his mother
> beyond his childish powers could also have convulsed him. Unable to
> contain himself when he heard their stirrings, he burst into their room
> as his parents were about to assume the primal position. Leaping into
> their bed to interpose himself between them, he discharged the only
> fluid possible from the "little organ of which he was the proud posses-
> sor." Growling like an animal in pain, his father may have tried to
> seize him but his mother tenderly intervened, kissing and fondling
> him as she carried him back to his bed, believing he had had a night-
> mare. (38–39)

The possession reading assumes a perfect fit between Freud and the
Oedipus complex, while recognizing only Hellraising where others might

attend to Freud's raising of ghosts. I have tried to show in my collected work how Freud's attendance at the father function served a saving fiction, one best suited for and tied to the transference neurosis, the replacement of the disorder brought to session with a variant that can be contained and that would in turn allow, through its cure and by inoculation, the presenting problem to contain itself. But, in other words, the center staging of father also doubled as diversion away from the crypts of the undead that Freud kept hidden away and safe in so many of the cases he studied and embodied.

In *The Interpretation of Dreams* an oneiro-auto-biographical relay keeps Freud occupied or cathected with the significance of his urinal streaming. At one point of rescue he skips over the stream and arrives instead in the vicinity of his adored teacher, Brücke (a name that, in a word, means "bridge"). When listing the Devil's borrowed pagan attributes, Jones points out that the Devil's habit of building bridges hails from Thor, whose thunder hammer resonates with what knocks out flatus, the Devil's primal leitmotif, musical accompaniment, or background music (161, 167). However, in Freud's case, the bridge is overwhelmed by the enigmatic force of doubling (two boards, two benches, two children) at the same time as it comes into focus as self-dissection of his pelvis. The association that fits at this crisis point is a mummy narrative, Rider Haggard's *She*. Mummy draws up any bridge to be built to the Devil father. She robs Freud of the support of what is not his own, and in the ensuing silencing: death or a dead person makes a ghost appearance. Another near-miss encounter with the Devil father turns back into another episode in the recurring series of Freud's haunting.

Amityville Horror, which isn't about a haunted house but about possession of the stepfather through this house of evil, is based on an actual case on which Ed and Lorraine Warren served as expert consultants. After they examined the precincts, their answer to the question, Are ghosts present? "This was the appearance of something far more ominous than a ghost could ever be: the manifestation of a comparatively rare phenomenon known as an inhuman demonic spirit. A preternatural entity, the inhuman spirit is considered to be possessed of a negative, diabolical intelligence fixed in a perpetual rage against both man and God" (Brittle, 5).

The house looks like a jack-o'-lantern. The titles also rise as children settle the score they sing: *The Amityville Horror.* The house, a crime scene in 1974 with execution-style family murder, could be anywhere. But it's on Long Island (it's amazing how Long Island miniaturizes the rest of America stretching toward the other shining I see Manhattan). The countdown begins: One Year Later. A couple can buy the place cheap. "All these people died here, doesn't that bother you?" "Houses have no memory." Wife's uncle is a priest who arrives to bless the house. Everyone is out back. He proceeds with the ritual room by room. He runs up against a room in which bees are gathering. Whatever he can't drive out drives him out. Later the priest tries to call his niece, Kathy. But there's only static and disconnection on this live line. Her aunt is a nun. She arrives for a visit. But she doesn't get past the front hall. "I can't stay. Forgive me." She has to stop her getaway car to throw up onto the road. The Father applies for exorcism. "The murderer said he heard voices. I heard the voices, too. Explain how the car went out of control. I am a trained psychotherapist. What I heard there was real." "You think your secular education gives you the right to question the church. Even psychotherapists lose touch with reality on occasion."

Kathy's husband, George (he's her second husband, and the children aren't his, which must mean she's a widow since she's so Catholic she made George convert), is getting surly, into his role as double. Careful when you ax him anything. Police officer to George: "Are you related to the family that was here before? You look a lot alike." Kathy's daughter has an imaginary friend named Jody: "She's nice." Jody tells her about the little boy who died. "She wants me to stay here forever so we can always play together." Kathy has the Father on the line. He's about to tell her something important, but it's wiped out by static. He has some kind of stroke. Bartender to George: "You look just like that kid, the murderer from last year." Their circle of friends counts a woman who's mediumistic. First time she pulled up to the house she wouldn't go any nearer. Now she's done her research. A refugee from

Salem built his house right where the horror house now stands. There are people buried here. They start digging up the cellar. She believes they have found "the passage to Hell." But George sees an apparition of himself.

George: "Oh no, I'm coming apart!" He was just dreaming. "What happened to your foot? It looks like teeth marks." "Will you stop nagging at me! You're the one who wanted the house so just shut up." "You bastard!" He slaps her hard but (still) feels remorse. When Kathy looks up the press coverage of the murder on microfilm at the library, she discovers that the murderer was indeed George's look-alike. It's the last night. The walls start to bleed, blood flows down the stairs. Kathy locked the children in the bathroom. George starts to chop the door down. Kathy jumps him from behind. Just as he's about to kill her, we see her face decaying. He stops short. She gets her regular face back. But the house is blowing up. The now healthy blended family unit escapes its former demonic system in the van.

In the 2005 remake *The Amityville Horror,* the writing on the wall (or refrigerator door) — "Ketch'em and Kill'em" — casts its spelling in proximity to the name Ketcham, which belongs to the father figure who immersed the house in his evil. The passage to Hell behind the basement wall has been remodeled in the new version as long corridor of an administration of torture, which back then claimed a multitude of Native American victims. Ketcham finally slit his own throat so his presence could live forever. While the Devil father is thus placed in prehistory, the stepfather comes into possession of the primal father position and body. The contrast between the unabashed working-class body of the stepfather in the original — bristles and cream — and his sculpted smooth body in the remake trains the laser hair removal beam on this fatherly figure and body, explicitly the substitute for the father in Heaven the second time around. "Houses don't kill people. People kill people." The remake incorporates home-movie-style footage as date mark of authenticity. We watch the family scenes once, then alone in the basement with the stepfather, then as memories flashing back across his mind. While we glimpse hallucinations or spooks at various intervals, only in this recycled material do we see familiar faces metamorphosing into demonic physiognomies. Stepfather gazes upon his family from the vantage point of an absence he shares with the dead father (before possession makes him host yet another dead father as his murderer). The shift to the demonic skips the duties of mournful substitution: "Don't talk to me like one of your kids!" A stepparent is always a body out of the bag up for grabs. The new body is so out of context in the 1974 setting (only prisoners back then gave this kind of attention to the details of one's mirror body). But that's what gives his shirts-off relationship to the eldest slightly plump step-son that prison-rape edge. William Tell me: hold the log while I cut between your hands with the ax. Sob! Tremble. Tell me you like it.

Amityville II (I see you) bears a subtitle: *The Possession.* The new owners are here. "Dad's such a creep." He's one of those "yes, sir" Dads. Wall opens, and POV looks at woman of the house from behind. She feels a shock of cold in her back. The shaving mirror, like the POV camera, has a life of its own. On their own, paintbrushes depict a demonic figure and inscribe the slogan: "Dishonor thy father." Father takes it personally and starts up with the abuse. Eldest son holds rifle to father's throat to stop him. Mother: "My God, what's happening to us?" Between earphones the son hears a word for our sponsor: "Why didn't you pull that trigger? Why didn't you kill that pig?" Camera turns around son with gun, turns him topsy-turvy. POV keeps swooping down on him. When POV visits sister, it's the brother. He's got incest on his mind. "Let's play you're a model and I'm a famous photographer. Take off your nightgown. Just for a second." She does it. He took her panties from the laundry. "But why?" He kisses her. (In confession she fills us in: "I went all the way with my friend.") While the priests consider exorcism—one asks the other if he believes in ghosts—the son is still following the bleat of a different sponsor: "How pathetic. They'd be better off if you killed them. You think so." Son with gun shoots father, then mother. Phone calls from the dead, blood writing on the wall, zombies coming up the basement steps. The killer brother is beginning to look like Regan possessed in *The Exorcist.*

Now it's the sister's turn. "While listening to my confession, you thought of making love to me." It looks like the house bursts into flame, but not really. The priest has absorbed the possession.

Possession, already nine-tenths of the old saw about exorcism and therapy, takes steps toward recovery, which alternate with the interventions of exorcism. The person possessed has passed through a crisis and is now grounded in a delusion or a reality that allows this crisis to settle down for a demonic spell and thus become legible, audible, or, if you prefer, treatable.

The Exorcist was projected as Devil fiction under William Friedkin's direction. William Blatty's novel, by contrast, packs an occult background of haunting that is styling with unmourning way more than it hails Satan. Early in the book Chris MacNeil comes down with a near-psychotic look into the void or death.

> Chris slept. And dreamed about death in the staggering particular, death as if death were still never yet heard of while something was ringing, she, gasping, dissolving, slipping off into void, thinking over and over, *I am not going to be, I will die, I won't be, and forever and ever, oh, Papa, don't let them, oh, don't let them do it, don't let me be nothing forever and* melting, unraveling, ringing, the ringing—*The phone!* . . . She hung up. And for moments sat motionless, thinking of the dream. A dream? More like thought in the half life of waking. That terrible clarity. Gleam of the skull. Non-being. Irreversible. She could not imagine it. *God it can't be!* She considered. And at last bowed her head. *But it is.* (15)

What makes this existentialism intro a close call on the psychopathology continuum is the ambivalently held lifeline that rings her out of it, connects her back with the paternal outside. Without the rescue ring, however, the "thought" is the kind of abyssal contemplation of nothingness that, outside philosophy's lazy thinking, signals the crisis of uncanniness or uncontainment that a young child first faces when Mother, who cannot hold her own static safely inside their duo dynamic, rears little one between being nothing and outward-and-bound raging. In Chris's case what brings up her own rearing first raises its unburied

dead: she lost her firstborn, Jamie, when he was three. She cannot contain or bury her feeling at a loss. She admits to herself that to protect
herself she stopped loving her husband: either he was no longer Jamie's
Dad or Jamie was dead. Ex marks that spot she was in. She cannot
admit to herself that she loves her other child the way she loved Jamie.
Regan, the replacement child, goes by the name Rags. That's right: from
riches or Jamie to Rags. Does Rags suggest the Cinderella-style mourning
habit as cover for self-effacement or degradation? The relay of painful
examinations, explorations, treatments that Regan must undergo—
which in the film, as in the added-on arteriogram scene, finds the Grand
Guignol place set for it in horror films—signifies in the novel that everything that didn't help in Jamie's case will also not help Regan. But then
the repetition reverses itself and makes a difference. The double approach
(at once psychoanalytic and occult or supernatural) that Regan's possession finally demands assigns an exit, for mother and daughter, from
the impasse of unmourning.

Consider the double occupancy (which lies completely outside the
provenance of Devil fiction) registered within the first nonmedical,
non-neurological definition of possession Chris encounters. "Immediately derivative of the prevalent belief in demons was the phenomenon
known as possession, a state in which many individuals believed that
their physical and mental functions had been invaded and were being
controlled by either a demon (most common in the period under discussion) or the spirit of someone dead" (194). This dead someone, given
the precedent of Jamie's death, must have gone down in an unmournably close relationship, connection, and call.

When the shrink in Blatty's *The Exorcist* explains "somnambuliform
possession," he again assigns the demon role in possession to "times
gone by"; "In relatively modern cases, however, it's mostly the spirit of
someone dead, often someone the patient has known or seen and is able
unconsciously to mimic, like the voice and the mannerisms, even the
features of the face, at times" (188). But the psychiatrist seems to point
to the more primeval candidacy of demon in Regan's case when he cate-
gorizes the possession by or as incorporation of people known to the

patient as always a less tumultuous case in point. Certainly a strictly inter-personal understanding of incorporation cannot account for the trans-mission of one mother's unmourning for Jamie to or through Regan, who never knew him. The measure of Regan's transformation in her pos-sessed condition is given by a continuing letter or journal Regan earlier recorded on tape for her father. To play back those tapes, made for an uncertain, unreliable father, is to know that the Regan up there is the shell of her former self displaced by an alien force. When one of the two priests officiating at the exorcism starts documenting the sessions on the tape recorder, the demon welcomes the change—and the chance: "I have always rather liked infernal engines" (266). (In both novel and film versions, the Devil's discourse blasting out of the little girl formerly known as Regan can be decoded only on tape as English spoken in re-verse: "I am no one.") That the possessing demon addresses the exor-cists (in particular Karras) as though they were the ultimate captive audience and prize and Regan just the medium extends the novel's analytic-occult frame to include the melancholic overlaps between Chris and Karras in the symptom picture of Regan's bid for certainty. It is also the (double) diversion that keeps the focus off Regan's agency in the self-analytic dynamic of possession and blurs, rather than clarifies, the telepathic skip of generation, of the interpersonal relation, in the trans-mission of undeath. While the novel asks us to take its mixed bag of tics on faith (Regan's possession persona refers directly—by contrast, con-tact, and absence—to the missing father but also comes in as baby blast "booming and yet muffled, croaking, like amplified premature burial" [331]), the film version is streamlined for certain dealings with the Devil that are set against neurotic ambiguities to be bypassed.

In the actual possession and exorcism on which Blatty based his novel, there lies in the background of the Protestant boy on his way to possession his Aunt Harriet, who was an adherent of Spiritualism. "At-tempts to communicate with the dead have traditionally been conducted through a medium. He or she summons up a spirit, who then takes over the medium. This is a form of possession. Spiritualists like Aunt Harriet did not look upon their beliefs as an acceptance of possession. But, whether using a séance or a Ouija board, Spiritualists did dabble in the same phenomenon that the Bible so vehemently denounced" (Allen, 5). Following Aunt Harriet's death, scratching sounds can be heard in Robby's room. Is it you Aunt Harriet? She knocks the requested number of times to signal her attendance.

The Ouija board and the Spiritualist séance have been singled out as disposing instruments for possession (in addition to Satanic child abuse, which rather emphatically puts you in the already position, I mean the ready possession). "In the context of Possession, all disposing factors produce within a person a condition of those two faculties of soul—mind and will—that is most aptly described as an *aspiring vacuum*. *Vacuum*, because there is created an absence of clearly defined and humanly acceptable concepts for the mind. *Aspiring*, because there is a corresponding absence of clearly defined and humanly acceptable goals for the will. In the case of the Ouija Board, or that of the Séance . . . , the participants must dispose themselves precisely with a view to being opened up; to becoming desirous and accepting of whatever happens along" (Martin, xxi).

In Friedkin's *The Exorcist*, before Regan shows and tells that she is possessed, there is one break in her behavior that precedes what follows like what's already at the breaking point of pathogenic crisis. One situational point of crisis precedes this breaking point: her father, Howard is his name, didn't call on her birthday. Let the case record show that Regan has an imaginary friend, Captain Howdy, who's always on call, her own personal Howard. We first meet Captain Howdy when Regan's mother discovers the Ouija board with which Regan has been playing in the recreation (re-creation) room. Can she play, too, the mother asks? Regan says Captain Howdy says, No. The Captain as the improved version of a father not to be counted on ultimately holds the place for the possessing demon.

Witchboard is directed by the sentiment that occupies the split between *Exorcist* the novel and *Exorcist* the movie (and which is internal to the constitution of Devil's fiction as monopolizing an exception to the rule it contradicts and implies)."How can you believe in spirits, if you don't believe in God or Satan?" Spirits are lousy spellers and they lie. Spirit David, a dead kid, is the special spook of this Ouija board. Soon Linda can't stop using the board. Progressive entrapment. Then the spirit changes. First the spirit breaks down her resistance, then he possesses her."So what you're telling me is: I'm living with Linda Blair." In the end the couple can marry after the board is trashed, shot up. Women cleaning up the mess of the former apartment find the damaged board."Do you think it still works?" The camera zooms onto the yes blurb. The Ouija viewfinder confirms the answer. Contact has thus been made between camera and board. In *Witchboard 2* the camera becomes the demon, keeping just ahead, tracking the deadly merger with the driving machine. A serial dream of murder is a groundless projection whereby the Ouija player is being manipulated by the demon to let it in. The sequel's subtitle: *The Devil's Doorway*. A Jewish New-Age occultist warns the kids that spirits are all around us trying to step through. The spirit told the kids that she was murdered."They always say they were murdered. All spirits are liars." How can they be sure the spirit is who she says she is? They use the automatic writer or psychograph. If she's for real, it will be her handwriting."Susan is dead and wants me to find her body." This is where the camera or demon takes over: the demon doesn't want the kids to discover there is no Susan, dead or undead. Witches contact demons, not the dead. But in a world of unmourners the demon cannot wait for witch contact. What looked like the addiction of the Ouija user was a demonic possession that cut out the middle woman, the medium, the witch.

On the evening of Regan's turning point, her mother, Chris (who in the film version, too, is a movie actress on location in Washington for the making of a picture that borrows current student unrest as its background story and setting), is hosting a party. Regan, who already said goodnight, comes back downstairs and stands at the threshold. The priest entertaining the partygoers at the piano notices her first. Regan says to one (astronaut) and all: "You're going to die up there." Then she urinates on the spot. Up there is where the little girl is without her father. Is her mother's director her mother's boyfriend too? In her father's absence Regan imagines her mother, her mother's body, in sexual contact with another man, the director, who will end up being the sole victim of the Devil taking possession of Regan. Her face is transformed to strike a match with her inner alien visitation. The original face to face has been replaced but not lost. And the body that was abandoned to the flush of its flowing away from itself is now at the disposal of her invading Devil, a whoremaster who offers up all her orifices for penetration. Her open body at the same time remains off-limits to Fathers of the Church. The Devil that got into her inhabits the imaginary space that's part womb, part anus, a bodily underworld and Hell. All the orifices open to penetration spew forth only excrement. Her open and shut body introduces certain boundaries into a field of staticky substitution.

The priest Karras occupies the place of the other possession—that of melancholic, haunted relations with the dead—which is kept, by the process of elimination, from ambiguating Regan's possession. Suicide is on his schedule no matter how one turns the storyboard. At the time of the party where Regan, the time of her life, shows what a pisser she can be, Karras's mother had already passed away and come back to take him with her. There's now a place for them.

The move to normalize or Oedipalize the possession via identification between mother and daughter changed nothing but the possessed child's gender. The case of possession on which Blatty based his novel, like the tape-recorded exorcism conducted in Rome Friedkin studied to prepare for the film project, starred a boy. But the only difference belongs to the Devil who takes possession and thus penetrates little boy and little girl alike—it's all one and the same fuck doll to the pre-Oedipal father—inside and out. (The Devil's legendary penis, besides being snakelike and in parts made of iron or horn, is also multiple to multiplug as many orifices at once [Jones, 172].)

Karras, a psychiatric counselor who's also a priest—the modern, updated version of a traditional exorcist—is a Father of the church in the irreplaceable absence of Father. He is bodily attached to and detached from his mother, as he binds her legs, across the distance of his priestly vocation and in the proximity sealed by his chastity vow. By not taking his medical career to Park Avenue, by keeping his training in the service of the Church Fathers, he becomes ultimately responsible for not affording his mother a livable position on her way out of his life. She dies on him but not in him. The Devil speaks to him through Regan in his dead mother's voice. While it looks like he takes in the Devil in Regan and then kills himself, the scene or motivation could also be read in reverse: he leaves the Devil and Regan alone to seal the deal of Dad certainty. Two Fathers of the Church, figures of a relationship of adoption or chosenness, and the prospective father, the movie director, who would lay his claim to her over her mother's body, are killed off in conflict with the Devil in bodily possession of the girl who knows who her father is.

After her release from the Fathers of ambiguity and the Devil of her bodily possession, time starts up again for Regan where it left off with the soaking she gave the threshold. The actress mother has been put in her place by the daughter who upstaged her acting by hosting a possession, one that brought in two father figures who were off-limits with regard to the mother's body, tortured inside out on center stage. The only souvenir she takes with her out of the film and into the demon-projection-free future is the parting close-up point of view of Father Dyer's collar or neck. She kisses the Oedipal father—the father as die-er, as model for mournable death—goodbye. (If this were a vampire movie, the enigmatic moment of the cleansed survivor's insider view would spill over as the living on of undeath between the lines we are given in closing. This overlap between them gives the novel's melancholic condition a parting shot on screen.) But looking not at him but at his collar, looking thus at this father as beside the point, Regan could also still be in league with the Devil who steadies her gaze. The mother has just assured us that Regan remembers nothing. But then she fixes our gaze upon the Father's collar in place of the unsettling souvenir that she was the collar of two fathers, one suicidal and one dead. In spite of the inevitable contradiction or incompletion that invites sequels, Regan at the close of these projections appears to be released, in the first place, from the neuroticizing influence that her disintegrating family held in store for her.

Exorcist II opens with priest performing an exorcism inside a structure of slats alternating with gaps of light, like the frames of a film. He splashes one possessed woman with holy water. "I feel sick. Why me?" She sets herself on fire.

Linda Blair is back as teen charge. The woman in charge of the research lab facility and therapy center is treating Regan, who's on the couch. "I'm just wasting your time. You know why I come here. To make my Mom feel better." "Those bad dreams are still inside you." "There's nothing wrong with me." They have something to look forward to, however. The therapist extols a new dream machine that will allow them both to watch her dreams together. Her lab is organized around the prospect of being of one mind. The film's cautionary proviso: if we're not ready, the Devil could triumph through this merger.

The exorcist gets a new assignment: investigate the circumstances of the death of Father Merrin during that exorcism in Georgetown. Some say he might have been a Satanist. When the priest arrives at the therapy center, Regan can tell it's about her. The therapist thinks that Regan was damaged by the exorcism. While the priest cares about her soul, the therapist wants to protect her mind and body. He says evil, she says mental illness. The therapist and Regan treat themselves to strobe-light hypnotism. The therapist is thus able to join Regan in her deep hypnotic state. She, too, can now see Regan's room back then in Georgetown. But when Regan comes out of the hypnosis, the therapist is stuck inside the dying exorcist. The priest is deputized, hypnotized to go back and rescue her. We see the exorcist from the first film, not yet dead. The new exorcist sees Regan's resident demon clutching the therapist's heart. He hollers and the demon lets go. Back inside her sound body, the therapist explains that what they experienced was "syncing with another mind." But the priest is convinced of the treatment's supernatural application. That sinking feeling was "utterly horrible and fascinating." But a word of caution: you can't be sure that what you saw was real. "We don't know all that much about synchronized hypnosis yet. It could have been fantasies, dreams."

Priest and Regan do the hypno sync. We're in Africa with a much younger Father Merrin. The village is beset by a plague of locusts. The demon or demonized responsible for attracting the plague announces: "I am Bezuzu." Regan says that's her dream name. Bezuzu is king of the evil spirits of the air. Regan is in sync with a really big locust. Her voice is weird: "Come, share my wings." In Africa there was a boy who pulled out of Bezuzu's possession unharmed. He must be a man now. Father Merrin prophesied that a new human being would arise to counter evil. The possession survivor, Kokumo is his name, might well be the new one.

Convinced that we make our own demons in our minds, the therapist ignores Regan's conviction that her soul is being killed, and hospitalizes her mind and body. Alone at night Regan pulls the sedating drip out of her arm and gets the bedside light to flicker fast. She connects with the priest out in Africa: "Call me by my dream name." Thus he finds Kokumo. We flash on a modern lab in which primal guy Kokumo is a scientist studying locusts. He is trying to raise a good locust, more like a grasshopper, which would calm down the rest of them.

Regan breaks out of the lab and takes the synchronizer with her. She and priest go back to the exorcism. Possessed Regan to Father Merrin: "You're dying—and your hopes die with you." Regan turns out to be, like Kokumo, one of the new ones, in possession of the new strength. That is why she was attacked by the demon in the first place. Split up into different groups with varying, even competing agendas, the characters are reunited—with the house in Georgetown. Locusts attack. Regan enters her old room and encounters the Bezuzu Regan, who flexes her powers for one last stand. She becomes the sexualized teen Regan. Remember, the good locust will break the chain reaction. "You must tear out her evil heart." The locusts burst into the bedroom. The house is shaking apart. But the locusts are stopped in the tracks of their closing vanishing act, because the priest took heart. The shrink is really sorry. She understands now. The world won't — not yet.

A decapitated head can keep seeing, registering, for twenty seconds. The killer is an artist. He lets the victim see his body dropping away from the head, head not shoulders. "Name?" "Legion, for we are many." The case terminated fifteen years ago. *The Exorcist III. Legion* picks up where *The Exorcist* went slack. Now it's back, down to details. The newspapers were never told. The man in cell eleven is Damien Karras. "It's a wonderful life." "Who are you?" "I am no one." While he was being crucified, the kid was kept aware, paralyzed but conscious. Detective meets Father Dyer. "I wonder if we both are dreaming this?" "I'm not dreaming." Dyer is finished dying: he's been murdered, too. His entire blood supply is collected in glass jars and not a drop of it was spilled, not even a smudge on the jars — just the writing in his blood on the wall, "It's a wonderful life." That was the title of the film the detective and Father Dyer watched on the anniversary of Karras's fall. It's a wound-erful life.

NOTEBOOK FOURTEEN

According to the epigraph to *Lost Souls:* "A man born of incest will become Satan..." An exorcism is called for. The doctor, who's not in the occult groove, offers to go in with the priest. "You wouldn't last five minutes." They enter the room of exorcism. "Hello, Henry. You know why we're here." "I've been really looking forward to it." He starts masturbating. We see that the exorcism is being taped. The Winona Ryder figure tapes the windows shut tight. Winona flashes back to her own exorcism.

The talk show features Kelson (quel son!), who is the author of a book on sensational murders. Hostess takes a running start: "the closer you get to evil..." "There is no evil," he interrupts. His diagnosis of the crazy murderer who heard demonic voices is "malignant narcissism."

Winona visits the famous writer who said on TV he doesn't believe in evil with a capital E. She gives him a tape of the exorcism. If he's interested, she'll be in front of the library tomorrow. Not only the day turns. Winona witnesses little girl at snack bar turn malicious: "Jesus is dead." Winona tells the author that he's turning into the Anti-Christ. He's already contaminated, that's why he couldn't hear the tape that drove the lady next door to kill herself.

"You're not real, but he is. Henry, I know you don't want to do this. Put it down." She runs, locks him inside. Henry keeps on floating toward her. Disarmed, Henry starts breaking up and open as demon.

"We won, Christ triumphed over Satan." "Does that mean that Satan was the weak one?" "Satan will make Christ crawl!" Winona tricked the possessing demon into showing himself. "They had their 2,000 years, now it's our turn. Absolute power, absolute knowledge." She urges him not to kill the bad guy. "You have no idea how much you look like your mother right now." He shoots him. Digital clock shows 4:55—then suddenly it switches to 6:66. She fires. We-win Winona.

According to Luther Link, the persona of the Devil in representation yields to its diminished returns. "He may have many masks, but his essence is a mask without a face. The apparent face of the Devil from the ninth century to the sixteenth is usually banal: it is a pasteboard mask with neither personality nor feeling behind it" (15). "Neither frightening nor fearful, rather than appearing as a real adversary of God, he seems to be just a pest" (131). At the same time, "the old lack of iconography is useful because . . . the Devil has the 'face' of your opponent." And: "The faceless Devil is an effective way to avoid considering the opposition and automatically to place God on one's own side" (183).

The supplemental representation of the Devil's evil influence was in renditions of sadomasochistic sessions administered by demons to the damned. As this pictorial combo demonstrates, the Devil's figural status as cipher is the best possible channel for evil. "Insofar as the Devil does not refer to real evil and is a rhetorical device, the Devil becomes a justification for real evil by users of that device" (59). "And if what the Devil looks like was largely determined by the costume used to impersonate him, this is fitting: the Devil is only a costume, even if it has become inseparable from the skins of those that wear it" (193).

The *Fratze* or grimace—or farce face—that Mephistopheles wears in Goethe's *Faust* pops up in the corner of signature events as the signature sealing the Faustian wish as administered command. First contact with the Devil on the way to her possession pops up for Anneliese Michel in the face to face. It is the signature moment initiating her possession/ pact. Gazing out upon the Bavarian scenery, she experiences a religious high—then she sees the *Fratze* of Satan. But when you look through the window, you also see your reflection in the pane/pain. As Anneliese informed Dr. Lüthy: "I often see *Fratzen,* ghastly, distorted faces; the devil is in me, I am all empty inside" (Goodman, 36). Father Hermann reported that "she complained that she was no longer herself. 'I am not my own ego anymore.' Occasionally she saw distorted faces, *Fratzen,* which she was unable to describe in detail" (42). But even if the face that empties you out is hard to identify, still it is possible to name the demon, and thus identify him within the Oedipal registry. Demons withhold their names from the priest who tries to trick them into showing and telling their labels of identification. "What cannot be named is difficult to exorcise. If the priest can trick the demon into revealing his identity, he gains a measure of power over him" (94–95).

At the trial of the exorcists for the murder of Anneliese Michel, Felicitas Goodman summons testimony on behalf of the priests from the demon inhabitants of Michel's ill-fated possession. The names of the *Fratzen* occupy the headlines of Western projections:

> There are some corroborating witnesses they paid no attention to, witnesses that the Court did not think to call and the defense did not cite either. These witnesses are the demons: Judas, the betrayer; Lucifer, the fallen angel; Cain, the slayer of his brother; Nero, the mass murderer; Fleischmann, the fornicating priest; and Hitler, whose name sticks in the German throat like the dead rat of the Russian proverb ("You cannot swallow it and you cannot spit it out"). Turning him into a demon and exorcising him was a masterful stroke. A ghastly lot. But they are nevertheless of the separate reality, and they know more than humans. (249)

Rather than meet the Devil with his match and maker in magic, ritual, or belief, the medical establishment treated Anneliese for epilepsy, which could never be diagnosed in fact. Anneliese submitted to the exorcism and to the regime of her doctors: she took her pills "religiously" (58). According to Goodman (who was born in Hungary and attended school in Transylvania), Anneliese died not of exorcism but of blood poisoning from the anticonvulsant medication she was taking. The foreign body of this medication trapped the demons inside her. As one of the demons exclaimed to the exorcist when the latter wondered if it wasn't getting late and wasn't it time for them to leave: "Yes . . . I can't stand it . . . we want out . . . out . . . out . . . out" (146). Unable to make their exit, they were along for the recovery phase of the exorcism/possession during which

Anneliese was free again to attend church and pray. The demons suffer terribly. At this point Anneliese can't tell if it's the Savior talking to her or the demons.

> The demons collapsed. Very shortly thereafter, on Good Friday, the Savior also died, as he had the first time. In a cataclysmic *Götterdämmerung*, a twilight of the gods, their entire world was obliterated, was wiped away, and vanished. Despite all his exorcistic ploys, Father Renz could not bring it back to life. "It was no longer possible to tell whether what Anneliese said was hers or a demon's," he remarked. "She screams, and I don't know why." (250–51)

Like Regan in the novel *The Exorcist*, Anneliese was the second child. In her case it was her older sister Martha who died in childhood of a kidney ailment. Anneliese was a sickly child whose mortality timer was forever under the parental purview. At age sixteen, she, not unlike Regan, crossed the threshold of this timer on her own person: "shortly after midnight she woke up and could not move. A giant force was pinning her down. It pressed on her abdomen and she could feel her warm urine spilling out" (14). A series of lung illnesses connect this double episode with the stay at a sanatorium where the *Fratze* interrupted her communion with nature. The possession wasn't open only to "the sinister part of the world. Her kin came to comfort her, Anneliese told Peter later: Oma Fürg, who had died three months earlier, and her dead little sister Martha" (83). In the course of the possession/exorcism, Anneliese "became telepathic, . . . began divining. . . . The dead visited her" (236). She is in the open and shut state that kept Regan from being neuroticized by her mother. "She said that they were using her vocal cords, and that she was only a spectator who could not prevent what they were doing with parts of her body" (138–39). Unlike Regan's clean break (in the film version), Anneliese succumbs to undeath, namely, her own. According to a popular commentary running counter to court and press following the girl's death in the course of exorcism, Anneliese was gone in order to come back: "A number of persons, both men and women, now reported on being possessed, some by the Devil, but most of them by Anneliese. Messages, purportedly from her, spread by word of mouth." The message was that, indeed, the exorcism had not killed her. "She died because she chose to. She offered herself as a sacrificial victim for Germany, for the youth of the country, for the priests" (178). Whether or not all of the above, from Christ to Hitler, died when she died, certainly all of them, all of them were still up and about in the projective Sensurround that Anneliese's undeath kept on not containing or reclaiming.

The Exorcism of Emily Rose, based on Goodman's account of the Anneliese Michel case (though the Germanicity associations had to go), spreads un-canniness along the edges of the black boxes within boxes enframing this courtroom drama in which testimony is projected, illustrated, or illuminated as flashbacks, internal simulacra of the otherwise abandoned film medium. Boxed in with TV court drama, the legal profession must share the brunt and grunting of possession in the mediatic foreground. Father Moore warned the defence attorney that the dark forces surrounding the trial might try to get at her. She's the anchorperson of the uncanny spread of the outside chance that the supernatural exists. Three in the morning was the recurring time in Emily's case. The lawyer wakes up suddenly: it's three in the morning again. She gets up, goes to the next room: the tape recording of Emily's ventriloquizing demon is running. Three in the morning is the witching hour. It's the inversion of three in the afternoon, the hour of Christ's death.

Another possession option, in another possession case and book (and movie), involves only the close quarters of one guy moving into the apartment in which a dead guy he never knew recently lived. Oh yes, one more thing: the deceased is "lost" over years of abuse and exposure to witchcraft; the to-be-possessed young man is "lost" the way middle-class kids cut loose/loss through drugs. In Ramona Stewart's novel *The Possession of Joel Delaney,* Hans Reichmann, the resident psychiatrist who is up on both Freud and the occult, cites authorities to back up his diag-nosis ("a weakening of the personality through the compulsive process"), its occult synonyms ("possession" and "demoniacal somnambulism"), and the possibility that the dead person who is sharing a young man's body is not someone near and dear who died on not in him (169). For example: "Then let us take William James's *Principles of Psychology.* He tells of a fourteen-year-old girl living in prosaic Watseka, Illinois. She was possessed by a neighbor's daughter who had died in an insane asylum" (171). She knows her neighbor's daughter. But the only thing close about this relationship is the close call with insanity. All one needs to do, however, is introduce a demon that had to move upon its meat vehicle's death from one possessed loser to another, and we are back inside the demonic principle of possession in contrast to possession as incorporation of the identifiable dead. *The Possession of Joel Delaney,* however, needs to take possession interpersonally. It must therefore all revolve around the sister—and the mixing of "lost" metaphors whereby she is able to draw the line between hers and his.

As brother Joel lies dying, his sister Norah is able through identification to travel the itinerary that got them there:

> It's strange what happens to you at a time like that. I had a serial sense of his life, as if I were he and were drowning. I recalled the summer he'd raised rabbits in the backyard, the way I used to take him to the movies. I saw him clearly, buying popcorn in the lobby. Even the last troubled years in New York returned, the misty nights he'd sat in empty cafeterias, the rainy afternoons prowling museums, a finely-featured lonely young man searching for a way he'd lost, trying books and arts and the hallucinogens. While another lost boy was also seeking a way back to a world that had crowded him out. (237–38)

However, when she sees him rally, an upsurge that shows that the other lost boy is back, she shouts, No—and watches them both die. In the projective field of representation, in other words in the film version, it is more difficult to conceal that Joel's double occupancy might just as well be the difficult articulation of an exclusive relationship between siblings.

Is *The Possession of Joel Delaney*—the movie—a vehicle for Shirley MacLaine, therefore, to act out or work through her outer-movie role as more-than sister? Her brother Joel isn't coming to dinner. She calls. At the other end of the line he's gagging. She goes to his place. He's flipped out and being taken in cuffs to Bellevue. In his apartment she's amazed at what he did with the place, it's so cultic, primitive, black magical. She finds a switch-blade. His girlfriend suggests that he probably tried to kill himself. At Belle-vue she tells Joel all he has to do is admit that he took LSD and he can leave—in the custody of a psychiatrist. She says it will be like old times. He'll stay with her.

Joel finds the primitive masks on her walls fascinating. He looks out the window and sees his hand reflected. He flashes back to the hand drawn on the wall of his apartment. He tells his sister that he met a lot of women like her in Tangiers who went there to get laid, came back, re-mained the same. The break in his personality is given a Spanish-speaking voice.

The girlfriend of suicidal Joel is the murder victim. The police wonder about any Puerto Rican friends. This murder is so much like cases in the re-cent past set in that specific milieu. A mother from this setting tells Joel's sister: "My son's spirit entered your brother's body." She accepts the invita-tion to an exorcism. "These people came to help you. Did you bring some-thing of his? His spirit will enter someone in the room, and the high priest will try to throw it out." She has to believe—and bring back her brother—otherwise the exorcists can do nothing. Whether possession or insanity, namely fragmented ego, it really comes down to the same thing. "Is my brother so vulnerable that he can be invaded by a man who is dead? I refuse to believe it!" She heads out to the beach house with the kids. While making breakfast, she finds a decapitated head on top of the fridge and Joel standing by with knife in hand. He's prepared to order a double decap. But then he walks the three of them into the living room at knifepoint. "Be nice and I'm nice." Double Joel plays with knife around little girl's neck. He dances with sister, then with niece (and knife). He tells the boy to dance. "Take off your clothes." Boy dances for Joel in the nude. "Are you cold? I was always cold." Double Joel identifies with the boy dancer. His sister isn't taken aback; perhaps it takes her back to the early years of their sibling rela-tions. After the police shoot to kill the double Joel, it almost looks like the possession has been passed on to the sister.

NOTEBOOK FIFTEEN

The Dunwich Horror opens with Americana gothic figures in black attending a birth. That was the prehistory. Now we're at college. Prof entrusts coed (Sandra Dee) with the task of returning the *Necronimicon* to the archive. But a young man (Dean Stockwell) intercepts her passage. He wants to see the book before she returns it to the library. That's impossible. But the coed, Nancy, has been hypnotized and doesn't see any problem with letting him consult the work. As he peruses the pages, kaleidoscope effects fill the screen. Professor demands the book back from, it turns out, a member of the legendary or infamous Whateley family. Professor: "You see man as a dismal creature." "Look around, they kill what they can't understand. In ancient times that book was said to unlock the gates to another dimension, another race of beings." Nancy and Wilbur Whateley are off to neck, to his neck of the woods. At the gas station, as soon as the attendant recognizes Wilbur, they are refused service. "They've treated me like that since the day I was born." His home or, rather, manor is, of course, the Vincent Price is right estate. But Wilbur also has cool stuff, like a mood lamp that makes Nancy hallucinate kaleidoscopically. She dreams that it's primal time and the hippies are jumping around at the orgy. She runs in the dream from the dream. She tells Wilbur her dream. "It sounds sexual to me." "OK, Dr. Freud." The professor and Nancy's best friend, Elizabeth, arrive. Now Nancy is staying the weekend. "Bye Elizabeth." Wilbur and Nancy take the tour. "That's where the people of the town strung up my great-grandfather and burned him and the tree to the ground. He wasn't afraid of God or the Devil; he thought those two were the same. He wanted to bring back an alien race." In town the professor and Elizabeth scoop the poop on the Whateleys. "Some say

Wilbur and his grandfather aren't alone. There's something else." Wilbur's mother, Lavinia, had twins. One was (allegedly) stillborn. The local doctor remembers that her insides were all torn up. He was able to save her life, but her mind was gone forever. Lavinia lives on in her asylum cell. Nancy, now in a mini poncho outfit, feels a little dizzy again. The tour takes them up to an open stone altar. "What is it?" "Legend has it it's been here forever." In name the place is attributed to the Devil. Fertility rights were practiced here. They waited for the moment when the gate would open and the Old Ones would come through. Nancy's a virgin. Soon some dreamy ritual scene, everyone attired in Satanic chic, can commence. Wilbur's torso is decorated with tattoo graffiti or hieroglyphs that ring around his body, ring around the body. Elizabeth is back. She explores the upstairs and unwittingly releases the twin. Her destruction by tentacles is largely psychedelically mediated. House catches fire. The POV is psychedelic. Wilbur and Nancy prepare to open the gate where the spheres meet. The twin is loose, lets loose: psychedelic flames of destruction rise up in her wake. Wilbur spreads Nancy's legs and positions the *Necronomicon* in between. (Sandra Dee has amazing skin tone, especially along the sides of her hips and thighs.) But the professor arrives in time to utter the counter spells. Wilbur ends up struck by lightning. The twin goes up in smoke. Nancy gets up from her altar ego. "It's all over now. The last of the Whateleys is dead." But then we get an X-ray crotch shot of Nancy's psychedelic baby. Nikolas Schreck points out that the film tried to hitch its chart to the success of *Rosemary's Baby*. "Despite its attempt to bring gothic occultism into the modern age, *The Dunwich Horror* seems far more dated today than the earlier period pieces it sought to supplant" (147). You'd think someone who changed his name to Schreck would dig dated. But from the point of view a reader must adopt, one that lies half submerged in the amorphous horrors of Lovecraft's fiction, the film version is certainly a happy faced update. Replace the groove of this film with the grave — and then wallow in its gravity, its decay — and you might begin to get back to the Lovecraft original.

Evil Dead II offers commentary on the body one is stuck on. In its own medium (and strapped to the laugh track), this movie is the more faithful cover of Lovecraft's calling, his craft of disgust. The overkill of the undead girlfriend that ends with a vise and an electric chainsaw was already sparked when the couple embraced and the new pendant he gave her hurt her. But then she says she loves it. That's why when he goes for champagne and discovers the tape recorder, she tells him to look what's on it so that it remains her fault. The reading out loud of the *Necronomicon* on tape is enough to summon demons, each with its own camera POV. The tape recording or, in film, the audio track summons the split-off visual apparatus of filmmaking. And the camera's arrival means that the limits of bodily experience and endurance will be tested and tried, dead or alive. How quickly the substitute bites the hand that weds it.

Lovecraft decided that a certain laughing stock of occult characters was no longer viable and that occult fiction must draw on sci-fi resources for tales that would be devoid of the "bland optimism" the narrator/editor imputes to theosophy but that just might characterize mainstream science fiction's rapport with the void out there. Lovecraft drew deliberately, then, on two deep impulses for his stories: first, the "sense of impatient rebellion against the rigid and ineluctable tyranny of time, space, and natural law," as he wrote in a letter to Harold S. Farnese, dated September 22, 1932, and second, "a burning curiosity concerning the vast reaches of unplumbed and unplumbable cosmic space which press down tantalisingly on all sides of our pitifully tiny sphere of the known." The unsettling (or uncanny) effect he deliberately aims for in his work is a "*sense of outsideness.*" As he goes on to explain the term that he has just underscored in this letter to Frank Belknap Long, dated February 22, 1931: "I refer to the aesthetic crystallisation of that burning and inextinguishable feeling of mixed wonder and oppression which the sensitive imagination experiences upon scaling itself and its restrictions against the vast and provocative abyss of the unknown."

In "The Call of Cthulhu," the unpronounceable beings from the stars but before human time are amalgams of so different creatures in part because they inhabit the limits of representation but also because they are part of the discourse of disgusting prospects of mixing (with) bodies. One name for any one of these possible creatures is Thing. Thing is transmitted via dreams of artists that inspire uncanny artworks—but *as* art they by and large stay at one major remove from direct, chilling, killing contact with Thing itself. Norwegian sailors die upon contact with Thing. Several are devoured, one goes mad, and the sole survivor is apparently assassinated back in Oslo: by the guardians of Thing's cult. But what also marks these Norwegian sailors or seamen—or semen— is that they don't reproduce. The bloodline linking the granduncle's estate and the grandnephew's execution, exploration, supplementation of that legacy is also nonreproductive. Like the last of the Norwegian sailors who witnessed Thing, the granduncle, a widower, has no progeny. According to the sailor's account, when he reversed the vessel and sliced through Thing, he also witnessed it recombine again as unicellular organism and immortality.

But while Thing communicates through the arts and to witnesses and chroniclers who do not procreate, and while it appears to contain and run on powers of replication rather than the powers-that-be of reproduction, there is also a mortal cult of followers that guides and guards knowledge of or belief in primal creation. For the most or moist part, these seeming Devil worshippers who indulge in "deliberate blood-thirstiness and repulsiveness" (189) are characterized as mongrel (including the isolated degenerate Esquimaux). They are clearly the product of mixing bodies, mixing with bodies. Our first contact with the cult we must renew after the fact, after we are given to suspect that the granduncle was in fact murdered. Right before the granduncle dropped dead, he was "jostled by a nautical-looking negro who had come from one of the queer dark courts on the precipitous hillside which formed a short cut from the waterfront to the deceased's home" (175). But this skewed setting is the rehearsal or repetition of all the scenes of contact with Thing, including notably the Euclidean-geometry-defying encounter the Norwegian sailor survived to chronicle. Out of a darkness that is precipitous, and displaced or dismantled by a short cut, appears the threat of a black sailor, seaman, or semen, the seed of mongrel mixture that transmits, represents Thing. The racism thrown into or coming out of the mix of metaphors of disgust with the body that is Lovecraft's main medium, at least in "The Call of the Cthulhu," is, like all racism, a symptom of disturbed relations with the body, with one's own body, and that means with the mother's body. Here the racism in the story is as much symptom as product of Lovecraft's experiment. In "The Dunwich Horror," by contrast, the prehuman demon spawn is allied with Caucasian inbreeds, like the shapeless albino Lavinia. In "The Call of Cthulhu" the brood and breed that transmits the cult, as mongrel, represents and represses the sexual mix with the other body, the off-limits body. We have thus an Oedipal plot here, the story of semen, off-limits bodies, illicit coupling, and short cuts. But Lovecraft's medium takes its inspiration, force, or even vitality from the pre-Oedipal plot or splotch as it gets recycled in the discourse of disgust. "The odour arising from the newly opened depths was intolerable, and at length" we hear "a nasty, slopping sound down there." "It lumbered slobberingly into sight and gropingly squeezed its gelatinous green immensity through the black doorway into the tainted outside air of that poison city of madness" (213). In the Norwegian sailor's account, the opening up of materialization is neutral but soon brings up visceral phantasms. "The aperture was black with a darkness almost material" (213). A darkness almost material, almost maternal: In *Hellraiser II* the daughter in search of her father opens up an entry in her hospital wall that seems wide enough. Soon a penis breast buttock turd with teeth wants to get to gnaw her.

When the Norwegian seaman bursts Thing's bubble, what slimes him cannot be wiped away with paper: "There was a bursting as of an exploding bladder, . . . a stench as of a thousand opened graves, and a sound that the chronicler would not put on paper" (215). It is hard to pronounce or inscribe any of the sounds emanating from this before form of existence. "A subterrene voice or intelligence shouting monotonously in enigmatical sense-impacts uninscribably save as gibberish rendered by the letters Cthulhu and R'lyeh" (181). Or again: "a voice that was not a voice, a chaotic sensation which only fancy would transmute into sound, but which he attempted to render by the almost unpronounceable jumble of letters, 'Cthulhu fhtagn'" (181). Writing's rendering is not affirmed. And the sounds of primeval voices are as disgusting as all the rest that is corporeal: even the mother tongue is mortified in mixed metaphors of illicit mixing.

The story goes that the mongrels assassinate individuals who know too much about their cult. But it seems rather that the assassinations intervene to save the pieces *and* the piecing together of the unwilling or conflicted chroniclers. The granduncle would have destroyed his research if he hadn't been overtaken by sudden death. The Norwegian sailor made no provisions for his account to be read or preserved. And the main editor, the grandnephew, hopes at the end that this archive that has come to him by accident will not be transmitted, that the yuck stops here. But of course we hold his portfolio, Lovecraft's story, spread-eagled in front of us. The opening line of the posthumously transmitted text or legacy (that was "found among the pages of the late Francis Wayland"): "The most merciful thing in the world, I think, is the inability of the human mind to correlate all its contents."

The grandnephew is able to piece together and correlate the contents of his and his granduncle's research, even if at the same time he, like his granduncle, would like to destroy the results before they can be transmitted. Artists pick up dream signals from the primordial beings but are spared the comparison shock of the big picture. "I know that panic would have broken loose had they been able to compare notes" (183). But it all begins (as always) "from an accidental piecing together of separated things" (174).

Only mongrel semen passes through the womb of reproduction in this story. Nordic semen doesn't reproduce. It bears witness to Thing, passes it along as art, and dies, decreeing, loud as denial, that the testimony disappear with it. But the chronicle gets passed on through and across death. The narrators, chroniclers, witnesses, and author work in the medium of disgust that denies wanting to mix with the (maternal) body or be equally penetrated by the pre-Oedipal father. (The mongrel cult followers specialize in ass-ass-inations whereby death unblocks transmission and preservation of their primal legacy.) Certainly the Oedipal father still gets his share of defiance and lip service. That the primal beings come before humanity, before time and space, and indeed from another space entirely, and are thus not, not even in evolution, linked to us, fulfills the wish that the father and father time be gone, that the son, via a time before, precede the father who is thus history, even prehistory, and definitely not in the picture. But that covers the desire part of the dread; the horror part belongs to the punishment that must follow. The zone that denies or defies the father is also one big threat that invites suicidal thoughts to cross the son's mind: "When I think of the *extent* of all that may be brooding down there I almost wish to kill myself forthwith" (210–11). The "almost" gives pause for the story we are reading to be the ultimate "survival," like that "strange survival," the primordial world of Thing, which is "something horribly remote and distinct from mankind as we know it; something frightfully suggestive of old and unhallowed cycles of life in which our world and our conceptions have no part" (189). Add a "y" to each "our" and you have your letter to the father. Otherwise a mumble-and-jumble discourse of mixed metaphors spreads dread across the coordinates of the big picture of infinite somethingness: "but I shall never sleep calmly again when I think of the horrors that lurk ceaselessly behind life in time and space, and of those unhallowed blasphemies from elder stars which dream beneath the sea" (209).

An incident that doubles back, through the footnote underworld in our annotated edition, into Lovecraft's own dream gives us the extent of refusal of the father. The artist's description of the dream power of his images that needs not observe nor be subservient to the scheduling or dating of historical time was in fact a reflection on dreaming that Lovecraft pronounced in his dream: "and dreams are older than brooding Tyre, or the contemplative Sphinx, or garden-girdled Babylon" (180). In his dream Lovecraft was at a museum trying to sell as work of antiquity an object he had just made out of clay. When the guardians of the museum (and of history) confront him, Lovecraft replies that his dreams are older, are before time, before linear time, the time of the father. In his dreams, then, the son comes before father (with his anal baby), and linear time is reversed. But the story also delivers the nightmare consequences—the punishment—of the underlying dream thought. At the same time the first representation of Thing evokes "simultaneous pictures of an octopus, a dragon, and a human caricature" (177). There is then between the lines of the attempt to represent the unrepresentable a doodling reference to the father, who sits for every caricature, and whose recorded shortcomings often aid in the son's identification with him. A relationship to the father gets mixed into the medium of disgust with the body. The patronymic, "love making," names the problematic mix of bodies and semen. The network of chroniclers transmits, under the cover of denial, an art complex that contains nonreproductive semen that must work with the mongrel semen to preserve the transmission of what was before the beginning of mankind, the forecast of the end as it was in the beginning, the world with end that all together work to push back. Among the chroniclers and witnesses there is also the desire to stop the transmission and destroy the evidence—which the mongrel cult must stop dead in their tracks. Lovecraft writes himself into the corner where he must cosign the demonic as principle of survival and deferral.

Lovecraft's father died of neurosyphilis when the author was eight years old. But first father collapsed while away in Chicago and was hospitalized for five years. The cause of the father's death was kept from the child, but we know just how known or knowing family secrets must be. The syphilitic body of the father threatens to return from the prehistory the son conjured to skip the paternal transmission. "The spells that preserved Them intact likewise prevented them from making an initial move." The death that preserved the father as legend to the map of the family line and name prevents him from coming back on his own. But all it takes is some accidental piecing together of cuttings or many other kinds of evidence, and the author son may already have summoned him—Them. Until then: "They could only lie awake in the dark and think whilst uncounted millions of years rolled by" (197). We are given a quote from the *Necronomicon* (Lovecraft's fiction within his fictions) to get a fix on the promise or threat of return: "That is not dead which can eternal lie, And with strange aeons even death may die" (198–99). This fiction of an ancient work is characterized as organized around double meanings. The lie we're given could also mean "deceive," as in the falsification of the cause of the father's death. If we translate "death" (as the lexicon of Freud's thought would encourage us to do) as "the dead," then a hope of mourning, the dying of the dead, is held up in contrast to the unlife the father is leading in a lie.

After the father's death Lovecraft lived alone with his mother. After his grandfather's death (his greatest blow), the grandson suffered a series of nervous illnesses that culminated after four years in the nervous breakdown that caused him to withdraw from High School. His mother helped out by telling all his friends that her son didn't go out during the daytime because of his hideous face. Lovecraft gets out of this dark period by a disgusted letter to the editor: the ensuing exchange around Fred Jackson, popular author of sentimental love stories published in the magazine *Argosy*, brought him to the attention of Edward Doas, then Official Editor of The United Amateur Press Association, who invited Lovecraft to join. That was in 1914. Five years later his mother entered Butler Hospital. After two years there, apparently insane like her husband twenty years before, she died. As soon as she was gone, he sold his story "Herbert West Reanimator" to a magazine for serialization in order to cover the funeral expenses. But at the same time, he attended an amateur journalism convention, where he met Sophie Greene, who would become his wife. But the marriage on the rebound from mother's death would end in impasse, long-distance separation, and divorce. Here we can turn up a contrast. Kenneth Anger replaced his patronymic with the name that shows defiance. To make his first Luciferian film, *The Inauguration of the Pleasure Dome*, he invested all funds that had come to him through his mother's death. Anger was able to enter as artist into a relationship with Lucifer. Lovecraft, too haunted by better halves to sign up with the Devil, nevertheless, like certain German Romantic authors, found himself aligned or allied with the demonic principle of repetition, but in the mode of disgust. Specifically he turned his same body relations into a discourse of disgust with embodied existence and defiance of the line of time, the discourse that permitted Mr. Sex to scratch the surface until it had all the depth there could be in the word thickened and stuck in the throat with disgust.

Kubrick's father was a doctor in New York. In *Eyes Wide Shut* a New York physician loses all foundation and certitude, ultimately concerning what crosses "his" mind in the procreative act. The title evokes the seeing eye of dreams, which doubles as the moviegoer or projector whose sight is for sore Is. The doctor's wife, Nicole Kidman, shares with her mate, Tom Cruise, the fantasy or fact of adulterous possession. Kubrick was clearly fascinated by the vulnerable perfection of this Hollywood couple. Following Kidman's admission of desire outside their duo dynamic, Cruise is haunted by a black-and-white insert—the hallucination or fantasy of his wife's infidelity, in which it seems he identifies, however, with the wife. He is driven to sign up along the Satanic margin of sex ritual where, however, the reality of lust begins. He's all eyes no action at the Satanic orgy. He asks the Satanic lap dancer who expresses concern for his safety childlike questions, trusting, absolute, helpless. He's on the stuck side of demonic repetition. He discovers that the sex setting is organized around life or death consequences. Kubrick is invoking the demonic in its Freudian setting of drives as the paternal legacy of feminization of the son in the Oedipal phase of couplification. Cruise was given a password for his uninvited under-cover attendance. But two passwords are required. When brought up before the tribunal of Devil father figures, he is informed in no uncertain terms that "here it doesn't matter if you forgot it or never knew it." Cruise is asked to strip for his sentencing. An already undressed woman sacrifices herself for him, takes his place. She is ready to redeem him. Interchangeability with the woman penetrated gives Cruise life. The highly neurotic, Oedipally complex nature of the doctor denies him a second password, the second signatory to the contract or contact with Devil fathers.

NOTEBOOK SIXTEEN

In Ken Russell's *The Devils* the Devil in Grandier (or in Loudun) is the desire for p-unitive relations with a righteous God. The elongation and the short of it is that the movie itself, however, opens with the king, by divine right, starring in a pageant in which he plays Venus being born. In the middle of the possession epidemic, he visits Loudun. Surrounded by an orgy of possession alternating with exorcism, the king is put off only by all the womb views in his face. Reproduction, as he tells his favorite, amounts to eggs dropped in dung. He offers to give the afflicted the royal treatment. He brought along a vial of Christ's blood encased in a treasure box. After its cure-all effect has been demonstrated, he reveals that the box was empty. Behind the scenes or in the front row, the powerbrokers want to unite one unified church with the state. The king goes along with it. But he stages his contribution to the elimination of Protestantism by making the heretics dress up as big birds that he pot shoots at his leisure. The officers of the Inquisition, raised for dais and in exaggerated garb to the power of high art, inform Grandier that none of this is political. That's denial, to be sure. But it's true, too. Grandier is on trial for heterosexuality.

According to Huysmans's *The Damned*, you write about the Devil when it's the times: if money isn't diabolical, then there's no other explanation beyond this impasse (13). But more to the point than such social studies hits home. When the Christian church becomes corrupt, as when priests abuse their charges, then it is instantly Satan's vehicle or institution.

"Without sacrilegious priests a tradition of Satanism is impossible." (47)

"At this very moment Satanic agencies are in existence and fallen priests are responsible." (178)

The protagonist, Durtal, decides, after two years of isolation from the literary world and from his craft, to write a biography of Gilles de Rais. Soon his research investment in de Rais' Satanic beliefs drops him off in a more current context of Satanism.

> What a strange coincidence. No sooner do I start to get interested in Gilles de Rais and the question of medieval Devil worship than I get whisked off on a conducted tour of contemporary Satanism in Paris. (216)

But Gilles de Rais is also a blot or block of narcissism and self-loathing inside the authorial frame of self-reference: "He was the Des Esseintes of the fifteenth century" (42). But this breach in the defense contract with singularity reflects the push and pull of the Devil's lack of revelation.

> "Satan does not exactly need to reveal himself either in human or in bestial form to make his presence felt. All he has to do, in order to affirm himself, is select the soul in which he wishes to take up residence, the soul he intends to ulcerate and incite to the commission of the most inexplicable crimes; and, to this end, he needs only whisper in the ear of his victim that instead of domiciling himself in his body without his knowledge, he will obey his summons, appear before him at will, confer advantages on him on the basis of a legally binding pact in exchange for certain concessions. The very fact of being willing to enter into such a pact will often be enough to bring out his presence in us." (95)

Because the crimes the possessed commits are inexplicable, the Devil gives this body of vice free will: a pact psychology allows the Devil to appear to be doing his victim's bidding. At that point—of coming full circuit within an utterly projective Sensurround—the Devil's presence comes to be known. The pact with the Devil occupies the bottom line of the legally binding deal or contract, which must be ironclad, include an escape clause, and be openly finite. Defoe claimed that the Devil holds a default policy whereby he works the fine print to get the services and soul of his clients for nothing. In *The Damned* the willingness to enter a pact indeed suffices: what follows, it appears to be the Devil at your service, clears you of responsibility for deeds to the Devil's possession that reflect your commitment and not any wish fulfillment of your own.

In Durtal's contemporary setting, the cult of Satanism confronts an entire institution or science of loss in Spiritualism. When the Spiritualism current is turned on at this intersection—as another occult force that ultimately "satanizes everything" (119)—it is at the same time observed that this intersection may itself have been overshot, exceeded. "Spiritualism...democratized the evocation of the dead and opened up a completely new path" (119). Hence, while fallen priests are immediate Satanists, the followers of such occult fads as theosophy and cabbalism are mainly "journalists down on their luck" (117). "What a strange age we live in.... It is just as positivism reaches its very zenith that mysticism re-emerges and all the nonsense of occultism recommences" (219). Bracketing out the occult return of what positivism repressed, there has all along been one continuity shot that could not be dispatched. "And just to think that this century of positivism and atheism has overthrown everything, everything except Satanism" (264). Not only does Satanism not yield an inch to positive thinking, it gets its offer of Dad certainty across in these times when rottenness is apparently more appropriate than splendor. Otherwise the cults of the demon and of God are undifferentiated and equally "insane" (218). Electricity and hypnotism, the great applied sciences of the nineteenth century, were in fact discovered in the eighteenth century. The nineteenth century introduced only "the adulteration of foodstuffs and more sophisticated manufactured goods.... It has even gone so far as to adulterate excrement" (104).

But one major overlap appears to contain the overspill or gap: in order to influence the living, practitioners of black magic tend to call on the dead rather than on demons even to perform the private parts of succubus and incubus. Thus, in reference to the succubacy of a living being, possession has become a redundant term. The involvement of the dead "combines demonism with the charnel horrors of vampirism," thereby striking a new low point on one and the same Satanic continuum: "Strictly speaking, cases of simple possession no longer exist" (122). It goes around and it comes around: "these so-called 'possessed' are the creations of the priests themselves or at least it is they who nurture such insanity; in this way they are assured of victims and accomplices, especially in the convents. All kinds of murderous and sadistic follies can be concealed under the venerable and pious mantle of exorcism" (57).

Black magic derives power from the ease with which we post our death-wish effects long distance.

> "But, my dear, to hear you talk, one would think it as easy to kill someone at a distance as posting a letter!"
>
> "Can't some diseases be transmitted by letter, cholera, for example?...But it's only the issue of transmitting something invisibly through space that astonishes you." (205)

In black magic, sparrow hawks, since particularly susceptible to the "influence of spirits," are used "'in exactly the same way as a hypnotist makes use of a patient or a medium employs slates and tables'"— namely, as "'telegraph wires for magical dispatches'" (238). But the time of transmission observes the linear time of cutting losses, specifically, of getting even: "Every person attacked by magic has three days in which to retaliate" (233). Participation therefore, being on the same schedule or page as the magician, proves one's best protection in the cross fire of black magic. Even attendance at a Black Mass must prove traumatic "if you do not formally take part in the ritual" (208). "In magic, any act which is known beforehand is doomed to failure" (233). "Countersigns" can be employed when you know in advance the exact time and date of the attack. You leave home, thus throwing the spell off and neutralizing it, or you can declare an hour beforehand, "Here I am. Strike me," thereby drawing off the fluids and paralyzing the powers of the assailant (238).

Modern occultists cannot compel angels to appear, and so they end up attracting only evil spirits via the "intermediate larvae" that, at least according to one priest, "inhabit an invisible, neutral territory, something like a little island, which is constantly besieged on all sides by good and evil spirits." "Now, because it is these larvae that the occultists evoke" (and with them, inevitably, evil spirits), so they "are always dabbling on the fringes of Satanism. In one way or another, this is always bound to be the fate of Spiritualism." Whereas "pure Spiritualism" claims that the phenomena observed in séances "are produced by souls called back from the dead," the most "tenable," even "veracious as well as straightforward" explanation relies on the theory of "elementals," immaterial beings that are simply in the air and manifest themselves under certain conditions (117). "Space is inhabited by microbes; is it any more surprising that space should also be swarming with spirits and larvae?" (118). Because the "notion that some imbecile of a medium can bring back the dead" is so "revolting"—we've heard already all about its status reporting a democratizing revolution—to accept the notion requires, as antidote, recognition of "the Satanic nature in such practices" (250).

To spin out this ectoplasm of Spiritualism's challenge more than half a century further, in the lifetime of the authors and the history of their subjects, consider Aldous Huxley's genealogical take on possession and summoning of spirits. In Huxley's study *The Devils of Loudun*, we strike up association with a name that's a place-name in order to view the double occupancy in possession.

> Professor Oesterreich, in his richly documented study of the subject, has pointed out that, while belief in diabolic possession sharply declined during the nineteenth century, belief in possession by departed spirits became, during the same period, much more common. Thus, neurotics who, at an earlier epoch, would have attributed their malady to devils, were inclined, after the rise of the Fox sisters, to lay the blame on the discarnate souls of evil men or women. With the recent advances in technology, the notion of possession has taken a new form. Neurotic patients often complain that they are being influenced, against their will, by some kind of radio messages transmitted by their enemies. (198–99)

The third technological variant restores the Evil in the dead or Dad. What you get by calling the possessing dead the Devil is, at the theoretical distance of advocacy, a more systematic view of psychic life than could be given by a focus fixed exclusively on the melancholic bond (or, for that matter, on an open invitation every body extends to let the unknown dead take up residence).

If indeed the Devil has passed out of the picture, Huxley laments, then along with the Devil "went any kind of serious consideration of the phenomena once attributed to diabolic agency. The exorcists had at least recognized such facts as trance, catalepsy, split personality and extrasensory perception" (188). What goes down in theory, goes double for therapy. The rapport between exorcist and the possessed is the "relationship" so important in treatment of functional disorders. "Dr. Ehrenwald and others have pointed out that this kind of rapport between doctor and patient is sometimes established in the course of psychoanalytic treatment. The relationship between demoniac and exorcist is probably even more intimate than that between psychiatrist and neurotic. And in this particular case, let us remember, the exorcist was obsessed by the same devils as had invaded his penitent" (212–13). Finally, viewed from within the discursivities that maintain or are maintained by Christianity and Devil worship, consideration is given the balance to be struck up among father, son, and spirit—Christianity, in a word (in the world)—in order to contain the one-sided imbalance that opens wide in spirit for the return of the dead.

> Where union with the Spirit is sought to the exclusion of the other unions, we find the thought-patterns of occultism, the behaviour-patterns of psychics and sensitives. Sensitives are persons who have been born with, or have acquired, the knack of being conscious of events taking place on those subliminal levels, where the embodied mind loses its individuality and there is a merging with the psychic medium (to use a physical metaphor), out of which the personal self has been crystallized. Within this medium are many other crystallizations, each one with its blurred edges, its melting and interpenetrating boundaries. Some of these crystallizations are the minds of other embodied beings; others, the "psychic factors" which survive bodily death. . . . Foredoomed to failure are all those who aim exclusively at union with the Spirit. . . . For them, there will be no union with the Spirit; there will be a mere merging with spirit, with every Tom, Dick and Harry of a psychic world, most of whose inhabitants are no nearer

to enlightenment than we are, while some may actually be more impenetrable to the Light than the most opaque of incarnate beings. (83–84)

Hovering above a footnote to Aldous Huxley's *The Devils of Loudun*, which Julian Huxley urges his readership to consult in the matter of "some horrifying practical results of accepting a daimonic-spirit hypothesis," we find an outline of the spirit hypothesis, which is identified right away as "more complex" than the magic hypothesis and god hypothesis outlined above. "When sacred power is supposed to reside in the spirits of the dead, we may find special rituals of burial designed to keep the dead from plaguing the living, or the cult may develop into an elaborate system of ancestor-worship" (153). To that date, religion, understood as a social organ that functions to adjust man to his destiny, had been based on the supernatural hypothesis, the coupling of the god hypothesis and the spirit hypothesis, which, however, "appears to have reached the limits of its usefulness as an interpretation of the universe and of human destiny" (155). Collective awareness is now "the distinctive and most important organ of the human species" (179). He closes by citing his "grandfather"—also the grandfather of Aldous Huxley—who in a "famous essay... defined agnosticism" (189). The Huxley genealogy of famous men carried for at least three generations an investment in mining to evolutionary theory (like coals to Newcastle) whereupon they became spin doctors of the projective process of culture, from religion to literature. Julian Huxley: "the present is the first period in the long history of the earth in which the evolutionary process, through the instrumentality of man, has taken the first step towards self-consciousness" (160).

The instrumentalization of evolution (or technological progress marching as to/through war) as the self-consciousness of the present (tense and tensions) assembles lines of God-saving UK militancy. *To the Devil a Daughter* is a Hammer production that shares with the book by David Wheatley not really even the title but only the scene of annulment of the father's pact with the Devil, which is the hurdle the Devil busters must clear before father can huddle with them and coach them along to their score. Though the title remains the same, its meaning is reversed from book to screen. The book's Satanists struggle to sacrifice a virgin daughter on her eighteenth birthday to the infernal priest's homunculus, whose artificial life will lift off where she leaves off. The film virgin, I mean version, is about the Devil siring daughters via elaborate alternate plots that are magically and telepathically connected. Our representative in the film is an author of books on the occult (like Wheatley, who was responsible for several so-called Black Magic Stories). In the book Wheatley hands over representation to a woman writer of mysteries, which she sets in the Cold War but animates with memories from her hot-war service in the offices of espionage. Like Ian Fleming, Wheatley entered the Cold War's field of representation with his World War II arsenal of fabulations. But whereas Fleming's corpus remained haunted by a double war from which he struggled to rescue his own ambivalently held paternal introject (but that's another story), Wheatley's Cold War oeuvre is the continuation of the world wars spawned by Russian black magic (Rasputin) and Soviet atheism (= Satanism). The enemy factory or plant behind our lines in this novel, as in Wheatley's first Black Magic Story, *The Devil Rides Out*, which also made it to the screen (a memory implant of which already flashed before our eyes), is Spiritualism. The mystery writer knows from her war exploitations what Evil looks like. The girl next door isn't a mood swinger: on a daily basis she becomes possessed by the Devil when darkness falls. The author must therefore combat enemies who are the henchmen of the Devil: "'Communism has now become their most potent weapon'" (83). It doesn't matter that this is hard to believe. Satanism doesn't recruit from among believers in the Devil:

> "The Satanists... recruit their disciples from among the people who attend quite respectable spiritualist and theosophical societies, many of whom can easily be intrigued by a promise of revealing to them the real secrets of the occult." (81)

Wheatley's 1971 cash-in coffee-table volume *The Devil and All His Works* may illustrate the culture of the Devil, but the text is a greater history of Spiritualism, including Mesmerism, hypnotism, the works.

The Hammer production of *To the Devil a Daughter* lets roll London raised to the power of the 1960s where a horizon of kinkiness meets the prospects for Satanism.

To the Devil a Daughter pits the father and his representative, an author of books on the occult, against the demonic (and incestuous) Father of a church devoted to the demon Astaroth. The author tells his closest friends about the mission of protecting Catherine with which her father has entrusted him. "I could hardly tell her that her Dad's in trouble with a bunch of Satanists." Ann: "Oh, it all sounds so sick." "Ninety-eight percent of so-called Satanists are nothing but freaks who get off dancing naked in freezing churchyards. An excuse for getting some sex." But he's not sure about the remaining 2 percent. When the friends, a couple, are alone together, David says: "I can't wait to see this nun." Ann: "I always thought you were kinky." "You knew I was kinky." Later she will ask Catherine if she could try on the habit. "I promise to be good as long as I'm wearing it." As soon as it's on, she tries it out on David.

One woman's tortuous giving birth (with legs tied together!) is simulcast as Catherine's tossing and turning in her bed. "I had a horrible dream. I dreamt I was being born. I was clawing my way out. I was hideous and inhuman. They were revolted when they saw me. But Father Michael looked joyous." The author would like to know what Catherine's training consisted of. "I learned about the Lord, the problems of the world, and languages. Soon the time will come. The vacuum must be filled. Youth need something new and powerful." Now he knows he's dealing with that 2 percent and that the church isn't after Henry, the father, so much; it's the daughter, Catherine, the Satanists want. "Unconsciously she knows what's going on." As proof, he tells her nightmare to his friends. Ann: "That's just a Freudian nightmare."

"Henry is trying to recant, but it's too late. The pact was signed eighteen years ago." Father Michael gets Henry on the phone. "We've always been very close. We're close right now. I feel your pulse. It's too fast. You're going to die. Where's Catherine?" All along he's been wrapping rope around the receiver. A snake writhes around Henry's phone.

Father Michael is seated at a table with a pentagram design on it and set with five plates. He turns one plate over while calling Catherine. She feels it in her hands. He turns over another plate. She stands up and fetches a special necklace, which she puts on. Third plate. She walks out. But the author spots and stops her. When he tears off the necklace, Father Michael shudders from the breaking of the connection. "Who gave you this? What does it represent?" "It's our Lord Astaroth." "He's evil." "He's good." "They've chosen you, haven't they?" She shudders. "What did you see?" She keeps on flashing back to a ritual in progress. "It's as though even though I was unconscious I could see everything. It was as though I were inside everyone there." The golden sculptural representation of Astaroth is placed between Catherine and Father Michael. They each wear a golden mask of the Lord. Father Michael turns over the last plate: Catherine sees a monster in the mirror. Author John breaks the mirror. Father shudders with the breaking of the connection. The author wants to peruse the grimoire of Astaroth from the church archives, where the head librarian keeps track of the identity of each reader consulting such books and which pages were read. Thus, we can follow Father Michael's reading finger into the 1950 origins of his horrific plans for Catherine today—or rather tomorrow. Father Michael desired to worship the absolute capability of man rather than of God. "The result would be terminal chaos presided over by Astaroth." His ultimate purpose is to create an avatar, a personification that will renew mankind.

Father Michael holds up a doll to the Astaroth idol and calls "Catherine, Catherine." He makes the connection. Catherine sees that Ann, who was asked to keep an eye on her by John, has nodded off. She plunges a letter opener into her head. This time, in trance-it, she stumbles all the way to the Satanists. "Everything she does now must be of her own free will. Do you know what your future will be?" "Yes, and I am content."

The author and his remaining sidekick David find Henry in the middle of the pentagram he drew on his apartment floor one day to keep the Satanists away. "He's going to baptize Catherine again with the blood of Astaroth. For the rest of her life she will *be* Astaroth. They baptize a baby girl in the blood of her dead mother. Then they bring her up in seclusion like a nun. Then they baptize her again as the Devil." For the ultimate ceremony it's up to Catherine's foster mother to give her lifeblood for the protection of Catherine. Father Michael lets the blood flow around the ceremony space. He sprinkles blood on Catherine—then senses John's presence. "Why not enjoy life? Why not enjoy Catherine? You know the power she will have. You will share that power." Even as Catherine remains white-robed and lying on the altar, her nude double advances toward John. John counters that the demons are now angry with Father Michael for killing Astaroth, who has yet to be reborn in or as Catherine. "The blood protects me." "But the blood of your dead disciple on this stone protects me." John enters the circle of blood and casts the first stone. He rescues Catherine, who wakes up. She looks content.

Loose morals accompany the screen renditions of the Anglo-propaganda metabolization of Satanism out of Spiritualism to the U.S. installation of proxy protection against suicidal depression, which sure looks like it inhabits the haunted sensorium of communication with the other side, but the one-way adjustment is already in place: only denizens of Hell holler to be let go through these gates. *The Sentinel*, both the 1974 novel by Jeffrey Konvitz and the film version, caption that New York moment when everyone on the island sounded gay. Even straight women just in from the Catholic Midwest trying to make it big apple as fashion models spoke the artificial idiom of camp. The changes in the socius that Anton LaVey welcomed into his Church of Satan (and which were sympathetically portrayed as cultural difference in *Rosemary's Baby*) are admitted into *The Sentinel* at once as life and as the small change of the same big currency of sin according to our silent majority share in Christianity.

The alliance doesn't sit well with Konvitz, who is therefore a stickler for the fine print of ultimate sin: suicide or attempted suicide alone has Hell or penance to pay.

In *Simon of the Desert,* Buñuel's Devil sends the stalwart Simon to a nonstop New York disco for Hell. In *The Sentinel* a changing of the guard must take place over the Entrance to Hell located inside a Brooklyn apartment building. A model rents one of the apartments crowded with eccentric neighbors. But then it turns out that she and the catatonic priest upstairs who just stares out his window are the only residents. In fact the people she claims to have socialized with are long dead, all of them executed for murder. The model has a traumatic past she flashes on. Back home early from High School she walked in on her father's orgy. He slaps her and rips off her crucifix. She gets the other fix: she slits her wrists. The slice is right. Now the model has been in a relationship with lawyer Michael for two years; he wants to get married, and she wants her own apartment. Two years ago his wife committed suicide. But what's that racket upstairs in the empty apartment? When she goes up to find out, she walks in on her flashback. She stabs the zombie father. She goes to church. "I've rejected Christ. I need to come back." "Is there anything else my child?" "I committed adultery. I tried to take my own life. Twice." "Is there more?" "I stabbed my father who was already dead." When she goes back to the church, the priest she encounters doesn't know which other priest she's talking about. She keeps on dreaming about the blind priest sitting in front of his window. Michael arranges for the blind priest's files to be stolen. It's a relay of files. One dies the day the next one disappears in one place and then pops up in front of the window as priest or nun. All of them at one time attempted suicide. There's a file already set up for the model, who is scheduled to disappear tomorrow and become a sister. All the dead neighbors she kept meeting are demonic reincarnations who crowd the stairs up from Hell trying to make her kill herself. Knock, knock, knocking on Hell's door. Michael is another damned corpse back from Hell: he tried to murder the Sentinel priest; he already murdered his wife.

Sometimes suicide is murder. Her dead father grabs her. "You are the Chosen of the Lord God, our Enemy. Now you must destroy yourself, be one with us." Instead, the model raises the Sentinel cross. The denizens of Hell start bleeding and rotting. Even when the building is torn down, its modern replacement houses a blind nun who sits in front of her window all day. She'll be seeing you.

In Konvitz's sequel, *The Apocalypse,* the penance the suicidally depressed must endure as God's bouncers is advanced from zomboid transmission of the seal on Hell's locked gates to omniscience not of this world. Konvitz also dislodges Hell's hole from New York City, where it is literally open and shut at a specific address: now the entrance is anywhere and everywhere, and the Sentinel exchanges sentient life for the status of all-seeing I. But the plans for Sentinel succession cannot escape the worldly surveillance of Satan (or Charles Chazen). That's why the Church pursues several plans at once, both the true plan and the blind ones, to keep us and Chazen guessing. By the end of the line we've been given three candidates in succession. Their candidacy doesn't even cross their own minds: their past lives in suicidal depression are locked up via "repression." The first two are a couple of replicants of family value. The wife turns out to be a female impersonator who at least has her bisexual husband convinced that she has a "woman's soul." Their baby boy was adopted. While this is sin, Konvitz stops short of assigning it the penance of Sentinel duty. There is also suicidality in their repressed pasts, which alone qualifies them as candidates. The final candidate, a priest, doesn't have lifestyle issues in his repressed past: he only assisted his mother's suicide and then attempted his own. But Chazen can bypass repression and bring the past back in a New York flashback. Thus, he induces suicidality in the priest before the transition is complete. The new Sentinel, who is situated for a change in Los Angeles, is the zomboid priest as body suit for Chazen—who in his own time is now free to open the surly gates.

In the late nineteenth century of *The Damned* the current manifestation of a need for the supernatural "in the form of Spiritualism and occultism" is what holds out hope, at the start of Huysmans's novel, for the otherwise disorganized state of letters (7). In Huysmans's sequel, *En Route*, in which Durtal reverses his direction and embraces Christianity, Spiritualism is cited once, but as bottom-line proof with which the good Durtal counters the Devilish sophistries of his double self. As evidence for the existence of the supernatural Durtal submits his "Spiritualistic experience, where no trickery was possible" (236). In contrast to the sublimity of the Eucharistic mystery, Spiritualism is still the "latrine of the supernatural," but turned now against the Devil of the material world, it gives the degree of certainty that can take it all on faith. In *The Damned*, Durtal's move to write a biography of Gilles de Rais was a move away from the modern novel, from Naturalism as "incarnation of materialism" that "promotes the idea of art as something democratic" (3). But Durtal doesn't simply move away from Naturalism, he moves through it, through its abolition of "the mechanical creatures of Romanticism" and "the sort of pedantic idealism and spinsterish vacuity that celibacy encourages" (4). En route, Durtal embraces "the Catholicism of the Middle Ages, a mystic Naturalism" (11). At a time when religion alone administers healing, religion demands in return at once a desertion of common sense and an abrogation of the power to be astonished. In this way mankind comes to be cured of the supernatural (12). The supernatural returns, however, via occultism and Spiritualism, with Satanism waiting in the wings to collect these returns — or to contain them within and for the Christian frame of reference that Satanism ultimately shares. Durtal thus enters recovery on a mission: "to call to life the formidable figure of that Satanic monster who, in the latter stages of the fifteenth century, was the greatest scoundrel, the most exquisite sadist and the most terrible artist in crime the world had ever known" (19).

Saints and Satanists, who "form the only connecting link between the Middle Ages and the present day" (103), were the bookends of de Rais' psyche. He fought by the side of a saint, Jeanne d'Arc. Perhaps it was too hard to emulate her. When she died, he turned, without transition, to "the patriarchs of the fifteenth-century imagination," the sorcerers (45) — he turned to evil, which became him. "One can take as much pride achieving greatness in crime as a Saint greatness in virtue. This is the whole story of Gilles de Rais" (46). Gilles de Rais was unable to summon Satan with the aid of his sorcerers. But Satan "was about to materialize within the unwitting Maréchal in order to entice him, spectacularly, into the joys of murder" (96).

Satanic orgies alternate, more and more rapidly, with "leaden states" that Durtal refers to as phases of de Rais' "vampirism" (135). He ends up haunted and hears the undead children, his victims, "crying for their mothers and pleading for mercy in his own voice" (146).

But in this failure of Gilles de Rais there lies an affirmation, too. "The Devil dupes everyone who falls into his clutches." You simply cannot be as evil as you can be good. In the pursuit of evil you cannot but run up against your limits: your voice in the children you once sacrificed to Satan with ease and pleasure. Identification outlasts projection. It is not possible to be identical with yourself under the aegis of evil. Identification catches up with projection and brings up the lost other where the Devil claimed only to be bringing up the rear. "But if, for certain souls, an infinity of love and goodness is attainable, the utmost possibilities for Evil remain beyond our grasp" (145). It is possible to be, to become, to know a saint. One says of such a person, he or she is too good for this world. Good is perfectible. Evil is not perfectible. Or, in other words, it is not possible to be too evil for this world.

Thus, there is a lot of worldly good, which in remaining Evil's equal, proves to be the flaw in the appointment with saintly goodness that must therefore undergo the workout for better sin atonement. Durtal advances into *En Route,* the sequel or sequelae of his *Damned* case, determined to make the next station of his crossing over into the Middle Ages his conversion to Catholicism, the other continuity shot (other than Satanism, which he tried last time around, but then gagged on the bad sex). But seriously, Durtal is in fact in recovery from his last hurrah of evil not only up close and cursed on all the magnetism tapes of modern Satanism but also from the remove of biographical writing. Another midlifer in Middle Ages crisis seeks recovery in the Church. The first delegate in the relay of fathers guiding him assures him that he can help himself—to the resources of his peer group: after age forty sex isn't a drive, it's an idea, in the imagination only, which means, though it thus has the tenacity of the imagination, it is far enough gone to forego it. But even as Durtal finds, from one extreme to the other, that he is a believer, he must also recognize that the "divine action" that pushed him this far also up and left him there without a trace to hang on to (17). This double momentum scatters the dotted lines along which anti-embodiment might otherwise cut in.

Durtal is "haunted by Catholicism"; he yearns for the church as the "hospital for souls" (22), which means that he is unconvinced that he can shake his debauched self or history: "my heart is hardened and smoke-dried by dissipation, I am good for nothing" (15). But that's good enough when it comes to a certain maxi shield of mystical nuns. Durtal's first guide grabs him by introducing him to the "plan of substitution." There are mystic nuns who gladly atone for the sins of others. Not only do they purge the faults of others, but they also succeed in "preventing them, hindering their commission, by taking the place of those who are too weak to bear the shock" (39). The nuns in these contemplative orders "take on their backs, so to speak, the diabolical expiations of those insolvent souls whose debts they pay to the full." Like "lightning conductors of society" (40), the nuns, who, unlike a sinner like Durtal given to equivocation, will have none of it, "draw on themselves the demoniacal fluid" (41).

The Order is a tall one. God doesn't care, and evil is just a medium of knowledge. The Order is an out-group that's an in-group, too. The members were banished from the church—a church that no longer believes in itself, namely in stigmata, exorcism, demons. The priest who breaks rules (and hearts) was trained to bust ghosts, demons, and all manner of undead. Apparently the so-called Sin Eater falls into his area of expertise. He receives a special dagger with owner's manual instructions for killing the Sin Eater. At the end we discover that it was the last—and lasting—ruse used by the Sin Eater to make the young priest into his successor. The special knifing isn't how to kill him, it's how to become him. The Sin Eater is also known as the Other. All along the priest, while being trained to slay demons, was really being shaped by the Other. His church father was excommunicated because he surrendered the boy to this raising. Sin Eater killed off the boy's parents, saw to it that, as a young man, he would fall in love with the woman sent his way (they meet at an exercise class — no, at an exorcism) only then to lose her. The Other kills her, making her death look, as he did with the mother's death, like suicide. When the priest finds his true love dying, he recalls the rites he witnessed the Sin Eater perform once and frees the dead body and soul of any burden. But this is how he also discovers in the course of the one-course meal that she didn't commit the mortal sin of suicide. He stabs the Sin Eater, and the rest is the former Eater is history. But even though the new Other was forced into the position through the administered experience of loss, he discovers that there are benefits, too, in keeping the ledger of sin or knowledge, which are to die for. One doesn't receive immortality, only hundreds and hundreds of years, during which time one Other gets all used up and must find another Other to take over so he can sign off. But what gets transmitted intact as endowment for interminable growth is the knowledge the sins leave behind once the Other consumes them. The Sin Eater treads a path to Heaven that doesn't require the mediation of Christ or his church. "Knowledge is the enemy of faith." But the Sin Eater "is all that remains when everything turns to dust." In one infernal minelike station through which the priest must pass in order to locate the Sin Eater, the cult leader of the advent of a third cross refers the priest's question to the dying. At the leader's command a fallen priest (he keeps several in store for such occasions) drops in for his hanging. He twists and shouts out the answer the priest seeks. The dying, not the dead, have the power. That's what the Other learns in contrast to his former training as ghost buster. You can't hold on to mother, and she won't come back. But on her inevitable way out, for example, as she lies dying, obtain with her sins the free gift of knowledge that in time answers every question.

Aspects of the father extend in certain Devil fictions to a fraternal relationship, specifically, in *The Minion,* for example, between Christ and the Anti-
Christ. According to the Nicene Creed, which is one of those secrets the
Church doesn't advertise, Christ and his brother, the Anti-Christ, parted company when the former spent three days among the dead. Christ trapped
the great deceiver and enemy of mankind inside the bottomless pit. The
Devil isn't without powers, too. That's why there is a key to the Devil's place
of incarceration that can never be destroyed but always only hidden. The
Devil has a familiar, the minion, who is dedicated to the liberation of his
master. The minion is strongest when faith in God is at an all-time low. A
monastery was built on top of the pit in Jerusalem, and the key was hidden
far away, in the as yet undiscovered new world. The movie begins in New
York City just days before the final Christmas of the millennium. The weather
has been too warm, ominous. Workers repairing water mains underground
fall through the floor into some kind of ancient crypt. Indian burial ground?
"We have an archaeologist on call for this sort of thing." The other worker
wants to pocket a few artifacts, a "Christmas bonus." But when they see the
seated skeleton of some medieval figure, they both get out of there. It's
quite a find. An Irish monk wearing a Knight Templar tunic and around his
bony neck a Celtic amulet. The archaeologist is excited. But a heavy breathing POV is beginning to breach the sealed-off area. The guard is killed. The
intruder reaches the ancient crypt and cries out to the skeleton: "Templar,
you have failed." But then some warrior priest intervenes and stops the
killer with a blow to the back of his head with a glove of knives (the Templar
weapon of choice). He shouts at the archaeologist: "Don't look at his eyes!"
Apparently evil is located in the lower back portion of the brain. But the
minion never dies, and with one eye-to-eye look can transmit it all, both the
minion-being and the mission to obtain the key and free the Devil. To regain
control of the find, or to get the rights to the story of the Templars, the
archaeologist suggests dumping the key in a radioactive waste site located
within the Indian reservation where her grandfather, who has access to the

site, resides. She calls her grandfather. She now knows that what he told her about good and evil is true. The minion keeps catching up with them. The chase brings the showdown to Jerusalem. The latest minion meat vehicle gets to the point of inserting the key into the door: the key starts turning on its own. But the archaeologist and the Templar arrive just in time to remove the key from Satan's prison door.

Mine

NOTEBOOK SEVENTEEN

Milton's Lucifer falls with his cohorts from Heaven's unrepresentable space to the Hell that is always on Earth: the rebel angels are cast so deeply into the material of representation that they end up inventing the primal technology of mining. Soon they will devise infernal engines that almost win a battle while staying on the losing side of the war against Heaven. The bottomless fall of Lucifer must be represented as unrepresentable. An allegorical timeline allows Hell to be like earth before there is earth. And the angels also already bear arms. But every sword comes from the stone, the mine. In Heaven there's a cavern where day changes into night. That's how there is mining before the discovery of mining at the bottom of representation of the unrepresentable bottomless fall. As Milton digs into and through the darkness, one is reminded that he was a blind man dictating the struggle to see the light at the end of the darkness. But there's also a historical setting of losses inscribed within Lucifer's renewed attack against heaven. In the mine from Hell the demons learn how to dry the volatile molten core and contain its underworld power in dust or powder. The engines that do take the angels by surprise at first blast represent the outmoding of armor and sword as functional defenses. Instead the trappings of chivalry are allegorized, still on the winning side of the angels, as conserving cans of former, now lost or breached, vital signs and defenses.

When Milton met Galileo, the latter was blind. In *Paradise Lost* Milton includes reference to Galileo's telescope. Blind seeing—and creating and projecting—is the desperate bid the Devil makes for a finite but certain lifeline or bottom line that guarantees and generates creation out of nothing. Lucifer and his followers fall into the void—but then they hit bottom. The world—together with the underworld (on earth as in Hell)—occupies the dotted line that even the abyssal fall will fill in. There's the Christian or AA view of "hitting bottom" and the death before resurrection into or as more spiritual modes of existence. Then there is the alternative inside view of a bottom line that we hit and make resound at the end of one endless free fall.

Freud stumbles on the primal scene of technology deep inside mother nature when he looks for analogies for the ready-made status of his seventeenth-century case of demonological possession: "This demonological case history leads to really valuable findings which can be brought to light without much interpretation—much as a vein of pure metal may sometimes be struck which must elsewhere be laboriously smelted from the ore" (*SE* 19: 73). And again: "a demonological case history of this kind would yield in the form of pure metal material which, in the neuroses of a later epoch (no longer superstitious but hypochondriacal instead) has to be laboriously extracted by analytic work from the ore of free associations and symptoms" (87). Demonology—contract, possession, exorcism—is the sword in the stone; your usual neurotic case is a dig for the ore from which the study must be fashioned before it can be extracted from the stone, from the materiality of the (endopsychically structured) transferences.

Ernest Jones argues that the Devil in legend is associated with analytic and literal underworlds. "Psychoanalysis has shown that the deepest source of the child's defiance of his parents is his refusal to control his sphincter at their bidding, and in consequence the acts just mentioned [like farting] have been used the world over as a sign of defiance or contempt" (176). Hosted by our own petard, the Devil also displaces upward from one's own person to the greater range of what can be called "mine." "The Devil dwells in remote places, being especially fond of dark forests and of treasure spots, such as gold mines. He penetrates into caverns and into the very interior of Mother Earth, i.e. into places quite inaccessible to ordinary beings (= children)" (173). When it's gems they're digging down there, miners, before they are discharged from the mining compound, are routinely strip-searched and every orifice opened

wide to stop the inside chance of stealing away with diamonds or whatever. In Dante's Hell, usurers and sodomites hang together under a golden
shower of fire.

The Gate. Holey shit. Two boys digging a hole left when a tree was up-
rooted, digging it more deeply. It's smelly. But the boys keep on extracting
crystals. One boy has bugs in a jar: "How long do you think they can live
without air?" "That's cruel." "That's cool." The father grounds them. The hole
is refilled. "What's with you today?" "It's the hole, it's weird." Father to son:
"Terry's Mom died — he's been strange ever since."

Gate II I see you. Terry: "Dad, I couldn't stop thinking about it. It was the most
exciting thing that ever happened. The problem isn't that we summoned
the demons, but that we didn't do it right. You're the only one I can talk to."
We see the dad passed out drunk.

Terry's ceremony conjoins candlelight and electronic digital gadgetry.
He also submits a photo of dad. "Protect this traveler into darkness." He thinks
the sentinels have arrived. But it's a group of suburban hoodlums. Terry corrects their assumptions about what's going on here. This is demonology:
"Satanism is for pussies." Demonology? "It's only the most powerful religion
on earth. Evil against evil." He picks up the ceremony where he left off. Time
to offer blood, the gift of death. He can't bring himself to slit the throat of
his pet hamster. The bully helps out. "What's that smell?" "That's the smell of
the dead." A tiny demon appears. The bully shoots it. Terry protests, but the
bully makes him take it back: "Say it:'I'm the asshole.'"

Terry keeps demon corpse in a jar. He ties his dad's tie for him. Dad's
company wants him back. Terry finds the music box of his dead mom. His
dad filled it with mourning souvenirs. "Everything's going to be different."
"Yeah, Dad." Dad takes a swig from his bottle before starting the car.

The bully's girl is into the spiritual side. "What did you wish for?" It's not
a demon, it's a minion. And it's alive again. "If demons were rock stars, minions would be roadies. The earth was their playground before they were
trapped between worlds billions of years ago." "Why mess with something

so dangerous?""I want results. I want to give him his life back." The girlfriend goes ahead and fires up the minion with her material requests. But after a time all the goods turn into shit, literally. Dad was badly hurt. They visit him in the hospital. "It's OK to touch him," girlfriend says to Terry. "It's OK to touch me, too."

Mom's music box is the vessel of the dead required to cast the spell that sends back the minion. He was thinking in three dimensions, like they would come in through some hole. But they are entering through—inside—them. Terry dies. After conclusion of graveside service: knock, knock, knocking inside the coffin. Terry gets out. Dad and girlfriend embrace him. Then the dead hoodlums crawl out. "Demons, man. Who needs chicks when you got demons."

The first constructed and imagined automata wore mined ore: gold, copper, gems galore. A certain upward displacement or mobilization keeps what's mine stowaway in every artificial habitat. The high-rise office, the plane cabin, the viewing space in front of TV or monitor are among the many interchangeable places modeled on the close quarters of mining. Inside his delusional system, Schreber also descends to the depths of mine shafts just as readily as he shoots up into outer space.

William Randolph Hearst began construction on his castle in San Simeon in 1919, the year of his mother's death. The concrete and steel combo was selected for building material in aftershock of the San Francisco earthquake. The castle was Hearst's monumental souvenir of his two-year trip through Europe alone with his mother when he was just a boy. The property had been the camping site for family fun in the days of his father. It would appear to be a double construction: part Oedipus complex, part crypt (or Hearse Castle).

The ongoing collection of European antique artifacts, which the castle could never completely house or catch up with, was the continuity shot with the maternal tour. In Hearst's day big collecting belonged to the cult of the new and improved: should that side altar look good in a corner of the rec room back home, then its purchase made a chunk of change. The European church was left behind a fragment missing a corner or one side. The resettling of citations from something old in something new (and bigger) reflects the Devil's revalorization of substitution as upgrade without complication. What Hearst thus collected was not so much collectibles as the dregs and facticity to which Europe could be reduced. Hearst also collected newspapers. If he took a controlling interest in the press, then it was for the chess game of power breaking with the news itself. It helps that newspapers isolate events from the outside chance that readers could ever experience or know them. Hearst's collection drive did not, however, support itself. All of the above was bankrolled by the fortune father had amassed through mining, which he had worked from the very bottom all the way up to the office along one continuum of artificial space. Before there was beach culture and all the other chain operations of California's missing death cult, there were the ghost towns of once booming mining operations that suddenly came back up empty.

By binding the metabolic phase of Gluttony, which we saw with Flusser as the Devil's inside track in technologization, to mining as primal scene, it proves possible to add to the duo dynamic between works of mourning or unmourning and the Oedipus complex (whether as diversion from or as inoculative intervention in those works) a third party, which the Devil would host.

Mining was the first technology to be institutionalized as science, discipline, and business. Paracelsus already knew enough on his own to go study down in the Tyrolean mines, a unique lab space for experimental treatment of accidents and diseases. In the Central European culture of *Bildung*, the home turf of such doctors of monstrous body *Bildung* as Caligari, Mabuse, Frankenstein, the first mining academies were opened in the 1760s in Freiburg, Berlin, and Prague. By then Novalis could be both a mining engineer and the author who, in "Hymns to the Night," would dig deep into what's mine about the other's death. In Sweden, never so far away from Central Europe—the how-to manual that gives

Dr. Caligari his remote control over a medium is the property of the University of Uppsala—mining also fit the corridors of modern institutionalization. Before his turn to the world of spirits, Emanuel Swedenborg was the inventor of iron smelting, salt pans, and docks and locks. He also officiated on the Royal Board of Mines. In his *Inferno* (where he describes how infernal electrical devices are in hot pursuit of him) Strindberg summons Swedenborg twice to describe or recognize Hell. The first reference is given in passing. The hotel boy places the chamber pot on the table next to Strindberg's bed—whether by accident, because the room is small and cramped, or, Strindberg's preference, by design. "If at that time I had known anything about Swedenborg I should have realized that the powers had condemned me to the Hell of Excrement" (134). Here's the more complete rendering:

> This is the picture Swedenborg paints of Hell. The damned being is lodged in an enchantingly beautiful palace, finds life there sweet, and believes that he is among the chosen. One by one all the delights begin to vanish like smoke, and the wretched creature finds that he is shut up in a miserable hovel, ringed round with excrement. (218)

As painstakingly described or documented in *Inferno*—largely because it is the prize for which he is persecuted by infernal forces—Strindberg's pursuit of the alchemical solution for making gold out of darker, baser substances aims at proving, ultimately, "that in fact people had always made gold when they thought they had merely extracted it from ore" (200).

Already beginning in the sixteenth century, and then going through more and more phases, complete with military distinctions, mining and warfare served as the chief venues for technologization. The use of explosive mines, which is as old as war, disappeared from war's theater at the end of the eighteenth century only to reemerge in the Russo-Japanese War, the first war to send psychiatry to the front to treat psychological casualties of detonations. The shock of the mines technologized and internalized the trauma of warfare that marked the spot we were already in with early conflict on the inside and thus with the eternal flame of unmourning.

During World War I, trench warfare turned European borders into a no-man's-land that was at the same time one big mine (also in the other sense lying out there waiting for detonation). Cinematic projections (the only entertainment that could satisfy in the modern work and war world) and psychotic hallucinations (as in the drug-induced gadget loving of Ernst Jünger or the double case of Fritz Lang and Hitler) were sprung from the detonation of crypt trenches. This tunnel vision of trenches or mines rehearses or repeats the nonperipheral vision of cinematic picturing. But does it hold the place for one and all of the war zone's missing death cult? Given time, yes. But in first place it is the momentum of substitution not for loss but for or as disposability that is being projected or forecast. Each period of contact with the war becomes a finite span of time to be protected within the ever renewable pact psychology whereby the second nature of mass destruction is staggered, rendered habitable. Under conditions of total war, living is about dying one's proper death at the proper time.

In my repertoire of reflections on occult and technical media, Edgar Ulmer's *The Black Cat* has afforded cinematic playback of a certain interiority of mummified bodies holding the place of our always narcissistic bonding, at the front of the line of "self relations," with the mother's body. These mummified women in their Snow White coffins are emplaced right where the long-range guns had fired in the lost war. They are the batteries of the narcissistic charge set off by trauma and charging itself on hold, a blast from the past war held back in the crypt of long-distance relations. Up above the mausoleum holding down this fortress of the lost war rises a modernist villa designed by architect Poelzig (who was in command of the battle stations below in the lost wartime). He keeps on marrying, losing, and mummifying interchangeable women. The psychiatrist Werdegast, the other psychological casualty of the same station identification in wartime as Poelzig, leads a young American couple on honeymoon to a Dad reckoning with certain legacies that cannot be left in Poelzig's care. In the end, Werdegast sets off the telegraphic detonation of the "undermining" of the fortress crypt. The citizens of the European techno death cult, just as the Frankenstein monster says of himself and his mate at the close of James Whale's *Bride of Frankenstein*, "belong dead."

But it's time now to reconsider the uncanny precincts of *The Black Cat* from within Poelzig's perspective, which is also Dadicated, but to the pre-Oedipal father. Poelzig's rapid turnover of embalmed shells is part of the Satanist service over which he presides. But although Poelzig recognizes in their shared war shock condition their membership among "the living dead," it is Werdegast alone who cannot not recognize a loss when his daughter (the double of the wife he left and lost in the architect's scare center) is declared alive after all (she shares Poelzig's playing-dead bed), only then to be found dying, right before his eyes. Werdegast moves to protect the substitute, the American wife, with his life, and sends the American couple out of the crypt into the space of substitution, circulation, survival.

When he shared the train compartment with the couple, Werdegast was on the hypnotic beam of the wife's resemblance to his missing wife and daughter. The cab the three travelers share upon arrival crashes. It's thus in a state of shock that the wife is introduced into Poelzig's home, which the American husband thinks would make a great insane asylum. Going "mediumistic" is how the shock induction into a hypnoid state is described. Under these conditions Poelzig of course sees the young woman as perfect for the sacrificial part to play in his worship of Satan.

By World War I all the conditions could be met for the epidemic outbreak of war neurosis, the doubling of the ego between peace ego and war ego, the blanks Werdegast and Poelzig fill out in their living dead conflict. The undermining of the crypt of the lost war also gets under the skin of the subject of cinema. Celluloid and dynamite are by-products of the same discovery. The skinning of Poelzig by Werdegast is shown as shadow play, as film within the film, and thus proposes, in what need not be shown, the surgical wear and tear of cinematic representation on bodies, on bodily senses, the stripping away of dead matter from the body that the camera I enters (or entertains).

When Werdegast avenges himself on Poelzig's body by flaying him alive, he still fits Walter Benjamin's composite picture (in *Origin of the*

German Mourning Play) of the melancholic in which sadism is admitted if not as factor then as fitting analogue. But Poelzig's demise is on one continuum with his own Satanist service of human sacrifice. The living end he in turn is served should not be confused with the melancholic undeath of Werdegast. Poelzig, who recycles interchangeable bodies, bodies uncompromised by the loss that substitution supplements and admits, until they give out, whereupon they are put on display in his trophy room (the space that for Werdegast is a crypt), lives his ending, down to the last layer to be peeled off the surface and added, via film's self-reflexivity, to the infernal reeling of going, going, gone mediumistic.

All key inventions of the Industrial Revolution were punched in by innovations required for safer, faster mining. The steam engine was first developed to drain groundwater from mines (drowning was a common fatality for miners). The first steam-powered locomotives hauled ore. By the early 1800s the British town of Newcastle was surrounded by a dense network of railways between the mines and the waterways. Canals were first built to improve on natural waterways for easier transport of the ore. Even the so-called Second Industrial Revolution was built up on the long-distance extensions and networkings of the mining industry. When the trains that first transported ore were reopened as vehicles for all travelers, the reception of accident was also opened up along this extension of the underworld. Like the miners, train travelers, while passing through tunnels, experienced the same loss of contact with nature. For both miners and train passengers, this tunnel vision belonged both to the safe passage of technologization and to a danger zone.

Train wrecks were common enough, at least for phobias to be a common consequence. Passage through tunnels—the way mining first entered mass culture—was particularly risky. Trains contributed the first public form or forum of psychic trauma when the shock of real or anticipated accidents was recognized as the cause of psycho-cultural disorders. Amusement parks and films supplied the catastrophe preparedness by injecting doses of train wreck into the sensorium to absorb future shock. We withstand shock by getting wired: we learn to get a blast out of being terrified through a culture industry of simulations of catastrophe. This development overlaps not only with the early history of cinema (consider, for example, the "traveling shot" as well as the special effect of the frontal shot of the approaching train with the movie-goers strapped to those tracks) but with that of psychoanalysis, too.

Freud's train phobia was based, according to his auto-excavations of early memories, on a childhood recollection of a train trip taken with his mother some time following the death of his younger brother Julius. Freud remembered that he got a primal first look at his mother's nude body in the railway compartment they shared. But when he looked out the window of the machine on wheels at the industrial mining landscape they were passing through, techno chips passing in the night, he thought he saw an underworld of tortured lost souls. It was at this time that Freud commenced carrying the secret cargo his mother slipped inside him while in transit: the unmourned remains of Julius. But the encrypted passage is stowaway in the main-text psychoanalytic interpretation of every means of transport in terms of sexual trafficking. Looking out train windows also saw the train or training of free association as well as, to come again full circle, the framing and editing of cinema's doubling of perception.

Soulkeeper mixes sacrifice, sex, occult sciences, and warfare in the happy medium of simulation.

Civil War battle reenactment. Lincoln lost his mother when he was ten. The actor or body double performing Lincoln starts his speech. But when he speaks of "big battlefields," he's confused by big boobs. He does a remix instead of all the president quotes he dis-remembers, like Kennedy's: "ask what you can do to me."

At the bar. "Do you believe in the supernatural?" UFOs, ghosts, Back Street Boys. "Do you believe in the power of the human soul?" Two women lead them to the man with the French accent. He appeals to the dead mother in the one man's case, psyche, recent past. "I am not a soothsayer, I am a potential client." Evil souls remain closest to the earth. Salvation is possible only for those close to the Devil himself. They're off to find the rock of Lazarus, the wonderful portal between worlds.

The double, Freud's summary term for all the modes and features of afterlife or unlife, was originally, as he puts it, a form of insurance, which the ego took out against its own unthinkable mortality. The opening up of the train complex of traumatic neurosis, phobia, catastrophe preparedness, which came up straight from the mines, was accompanied by the spread of the concept and institution of accident, health, and life insurance. Originally instituted in Roman times as a means of setting aside the funds required for one's own burial, insurance spread its calculation of risk between life and death with each vehicular extension of our long-distance community (and immunity). Thus, shipping was the first risky business to be insured (all forms of property soon followed). But by train and plane time, in time, that is, for world war or total war, accident and health insurance were society's facts of life. The psychological casualties of train wreck—persons suffering, for example, from railway spine—were therefore doubly registered, once as neurotic, and once more for good measure, as virtual malingerers, as pension or insurance neurotics. This sliding scale of valuation, along for the more psychological modes of diagnosis, was thus in the ready position in time for World War I and its shell-shock epidemic. If in the second half of the nineteenth century, science fictions about underground worlds often share a fantasy of classlessness brought to us by some new technology or energy source that, even more than electricity, makes life in all lanes automatic, then this science fiction of energy or technology makes displaced reference to the real-life mix and match of insurance coverage and catastrophe preparedness. This new mode of group psychologization or technologization did undermine historical conflicts, like those of class, in exchange for a bond between self and other forever (and never) based on risk. The relationship to one's own death, which replaces or instrumentalizes the other's death, as in so many fantasies of being one's own double, becomes contractual: death is admitted but written into a schedule that makes at least the moment of signing deathless quality time.

No group or pact psychology without catastrophe preparedness. The first disasters to be contained by the group they at the same time built were the techno-accidents and crashes that reminded everyone of earthquakes.

· Natural disasters were simulcast (via antidotal group identification or shock absorption) alongside the accidents brought to us by technology. In other words: no group psychology without media technology (which transmits, on station identification, our participation in or anticipation of catastrophes preprogrammed to tune in as techno-accidents). In Auguste Villiers de L'Isle-Adam's *L'Ève future*, the techno platform, on which Hadaly (the narcissistic object and increment of group or mutual identification) shoots up from the crypt once Edison turns it on, shakes to the sounds of earthquake (or mining accident). Shock is always getting injected shot by shot into its reception. The shot of trauma induces— addiction style—auto-micro repetitions looping back onto larger repetitions (phantasm reruns or unconscious blocks of time). At this living end, the techno-underworld becomes again the last resort of blow-up-dolly perfection—but its momentum remains that of deferral or controlled release of suicide.

Telegraphy was first put to practical use in making tunnel passage safer for train travel: the all clear at one end was thus communicated to the train entering the tunnel at the other end of the line. Telegraphy gave us the first means of long-distance remote-control ignition of mines and other wartime or industrial explosives. Amusement parks, which to this day are built up on top of this second phase of mining technology, began with the tours and celebrations held in caverns, mines, and tunnels where visitors were kept safe from but real proximate to (simulations of) risk and accident. The first large-scale developments of this theme of thrill inoculation could be found inside works of science fiction about underground civilizations. In William Delisle Hay's *Three Hundred Years Hence* (published in 1881), the underground setting is all world's fair in its mobilization of every representative architectural style imaginable—pagodas, mosques, temples, Swiss chalets—to cover the mineral slopes of the artificially illuminated, animated underworld. Electricity turned on the last resort of the subterranean fantasy. Light and music could now beam up from nowhere. But the backgroundization of the senses always tunes in the death-wish static of identification overload.

Edward Lytton's *The Coming Race,* which first appeared in 1871, and thus ten years before *Three Hundred Years Hence,* occupies the recent past that a novel of wish fulfillment was better off forgetting. The first person narrator/protagonist is a financially free agent whose last parent, his father, died when he was just twenty-one (1). In the course of journeys subventioned by his survivor status he meets a professional engineer who invites him to "visit the recesses of the...mine, upon which he was employed" (1). But the engineer's been working on a deeper a-maze-ment, which our agent in the novel persuades him to disclose:

> "I saw, to my unspeakable amaze, a broad level road at the bottom of the abyss, illumined as far as the eye could reach by what seemed artificial gas-lamps placed at regular intervals.... The superstitious belief, common to miners, that gnomes or fiends dwell within the bowels of the earth, began to seize me." (3)

They agree to go down there together so they can halve and hold the engineer's dread. But already during their descent the engineer falls to his death. Now the engineer's dread goes to the protagonist's head. On his own, then, the protagonist encounters an ancient, highly developed or evolved race served by automata, equipped with electrical wings, and surroundasounded by music: "A strain of low music, above and around, undulated as if from invisible instruments, seeming to belong naturally to the place" (8). While all the technologies in this new world are ahead of what is available above ground (or in the mines next door), they can still be analogized with what was brand-new in the industrial era. The biggest machine he encounters is comprised of components "resembling our own steam-engines" (12), while the telecommunications metallic plates inscribed with hieroglyphs "I rightly conjectured to be of the nature of our telegraphs" (13). And where the technical analogues are, the occult ones must follow.

> The strangeness of all I had seen began now to operate fast on my senses; my mind itself began to wander. Though not inclined to be superstitious, nor hitherto believing that man could be brought into

> bodily communication with demons, I felt the terror and the wild
> excitement with which, in the Gothic ages, a traveller might have per-
> suaded himself that he witnessed a *sabbat* of fiends and witches. (15)

We confront two forces in this new world. First there is vril, the nuclear-
like potentiation of electricity that includes magnetism and galvanism.
Once applied as weapon, vril proved so powerful that wars were soon
history. Second there is the new woman, or gy (pronounced, we are informed, like "guy"), who is the one who comes courting. Soon our protagonist is wooed. But he flees this chance or change. The narrative is
bracketed by two reflections on the dreadful quality of this "coming
race" that slips between the lines of their completely civilized, benign
demeanor. If by the end he finds that his own extinction is in their faces,
his first insight, the running start to this conclusion, bounced off the
closed circuits of Devilish finitude and Christian idealization, wherein,
precisely, the dead have no place.

> On that brow, in those eyes, there was that same indefinable something
> which marked the being of a race fatal to our own — that strange ex-
> pression of serene exemption from our common cares and passions,
> of conscious superior power, compassionate and inflexible as that of a
> judge who pronounces doom. (122)

> They seemed as void of the lines and shadows which love and sorrow,
> and passion and sin, leave upon the faces of men, as are the faces of
> sculptured gods, or as, in the eyes of Christian mourners, seem the
> peaceful brows of the dead. (10)

In the language of dreams at least, or at the latest, building upward
can also mean to build down there, in the underworld. We saw the interchangeability of one space, now high, now low, in Fritz Lang's *Metropolis*. Ernst Kris also takes building to the group-psychological high-low
point: "Painters conclude pacts with the Devil in order to compete with
God, while builders, heirs to the builder of the Tower of Babel, commit
suicide" (166). The underworld is the internalization of the Tower of
Babel. Heinrich Schliemann's excavation of Troy shared not only with
Dante's Inferno the same nine circles but also with Babel the diminish-

ing width of the bottom—the diminishing return, in other words, of the top. On his way to the internalization or excavation of a suicide pact, Schliemann traveled to California in search of his missing brother Ludwig, who had immigrated to the Coast in 1849. When Schliemann followed one year later, the brother was already dead. But the survivor was there in time for California's declaration of statehood—an event of such performativity that Schliemann was instantly turned into a citizen too. It was, then, the brother's legacy (which Schliemann expanded by introducing the sale of conserving canned goods first to the gold-rush miners and their hangers on, then in Russia, where the Crimean War in particular helped him out) that backed Schliemann's final confrontation with the perfectly, prophylactically preserved Trojans, which he dug up only to watch them break down to dust to dust. Whether or not Schliemann's uncovery and recovery efforts remained within the limits of literary phantasm, their double plot pumped it all up with the stowaway identifications of unmourning. How else could this Blitz of a forgotten or denied past (which archaeology always, traumatically, secures) pack enough momentum to cause one once skeptical professor, who had ridiculed Schliemann's project in print, to commit suicide.

Phantasm opens with teen sex in cemetery. She's on top. But that's so she can knife him better. Her face switches with an older face. It's ruled a suicide. Someone goes to the cemetery to grieve. Someone else arrives by motorbike. "The funeral is about to begin, sir." The biker attends the funeral at the distance of binocular viewing. The view is double-breasted.

Biker visits grandmother. Grief counseling for the child of dead parents: "In two years you can get over most anything." Grandmother teaches him a lesson in fear. He must submit blindly and stick his hand inside the black box. "That really hurt." "It's all in your mind."

They're taking the dead and turning them into dwarves who still weigh the same. The wait is the same. "What about Mom and Dad? Are they up there, too?"

Adelbert von Chamisso's *Peter Schlemihl's Strange Story* identifies (with) the figure of the outcast in the mode of (self) deprecation. But rather than serve as fall guy who buys someone else's shadow, he finds someone to take the fall for him and buy his own shadow. What he doesn't know is that he's dealing with the Devil. Schlemihl first meets the little gray man (who turns out to be the Devil) at his millionaire uncle's estate. Whenever the uncle or any of the guests in his party utter a wish in passing, the man in the gray coat, otherwise overlooked by all, pulls, slapstick-style, whatever is desired out of his pockets: first a telescope, then a large Turkish carpet. Finally, he pulls out a magic purse, a kind of double of the Devil's deep pockets. In exchange for the shadow the Devil takes along with him, cash and carry, the Schlemihl receives the purse of fortune: the gold pours out but never runs out. Later the Devil asks for the formality of Schlemihl's signature in blood. Schlemihl declines, as is still in his rights and will power, and heads for the mines as the place of employment that will leave him alone without his shadow. (Full illumination of his shadowlessness is one major drawback to his exchange; like evidence of vampirism it inspires Christian peasants to wave crosses, stakes, and torches.) The fit between his shadowlessness and the artificial world of mining was first tried out when he obtained an invisibility device that otherwise fails to conceal the shadows still cast by see-through bodies.

Schlemihl purchases what he takes to be mining boots, which turn out to be seven-leagues-boots, as he discovers upon entering step by step a field of projective representation. As this representational field flashes by him or as he flashes by it at top speed, he obtains another form of invisibility mixed into what's all a blur. On the way to the mine—in techno boots—he enters all that folds out along the projective lines of illumination of the mine space:

> I was very much lost in thought, and hardly noticed where I set my feet; my mind was on the mine. . . . I had scarcely walked two hundred paces when I noticed that I had wandered off the beaten track; I looked around in search of the trail and realized that I stood in the midst of a vast and ancient forest. . . . Proceeding another few paces,

I found myself surrounded by barren cliffs....I looked around and noticed that the forest had disappeared behind me....The sheet of ice on which I stood, and over which a thick fog hung, seemed to stretch for miles around me....I had no idea how I had got there....Another step, and I landed at the icy edge of an ocean....Then I ran on for a few minutes dead ahead....I looked around. To one side stretched cultivated rice fields and to the other mulberry trees. I sat down in the shadow of the latter and peered at my watch; not a quarter of an hour had passed since I'd left the marketplace....Two Chinamen, unmistakable in their Asiatic features (even if I were to doubt the authenticity of their costume) addressed me in which I imagine must have been the common local greeting. I got up and stepped back two paces. The Chinamen were gone, the landscape was altogether different: trees and forest stretched before me instead of rice fields....Intending to approach one tree for a closer look, I took a step forward—and once again, everything had changed....Wondrously changing vistas, flora, fields, mountains, tundras, and sandy deserts unfurled themselves before my marveling gaze. (76–77)

Schlemihl uses this projective velocity to circumvent his traumatic losses and, funded by the loot he can pick up in uncharted lands, proceeds to wrap around his ruined life a vast research project of scientific archivization or natural historicization of life-forms.

NOTEBOOK EIGHTEEN

In *Def by Temptation,* Succubus gets her actor mark to sign up by way of giving her his autograph. The brothers were in ministry school together. The older brother became an actor, instead. The younger brother is the priest. He interrupts the contract sports Succubus was planning to play on the actor.

Bar scene, bar none: Succubus puts the moves on her new john. "This is too good to be true." "You're right." He freaks out over the cut marks. What will his wife say? "I've given you something there's no cure for. It'll grow until it consumes you."

In *Bedazzled,* the remake, the Devil, made over as a woman who says she's "hot," suggests to her client that they take a peep behind the scenes to see what the woman of his dreams is looking for in her man. The Devil with a red dress on reads from the woman's diary out loud: "Where are you my sensitive man?" We know where the woman is: she's at home during their visitation. They, however, are not only see-through but walk-through, too. The woman passes right through him. "We were like one person for a moment—like *Ghost.*" In the sensitive scenario, he's so "tiny tears" that his beloved is driven to gangbang the next best men on the beach who come by to kick sand in his face. When the client asks impatiently, "Do you think everything is sex?" the Devil automatically answers, Why no, and names the other six mortal sins.

In the series of double father figures in E. T. A. Hoffmann's work, which Freud identifies with the demonic, we can count Torbern, the underworld spirit or demon who lures the protagonist, Elis Froböm, just at the moment he finds himself without parents (and siblings), down to the lowering of the young man's doom in the mines under the covers of fantastic reunion with the pre-Oedipal mother in her incarnation as the underworld's ice queen.

At the start of Hoffmann's "The Mines of Falun," Elis Froböm has already suffered three strikes of loss, but he wasn't out, he was in, alone with his mother after two brothers died in battle and father was dead by the same storm from which Elis was rescued. Elis's survival thus murderously holds the place of the father's death, with the double barrel of loss of brothers finishing off the Oedipal fantasy. But Elis continues to live like his father as seaman. In identification with his father he just goes—and then, when he returns, he is forever gone to his mother, who has died in his absence. Mother's death doubles the whammy of Oedipal blockage: the undead mother cannot be substituted for—not by living women. The barmaid hired by his fellow seamen to lift Elis's spirits receives only the short change, the interest of or on his investment in the other woman. But, at the same time, he gives the young woman already shadowed by death coming soon the cloth (and shroud) he had originally brought home for mother. Although she returns the money when she departs to be counted from that moment on missing, she takes the cloth with her in the now double wake.

After the "other woman" has thus split the scene of parting, Elis only wishes he were already buried beneath the ocean floor. He is in despair, the multiple undoing of the pair. But a voice addresses or interrupts him, the disembodied voice of a demonic figure who approaches Elis from behind, and establishes immediate transferential rapport. He introduces himself as voice and listening ear, as analyst positioned behind the analysand. Elis talks up a cure; he admits to the old miner (Torbern is his name) that he was trying to divert himself from deep depression by joining up with the other seamen on a leave of the senses. But he is now overwhelmed, buried alive, by sensations of bleeding internally, eternally to death, into the dead.

Torbern, who will continue to bring up the rear, recommends for now a career switch away from the open sea, the open circulation of semen, down into the underworld passage of mining. Torbern illuminates the underworld awaiting him, behind him, the alternative world of searching deep down inside the bowels of mother earth for minerals, gems, in a word, for ore. Either you pick up your spirits, your current life in pieces, or you dig ore.

Like the seven dwarf miners, and like the garden figurines of a still current predilection for kitsch in Europe, Torbern is heir to the subterranean demons Agricola already referred to, pranksters who liked to mimic miners and thus cause all kinds of double trouble. Mining accidents were often attributed, in these convenience stories, to demonic gnomes.

When Elis rejects the molelike existence of miners, Torbern counters: "If the blind mole burrows by blind instinct, it may be that the eyes of man acquire more penetrating sight in the deepest depths of the earth, until they can recognize in the wonderful stones they find a reflection of that which is hidden above the clouds." Elis's "ego" is captive audience to Torbern's conjuration of the wonders of the deep, as though he had already gone below with him, as though he had already identified with this underworld position. Then he has a dream. He can see right through the ocean, now a mineral mass and crystalline floor or block; above is a black shiny stone ceiling sealing off the horizon. Flowers of metal rise out of this ground. Beautiful maidens are on display, whose hearts break open by the roots growing up toward the glassy surface. Burning desire drives him down to the mine maidens. The older miner reappears, monumentalizing all-metallic on the spot, while lightning flashes on the stern face of the Queen. Elis's desire, no longer dead, is dread and alive. He sees the stars, the outside world, through a crack in the stone roof. Then he hears his mother's voice. It looks like he can see her up along the crack of sky in the crypt ceiling. But it is a living young woman after all who reaches down for Elis's hand (in marriage). Elis demands to be allowed to join her. He proclaims that he still belongs to the upper realm. But Torbern warns Elis to remain faithful to the Queen. Elis looks again upon her face and feels his ego flow out into the gleaming stone. He wakes up screaming.

Two thoughts now keep double-crossing his mind: on the one hand he just really misses his mother, on the other, which is the hand to be given in marriage, he wishes to run into that barmaid again. Thus, he sets the substitution of women going down or out the crack in the crypt lid. But in the mode of "The Sandman," Elis at the same time fears that it will not be the barmaid turning the corner but, in her place, the uncanny trickster, Torbern. He dreads that corner and encounter but at the same time desires only to hear more and more about the underworld. Elis departs, more or less on automatic, for Falun.

Like the double who upon closer inspection remains always in some other place, Torbern would appear, like an apparition, to accompany, guide, or shadow Elis's journey. Then Elis gets his first sight of miners crawling out of their hole in the ground just like worms. He flashes back to the yarn spun by sailors about fever dreams that afford an inside view of monstrous life-forms at the bottom of the sea. The seaworthy interpretation of such dreams was that the dreamer's own death was coming soon. Elis analogizes that viewing, attendance of one's own funeral, with his own X-ray vision of the mined earth. But then a drop scene interrupts the psychotic breakup of connections: a local celebration surrounds him, and in its tow he too enters the home of a father and his daughter Ulla. Elis recognizes her immediately as the dream maiden who had extended a helping hand to him down there in the crypt. Déjà vu helps extend the original substitution series by one, if not the same one. Elis stays put, alternating workdays down in the mine with free time spent with Ulla aboveground.

To get Elis to make his move and take his daughter's hand already, the father stages Ulla's engagement to another man, while at the same time asking Elis to continue living with him as his son. Elis slides from this Oedipal frame-up down into his desperate last-ditch effort of auto-recovery along the same lines that get him there, the cracks of psychotic breakdown. He summons Torbern, his pre-Oedipal father: he wants all the magic back, in his back, to see the maidens, metallic plants, and the Queen. The Oedipal father retrieves Elis from this underworld and gives the boy another break by interpreting the break down into the mine as just his way of shaking on it. Father pronounces Elis and Ulla to be joined in matrimony. But by now Elis just can't shake his underworld thoughts. "He felt himself split into two: the better half, his real being, descended with him into the bowels of the earth and reposed in the arms of the Queen, while in Falun all was dull and gloomy" (334).

Ulla's alarm prompts father's reassurance that their wedding night will be all the cure-all the doctor ordered for fantasies centering on the under zones of mother earth. But father, who would appear to hold the movie rights to the Hollywood version of the story, drove Elis just in test to make the break that now makes his delusional ties with the Queen the strongest they've ever been. Elis cannot but identify his authentic ego as residing with her. But he cannot give away their secret to Ulla. To utter the Queen's name would be to petrify it all as under the gaze and curse of Medusa. The thought alone transforms his beautiful vision into pure Hell. Finally, on the morning of the cure, Elis feels compelled to go down just once more to find the prize he saw so clearly in last night's dream vision and bring it back up as wedding present for his bride to be. Or not to be. Only by going down, one last time, will their inner beings coalesce with the wondrous branches growing right from the heart of the Queen at earth's center. But then—one can never be careful enough about what one wishes for—he gets buried alive.

In *Demon Wind* the spectral mother defeats the Devil father-and-son in the future space of generation and mourning. But the phantasm lines that draw out the conflict still confirm the sway or say of the primal Devil father. It all begins in prehistory: an American Gothic couple is destroyed inside and out by demon possession. In the modern day of the film, a couple drives to the husband's father's farm. Silence. Wife: "Since you've found your father, you haven't looked at me." "I need to have answers about who I am."

He enters the house. The setting is just as it was in prehistory. But there's a blackened corpse lying over there and one cracked medallion. "It's my grandmother." The writing's on the wall. One of the women starts reading it out loud. The spell is cast. It's shake and quake time. All kinds of weather or not they're prepared for it. Children in old-timey outfits walk in out of the fog. They steal away with the woman they abduct. A burning doll is all that remains in her place. But the couple therapy isn't over. The partner's ears burn, baby doll, burn. "You lied to me." That's the last we ever hear of the missing woman.

The son on a mission finds his grandmother's diary. In it she warns future kin against the evil coming through her. She gives instructions on how to kill the son of Satan. The great-grandfather built the farm. He was a follower of Father Enders. But Enders turned toward Satan. He tried to raise him or his son. Three children were sacrificed. But the congregation went up in smoke.

The son wakes up—they're all still there, in this together, but then on double take he sees that they're really zombies. Now son is back with Dad committing suicide. But the father takes a break to attack his son. "It won't work. I'm not afraid. We're alive, you're dead." The last spell in this father's mother's diary lights his pyre.

Fifty years later the corpse is found (whose corpse?), and it is perfectly preserved: young man looking like he's only sleeping. An old woman arrives right on schedule. She comes to the mines every Feast of St. John, the day that was to be and was never to be her wedding day. It's Ulla, who got this reunion schedule back then from Torbern as consolation prize. And she alone recognizes the mummified corpse: it's Elis who's back, forever young. Old Ulla embraces her undead betrothed, dies on him, their consummation now complete. She is no longer a living woman, no longer the killer substitute. But she was around long enough to mourn for the two of them, for what was bigger than both of them. Now Elis's exquisite corpse can be all it can be, just dust.

Elis's dead siblings were last seen in the prehistory of Hoffmann's story, in the finish line given any rivals for Elis's solo bonding with mother. His doubling of the father's departure would then figure as punishment for the wish for merger with mother and for murder of all rivals, with the father trailing in reverse, that is, holding up his ending at the front of the line. And then the story proper begins, over the doubling and dividing body of the lost mother. But the double-header Oedipal plot lies between the mother and the barmaid. Torbern and the Queen, the two underworld figures, come from behind the mother's death by way of another transmission.

Like Nathanael in "The Sandman," Elis is not a suitable candidate for contractual relations with the Devil. He's haunted by a loss that won't admit substitution without serious complications or conflict. The pull of the underworld of loss preservation isn't greater than the push up to the outer rim of substitution that even had the living mother's (mixed) blessing. Torbern, as demonic figure, is accordingly interchangeable with the Queen, the pre-Oedipal mother, the one and only with whom we reunite in regression when we are at a loss that can't bear or stand replacing. Because he cannot enter the underworld on the Devil's terms, because service to the Devil does not replace his sorrow or Sloth at the start of the story, Elis must remain in one of two states: undying submission to the underworld queen or investment of the riches of the deep in coupling with Ulla up above (in love). Both sides are linked but cannot be superimposed one onto the other.

The melancholic side has another side or crypt wall that's even harder to situate. First Elis needed his mother alive at a long distance in order to found the economy of homecoming in which his siblings, lost in the war zone, were stowaway, linked to but separated from the mother who couldn't accept their absence. The father's death must also be unacknowledged. Thus, Elis could replace his father in returning from and narrating his voyages and dropping the profits in his mother's lap. With mother gone, Elis hits bottom: Torbern and the Queen await him in the vast artificial world of mining, crowded with treasure and signs that extend the familiar frame of reference to the skies and beyond. In the end Elis becomes the mine's treasure: unidentified he is interchangeable with his missing brothers. But Ulla, still alive, brings mourning to bear—with the Oedipal father's vengeance—upon the crowded unburial plot. The shiny preserved body turns back around into waste matter, the excremental production that long time ago took over where reproduction or substitution was left off.

The disconnection is all that remains, the disconnection between the unchanged, unmourned, unmournable figure, a kind of para clone discharged from the underworld, and the woman from the world above, the world of living on, an old woman who could have been the substitute, who could have reproduced a line of substitution, but that's all in the past. Present tense: she still can mourn (and die). All of the above transpires with just a few adjustments (the protagonist is rejuvenated rather than mummified, the enabler is the Devil rather than another uncanny or demonic underworld figure) within the relationship commemorated in *Damn Yankees:* "Goodbye old girl."

The demonic compact is refused over and again in the literature that took its confirmation or reservation from the Falun mining story—because the candidates or clients prove inhibited, stuck on some loss in the past, a lost love, prove neurotic to psychotic or, in other words, haunted. But the demonic proves to be, just the same, an unstoppable force. It creates the scene of disconnection or death cult at which living mourning but no future generation living on is in attendance. In Hoffmann's "The Sandman" (as in Freud's "The 'Uncanny'"), protagonist Nathanael's efforts to couplify and substitute are repeatedly disrupted by the demonic Sandman, the evil father, who, up in the Oedipal zone, castrates Nathanael. The repetition compulsion that Freud links to the death drive and to the figure of the Sandman is called uncanny. In *Beyond the Pleasure Principle* Freud calls this uncanny convergence of repetition and death drive simply demonic. It is in the literary genre of near-missing relations with the Devil that the demonic as principle or drive nevertheless fires up.

NOTEBOOK NINETEEN

In *Sometimes They Come Back... for More* two MPs are dropped into Ice Station Erebus: officially it is a research facility, "unofficially it's an illegal mining operation courtesy of the Pentagon." The day before, one of the engineers "went postal." They must find survivors, arrest the mad man, and secure the facility. When they stumble across their first corpse outside in the deep freeze—it's the commanding officer—we also see in place of the dead man a woman's naked body from a different time zone (the light and the colors are completely different from the icy desolation of the station grounds) in the split second set aside for flashback, phantasm, or some spell or warp. Back inside, the two MPs find a survivor, the medical orderly, but first they must negotiate a peace because she is so terrified that it may be Schilling, the mad killer, coming for her. When the MPs look at their next corpse, we see that it is his not her flashback: now he sees naked women that he once buried in that other time zone. There he is, the second survivor, Shebanski, an engineer, who wants out of there right away. But they were dropped in; the transport couldn't land because of the storm. But then they need to radio for help right away. He wants "to get the Hell out of this iceberg": "If you guys are waiting for Hell to freeze over, you're a little bit late." She-MP says nobody else is going to die, none of the four. Loud rattling sounds coming from the roof unsettle them at night. But nothing could survive out and up there. "Nothing living." The mine was shut down because of noxious fumes, sulfur buildup, but Schilling went down there anyway. Then he returned with a knife and started his chopping spree. The second corpse the MPs looked at is gone. She-MP hears someone calling her name. Then she's gone and dead and then gone again. In the meantime the radio has been trashed. Then they find what looks like another corpse in deep freeze. While the doctor examines this one, he has a jump-started and jolting recovery. But then he only has words of warning: "He's coming. You can't stop him. The dead will walk. Destroy this place." Shebanski concludes: "The bottom line is we're all fucked." Inserted foreign-body style, like his flashbacks (and there's been one more of those too, with women dancing, writhing orgiastically), He-MP finds an engagement ring: when he examines it, there's a date, could it be 1916? He hears someone greet him, "Hello little brother. Have you seen Mary?" When She-MP's corpse is missing, he flashes back to a funeral pyre. They go into Schilling's room. Someone has been in there. A Satanic star or pentacle has been drawn across the map on the wall. What are the coordinates that are being linked? Birthplaces? Now he tells us, that is, He-MP tells the doctor: "Schilling is my half brother." They were in the war together, they lived like animals, but he met a nurse named Mary; his half brother took her from him. The souvenirs identify the war as World War I. He-MP wants to flush Schilling out of the mine, taking it level by level. The engineer is supposed to accompany him, but he builds a mechanical seeing-eye device instead that tours the mine and transmits what there is to see to their surveillance monitor. The tour of the mine looks a lot like those miniature video tours of intestinal tracts on the lookout for suspicious cell activity. At the bottom of the mine they see an altar, another pentacle, then they see Schilling and the corpse of She-MP. He-MP says the group of three needs "to stick together," like the multicellular alternative to the unicellular force that is with Schilling and the dead. After the zombies attack, He-MP discovers that Shebanski was Schilling's plant, his undercover medium, and shoots him dead (again). It's just the two now, the couple by elimination. But there's also the couple of brothers that overlaps with the survivor couple. The doctor is getting nervous about Schilling's powers. If Schilling is a demon, then "who are you?" "I don't even know." The book titled *Raising Demons* that the two found in Schilling's room spells it out. "If a demon can complete a circle of eight on a certain day that comes along every thousand years, then Satan can be raised. Six human beings, the demon, and one of his own blood." He-MP must be a demon too. But he tells her: "I need you not to be afraid of me." Soon the doctor is gone, too. He-MP goes to the altar and tells Schilling to let her go. "Don't tell me you're still mad about what's her name, that was eighty years ago." "Her name was Mary. I worshipped you and followed you for a thousand years." "We were brought into the world for one purpose, to bring about his return." If the Devil father doesn't return, then their demonic timeline will come to an end too. Schilling is able to set a spell on his brother. As He-MP is about to sacrifice the doctor, she says: "I'm not afraid of you, Sam. I love you." In the end it's Schilling who gets skewered. Mary makes a silent but smiling ghost appearance. It was her engagement ring. He gives it to the substitute. Mary vanishes.

The series of films this one concludes begins, in *Sometimes They Come Back*, with a story of haunting and unfinished business that can be put to rest when the traumatic incident is repeated with ghostly killer bullies, but with a difference that the grown-up younger brother and survivor of the brother killed by the gang many years ago is now able to make. The result is that the bond of haunting with his murdered brother can be given up. Now he can renew his vows with wife and son and live with them in the present. This "giving up" is made easier by the promise of reunion in heaven. Unavenged, the brother's ghost was in limbo. Now he is free to join his parents. One day they'll all be together again. It makes it easier when you can skip the pain and spookiness of mourning. That's why, in *Sometimes They Come Back... Again*, the bully types are Satanists who come back as demons. Back then they sacrificed a little boy's eighteen-year-old sister. He witnessed the murder, and as he withdrew—they saw that they had to take care of him, too—he accidentally knocked cables into the puddle in which the gang was standing and then stir-fried. This primal scene is played out in what looks like the entrance of a mine but is called a train tunnel that is no longer in use. The return of the past in the first film was set on a train tunnel no longer in use but that in the past was functional: a train crashed into the car with the bully gang inside, and thus the brother's murderers also died. Now they're back (again), and they are demons who are after the grown-up boy's eighteen-year-old daughter, just the virgin they need for the rites of their "cabbalistic sabbath." The leader brings back each gang member with yet another murder. But how did the leader come back? A priest instructs the father with a virgin daughter to protect: "A poorly extinguished fire is easily re-lit." The gang members are "evil incarnate. All that was human has been sucked out of them." The demon leader must be desecrated. They find something that is required, an amulet the demon has touched, that the dead sister touched, and that the daughter touched, too. But the father must also sacrifice one digit to send the demon gang back to Hell. He cuts it off. Then one day he's listening to a client (the brother/father is a therapist), and for a split second the client looks just like the demon ringleader. In the three films, then, we enter the Devil fiction only with the first sequel, when the dead come back, but again. Crimes in the past were decked out as Satanic rites. Unfinished business, like poorly extinguished light, brings them back as demons. In the third film, we have two sons of Satan who are divided in their allegiance to the Devil father over the dead body of a woman. One brother is haunted, a perpetual mourner, and thus resistant to the purpose of his and his brother's existence. In the end, with the Satanic side of his life of living on gone, he at the same time puts to rest the woman, the outside chance of substitution, who was sacrificed by the evil brother or double, and forms a substitutive couple with the woman he this time succeeds in rescuing from the evil double Hell-bent on raising the Devil father.

The accident happened, because it recurred. A young miner, Matts Israelsson was his name, disappeared in any one of the cave-ins going down in the copper mines of Falun, Sweden, between 1676 and 1677. He went down alone that night, they say, to light his pyre. To his fellow miners he was known as Fet Matts, presumably because he had a weight problem, or perhaps because he was just the type to sweat a lot, like Hamlet. He definitely had a problem waiting. His disappearance, which in turn disappeared, never getting a real date, began to be reversed when, in 1719, a young man's corpse was discovered during renovations or expansions of the same old mine, which was by then so steady-state, production-wise, that the company was going for more, and more accessible, infrastructures of profit and savings. It was a connecting tunnel that yielded the spectacular disconnection of a loss come back, intact and undisclosed. While the body the miners discovered still marked the spot of accident, what with legs severed but lying by, as parts with their whole, nevertheless this unidentified object was, science fiction aside or inside, perfectly preserved. Even the tobacco in the dead miner's matching container was decay-proofed by the mineral solution that treated the whole corpus to mummification.

It was also a flashback to the inaugural image for the introduction of discourse into mining. Preceded only by a long itemized dedication, the opening line of Georgius Agricola's *De Re Metallica* calls the metallic arts to assembly lines of part for whole: "Most illustrious Princes, often have I considered the metallic arts as a whole, as Moderatus Columella considered the agricultural arts, just as if I had been considering the whole of the human body; and when I had perceived the various parts of the subject, like so many members of the body, I became afraid that I might die before I should understand its full extent, much less before I could immortalize it in writing." Fear of dying and the bodybuilding of a discourse out of parts and compartments animate mining for a monstrous parting. Just add a century or so and we have the mummified body. The "and" Agricola dealt us with his representation of the science of mining in terms of his relationship to his own corpus or body, dead or alive, enters the stage left without recognition or identification. Because the body without context did acquire a witness, and thus made the primal scene, when an old woman arrived just in time to identify the preserved corpse as that of her fiancé, lost forty-three years ago. What cuts in right here is the scene, with names and places forgotten or displaced to protect the innocent of mourning. Once the forget-together was in place, it could also skip a context, even a country. This scene became the primal opening of a certain German Romantic reception, an opening that belonged, between those lines, to a death cult inside our mass media culture, our state of ongoing technologization.

The skipped beat, which Sweden had to hand to Germany to protect, project, and police, was picked up in 1808 by Gotthilf Heinrich von Schubert who recorded the incident in his *Views from the Dark Side of the Natural Sciences*. The volume was turned up full blast, and the reception of the mining scene finely tuned, throughout the movement or momentum that was German Romanticism. While Wagner too planned an opera around the synapse of this connection, but only in synopsis form, Johann Peter Hebel, Achim von Arnim, Friedrich Hebbel, and Hugo von Hoffmannstahl worked it on out and built it into the corpus of a reception. Here is von Schubert's opening cover. It is the scene as it gets encapsulated right at the opening of a reception, and right before it is swallowed whole, on eternally postponed time release:

In like manner, that remarkable corpse, the one described by Hülpher, Cronstedt, and the Swedish scholarly journals, also decayed into a sort of ash, even after they had placed him, to all appearances transformed into stone, under glass to keep out the influence of air. This former miner was found in the Swedish iron mines in Falun in the course of tunneling a connection between two shafts. The corpse, saturated in sulfuric acid, was at first soft and supple, but then petrified through contact with the air. Fifty years he had been lying low at a depth of three hundred meters in that acid water and no one would have recognized the unchanged facial features of the youth who died in the accident, no one knew the time he had passed in the shaft, since the local records and legends concerning all accidents were unclear, if it had not been for the recognition of his once beloved features, recollected and preserved within an old faithful love. For as the people crowded around the salvaged corpse to gaze on his unknown still-youthful physiognomy, there arrived a little old gray-haired mother, on crutches, who sank to her knees with tears in her eyes for the beloved dead man who had been her betrothed, and she praised the hour that had granted her, right at the portals of her own grave, such a reunion, and the people watched with amazement as this odd couple was reunited, the one who retained his youthful appearance even in death and down in the deep crypt, and the other one who had preserved the youthful love inside her faded and decaying body. The group looked on as this fifty-year silver wedding anniversary transpired between the still youthful bridegroom stiff and cold, and the old and gray bride, so full of warm love. (215–16)

So who's mourning now? Who's dying now? This was the beginning of the Romantic safe text of disconnection in place of sexual union, a text or corpus kept safe, in the safelike preserve of a mineshaft.

Follow the directions Wagner gives for the opening scene of the second act of his unrealized "Mines of Falun" opera. He places the mine right where his opera would be, once he hid the orchestra and turned off the house lights: inside the electric-theatrical prehistory of cinema.

The theater represents the depths of a completely unilluminated shaft. A weak light beam approaches from above.... The back wall of granite brightens gradually and seems to draw back. A growing bluish light spreads everywhere. Wonderful crystal formations reveal themselves to our gaze. They take on gradually the forms of flowers and trees. Gleaming precious stones glow on them; other crystal formations take the shape of beautiful maidens, intermingling as in a dance. Surrounded by a curious glow there sits in their midst a beautiful woman, preciously adorned. One hears from up above Ulla's voice: Elis, Elis, I am yours! In an instant the shaft is transformed back into its earlier state.

In his version of the Falun story, Wagner adds a buddy double, Joens, to complicate Elis's courtship of Ulla. Each doesn't know what the other thinks he knows. Joens declares his interest in Ulla, which Elis interprets as praise for his own good choice. When Ulla bisects the cross fire of misunderstood wooing, she takes Joens's suit to be on Elis's behalf. Ulla's father caps it all by accepting Joens's proposal. Elis is shafted. But Wagner doesn't make the jump cut to the parting shot: the exhumation of Elis's preserved corpse fifty years later and aged Ulla's identification with the undead died young.

Two years prior to the date of his Falun manuscript, Wagner opened a feuilleton review of virtuoso tenors within the debris of mining allegories of our relationship to the "genius of music." This jewel lies at the bottom of the deepest recess beneath the condemned site of countless lost civilizations. "Superhuman" figures could see through the ruinscape and gaze upon the treasure's gleam. But when they tried to clear away the monument rubble from the distant jewel, the "inert mass" didn't budge. Centuries later someone has a plan to proceed in the well-tried manner of mining to extract the treasure. Tunnels and shafts penetrate the "bowels of the earth" where they interconnect via countless passage-ways until, in the resulting labyrinth, the treasure is lost. One day the miner from Salzburg (the miracle minor Mozart) arrives at the aban-doned and crumbling mine. While studying its useless layout, he glimpses the jewel through a fissure. At once he oversees the whole labyrinth and recognizes the pathway leading to the miraculous stone. Soon he stands before the "divine Talisman." (In *The Devil Rides Out*, the novel, the "Talisman of Set" that all the fighting is about is Osiris's penis, the miss-ing link between the living and the resurrected, between the Devil and the undead.)

While a kind of contact high around the miner's discovery is enjoyed by one and all, far and wide, the miner himself disappears. Then the miner from Bonn arrives in search of the Salzburg colleague. As soon as he picks up a clue to follow out, he sees the jewel and is blinded at sight. Doubling over with vertigo, he topples into the abyss. The shafts col-lapse upon him. Roll over Beethoven, no one's seen you no more. My parenthetical free association above reserved a place on the connection to make with Wagner's version of falling for Falun. By force of implica-tion and elimination, the exquisite corpse in mineral safe deposit is the prized musical genius or spirit, which, according to Wagner's earlier allegory, is always in some other place.

Emil Franz Lorenz argues that Wagner—like Hugo von Hoffmans-thal in his version of the Falun story—was making a formally justified decision in choosing one out of the two Falun stories that Hoffmann, in conjoining them, had proved to be distinct. One story (the prehistory) ends with Elis's live burial in the mines that double as his unconscious. The delayed epilogue, which the epigones skip, is another story entirely.

But I would shake down Hoffmann's stereo delivery as follows: the first story of unmourning is sealed in the second story's disconnection between mummy and mortal bride, a block that endures for as long as it takes to fill without exceeding a lifetime or some other span of remembrance. What thus dangles at the end is the incorporation that Hoffmann's narrative as the retelling of Novalis's work of mourning cannot expel from its interior (or anterior). While J. P. Hebel and Achim von Arnim had done some prep work in demarcating a prehistory of the Falun incident, Lorenz underscores the close proximity between Hoffmann's introduction of Elis's cathexis of mining as well as his extension of this diversion to include the outside chance of substitution or marriage and Novalis's earlier affirmations of the work of mining in his narratives *The Apprentices of Sais* and *Heinrich von Ofterdingen*. There is also, however, Lorenz quickly points out, an overriding difference between the corpora that the psychopathologization of the mining pursuit in Hoffmann's "The Mines of Falun" brings out. The mental status of mining in Novalis's two narratives remains within the healthy association between scientific pursuits and curiosity in childhood (= childhood sexual research). Hoffmann restores hymnic night or nothingness to the narratives of substitution that followed Novalis's bouncing bio from dead Sophie to replacement Julie. After Sophie's death Novalis doubled her departure by moving to Freiberg, where he enrolled in the study of mining sciences. But in the course of this dedication he found substitution with Julie, the daughter of local mining superintendent *(Bergrat)* von Charpentier.

In *The Apprentices of Sais* the story of Hyacinth is one of working through the turbulence around his maternal imago set off by a traveler who, passing through, set a spell on Hyacinth. He tells tall tales for three days with time out between the legs of his journeys to "crawl down deep mining shafts" with the boy. The boy now broods in isolation from his parents and girlfriend. An old woman prescribes for Hyacinth a round-trip away from his impasse and then back to himself. He hopes to find "the mother of all things, the veiled virgin." He does reach the sacred residence of Isis. Since only in his dreams can he enter, he takes a doze or dose. As he passes through the splendor of her digs, he senses his last earthly impulses evaporate. But when he lifts the veil of the heavenly virgin, he finds his girlfriend underneath it all. *Heinrich von Ofterdingen* picks up where the Hyacinth fairy tale or daydream fantasy was to be continued, but as the work of *Bildung* that carries over the fantasy figments or fulfillments into the registers of waking narrative or life. Hoffmann brings up the arrears or the *After* ("asshole"), which was originally working part of the title: "Heinrich von Afterdingen."

From Ernst Bloch and Ernst Mach to Friedrich Kittler, readers of Ernst Kapp's premier theorization of our prosthetic relations with technology try to screw it off around the absence of any fit with or model for the wheel. Marshall McLuhan oddly advances the wheel as his first example of the gadget-loving prosthesis. But more frequently it is judged a stretch to evoke behind the wheel the body's orbit with limbs outstretched, whether as Dürer's proportional gridlock on the human body in motion or as the cartwheels children turn. But thanks to Hoffmann rereading Novalis revising himself, we can see that "O" can replace and conceal the asshole. Anal projection is, after all, on one bottom line with the primal sensorium of incorporation.

The story of the underworld accident in Falun—which gives us two chances, the one that gives us pause, the preservation of the hiding of loss, the other that gives us the outside chance of ultimate mourning or unmourning through the big reunion that's also a major disconnection—is the legend to the map of our mass media Sensurround.

It proves possible, according to Allan Sekula, to extract the photo-archival history of mining's documentation, and with it, a certain genealogy of media, already between the lines of Agricola's sixteenth-century treatise on mining. While the illustrations in Agricola's study are more models than plans, their enabling conditions are the same: "Thus, two fifteenth century inventions, printing and perspective, provided necessary technical and conceptual groundwork for sixteenth century illustrated books on anatomy and engineering" (205). Mining was thus, along with anatomy, the first technical-scientific enterprise to make it into pictures. Pictures are always seconding the motion of the acceleration they represent as faster means of knowing, both at a glance and from above. Agricola's introduction of cutaway views of mining, in particular, begins "to manifest an ontological similarity to mining itself. The eye digs away from the side, a metaphorical miner cutting at right angles to the actual diggings being pictured. The line of sight intersects the plane of physical toil. A hierarchy of labor and knowledge is charted here, at this intersection of 'digging' and 'looking': the mole-like work of the diggers is subordinated to command from above and beyond the mine.... Quite literally, the line of sight assumes the privileged status of supervision" (209).

In Shakespeare's *Hamlet* the ghost is also "old mole," while the grave digger, hailed as the master builder, puns around Hamlet's question about the current dig's intended content. The grave digger says the grave is "mine" because he's digging it. The trouble with the corpse (Polonius's body, for example) is the trouble with this grave. Someone is always left over, missing, in the one-to-one correspondences between dead bodies and their proper interment. The rejoinder or reply in *Hamlet* is called by Hamlet, in the series of his cagey dealing with the spies, Rosencrantz and Guildenstern, "replication." One such rejoinder, in the context of what's mine, is elaborated by Hamlet as he plots the demise of the two spies (R and G): "For 'tis the sport to have the engineer / Hoist with his own petard; and it shall go hard / But I will delve one yard below their mines, / And blow them at the moon." And Hamlet closes the parenthesis by exiting with Polonius's corpse.

Swedish tourism to this day recognizes the story of Fet Matts only as oddity or anecdote, a sideshow in the natural history of science, in a prehistory that belongs in the home Swede home. Sentimentality, even in its German-theoretical setting, must find its balance over against acts of violence it in every sense contains. Thus, German Romanticism was there when Mercedes test-drove models for safety measure using dead children as the proxy drivers. Indeed, those corpses probably did give a better indication than just another dummy of what a driver might be expected to suffer or survive in a crash. It's possible to take off the kid love when techno precision rises to life or death stakes.

The Swedish history of the Falun reunion didn't stop dead in the tracks of the Romance. It was always all about this body that the authorities kept aboveground to display as a "curiosity." And the ex marking the spot of witness, who figures so identificatorily in the German reception, was a quite forgettable participant in the line of her ex's relic production: she didn't have any wait problems, but was quite remarried and remuneratable when the trouble began with a corpse that primal tourism just couldn't bury. She gladly made the fast change from mourner to beneficiary when she took money for the claimed body's unburial and display. The mummy miner was a good sideshow to supplement what was left of the attraction, by 1719, for example, of what had been mines. In the case of Sweden, tourism (and in the first place tourism of the Falun mines) was introduced to pick up the slack or slag where mining had started to go unproductive.

The mines became the big part of the grand tour of Sweden. A saying from the seventeenth century can be found recycled on brochures published by the Dalaran County Tourist Office: "He who has not seen Stora Kopparberget has not seen Sweden" (3). When Matts Israelsson disappeared, the mines were still on a peak: the mining company today known simply as Stora, which was founded in 1288 as the first stockholding company in world history, was still in the seventeenth century, the century of Sweden's successful bids for world power, the largest supplier of copper on the planet. But the supplies started bottoming out around the time the preserved body was found. The history of these copper mines runs the same course as that of Sweden's imperial aspirations. By 1719 Sweden had been forced to withdraw from the running for world power. The retrenchment of these aspirations within the new industries of culture belonged equally, say, to the exploits of the Actor King and to the ongoing exploitation of the mines for tour appeal.

Linné visited the mines in Falun in 1734. As a whole he characterized the attraction as "Sweden's greatest wonder, but as terrible as Hell itself" (Dalaran County Tourist Office brochure, 4). Linné also attended the viewing of the preserved corpse, which he saw as not so much "petrified" as "encrusted or transformed into a stalactite." When it was first found, it was completely supple still, like the body of miracles belonging to some saint. Five years before Linné took the tour, the body, which had started to harden and decay around the edges, was restored and wired in place. By 1749 it was determined that the corpse, being no longer presentable, should finally be buried. But the trouble with Matts was that several exhumations followed. In 1860 the remains were up in the church attic. To date, 1930 was the date of his last burial. Follow the bouncing corpse: a certain history of Sweden gets inscribed with each advance or placement of the eternally decaying body now inside, now outside a place of proper burial.

In 1992 the mines ceased copper production and became the exclusive preserve of tourism. Stora does, however, continue to supply the pigment used in the blood-red paint, the local color, *Falun Rödfärg*, still applied with the age-old guarantee of its preservative effect on the wood it stains.

Friedrich Jürgenson, an artist displaced by the events of World War II from Russia to Sweden, discovered the Voice Phenomenon: the dead can rearrange white noise, the static between radio stations, even the sounds of regular recordings into communications from the beyond that only the tape recorder can register. Just let the tape recorder run, then play it back, over and over again: the record that speaks for itself makes contact with the deceased.

For Jürgenson his first contacts were all with the World War II dead, who were now all in it together: Churchill, Hitler, Göring, a Russian Jewess. "I followed attentively the tape recording, to the point where the woman's voice with a Jewish accent announced Hitler's presence. . . . 'Heil! [. . .] that was Hitler, he isn't ashamed of himself!' And then followed those strange words, which were added by the woman with a changed and disconcerted voice: 'That was Hitler—he sees you! I tell you, Hitler—he loves me!'" Death is the greatest healer. Jürgenson in Sweden became the talk show host with the most ghosts from World

War II. "Wasn't it remarkable that Hitler and Göring, these two fundamentally different figures, to whom fate granted the leading roles in
apocalypse number two, should be making themselves known to me on
the tapes. Hitler conducted strange monologues, and Göring sang happily on my tapes" (89–90). Next page, next chapter Jürgenson discovers
that it's easy to get stuck in the "suburb," as the dead named this outer-
lying region, where the victims and perpetrators of psychologies of
resentment and hatred, whether the criminals or the scapegoats, are
sent first. Behind the tape recorder and radio connection with the voices
of the dead, the living dead inhabit caves and caverns in the suburban
underworld.

On the external side of Jürgenson's own listening, there's an excavation project in Pompeii, which he attends as filmmaker documenting
the archaeological process for Swedish TV, which stops and starts in
alternation with his accidental discovery of the Voice Phenomenon. The
Pompeii project is interrupted at first, but then, with one last time-out
for its deferral on the better behalf of connecting with a friend's murdered daughter, is really happening, under way by the end of the book.
"Below me the not yet unearthed section of Pompeii dozes on. Amazing,
that it was right here that seven years ago I was to begin the excavation
of a house, 'Casa Svedese.' Instead I penetrated the darkness of an unknown grotto of a spiritual nature. Today, however, now that the 'bridge'
is already pretty much firmly established, I have returned to the same
starting point" (248–49).

The dead deposited in the passageways of the Pompeii-like underworld are the only unfortunate ones: without being able to rise on their
own to consciousness, they are mired in repetition of trauma. Jürgenson is thus enjoined by the other side to help awaken these dead and
thus break the recycling of the pain. That's why the healing of the World
War II era rose first to the top of the agenda.

The cinema of Ingmar Bergman goes as deep as his proper name:
somewhere between German and Swedish, the Bergman could be another name for "miner." In 1960 he made a comedy for a change of his
art prefaced and based on the folksy adage that "a chaste woman is a

stye in the Devil's eye." In *The Devil's Eye,* the Devil (who surrounds himself with Sadean libertines as ministers) is troubled by the young Swedish virgin who wants to save it up for the wedding night. He releases Don Juan from Hell to attend to the maiden's seduction. She relents only out of pity; Don Juan in turn will not accept charity sex. For the first time he falls in love with the girl who cares less; for failing the mission, his extra punishment is to listen to a demon's report of the maiden's deflowering on the night that's the night. But because she tells her man that she has never kissed another before him, her lie remedies the Devil's stye. When Don Juan takes his usual punishment in Hell, it consists of the repetitive seduction of former flames he can never put out in the living series of his consummations.

The Marquis de Sade also took the tour through the "model of the North," but in 1775: "After I had spent some three months in Stockholm, my curiosity was directed toward those famous mines about which I had read so much and wherein I imagined I might encounter some adventures similar to those related by the Abbé Prévost in the first volume of his anecdotes" (726).

Sade visits the Taperg mine, which he contemplates as emptied out by just about everyone's indebtedness to the English. This "subterranean" monument to the "avarice of a handful of men . . . capable of dominating so many others," must resemble the catacombs, which he recently toured in Rome and Naples. But: "I was mistaken. Though situated far deeper in the bowels of the earth, I was to discover there a solitude less terrifying." In the bowels there is a less terrifying solitude. What's more, the bowels are habitable, containing in the case of this mine a "veritable subterranean city: streets, houses, churches, inns, much hustle and bustle, work being performed, police, judges: in short, everything the most civilized city of Europe might offer" (727). In the spot of civilization he is in, deep in the bowels, Sade dines on "a kind of Swedish bread commonly used in rural areas made of the bark of pine and birch trees, mixed with straw, some wild roots, and kneaded together with oatmeal. Does one need anything more to satisfy one's veritable needs?" The tour of the mine is set up as preamble to the story of lovers betrayed, to the story's living ending in the punishment of the guilty party inside these mines, an ending overtaken by a still unassuaged avenger penetrating even "the bowels of the earth" to pursue the prisoner. But the filler or background that's on tour has already gone the full circuit of Sade's discourse within a communion feast in the bowels of the earth, one that will surely make him feel his digestive tract, from his bowels on out. It's the feeling, the satisfaction of one's veritable needs, that proves to be for him always a less terrifying sensation than all the many others that must have terrorized him.

> The Ratman case is a tight fit in these close quarters. In *Aberrations of Mourning* I do Ratman. But as placeholder for this reading or referral, consider *Ghoulies II*. They're back, demons from outer space. Precautions weren't taken, warnings heeded: now the mob of visitors to the circus want to kill the owner. He overhears such sentiments. He wears his sunglasses at night. He goes to the restroom wagon in the mobile staff camp. He needs to sit this one out. There's a ghoulie in the toilet. He pulls down his pants and centers his hole over the hole. Pause. SCREAM. Goal! To contain the alien demons, the good guys use a grimoire to conjure one colossal demon belonging to the bowels of the earth from which it emerges to eat the space critters. But how are they going to stop this demon? They feed it a makeshift explosive device dressed up like a space fritter. The snack blows it up and back down the crack in the earth.

> In *Little Nicky* every day in Hell begins with the Devil father shoving the biggest pineapple up Hitler's ass (who is dressed as housemaid, in his premarital mother's abject position as maid in Austria tending and cheating on the first wife of Hitler's Dad).

The labyrinthine underworlds we go down or out represent, Freud advised in his 1932 lecture on the "Revision of the Theory of Dreams," "anal birth" (*SE* 22: 25). A few years later, the Disney revision made Snow White work like a cleanser. By the time of its release, World War II had shut down the international circulation of all Hollywood productions, even when they were associated with Disney, whose good German name, according to Nazi propaganda, was really Distler. It was an agonizing time of transition for Nazi Germany. *Snow White and the Seven Dwarfs,* so long awaited by the other mass culture of Mickey Mouse, was the first Disney production to be held up at the border, because now the war was on. German newspapers gave long reviews of the Disney masterpiece being shown in London. Only the leadership could watch the film in the archives in Berlin. Hitler had his own copy. It was his fave. Only the neutrality of Sweden, once reviews of London screenings were blacked out by the war's escalation, provided Central Europe with some kind of access to the world of Disney.

Both Snow White's sanctuary with the dwarfs and her home with stepmother bear deep down relations with mines, crypts, dungeons, tight spots of anality. While the dwarf miners dig the excremental underworld for shiny diamonds, Snow White, first thing, cleans up their filthy bachelor cottage. It takes her loss to recognize their loss: they must not have a mother, she concludes. Back in the castle, following another mirror brief, the stepmother descends into her crypt lab and dungeon space, which bears all the filth Snow White is trying to wash away in another place. The original plans for the film, carried out to the drawing and cel stage, included, inside the dungeon, the stepmother queen's capture and chaining up of Prince Charming placed or splayed agonizingly on S/M display. The shiny apple offered by the queen in her dirty aspect is toxic, an excremental bit that gets stuck in Snow White's throat. On the outside there's Snow White, all shiny in her glass coffin. On the inside there's a catch, a catch in her throat: the apple of her mother's eye. Only the princely substitute can shake loose the unmournable loss of her mother stuck fast on the intake. The queen, who doesn't just put on a disguise when she adopts the witch role, failed to fulfill her contractual obligation to offer up the fairest in the land as sacrifice to her mirror demon.

Hearst's mother had built a "Wagnerian" castle in northern California in 1902, which she named—almost as leitmotif passing through Ludwig II to Disney—Wintoon. When it burned down in 1930, Hearst didn't build another castle, though it did cross his mind. Instead he erected his own Wintoon up against the momentum of the Great Depression as a Bavarian village comprised of fairytale houses named after Cinderella and Sleeping Beauty, for example. Only for Snow White, however, does a cottage fit the story as home for miners. The paternal backing that came out of mines thus entered the foreground of collection.

NOTEBOOK TWENTY

She's in the bar (again) after the especially bad day. A shadowy figure buys her drinks and listens to her gripe for days. "If you'll just sign here and here." He shows where on the cocktail napkin. "What's that for?" "All your problems could be a thing of the past." There is a slight fee involved. "In the end I always collect." "I feel a lot better." That's what *The Contract* is all about.

The sales boy (who was on the hit list) gets butchered. Intercut with death-wish wife in sexual reunion with the husband she already death-wished away. She finds the napkin with the death wish list and then hears on the news that the clerk was murdered. Now she knows that she must stop the hit parade. She rushes to the home of the babysitter, who's already hung up on the closing garage door. The assassin beats her up: "Don't mess with the contract. Don't tell anyone." But she keeps on showing the list and telling what it means. "This is a fucking contract." But after she stops the contract Dad in its tracks, she goes back to the whine bar where the Devil waits to buy her one drink at a time.

Uncontainment, a more literal rending apart in English what is due to the German word for the "uncanny," *das Unheimliche*, drives the essay "The 'Uncanny'" into the missing fire sparked between the nonsuperimposable doubling of secret burial plots onto both the Oedipal plot and the other Freudian discourse, brand-new in the complex, of Dad certainty, the demonic, and Death Drive. When Freud makes a move to improve on Jentsch's pre-psychoanalytic understanding of the uncanny, he also addresses change in the range of the demonic concept. Pre-Freud, the psychological-philosophical lexicon associated the demonic with automatic and autonomous-seeming activity. Thus Olympia (what a doll!) would fit this old playbill as demonic figure and, by Jentsch's extension, as the source of uncanniness in the story. But, Freud corrects his precursor via the Hoffmann story Jentsch first summoned for support, what's so uncanny is the Sandman. This figure is uncanny because his doubling or returning has its dislocating and uncontaining effect in time. In place of the father function, there is the bogeyman, the enforcer of rules in childhood run amok—precisely because when the mother invokes the Sandman, she cannot contain her own overwhelming dread of this unDad figure.

At the same time, if we keep the pattern up front, rather than keeping it, as Nathaniel does, in the unconscious, we can observe that the father on the rebound is a figure of certainty whose returns run like contract. Whenever Nathaniel seeks consummation of love or passion, the Sandman is back to make the disconnection (which is also just another form of correction). "There is no question therefore of any intellectual uncertainty here... and yet this knowledge does not lessen the impression of uncanniness in the least degree" (*SE* 17: 230).

Freud addresses the corpus of Hoffmann as exemplifying "the uncanny in literature." The best example proves to be not "The Sandman" but instead *The Devil's Elixir*. Unfortunately the novel's story was too overcomplicated for case note summation or transcription. Hoffmann's *The Devil's Elixir* "contains a whole mass of themes to which one is tempted to ascribe the uncanny effect of the narrative" (*SE* 17: 233). A "Note" signed S. F. that appeared (the same year as the essay "The 'Uncanny'") under the rubric "Varia" in the *Internationale Zeitschrift für Psychoanalyse* cites Schönfeld's words of comfort for the deranged hero in *The Devil's Elixir* (a novel cited overall here for its wealth of "masterful descriptions of pathological mental states"):

> "And what do you get out of it? I mean out of the particular mental function which we call consciousness, and which is nothing but the confounded activity of a damned toll-collector—excise-man—deputy-chief customs officer, who has set up his infamous bureau in our top storey and who exclaims, whenever any goods try to get out: 'Hi! Hi!

Exports are prohibited...they must stay here...here, in this country....'" (*SE* 17: 233–34 n.1)

This readymade gives Freud's own work of analogy whereby he animated
certain formulations of psychic processes and relations the double
whammy. The "Note" thus assigns *The Devil's Elixir* to a place of horror
alongside Schreber's *Memoirs of My Nervous Illness* (and in contrast to
the series of works of interpretation to which *Oedipus Rex, Hamlet,* and
"The Sandman" belong) as one of those works in which psychoanalytic
knowledge can be found endopsychically recorded and stored to the letter (before the letter) of Freud's public, published words of formulation.
Another figure on the sideline in *The Devil's Elixirs* (Euphemie) comments internally on the endopsychic relations Hoffmann's work, beside
and inside itself, would enter after the fact with or within psychoanalysis:

> "It is a unique trait of the insane that they often appear to stand in a
> closer relation to the psyche and at the same time in their own inte-
> rior are more easily, albeit unconsciously, receptive to a stranger's psy-
> chic principle, and can often see that which we have hidden away inside
> us and express it in remarkable accord such that we are often gripped
> with uncanny dread by the terrible voice of a second ego." (78–79)

In his reading of "The Sandman" Freud drops a footnote of bio
confirmation: "Hoffmann was the child of an unhappy marriage. When
he was three years old, his father left his small family, and was never
united to them again" (*SE* 17: 232–33 n.1). This note of dis-pair bounces
back as the first sentence of the monk's narrative incorporated within
the editorial frame: his mother never disclosed to him under what conditions his father "lived in the world" (9). As in Schreber's *Memoirs,* according to Freud, it is by the light of the sun/son that the father is read
(in the son's head). In the novel a certain Schreberesque breakdown of
rays of light (applied not only as analogy for a spiritual stance) drives
(not only metaphorically) the narrative of heightened vision. "Without
bestowing on earthly existence a false value, they had to recognize in the
diverse internally-determined way of life of men the necessity of such a
refraction of light rays *[Strahlenbrechung]* of the spiritual principle, without which everything would have remained without color or shine" (20).

Back inside Freud's "Uncanny" footnote, on the rebound, we are given a more staggered, transference-timed account of the disintegration of "father" via the pairs of Sandman figures. Still we can sense the rush of Olympia as that against which the coupling with father should have offered inoculation.

> In the frightening scene in childhood, Coppelius, after sparing Nathaniel's eyes, had screwed off his arms and legs as an experiment; that is, he had worked on him as a mechanician would on a doll. This singular feature, which seems quite outside the picture of the Sandman, introduces a new castration equivalent; but it also points to the inner identity of Coppelius with his later counterpart, Spalanzani the mechanician, and prepares us for the interpretation of Olympia. This automatic doll can be nothing else than a materialization of Nathaniel's feminine attitude towards his father in his infancy.... Spalanzani's otherwise incomprehensible statement that the optician has stolen Nathaniel's eyes... so as to set them in the doll, now becomes significant as supplying evidence of the identity of Olympia and Nathaniel. Olympia is, as it were, a dissociated complex of Nathaniel's which confronts him as a person, and Nathaniel's enslavement to this complex is expressed in his senseless obsessive love for Olympia.

At this point Freud must interrupt the train of analysis, which would be speeding to a terminal of demonic doubling (in which coupling is interrupted in the name of a punitive father who's a sure thing), to accommodate the Olympia episode, which is the pre-Oedipal bottom line in Nathaniel's case, and which makes "The Sandman" an example of the psychotic sublime, of psycho horror, and of psy-fi occult relations inhabiting the rewinding and rewounding of techno narcissism: "We may with justice call love of this kind narcissistic, and we can understand why someone who has fallen victim to it should relinquish the real, external object of his love." Freud tries to fold the digression back inside as subsumable by the father complex: "The psychological truth of the situation in which the young man, fixated upon his father by his castration complex, becomes incapable of loving a woman, is amply proved by numerous analyses of patients whose story, though less fantastic, is hardly less tragic than that of the student Nathaniel." But the Olympia complex is one part that exceeds the whole of the father complex, which raised now to the Oedipal developmental power of castration anxiety, has also been pulled out of the double trouble with the pre-Oedipal father. Death wish management along the Oedipal lines of mourning as substitution (over the body of the lost father) has become, after the fact, the overriding theme (which really doesn't override much, the too much that has been admitted over Olympia's techno body).

Olympia is the dolly on which the recording of a machine history from camera obscura to cinema lets roll. But Jonathan Crary was right to argue for a discontinuity or station break in a reception of vision as lined up in assembly with camera obscura, laterna magica, photography, and film. Crary documents a sudden appreciation of the bio-psycho ungroundedness of vision in the nineteenth century that could be found among the lenses, telescopes, and other ocular devices Olympia's father presumably manufactures and sells. Devices like the stereoscope deliberately produced special effects by underscoring the gap between vision and perception. In the case of Turner, the bright and blind spots in eyesight that caught the backfire from the stare straight at the sun give a supplemental story of the advent of techno vision in the physical ecstasy and torture of beaming up into it. It is the nineteenth-century refiring up of the underlying passion in the first Masaccio crucifixion painting to set its site of suffering on our own mutation as 3-D bodies or subjects. This passion is excluded in the histories of the seeing-eye machine that mark, after the fact, our progress as going to the movies. The Crary move is not, however, a paradigm shift as pride in new historicism might require. But it illuminates an underworld in the genealogy of visual media in which *The Devil's Elixirs* can be found testing the self-evidence of visual certainty or uncertainty.

The editor of the monk's posthumous corpus calls on the reader somehow to share the setting of his own first reading of the manuscript in the church garden to suspend any defensive move to write off these memoirs as merely "the disorganized play of the heated imagination" (7). The guardians of the archive, for one, have a projected sense of the performative stakes: they advised him, upon showing him the manuscript pages, to set them on fire, interrupt their transmission, contain their doubling-on-contact contamination. As editor and guardian, there-fore, of literacy, the first I the reader meets in the book makes the intro-ductory offer, in exchange for giving credit to the remarkable visions of the monk contained herein, of the pleasure to be derived from "the mani-fold images of the camera obscura that thereby opened up for you" (8). But then the editor picks up on an order that has been dictated to him from the corpus he introduces when he sets the stakes of certainty or uncertainty in one's following of letters or their visualization in terms of the Devil's own tempting offer. It is "possible that what we commonly call dream and fantasy could be the symbolic recognition of the secret thread that runs through our life, attaching it to all its conditions, as though *he* however must be considered lost who with this knowledge believes to have won the power to tear apart that thread and to take up instead with the dark power that rules over us" (8). One way to follow this thread is to consider the optical devices that give the measure of visualization or hallucination in the light of what they project onto the dark power.

Latter-day genealogists have attended to the new and unsettling con-ditions of silent reading that were posited with or as the Reformation and then climaxed in the contained derangement of interiorities during Romanticism. The roundabout argument is that what opens up with the silently read book or with the film screen is only partially consumed on location and is instead consummated in the master bedroom or back home by couples. I'm reminded of colleagues who study pornography and even fold this research interest into curricular offerings but never take into account or include the masturbation that is the other medium or mediation of these images. Didn't the book that you could drag into your private world or masturbate room lend its ciphers to the visualiza-tions that tend to come up when you're alone? The pornographic images on the Web are as abstract a medium for sexual imaginings and hands-on application. Home-alone libido antedates the invention of the print-ing press.

The Devil's Elixirs admits that it operates as camera obscura. Fried-rich Kittler shows that the protagonist, Medardus, Hoffmann's Monk, operates instead as laterna magica. Kittler catches him in the act of falling for his objects: his love begins in church niches, goes out into the world to find doubles, then doubles back inside the church. When you read alone, silently, the inner reading-eye sees statues of saints step down from their niches. All the doubling in Medardus's object world proceeds along these lines, moving from fixity in Church to animation, the motion picture in which the lover's interiority shares. "The reproduction of images turns around thus into production of images" (Kittler, *Optische Medien*, 150). Medardus doesn't get his girl: her double image, the Saint, is the cock blocker. He comes close only when he interrupts Aurelie's silent reading of the book, which actively contains her erotic imagination, and tries to fill in the blanks. But in the extended field of representation of silent reading Medardus only has blanks to fire. He gets to double the embrace, but there are no dotted lines to follow to coitus. When Medardus returns to the Church, he is assigned as work of contrition the writing up of his life painstakingly. In this way he will follow his fantasy into the world and feel again all that was gruesome, terrible, or ridiculous and fun. Perhaps he will again see double and reenter his world of objects. However, his visitation writing, accompanied this time by the absence of the spirit of Evil, the absence, in a word, of worldliness, will this time hover over all that happened "like a higher principle" and thus preserve him from contact with the unsettling traces of his once deluded impressions. If, as Kittler concludes, Medardus thus becomes author and the Church becomes literature, then the difference that the writing down makes hangs by the secret thread that must be followed "like" a higher principle lest the dark power ruling over us tears into our light writing, our seeing-eye texts.

The House of Exorcism that Italian horror built also draws Big Time from German Romanticism. Maybe that's why the woman-to-be-possessed, Lisa, is a German tourist who gets off the bus in the Italian town with a main square attraction featuring the Devil. The fresco Devil looks just like Telly Savalas. Lisa enters a store where mannequins, large and small, are made and sold.

The client in the store who already purchased the small figures on a carousel that Lisa fancied looks just like Telly Savalas, I mean like the fresco Devil. Lisa backs out of store and deal. Merchant to Devil double: "That's weird. That could be her or her twin." "She's the splitting image of Helena. You're thinking, Why not use that girl instead of Helena?" When Lisa gets back to the square, she goes into convulsions and then starts making animal noises.

We're back with Lisa, who is in the hospital by now. "My God that can't be her voice." "Your hands stink of incense! It's turn, now it's your turn. Finally a body, a living body. She will suffer, not I. It's her turn." "Lisa!" "I'm not Lisa, you stupid pig. I never was Lisa."

The hospital tests are all negative. It must be "a psychiatric problem . . . from the unconscious." "What we priests call the soul." "A case of hysteria, split personality. An occult invader, if you will." "You almost sound like a text of demonology." Lisa throws up onto the priest. "There's your fucking daily bread. Eat it. Like you did your whore cunts before you became a priest. You are evil, you and your church and your Christ." "Who are you? What is your name?" "I am the asshole of the world!" "Who are you?" "A whore like those you used to fuck!" "Where do you come from?" She comes from adultery and incest. "From a cunt, you jerk!"

While the guests sit around the dinner table, the blind mother of two sons touch-reads Lisa's face. The younger man brings a picture of Helena. "She" runs toward him in park, embraces him in the past. Lisa enters a room packed with mannequins. "Helena!"

"You're even more beautiful than Helena. She deceived me." He shows her Helena's corpse. But then he gives Lisa the chloroform treatment. "Now you and I will be together always. It'll be different with you." He makes love to her knocked-out body lying beside Helena's relic corpse. Now he hates the smell of death. Now he loves to yell at his mother: "It's a wedding ceremony, not a funeral." "What will that change?" When he stabs his mother dead, she returns as zombie. "No, mother! Please, no!" All the undead gather around the table. There's death in the heir.

Hoffmann's *The Devil's Elixirs* is uncanny or demonic in the sense that it leads us down endless passages of self-reflection between reality and illusion filling, fulfilling, revealing the chasm that is indeed inside this book. In other words, we have here a narrative of variations on what is in effect a repetition compulsion. But the novel that is read within this narrative, Matthew G. Lewis's *The Monk,* is in contrast a Devil fiction in which all the conditions are met for commerce with a personified Devil, although the terms of the contract are kept or revealed, ultimately, in a place other than the immediate Devil relationship. Another remove or displacement results from witchcraft's introduction. The too-passionate monk, Ambrosio, comes into first contact with the Devil through the mediation of his lover, Matilda, the woman who dropped her monk's drag to seduce him after she had already, in the guise of a young monk or novice, befriended him. It turns out she has direct dealings with the Devil. When Matilda learns that he lusts after Antonia, a change of heart that changes their relations, she insists without jealousy, from intimacy to best friendship, she offers to help him out with her black magic. But Ambrosio is horrified: "If on witchcraft depends the fruition of my desires, I renounce your aid most absolutely. The consequences are too horrible" (265–66). While lauding as merit his ability to look upon his own guilt with horror, he throws his violation of his vows back at her as her infernal crime of seduction. She matches those consequences of selling one's soul with the horror she excites in him: "That scoffing tone, that bold and impious language is horrible in every mouth, but most so in a woman's" (276). But then she shows him her magic surveillance mirror and gives Ambrosio a peep show starring Antonia preparing to take a bath. "Ambrosio could bear no more" (269). He yields completely. Besides he still has pause to think himself at a safer remove than the witch Matilda, whose mediated services give him a buffer zone and benefit without consequences: "as he employed her assistance, not that of demons, the crime of sorcery could not be laid to his charge" (270). In other words, he still has time to repent. He just has to avoid all contract with the Devil. In the end he finds out that Matilda was the Devil's own spirit made over to look like the painting of the Madonna that Ambrosio contemplated with a pleasure that was not without interest. Thus, the Devil all along watched him and entrapped him through a relay of minions and illusions until the monk is led to realize contacts that are sinfully criminal and then to sign the contract to defer the inevitable. But once the Devil has him, he wastes no time torturing his client to death. There is in place of relationship in the novel always and again the same short attraction span (and a lot of waiting around, planning, observing, scheming).

> *Return of the Blind Dead* sends a series of couples on a blind date with the undead Templars. Tonight is the night, according to legend, that they return to claim sacrifice. But the night is the night for sex. Knock, knock. A woman is home alone. It's her boyfriend. He shouldn't be here. Father is out. Suppose my father should find us. He reassures her and then gets what he wants: No one will know. After they finish, she mopes. She ruins his afterglow. Knock, knock. The Templars are here to fill the missing place of the father as finders, keepers, killers.

Ambrosio's only long-term sexual relationship was with the uninhibited Matilda. His attraction to Antonia is one of passionate overvaluation, idealization in the realm of the senses, which presses for immediate consummation. But when his attempt to molest the date-drugged Antonia is interrupted by the mother and he is thus reminded that there can be consequences to his acts, he looks on his beloved with loathing. He has killed the mother but is unable to proceed with sleeping beauty. "He had no desire to profit by the execution of his crime. Antonia now appeared to him an object of disgust. A deadly cold had usurped the place of that warmth which glowed in his bosom. No ideas offered themselves to his mind but those of death and guilt, of present shame and future punishment" (298). Once he does have his way with her, he would gladly kill her to erase the act and its consequences. This rapid-fire alternation between overriding attraction and loathing or horror, through which the second thoughts of ambivalence are circumvented, is the sensual or sexual counterpart to the refusal on the part of Antonia's Christian survivors to live with the mourning after. Agnes who, unlike

Antonia, survived the conspiracies spun around her endangered life is the sister of Antonia's betrothed, Lorenzo, and best friends with Virginia, whose match with her brother she wants to make happen. At the end of her tale of suffering and survivorship she comes to the point of present tension: "One only wish remains ungratified. It is to see my brother in his former health, and to know that Antonia's memory is buried in her grave" (397). Two pages later (Lorenzo and Virginia are already married): "Antonia's image was gradually effaced from his bosom, and Virginia became sole mistress of that heart, which she well deserved to possess without a partner" (399).

Ambrosio's negotiated end with the Devil comes quickly but also— in the mode of overkill—not quickly enough. The Devil only promised to deliver him from the prison. He didn't promise not to drop him down a chasm and make a smash. Ambrosio takes six days to die, the span of divine creation. The Devil hurries up with Ambrosio but only to delay the inevitable point of extinction through the micromanagement of Ambrosio's pain. Before he dashes the monk down the chasm (leaving him enough time in the dying to start up the pain of Hell in this life), the Devil torments him with the revelation of all the family members he unwittingly defiled and murdered. Thus, through the Devil's revelations his crimes join in his punishment. Even the Devil is caught in the rapid turnover of idealization into demonization.

Wishmaster features the creature that "feeds on wishes." Give him your soul and he gives you the death of your enemy. But one unhappy medium suffers from death-wish backfire over the parents who died in the fire because she couldn't save them. The Master smells her fear. By *Wishmaster 3,* like the subtitle says, we're "beyond the gates of Hell." One girl's trauma is to have survived the car crash that took out her idealizable parents (her father saved her before dying). The transference continues from wreck to erection. The Devil uses a professor's sexual harassment proclivities to entrap him. This Devil or Djinn specializes in granting your wish while at the same time opening the gates of Hell. But first he assumes the professor's form.

Jones argued that the secularization of sexual repression restricted sex to private fears. At the latest with the onset of the Inquisition, the theatrical defense mechanism of denial allowed everyone to satisfy the repression standard and just say no, but at the same time the endless discourse and pseudoscience all about intercourse with the Devil allowed everyone to get into it under the cover or aegis of being in the no. In *Love at Stake*, a film farce about the Salem witch trials, the man with a plan for getting property fast is about to announce a witch hunt but instead all of a sudden describes the benefits coming soon from steam-powered ship travel until he just as suddenly remembers himself and starts up again with the demonization project. Thus, there is a certain interchangeability between the pseudo knowledge allowed to be gathered about witchcraft and the scientific knowledge that was no longer under the same interdiction. But on the horizon of our voyage, the first prospects for human cloning hitting the headlines are still under restraint. The early church interdicted the belief in demons and witches. During the Middle Ages the church changed its position, accepted the reality of evil beings, and prosecuted them. The church continues to reject all forms and expressions of pagan belief and fantasy as in league with the Devil, and while witches and company are no longer prosecuted, the belief in the existence of the Devil's purely evil minions has been retained. When antimatter was located in the universe and substantiated, the Pope wanted to know if this, then, was in scientific terms what he called the Anti-Christ. Since psychoanalysis identifies the pursuit of knowledge as the sublimation and continuation of early childhood sexual research, it alone is given to read in this double disavowal a certain sense.

In his grid of good and evil fathers and sons, Jones diagnoses different traits of the Devil regularly recurring in folklore and legend. That the Devil is so often given to run up against a limitation that allows the client to escape (Goethe's Faust wasn't the first or last Devil's client to escape the terms of the contract through the deception or ambiguity of the fine print) underscores the fatherly status of the Devil from a young child's perspective. Gambling, from dice to cards, Jones points out, is often attributed to the Devil as his invention. Freud argued that the gambling compulsion recycled infantile masturbation. Take a look around Las Vegas and that's just what you see: babies with cash. Thus, the Devil tempts and pursues the client to the terms and termination of his will. But as persecutor he can be defeated through deception. "Slyness and guile are notoriously the only weapons of the weak child against a parent's opposition. . . . A powerful person who is easily cheated by a weaker one is naturally conceived of as stupid, or at least as naïve. This contemptuous view is one that children often entertain of their parents, partly for the reason just stated, and partly as an over-compensatory reaction to the other occasions when they feel their ignorance in contrast with the parents' knowledge" (Jones, 175). But in turn this also means that we keep on dealing by necessity with the Devil father. "Infantile conflicts relating to the parents found one of its earliest expressions in peopling the universe with a number of powerful supernatural beings who were sometimes friendly, often ill-disposed, but always in need of propitiation" (187).

While, bottom line, the Devil's source in the primal or pre-Oedipal father concerns the little one (girl or boy) in everyone, with Oedipal re-organization, the Devil, too, gets assigned to sons and the witch lines up with daughters. In *Love at Stake*, the setting for belief in and persecution of witchcraft lies in a certain hysterical excess of female sexuality that, according to Jones's reading, was, at least in the Middle Ages, a historical excess, too. In the film there is one witch who's come to town, a good looker, the hooker of all the male looks she attracts. But while the men are uptight or erect, the women are horny. Aunt Deliverance sings in praise of her pussy while the pet she carries with her everywhere and plays with in bed is being addressed. Devil worship and witchcraft would seem to have served time in history, within a concise history of Christianity. But the ingredients, Jones underscores in his 1930 edition of *On the Nightmare*, have yet to be exorcised. Also in 1930, in *Civilization and Its Discontents*, Freud points out that the economic function, psychically speaking, that the Devil once played in Christianity, was a blank being fired up for and filled with the Jews by the new Aryan worldview that needs to do a few splits to preserve the ever-endangered purity of its vision. No one likes to hear about "the inborn human inclination to 'badness,' to aggressiveness and destructiveness, and so to cruelty as well. God has made them in the image of His own perfection; nobody wants to be reminded how hard it is to reconcile the undeniable existence of evil . . . with His all-powerfulness or His all-goodness." Freud turns then to the current event coursing through this same structure of untenable positions. "The Devil would be the best way out as an excuse for God; in that way he would be playing the same part as an agent of economic discharge as the Jew does in the world of the Aryan ideal" (*SE* 21: 120). Freud's Devil's advocacy in *Beyond the Pleasure Principle* was the rehearsal dimmer of the mourning light in which he had presented his work up to that point. He knew he needed to shake on the password Death if he wanted his word heard in the recycling din that would be coming soon. Thus Freud divined in the modern revival of anti-Semitism resistance, ultimately, to psychoanalysis itself.

Devil Father Mine

NOTEBOOK TWENTY-ONE

Night Visitor opens in red-light district at night. Drive-through client. She gets in back seat:"Wait a minute. Who are you?" Scream.

Cute teen is late to school again. "My mother's hair dryer exploded. It almost killed her. She has to wear a wig now." The teacher is straight uptight with a twist. The latecomer, Billy, has a boy pal and a gal pal. When it looks like the pal part might change to friend, as in girlfriend, the other pal warns him:"You don't date your pal, butt sniff. It would be like dating me."

Back home a new neighbor is moving in. She's his mom's age. But she's a babe. She flirts with Billy. He has her bedroom under surveillance. After a couple of days of this, he realizes she's a hooker. He invites his pals over to watch. Boy pal to gal pal:"You want to see her just as much as I do!"

Back on the streets, the passing car tried to hire another prostitute. Upon entering the car something creeps her out. She tries to run away. The mystery john grabs her and with a sword slits her throat.

Billy is unjustly suspended for the prank his boy pal played on the teacher. The teacher is pupil-focused on Billy as trouble. Billy wears sweat-shirts that have two buttons at the top. Teacher asks him to button up. Whenever he's on his own, Billy prefers to show cleavage. While spying once again on the hooker neighbor, Billy witnesses an evil john murder her. It was his teacher! And the teacher sees him, too. Billy tells the police. This is most likely another one of his pranks? It's not like he likes the teacher. The preshrunk authorities know, without knowing what to call it, that it's all about negative transference. "I'm like the boy who cried wolf." "More like the boy who cried Devil."

We are let into the basement beneath the abode of teacher by day, Satanist by night. A woman is being kept tied up down there. The teacher lives with his retarded brother, who likes to play with the "furniture." "Furniture shouldn't whine." Why does he call her furniture? "People buy you." Teacher brother is back home. "Don't worry about Billy. When the time is right, Satan's disciple will take care of him." It's time for services: "Almighty Satan, Father of Evil, we ask you to accept our offering." He goes upstairs. Now the retarded brother feels sorry for the "furniture." He frees her and guides her up out of the cellar. But it's an act: he has guided her up into the secret chapel. "Welcome to Hell, my dear." She's knocked out with chloroform. "The dead shall rise. I will give to the dead power over the living so they will remember them." I guess this is the way he remembers, I mean forgets, himself as parental guidance. It's the transference as wish and command. "I evoke thee from thy resting place in the bowels of the earth. Look favorably upon our sacrifice." When he puts on the Devil mask, it's time to stab the victim.

Entirely without any prompting, like instant anamnesis, Billy thinks to ask his dead father's good friend, a detective, for help. "He thinks he's the Devil's representative on earth. Dual natures are very clever. Law-abiding by day; by nightfall they set up altars and recite prayers backwards." When the Devil-worshipping duo ends up with Billy's gal pal in the secret basement (hosted by the duo's own retarded), the high priest recognizes that the end is in sight, site-specifically in the transference: "That little tramp is one of my students!" The boy pal has been out of the picture for some time now. The evil brothers join him in the missing persons department of *Night Visitors*. The mother, who was doubled as the hooker next door, goes there, too. There's only the new trio at the end. The detective, who represents the recovery of the relationship to the dead/Dad, presides over the couplification coming soon between Billy and Kelly.

If *The Vampire Lectures* was about powers of transference to which the collection testified, then these "Devil Notebooks" wallow, more specifically, in negative transference. The battery running these "New Vampire

Lectures" at their core is also positive transference: the course was a close second in popularity, peaking in 2002 at around seven hundred students (just the quarter before the vampirism class had brought in close to nine hundred students—and counting). But the topic of mourning (or unmourning) keeps the vampire material always closer to the ultimately benign, in theory and therapy, transference interpretation. The Devil material about-faces mourning, and awards substitution not Oedipal-ambivalent necessity but priority over loss. This paradoxical creativity is submerged, of course, in reactivity. The Devil comes second, and the emotion that binds one to him is secondhand. That's why it is fundamentally a contractual relation, one that, by definition or stipulation, deploys finitude against ghostly consequences.

To "introduce" my earlier study of evil, *Nazi Psychoanalysis*, I constructed a paranoid narrator as the only perspective that could "overlook" the frame that would contain both words in my title. I needed to complain, reactively, about conspiracies of corpus desecration and improper burial. I had three stories to choose from: the colleague on campus who cheerfully announced to me his new class on the Techno Gothic in which he had thought to apply Freud to the haunting trajectories in the literary works and films in order thus to open up a certain reading of media technologies. Then there was the colleague, not from campus but from the same system, who—ever since moments after I delivered a talk on the internal momentum Weimar cinema owed to war neurosis (including, endopsychically, to Freud's theorization of shell shock) and then every time we ran into each other subsequently, moments few and far between—announced to me his new book on war neurosis and Weimar cinema, though, to give him the credit line of guilty conscience, he each time, on double take, recollected my prior part in our exchange. The story I chose to write about instead did finally catch the historian in the act of reading me. In a note sent by e-mail following the appearance of *Nazi Psychoanalysis* he rejected my charges and enjoined me to pull myself out of the gutter sniping. But here is my response: as founding member of a UC systemwide psychoanalytic organization, I attended annual meetings throughout the first half of the 1990s. At the start of each meeting, participants presented research-in-progress reports to the group, exchanged offprints, set in process discussion about new work that continued nonstop throughout the meeting. One of the two presiding eminences at these gatherings was the historian's thesis advisor or, as we say in German, doctor father. I suppose the historian in question could submit interpersonal proof that for the past fifteen or twenty years he had lost contact with his former advisor. I still wouldn't be convinced—because transference, as intrapsychic structure rather than interpersonal intention, would be on my side.

When it comes to vengefulness, Nietzsche's superman gets in our I and blocks our schlock. But Nietzsche argued that revenge at first makes or made us interesting by opening up a network of interiorities. But he couldn't leave it alone. It was high time, and he could see for millions and millions and millions. Nietzsche was right about the "It was" of time, about the wars of the world, and about the misunderstanding of his words. But the superman didn't happen. He was right about Christianity occupying interchangeable places with nihilism in its current late phase of lingering, malingering on. Man is indeed over and out, but the superman required to pass the test of the Eternal Return never did rise to or from this occasion. Yes, the revaluation of the good and strong and the Evil One left all that is evil in this Christian frame-up as the place where we are most alive. Over time the inevitable happened: Christianity *is* evil.

In "Cogito and the History of Madness," Jacques Derrida underscored the motivation or momentum of evil subtending the mere progress of René Descartes's analysis in his *Meditations* from the turn to the *malin genie* or Devil (to get out of the mire or mirroring of reality being but a dream or delusion) to the follow-up address to the existence of God. Nietzsche argued that the Christian system of valuation posited evil or the Evil One first: good (as in goody-goody or as good-enough or OK) was an afterthought. What was once good as the self-affirmation of the good and strong became evil. Even the world leader who wages war for God and the good against the forces of evil will enjoy his victories only *as* evil. But if—and Anton LaVey tried to make book on it—this could be raised to consciousness rather than remaining mired in moral masochism and the unconscious sense of guilt, then the Church of Satan (for example) might indeed prevail and evil would deliver the good.

It's not a good idea to leave the spirit of revenge in the hands of the small-minded. Freud argued that the superman belongs not to the future but in the past: he was the primal father who, as the pre-Oedipal father in individual development, is the model I am proposing for the Devil. But then the question arises or remains: can the Devil be pried loose from the Christian frame of reference—conceived not as an allegorically maintained ruin, but as the family dysfunction that the Devil helps reanimate when back home for the holiday reunion?

Perhaps the existing frame for superhumanity or transhumanity should be our institutions of higher yearning, like the Professor's academy in *X-Men*. As long as he is subordinate to an overriding Christian frame, the Devil cannot pass this school's admissions test. Remember, it was the students at the academy who one day came up with the term "X-Men" as nickname for their instructors. It was a transference gift. Freud gave transference the rigorous assignment of replacing "in the patient's mind the desire to be cured" (*SE* 23: 175). The study of our self-difference, our positioning in a network of transferences, would then cover our relation to super- or trans-humanity. Thus, the mutant charges give up totalizing notions of cure-all or fulfillment of assimilation demands.

A measure of the transferential force that is with you is the lengths one will go to lose the transference—the way we would lose the police—but with the result in the former chase of *autos* or "self" that a kind of junkyard or graveyard of unmarked sites brings up the arrears.

A few months after the appearance of *The Vampire Lectures* a professor in Australia shared his concern with me, via e-mail, that I must not know his book on vampirism since I hadn't cited it. He also called my attention to another work I had failed to mention. I knew about this work, couldn't avoid noticing its cover in the bookstores. As an undergraduate English major I witnessed the author ridicule as "grotesque" a junior colleague's presentation on Samuel Beckett and Warhol's serial work (in which the liberties he took were all within the frame, at least, of high art). That was in the 1970s. In the meantime, thanks to cultural studies, all these English Department types can publish on what was all along their only passion, B literature, a passionate relation, however, that—it's the logic of repression—gets reduced after all to their same-old scholarshit. So, no, I hadn't read that one, but on purpose. I answered that my Lectures book was not a contribution to vampirism scholarship. As underscored in my preface, the Lectures are canned discourse in which what was original in other works, including my own, is freely recycled outside the frame of references but in earshot of the oedipedagogical relation. What is original about the Lectures is its role or function as monu-mentalization of the transferences to which the collection owes its utterance, recording, and sense of audience. What's-his-name reacted in a rage that scholarship was out there so we wouldn't keep on repeating ourselves. For all he knew I had "transferenced" his work, his ideas, without issuing proper citations. I stopped then and there.

The effort to lose the transference today finds its host in Web conditions of fame and rage, of name and no-name. Several months later, it came to my attention, via the Web scan of any number of the eight hundred-plus students taking my class on vampirism at the time and again, that an Australian professor, the author of a book on vampirism that no one had ever heard of, apparently published a negative review of The Vampire Lectures in a new online journal, another of the many no-namer sites whereby the former British Empire finds another way to avoid being encompassed by the setting of the son. Of course I worry about what comes up when my students supplement our lecture relationship with name searches. But the spill contained itself in my students' recognition of what's all the raging. I let them be my hearsay. Apparently there was again in the review the outright refusal of the concept of transference even as a thought crossing the mind or net, which was already evident in the e-mail that I did read—and yes, I assumed there couldn't be another Australian academic author of a vampirism book that I'd never heard of. The rejection this time around was more fully projected as the joke on me of my own narcissism. It is an instance of what I would like to identify as, specific to the Web, the spectral rising up of the unread. But in passing his own review what's-his-name referred not only to the additive progress of scholarship but also to the new and improved social studies discourse whereby "Žižek" had made it no longer necessary, indeed it was now ill advised, to touch the sticky parts of Freud's science that he had apparently explained away, like the mother's body that even in its pressing missingness elicited what's-his-name's offer to throw it up all the way from down under.

While I must emphasize that I do not know him, and have not kept up with his work, and thus remain familiar only with his shorter diatribe pieces published throughout the 1980s in countless 1960s-style Lacanian newsletters, Slavoj Žižek may well have some explaining to do. "Žižek" serves as transference block in so many settings. I've observed on several occasions how the academic unsettled by the excellence of the just concluded presentation of a colleague will immediately rave to the speaker about the helpfulness of "Žižek's work." In the place of the third person (and three need not represent the father, when it's also making a crowd), praise for "Žižek" comes in handy for the person in second place who would like to bury work he cannot afford to attack because he could never outclass it.

It doesn't surprise me that "Žižek's work" is sponsored by negative transference. On recurrent occasions we were both invited to conferences at which Derrida was also to be present. But those were the conferences that always counted Žižek as no-show. During the 1980s Žižek laid the foundation for his readership in his compulsive or polymorphous publication, in every available print outlet, of criticism of Derrida. Derrida was Žižek's teacher once upon a time. I realize that Jacques-Alain Miller was ultimately entrusted with the Lacanian's formation. But the name brand is associated with reading of or with philosophy. In this regard Derrida was his teacher. This is not the only shadow cast upon a certain Lacanian reception by association with Carl Jung, whose entire oeuvre following his psychotic break with Freud can, archetypically enough, only be rendered intelligible in the terms of his negative transference onto Freud.

What's-his-name's review apparently opened with the proviso that friends of Rickels should read no further. But who's-it thus inadvertently touched his own woundedness and hit on the very point where Web access falls short of itself. Among those friends of Rickels are (and were) leading writers and thinkers who already and always will not have read any work or words by what's-his-name. If we could imagine such exchanges keeping to the standard of Old Testament justice, I for an I, ego for an ego, then my and my friends' reflex promise that an encounter with what's-his-name's publicity will never take place, should in return presuppose no-name's vow to keep out of our words, too. Web conditions notwithstanding or saluting: there are "Masters of the University"—and then there's everyone else.

Another Web review that caught the attention of one of my surfing-eye students, a review this time of *The Case of California* on the occasion of its 2001 reissue, was signed by a name to remember just because it can be pronounced "baby." They really are getting younger out there. Baby made allowances for my book being ten years old and congratulated his cultural studies generation for having in the meantime come a long way. Baby was especially grateful to "Žižek" for using the conversational skill of backing off with the pretensions and coming clear with the follow-up explanations. Is it Baby or "Žižek" who's the big explain-in-the-ass? We're asked to imagine a conversation in which Baby could hold up his end with explain-away wipes in ready reach. "Žižek," according to the hearsay versions of these two Web reviews, appears hoisted by his own retarding effect as explainer to the front of the line of those who no longer need to read save through him.

A certain compatibility between middlebrow culture and the demonic seconds the emotion of negative transference. The famous analysis of the passion play of music is not Kierkegaard's only consideration of the demonic in *Either/Or*. Boredom is also identified as the medium of the demonic. The big idea of being bored to death is already a middlebrow plaint. Rather than commit suicide, the one who is thus bored—impaled upon a want or shortcoming—determines to bear his mediocre life as testimony to God's own limits. Thus, middlebrow culture is demonic to the extent that it *thus* recasts life as the deferral of suicide. No longer the suicidal type, the demonic personality promotes himself as the typo—the proof is in the putting down of his author—in a poorly assembled Book of Life.

Negative transference is the paired opposite of positive transference. At the same time it is in second place (before it can be all over the place). "The hostile feelings make their appearance as a rule later than the affectionate ones and behind them; their simultaneous presence gives a good picture of the emotional ambivalence which is dominant in the majority of our intimate relations with other people" (*SE* 16: 443). Freud first borrowed the term ambivalence from Eugen Bleuler to designate mixed emotions in this setting of differentiation between positive and negative transferences. Freud introduces this splitting and pairing in taking up the challenge of understanding resistance. Once we identify transference resistance, there is no point in speaking of transference: "we must make up our minds," Freud writes, "to address only the positive and negative sides of transference." Positive transference based on repressed erotic impulses and negative transference both get pressed into the service of resistance to the treatment. "The hostile feelings" in the negative transference "are as much an indication of an emotional tie as the affectionate ones" (*SE* 16: 443). For example, the student evaluation that's all rage also always means that the student enjoyed the class too much. Although "all the emotional relations are genetically linked with sexuality and have developed from purely sexual desires," negative transference is able to go its own way, away from the ambivalence of emotional relations, and set itself up as the dis-pair of the sexual origin of the emotional tie and as limit concept of transferential treatment. "The breaking out of a negative transference is actually quite a common event in institutions" (*SE* 12: 106). Let us take "institutions" here to include every frame of transference that thus counts negative transference as one of those breaks it doesn't always get. "As soon as a patient comes under the dominance of the negative transference he leaves the institution in an unchanged or relapsed condition." Negative transference can cause the patient to split, to leave and leave behind, to split off the "affectionate transference," and thus foreclose the outside chance of ambivalence, in other words the prospect of mourning. Once "the capacity for transference has become essentially limited to a negative one, as is the case with paranoiacs, there ceases to be any possibility of influence or cure" (*SE* 12: 107). A certain pairing or dis-pairing of emotional ties, ranging from ambivalence to paranoia, crosses Freud's mind in the face of transference resistance. Negative transference already marks the spot Freud was in and that could come out, out—but only at the fundamental, fundamentalist remove of what Freud advertised as his role of Devil's advocate—with the introduction of the death drive.

In *Bless the Child* the Devil worshipper pretending to be a New Age priest has, through a murderous process of elimination, found the born saint whose powers he would harness, indeed hitch to the Devil's domination of the world. He tells her that he is her father now: "You never had a father before." He offers her the world as far as the I can see. When she nevertheless remains loyal to her beliefs, he tries to make his point by holding her over the edge above the street that's many floors below them: "If you believe, jump. You can trust my hand, you can see it, it is the hand of Satan. Where's God's hand? Will he catch you? If you believe, jump." And she says: "After you."

In *The Prophecy* and *The Prophecy II* Gabriel leads the second war against heaven over God's heir conditioning of man as the one with soul or psyche. Gabriel wants it to be "like it was: He loved us best. I will not allow some talking monkey to replace me." The first time around Gabriel's plan is to find the evil soul power (a recently deceased Korean War vet was holding down this fort) that was prophesied capable of leading to mankind's doom's day only in this way of leader-and-the-pack self-destruction. But one good angel displaces the evil soul from Gabriel's grasp of the prophecy—first by inhaling it from the corpse's mouth, second by depositing it inside a little girl mouth to mouth. In *The Prophecy II* a good angel mates with a woman of faith: their progeny, as it is written, will introduce the end of Gabriel's war. The angel father dies leaving the Christian super-savior family value of mother and unborn son to stop Gabriel (who at the start of the sequel is cast out of Hell by Satan, who takes a controlling interest in the soul power the other rebel angel just wants to eradicate). During their face-off, the mother-to-be defeats Gabriel through a literal leap of faith. Hell's Beals. Jennifer asked Gabriel, before they took the plunge, whether he had heard from God lately. I guess not. She takes his calls all the time.

She decides not to entrust her baby to the angels. The angel who died for her was worth more than the rest of them put together. Years pass, and she walks her son to the school bus. Another mother confides her anxieties about her own child's weekday departures. But the widow of an angel knows better: "You just got to have faith." Gabriel is now a panhandler at a city corner. He's waiting for the phone to ring, he just knows it will, the phone's going to ring.

In October 2003, at a conference held at UC Santa Barbara titled "Irreconcilable Differences: Jacques Derrida and Religion," Derrida underscored during the closing roundtable discussion that the faith that concerned him was a faith precisely without redemption. Someone in the audience uttered as reflex response that this was the definition of Satan. Derrida smiled. At some point by the 1990s religious studies had replaced social studies as the habitat for the dismissal of Freud's science. But eclectic psychotherapy (which genealogically must be viewed as "greater psychoanalysis") is still, at least in California, fundamentally Freudian when it comes to the fundamentals of belief or faith. The therapist is trained to consider, first, the political or religious belief systems brought to session as part of the presenting symptom picture. Transference is the bottom line here.

Sándor Ferenczi resituated the Devil within the transference dynamic, which he examined with regard to the suspension bridging blind belief and blind disbelief (and suspicion). Novel scientific views often trip one of two receiving lines: there's that measure of suspicion and disbelief that exceeds the limits of objectivity and betrays outright animosity and then there's that condition of belief that takes its cues from the good reputation and authority already accorded the personality of the scientist or his method. Ferenczi recommends the analytic session, which is the place where over time patients often undergo fundamental changes in outlook, as the perfect lab space for testing the contradictory attitude the public assumes toward novel claims.

Obsessive-compulsive patients repress their belief and maintain instead a kind of doubt addiction that is based on disappointment in the reality of the love advertised in their earliest relationships. In the extreme form, a patient is unable to form any judgment at all. If there isn't even a trace of the capacity for transference or belief—as is often the case in paranoia—then analysis proves impossible (136). There are two reasons for illogical disbelief: disappointment in the ability of authority figures to explain things or processes, and disappointment in their good will to give correct explanations (137). In the former case it is a reaction to the original trust in the omniscience and omnipotence of the parents; in the latter case it is a reaction formation in regard to the originally assumed and experienced all-goodness of the parents. In the first case, the only case, strictly speaking, that demonstrates disbelief, the authorities are de-deified; in the second case, a case of suspicion rather than disbelief, the authorities are still held high but in the negative mode.

Belief in God is replaced by belief in the Devil, whose omnipotence is dedicated solely to the pursuit of wicked designs. The Devil's replacement duty is particularly clear in paranoia or persecution mania. The negative father image exercises superhuman or supernatural powers— via all the other people at his disposal and through physical and occult powers "(electricity, magnetism, telepathy etc.)"—in order to destroy the persecuted. "There is moreover hardly an analysis in which the patient does not for a brief or longer duration identify the analyst in the father's place with the Devil in person" (137).

"Abnormities of belief: excessive trust, doubt addiction, as also fundamental disbelief and suspicion, are symptoms of regression to or fixation in that infantile stage of reality development which I named the *magical* and the *projective phase of the sense of reality*" (137). The religious phase of mankind corresponds to the subsequent stage of development

of the sense of reality when the child exchanges the limits of his own omnipotence, which he in the meantime must recognize, for higher powers
that must mediate or administer his wishes. Thus, the idea of omnipotence
is not surrendered. Those given to blind belief or trust in authority are
fixated in this stage of reality's reception (138). But even if we make it to
the third stage—the "scientific" stage according to Freud, the projection
stage according to Ferenczi—by giving up all our illusions of total controls or sources of power, we can at any moment encounter the return
of those points of view that we seemingly surmounted.

When wishing alone doesn't suffice, then the external world emerges
as medium for change to the extent that it must be altered if one's wishes
are to be realized in this world. Sense perception is the only guarantee
of the objectivity and reality of psychic content. "This is the 'primal
projection,' the separation of psychic contents between the 'I' and the
'Not-I'... 'Seeing is believing'" (139). The slogan of the senses is given
as English-language foreign body or introject in Ferenczi's discourse.
The alteration that this body will undergo gives the inside view of Ferenczi's relocation of projection in this transferential setting of belief.

But in time one learns that the evidence of the senses can also deceive. "Only the simultaneous and successive mutual control of the sense
impressions" leads back to evidential certainty. Logic and mathematics
are added to this sensorium of evidence, but since both are the result,
according to Ferenczi, of experience, the bottom line of evidence remains
intuitive perception and test result. The experience Ferenczi summons
here includes the increasingly important role played in this phase by
other people. With all other objects of the external world the child can
come to terms because even as obstacles they are constant: the child
can reckon or count on them. But other people are the objects that remain incalculable. This seeming lack of limits can cause the child to
transfer ("zu übertragen") or project omnipotence fantasies onto the
adults. Objects don't lie. If we were wrong about something we thought
we knew about them, then the mistake is only our own, the kind that's
easy to correct. The child originally uses words as objects. The child believes them and holds their truth to be self-evident. Ferenczi makes his

point within the German word *wahrnehmen*, "to perceive," which he then redistributes as *etwas für wahr nehmen*, "to take something to be true."

Any mistakes in regard to objects can be corrected in time. But this opportunity is denied the child with regard to the words of the parents. The blind belief that arises from this interdiction or impasse differs from conviction in that the belief is an act of repression, while conviction is carried via impartial judgment (140). All of the above is further complicated, rendering adjustment yet more difficult, by the uneven inhibition of the formation of the child's judgment. The child is supposed to judge correctly regarding "harmless" matters. Expressions of the child's intelligence are rewarded and praised as long as they do not address sexual and religious questions or the authority of the adults as questionable. Because I say so! Thought itself can thus be inhibited in a child. Those stuck in this corner easily succumb to energetic suggestion or the influence of energetic personalities. To believe because it is absurd "is in fact the most bitter self irony" (141). Children with a sense of reality that was able to develop ahead of schedule only comply in part with the parental demand that one exercise partial repression. Their doubt returns readily from the repressed—often displaced onto other thoughts. They assume certain dogmas without criticism but compensate with exaggerated suspicion of all other conjectures. A hypercritical attitude in one area is often balanced by blind belief in another matter.

"The greatest burden placed on his capacity for believing the child experiences in regard to his own subjective feelings" (141). The adults inform the child that stuff he thinks of as fun is bad, while the renunciations that are such a drag are nice and good. "The double meaning in the words good and bad (which signify good and bad tasting as well as well-behaved and misbehaving) contributes not the least to render statements of third persons regarding one's own feelings doubtful. Here we can seek at least a source for the special suspicion of psychological statements, whereas so-called exact, mathematically formulated statements or statements based on technical-mechanical methods of proof often meet with unjustified trust" (141). Thus, individuals demand special guarantees with regard to psychological discourse that they are not going to be deceived again.

In literature we can be instructed as long as we, the readers, must find the moral of the story ourselves. The teachings of psychoanalysis tend to be accepted most readily when packaged as humor or represented as the history of an individual. Only through exemplification—experience in detail—or along the painful pathway of transference can psychological evidence be obtained. Logical argument is not enough. You may heed the message but you won't believe it. The English-language introject can now be metabolized: "Feeling is believing."

> The message of *Dogma:* "It doesn't matter what you have faith in, you just have to have faith."
>
> Loki, the Angel of Death, hangs with Bartleby at the airport. Bartleby likes it there because he enjoys seeing through the reunions. "That guy doesn't know that she cheated on him twice while he was gone." They want to go home. If they walk through the arch of that church in Jersey and then die, they can't be turned out since their souls are clean. "We won't be angels, but we'll be home." "Last four days on earth. If I had a dick, I'd go get laid. Let's do the next best thing—let's kill people."
>
> "Voice of God," one of the Seraphim, contacts Bethany. Her mission: "Stop a couple of angels from entering Heaven and thus negating all existence. If they get in, they will have reversed God's decree. To prove God wrong would undo reality. Existence would become nothingness." The demon Asrael cast the big idea as spell on the two itinerant angels. He is also keeping God displaced to one of his sidelines, trapped in human form (God's favorite pastime is to go native).
>
> Rufus, who falls from the sky as a black brother, tells it like Christ is black (once Christ goes black there's no going back). Rufus (the thirteenth Apostle, excluded to whitewash the true biblical history) joins Bethany, the great-great-...-grandniece of Christ (Mary had kids with Joseph) on her journey to New Jersey together with two dopers she thinks "Voice of God"

counseled her to rely on (the confusion lies in the phonic interchangeability of "prophets" and "profits"). The foursome meets up with Serendipity, who dances at a nearby strip club. She's a muse who underwent a transsexual change since Rufus last saw her. The muse decided to write in her own writing. So she went out into the world in a body. But it turns out she can't inspire herself.

From out of the toilet in the club restroom emerges the Shit Demon. Shit Demon first grew out of the cumulative last bowel movements of all crucifixion victims on Golgotha. The mute stoner sprays the demon with air freshener. It claims that it "knocks odors out." The demon is knocked out. Truth in advertising: now *that* is Christianity.

Demons don't have bodies of their own (hence Shit Demon); Angels are like Ken dolls, like resurrected bodies (like the reassembled Osiris, like the Oedipal father as model of successful mourning going on substitution); the nonangelic dead, like Rufus, only have to worry about decay and necrophiliacs; God is a woman but not human who, however, likes on occasion to enter human form, the more abject the better (she's also a recognizable rock star playing a Christian rock star); Christ on the cross is too depressing and is going to be replaced by the figure "Buddy Christ."

The Angel of Death had to take early retirement when Christianity appropriated the Old Testament as its Before Picture, as the bad cop, bad breast, in contrast to its own good news. Equally severe when it comes to idolatry, Bartleby and Loki are precisely behind the times within the Christian schedule and frame of reference.

Bartleby knows that their return will bring mass destruction. He figured out that if man has free will, then angels are servants. Angel of Death: "I've heard this rant before. You sound like Lucifer." Man has the choice. But Angels were made to miss God. "We're going home. Even the Almighty Himself isn't going to make that otherwise." The allies take up position before the church of "Buddy Christ." Bartleby is still running amok. Loki explains: "Aeons of repression needing to be released. If only we could beat off." Bartleby:

"Though my kind came first, your kind was most revered. This failed experiment called existence will cease to be." Bethany figures out that God must
be trapped in one of her incarnation escapades. She locates a patient in a
coma on a respirator. She pulls the plug, thus releasing Godma in time to
greet Bartleby at the church door just as he prepares to enter and bring
about the complete reversal. They kiss and embrace. Bartleby weeps. Godma
blasts him with a sonic booming yell. Bethany was mortally wounded in her
womb area when she pulled the plug back in the hospital. Godma heals
her. What's more, that blast impregnated her. She is no longer the last scion;
now she bears the last scion. Rufus: "What about your faith now, Bethany?"
"When it rains it pours."

NOTEBOOK TWENTY-TWO

Horror Hotel opens with the Christian mob asking for the witch, Elizabeth Selwyn. We're in Whitewood, Massachusetts, and the witch stares down the "ye olde gift shoppe" Colonial crowd. But one cry of "Witch!" suffices to break the spell. "Burn the witch!" Her man denies and betrays her. "Hast thou consorted with her?" "No!" But to himself he says: "Help her, Lucifer!" In the present a professor's star student wants to fieldtrip to some backwater in Massachusetts. She's going to stay at Raven's Inn in Whitewood. "Witchcraft is not nonsense!" "The basis of fairytales is reality." "The basis of reality is fairytales." The student feels that the women back then may not have been "silly," after all: "Suppose they did have a pact with the Devil." Upon arrival: "I feel as though I were in the seventeenth century." "Here time stands still off the beaten path." A plaque in the inn claims to be the site where she, Elizabeth Selwyn, was burned. The innkeeper, the witch's look-alike, says the inn is full. But the professor's name gets her a room. The pastor in his empty church tells her that for three hundred years the Devil has held sway. "Leave Whitewood, before it is too late." On February 1 the witches mock the rites of the church. She discovers an underground access from her room. But once she's down the hole, the black-robed innkeeper catches her. "I am Elizabeth Selwyn." She stabs her latest sacrifice. Jump cut: Knife cuts cake at cousin Sue's birthday party. The boyfriend comes calling or investigating in Whitewood. But the witch flashes in his face (in the windshield), and he crashes. Her brother resides in his sister's former room. He soon discovers that the Devil gives his followers eternal life, but only if two sacrifices are performed each year. Rather than supply the other booster shot, he casts the shadow of the cross upon them—all of them, all of them flamers.

The other word for "primal,""primeval," also sounds like *Prime Evil*. In 1349 the Black Death decimates the populace."God has forsaken us!" Lucifer seized the opportunity. One priest has signed up with Lucifer:"Join us now and live forever or die for nothing!" Brother Seaton is still alive in New England today. His client:"She is my daughter. I swear it, in the name of Satan.""With the sacrifice of your child you will be granted thirteen years by the power of our Lord God Satan. You will not grow older." After thirteen years are up, however, he'll need another blood relation to sacrifice. Brother Seaton's sect broke away during the plague—but never left the church: there is power there. The followers don't die. But the vows once pledged are irreversible. The undercover nun stabs the Satanic grandfather before he can knife his sacrifice and extend his life. They're all in it together: irreversibly they start to decay away.

If this is the seventeenth century, then we are in Moldavia. The opening voice-over pretends this is a vampire movie:"Blood-devouring assassins." That pretend movie bears the title *Black Sunday*. But properly titled, *The Mask of Satan* shows us a witch, Asa, who, condemned by her brother, gets branded with an S for Satan."Cover her face with the mask of Satan, nail it down, may the flames obliterate her foul body." Her parting shout:"In the name of Satan I place a curse upon you. Your progeny will restore to me the life you steal!" A rainstorm extinguishes the purifying flames. Now we're in the late nineteenth century. Two professors of medicine travel by coach to Russia, where they will attend a conference. While the driver fixes the squeaky wheel, the professors follow eerie sounds into ruins. One coffin has a window for all to see the witch nailed by the mask of Satan. In the course of examining this find, one professor cuts himself on the broken window glass. He removes the mask while his blood drips onto the stiff. Above-ground they encounter a young woman we recognize to be the witch's look-alike. The other professor, more junior, not the one who let it bleed, immediately falls for her. Today is St. George's Day. Two centuries ago the burning occurred. Because there are many portraits of the family ancestors, the father knows that his daughter, Katia, is the witch's double. "It is as though the witch tormented her victims with her own beauty before killing them." In the meantime Asa has summoned her partner in demonic crimes back from the dead. The jump-started minion picks up the older doctor. The witch is waiting. "Just a few drops brought me back to life again. All of your blood will give me the strength for vengeance. Kiss me! You will be dead to men but alive in death." In the meantime Katia's father dies. "What is my life— sadness and grief—something that destroys itself day by day, and no one can rebuild it—Here is the very image of my life—Look at it—consumed hour by hour like this garden—Help me!"

A portrait hangs by the fireplace. A curtain hangs over it. A candle ignites the curtain. When the fire is put out, an opening is revealed behind the portrait. It's a secret passageway. "Then my father was not delirious. And his last words were: the silver griffin and the man in the portrait." They enter the passageway through the fireplace. They find a portrait. "It's the same girl as the portrait in the salon." But the portrait is another swinging door. Fireplace door slams shut. The man left behind to guard the entrance is strangled from behind. Inside the crypt the two men look at the witch. "She looks as though she just died." "Look. She's breathing."

They find the missing doctor, already in a decaying state. "But last night he was still alive. I saw him." "No. He was already dead." "But it's impossible. He moved. I even spoke to him." "Sometimes Satan even plays tricks with the dead. The witch turned him into the slave of the Devil, dead by day, alive by night. So he could carry out Satan's nefarious orders." They must hurry before the witch comes fully alive by possessing the living body of a woman, specifically her look-alike, Katia.

Katia is alone with dead father. He comes alive. "Father? Father?" "I am no longer your father. My blood is no longer your blood. The spirits of evil have rended that tie between us forever." Minion knocks unDad out of the running for her life. In the fireplace: burn Daddy burn. Minion gloats over the doubles lying side by side. "At last your vengeance is at hand, Asa. Now you will be free forever." It seems the witch only has to hold hands with Katia to swap vitalities and places. While minion fights Katia's rescuer, Asa gloats too much too soon. "The love of the young man could have saved you. But now you will enjoy a life of hate and evil in me." Cross around the collarbone. The young man fights his way past the minion, but takes Asa to be Katia. Just as he is about to pierce the wrong one, he stops short when he sees the crucifix around the neck. "But this is your cross, Katia, how is it possible?" Now he understands. She must turn around to get up and away. We all get an eye full of her memento-mori style backside sliding down bones into decay. "Lose yourself in my eyes! Don't you feel the joy and beauty of hate?" The crowd of angry Christian peasants bursts upon the scene. Asa gets torched with no rain on her charade. "Why was Katia taken away from me? And she is dying with Katia's beauty." The witch burns, but Katia starts to twitch. Before she goes, the witch loses the face she saved at Katia's expense. Katia and her admirer get her looks back, too.

In *My Mother: Demonology*, Kathy Acker digs writing in the throwaway defense mechanisms of the "male language," the language of "the patriarchy." Within a dizzying relay or rebound of exclusions and implications we can yet discern a line up of parallel universals. The first President Bush enters the writing-self's dream to report the words of his sister: "There are only dreams. This is the *nothing* which you men call *death*: therefore, in your male language, death and women are friends" (195). There is, then, another language to which translation or encryptment refers us. It is a language of memory—the translations or reformulations of the male language are essentially repressions or forgettings—in which "rhyme" (as the motor of contaminated and containing slang, jargon, slogans, or wordplay) doubles as "the mirror of history" (220). "Thus it became clear that puns, bad language, and memory are closely conjoined" (187).

In *My Mother: Demonology,* as in Daniel Paul Schreber's *Memoirs of My Nervous Illness,* the bad language of pun and analogy is dead-icated—and it's where the girls are. "According to history, any school of all girls is a school of the dead" (77). The writing that Acker summons demonologically must be reclaimed from projection. The secondariness or reactivity of projection in the wake or place of first contact (which subsumes reading, too, conceived as seconding of the motion of inscription) turns around in this process into new writing—original screen text—along lines long associated with the Devil. "I have sold myself to the Devil! As do those who write" (129).

Acker looks after writing—red writing—in all the wronged places and uncollected words of the middlebrowbeat. Thus, when the writing-self sells her soul to the Devil or goes down with the witch, she leaves evil to the banality bunch: "No religion: this is the one event that'll never change. No religion is my stability and surety" (13).

In his *Lucifer Rising* Gavin Baddeley establishes cinema as "the Devil's lantern" (87). The Devil may be the prince of all the occult figures out there, but all the other creatures of the night—of nothingness—always seemed a better generic fit with the film medium. Consider, for example, the cut-and-suture recycling of preexisting corpus parts comprising Frankenstein's monster—or, for that matter (or mother), Shelley's novel. The vampire, too, since constitutively mirror-image-less and therefore sheer image—the quintessential *Doppelgänger*—can be seen as rising up between the lines of literature in anticipation of cinema. Even when a film like F. W. Murnau's *Nosferatu* denies the undead full representation in its own mirror medium, the "phantom" is just the same represented *as* unrepresentable via special effects stop-starting the motion picture and showing off manipulation of the print back in the lab. Thus, by getting in touch with itself as artificial lab-spawned medium, cinema admits the vampire as its definition or limit concept.

Monster analogies with the movies parallel Freud's insertion of projection into the setting of mourning or unmourning. Untenable wishes recrossing the mind of the survivor cannot be admitted in close-up but only in the long shot of projecting them upon the deceased who, thus reanimated by the mean-spirited thoughts, expresses and acts on a hostility that, in its one-sided, one-way trajectory, gets the survivor around the original messy ambivalence to which the undead creature owes its new release on life and upon the living.

The Devil also emerges in the gaps and overlaps between psychic and cinematic projections—but not in the service of finding and keeping in place of losing and weeping. The Devil caters to hugely healthy nonneurotics or—same difference?—psychopaths, subjects, in any event, markedly devoid of inhibitions and precisely not grief-stuck on losses. The Devil's clients are able to substitute for what's missing without complication—indeed to the point that the loss is affirmed in exchange for a new invulnerability or certainty that is the Devil's best offer. Thus, the Devil never advertises immortality as the "free gift" you get for joining, but only finite quality time, time uninterrupted, uncompromised by the uncontrollability of mortality until the set deadline arrives on schedule, the line in time along which you sign when you sign up with the Devil. The Devil does not indwell the projection of the other (undead or live). The Devil's clients contemplate instead the projection out of nothing of a world of their own making.

What lies between, however, the Devil's inevitable medium in the egos of innocent bystanders, is his projective typecasting as laughable trickster. At the same time, as Freud observes of the doodling caricatures on the margins of the superego's dictation, the butt of all jokes is the child's early-easy identification with the father, the child taking it up the wisecrack. Already in Daniel Defoe's list of what all the Devil's followers can accomplish through their Dark Prince, we read the fill of what the movies have to show for reading its own projections in his magic lantern. The purpose of his minions is to undertake the Devil's "business in the world":

> To this purpose gave he them power... to walk invisible, to fly in the air, ride upon broomsticks, and other wooden gear, to interpret dreams, answer questions, betray secrets, to talk (gibberish) the universal

language, to raise storms, swell winds, bring up spirits, disturb the dead, and torment the living, with a thousand other needful tricks to amuse the world, keep themselves in veneration, and carry on the Devil's empire in the world. (245–46)

Wait a minute: where is talking the universal language in pictures? In theory, gibberish, like cursing, like music, indeed steps up in a list of the Devil's interests. In fact: *Incubus* is a Devil movie about temptation and possession that's spoken entirely in the made-up universal language of Esperanto (with William Shatner and company giving even it an American accent). Shatner is the pure soul that the succubus sister decides to go for for a change. The vain, corrupt, and infirm flock here to take the healing waters. The succubae lure the tainted. "Why do we have to lure them to where they're going anyway? Why not a pure soul?"

Right after Defoe defines the magic lantern as mere optic machine and means of representation in which there is, however, no Devil, he cuts the slack of analogy to define the modern condition of possession as just such optical machination:

> The magic lantern is an optic machine, by the means of which are represented, on a wall in the dark, many phantasms, and terrible appearances, but no Devil in all this; only that they are taken for the effects of magic, by those that are not acquainted with the secret.... I cannot but take notice, that this very piece of optic delusion seems too much akin to the mock possessions, and infernal accomplishments, which most of the possessionists of this age pretend to, so that they are most of them mere phantasms and appearances, and no more. (278)

In many vampire movies, the creature of the night fails to make or leave— or live—an impression in photography. It is the multiple mechanism of projection that is thus set aside in this splitting (and not a suspension of the film's fictive or medial status). Ghosts often appear only via photographic development both as Spiritist photography and in movies. In *The Omen* the overlap between the momentum of haunting for those so inclined and the uninhibited interventions of the Devil—the death wish—carves its scheduled enactment in photographs of the victims-to-be. In the remake of *The Omen,* the photographer carries both kinds of camera with him, the kind that registers an emanation as negative on film and the digital kind. That the scratching is also visible on the digital prints is viewed as proof of its supernatural significance. The photographic and film media were largely entrusted to occult figures of melancholia because of their fundamental relation to the vestige of the object reproduced. Thanks to digital mediation, the Devil's communications are no longer shadowed by the alternative tracking of the retention span of melancholia.

While the Devil has no use for vampire lovers, God worshippers, review journalists, suicides or any of the other immortality neurotics, it amuses him to watch your average inhibited imagination victimized by its projections. Anton LaVey, allegedly in his day Satan's representative, recapped the projections that rebound to the gory imagination of parental guidance:

> Your Apocalypse is here.... Credit me for the revolution, but credit yourselves for the forms that it has taken.... Whenever I got on TV or the radio, I was given a few seconds to say what they desperately needed me for.... If Satanism was so hot, why wasn't I able to talk about it?... A "Satanic survivor" could grunt out 15 belabored minutes of applauded testimony, while a real Satanist was lucky to be heard above two whole minutes of studio idiots gasping and jeering. Now, in your End Times, you blame Death Metal and its influence on youth.... YOU listened to the warnings and examples set forth by the Blattys, Pazders, Geraldos, Oprahs...and their identity-starved stooges.... YOU provided media saturation informing them what "real" Satanists do, what kind of noises they make when possessed. YOU encouraged them to rebel by the aesthetic standards YOU provided.... Your hysterical plan has backfired. YOU brought about your own Apocalypse, like the stupid masochistic victims that you are. ("To: All Doomsayers," 4–7)

LaVey always tried to affirm the projections recycled time and again to represent *and* repress the Devil as sleazy journalist, abject bureaucrat, or used-car salesman (whose favorite verb, as learned from social scientists, is "utilize"). Fyodor Dostoyevsky's Devil (in *The Brothers Karamazov*) is submerged in this b/anality of evil (and Thomas Mann's Devil is, of course, the cite-specific recycling of Dostoyevsky's depiction of a shabby near miss of a gent dressed so two-years ago). What is most endearing or amusing about LaVey is his upbeat conclusion, again and again, that the Church of Satan was winning. He was pitching his Church to the hardworking middle class and middlebrow, otherwise denied pleasure or power. Inevitably, the missing middle would rally to this cause.

Drawing on his career as circus carney, LaVey affirmed magic pranks (because they serve revenge), inflatable companions, and all the rest—a petty picture indeed—remaindered in the back of pulp magazines (watch the docu medley of LaVey's self-presentations—*Speak of the Devil*—for the complete lowdown).

LaVey's all-time favorite film was *The Abominable Dr. Phibes*. Phibes plays a deadly prank on the doctor who attended his wife at her decease. Of course he blames the doctor. Phibes has hidden inside the unconscious doctor's son the key that alone will open up the bindings that strap the boy to the point of reception of poison set to drip down on him in the amount of time in which the doctor failed to save the wife. During the time of this test, Phibes locks himself into the undeath position alongside his mummified wife. Around the crypt core in which Phibes and wife will no doubt remain hidden and preserved, the elaborate private circus, carnival, or musical theater in which he had propped up the home address of his vengeful fantasies systematically crashes down on schedule and by Phibes's orders. The son isn't sacrificed. In fact the prank Phibes pulls is his theatrical appropriation of the melancholia that might attend the setting of the son, but is not as likely a consequence of the passing of father or wife.

Dr. Phibes Rises Again opens flashbacking across the prequel, the story of revenge sought for destruction of Victoria and of his own face. A series of murders unfolds, each one greeted by songs of triumph and revenge performed by his clockwork musicians. His wife is neither alive nor completely dead: hers is a suspended life. It's three years later, and Phibes comes alive to the outside chance of finding the means in Egypt to effect resurrection for Victoria and eternal life for both of them. He summons Vulnavia to assist them. Vulnavia, who never speaks, is Phibes's bodily or motility prosthesis. Phibes does all the talking but only as voice-over. A machine transmits his words caught in the act of communicating in his throat. No one need read his lips. Vulnavia sees to that.

Under the Pharaoh's tomb the river of life flows every three years. When enterprising thieves steal the papyrus map to the legend of resurrection, they pick up bad Phibes. "We have been forced to kill for you Victoria only that you may live again. For here where the mystic lines converge, we will find the line that separates the living from the dead." During the voyage by sea to Egypt, Phibes watches home movies starring Victoria. Meanwhile another passenger on board is running out of his elixir of life. That's why he's heading in the same direction as Phibes. Their lifelines will cross.

In *Satan's Cheerleaders* we witness the struggle between the Teen Age and midlife criticism (of youth that is wasted on youth or in youth). Role-playing Satanists who, apparently childless, like to hunt, rape, and sacrifice maidens, meet the cheerleaders, whose Slothful member, Patti, rises to the consciousness that she is of the same body as Satan. The only player who is also a believer, the local Satanic High Priestess, recognizes Patti's doubling bond with the in-group the Priestess worships. However, like a true Satanist, she does not wish to give up her hard-won power and privilege. Vengefully, she aims destruction at Patti, which on the rebound turns out to be a showdown, in the course of which Patti acquires a staticky mediated voice whereby she rewinds the winds that the Priestess sent whistling to whip her out of shape. Patti was rubber, the Priestess was glue. The Satanists required a virgin for their ritual. But the cheerleaders don't qualify. The Satanist leader (he holds the daytime job of local sheriff) blew the wad when he raped the one midlifer along for the cheerleading as guide or advisor, the gym teacher, who was the virgin. Midlife criticism loses, but to the teenager, who was truly Satanic, whereas they only passed as or played at Satanism—as perpetual teenagers. In the end, Patti's avocation is to her advantage: she cheerleads the team to unstoppable victories.

If LaVey admired H. P. Lovecraft to the point of including the Cthulhu legend in his Black Mass, it is because Lovecraft, appearances and apparitions notwithstanding, could be viewed as cultivating, in the reversed mode of disgust, the same tenets as those guiding LaVey's affirmation or exhibitionism of our abject relations with the Devil. The Devil not only watches but also inspires a neurotic medium of disgust, which Lovecraft raised to the power of literature: a body or corpus gets built in slo-mo out of returning blockages or repressions, something any body might attend to while coming down off the exstatic cling of certain drug-induced de-repressions. The dread mongrelization that lowers the doom in Lovecraft's "The Call of Cthulhu" in-stalls itself as extended span of time right before and during the saving repression. Lovecraft does not make the jump cut to one more projection for the rote recognition of inhibited minds. LaVey, for his part or party, stays with the scandal in a meglo political mode. In "A Plan," for instance, he bases his forecast of a victory of Satanism over Christianity on the melting plot whereby a new majority of half Jews and other hybrids (coming soon) will turn to the pedigree and look of evil "rooted in Judeo/Nazism" (20). These children of mixed unions—following the lead of the half Jews—will deal with the "and" that was dealt them "through new common denominators that render established stigmas as inconsequential" (21).

> Hereditary Jewish culture is a perfect springboard for anti-Christian sentiment. The Jews have a foot in the door as the only historically consistent scapegoated enemies of Christ.... To be a Satanist is, by association, already to be aligned with the universal devil Jew. The Jews have always had the Devil's name. They just haven't owned up to or taken pride in it, but rather have attempted to defend themselves against it. Instead of declaring that Jesus was a nut and a shit disturber and he got what he deserved and we'd do it all over again, they decided to infiltrate the Christian world and survive that way.... Just as the Nazis "Aryanized" certain needed Jews, we will see even more of the same phenomenon, given the pragmatically Jewish/Satanic connec-

tion. Gentiles without a drop of Jewish blood might concoct genealogical evidence of a Jewish great-grandfather, thus making them by
heredity, generational Satanists. . . . The only place a rational amalgam
of proud, admitted, Zionist Odinist Bolshevik Nazi Imperialist Social-
ist Fascism will be found—and championed—will be in the Church of
Satan. (21–22)

LaVey's link to projection seems here creatively or therapeutically interventionist. To get to this point, however, LaVey deliberately inhabits and
passes through a cross fire of the projections that accrue to the Devil as
his medium.

I remember one Good Friday I joked around with the regulars at
the West Hollywood dog park that for us Nietzscheans this was a *Good*
Friday indeed, the one holy day on which a world religion admits that
God can die. At which point a very well-meaning, very nice neighbor
blurted out: "I didn't know you were Jewish!" Rather than instruct her
that Jews didn't gather together to celebrate the death of Christ, one
might have instead affirmed the projection—that for "Nietzscheans," as
for Jews and Satanists, too, as far as she and I knew, Good Friday was
the High Holy Day, and nothing could compel us to go along with the
Christian recuperation on Sunday. This is also the gist of LaVey's take
on witchcraft: the crime according to the Inquisition was the bond with
the Devil, and that must be affirmed in contrast to the New Age Wicca
view that tries to get around the Christian frame of reference, for example, by tying the original witch to mother religions. *The Mists of
Avalon* sought a similar revalorization of the Christian grail legend by
making Morgaine, otherwise the demonized intriguer, in fact the Wicca-
style high priestess of mother deities who, when she saw she was on the
losing side, nevertheless smuggled her pagan symbols and meanings into
a mix with Christianity, which would give the new faith maternal aspects
and dimensions. The author, Marion Zimmer Bradley, who succeeded in
being ordained somehow as Catholic priestess, held the view aloft (outside the pages of *The Mists*) that the Judeo part of the Judeo-Christian
tradition alone was down on women: or, as she preferred to address her
(historical) opponents, the "Hebrews" were to blame. Psychoanalysis

joins The Church of Satan in affirming as fundamental the bond between witches and the Devil. Judaism stands at the front of the line of
all the earlier religions Christianity rehabilitated (often by reinscribing
the symbols or legends of these displaced creeds as symbolic of the wish
fulfillment Christ's resurrection realized on earth as it is in heaven—more
often by demonizing the best of the rest).

A 2004 remake of an old idea—called "Lucid Dreaming" according to
my informant, again at the local dog park—extolled the benefits of controlling your dream world to the point that one might even summon
the body double of anyone you desire for dreamy sexual contact or congress. At this point we get reacquainted with the notion of the succubus
(or incubus) as the demonic occasion for turbulent dreaming. In Huysmans's *La-Bas* and *En Route*, the Satanist Madame Chantelouve exercises
this sexual power over or via the dream thoughts of the protagonist.

> A strange fact, which seemed to point the difference between this state
> and the unconscious uncleanness of night, was, beyond certain epi-
> sodes and caresses which could only follow each other in reality, but
> were united at the same moment in the dream, the sensation clear and
> precise of a being, of a fluid form disappearing, with the sharp sound
> of a percussion cap, or the crack of a whip close by, on waking. This
> being was felt near him so distinctly, that the sheet, disarranged by the
> wind of the flight, was still in motion, and he looked at the empty
> place in terror. (*En Route*, 169)

While writing *My Mother: Demonology*, Kathy Acker dreamed up
new writing sources and reserves. She trained herself to control her
dreaming, to pick up a dream right where she left off when she last awak-
ened, and to remember her dreams. She was not, however, interested in
the other world of dreaming. Or, as the writing-self advises in *My Mother:
Demonology*, "I have always despised fantasy" (225). Acker placed her
body and corpus on one continuum with as many projections as she
could throw a fit with. Dreaming relies on projection, as does the delusional system of the psycho, his and her new world or word order.
(Freud once noted in passing that even the ego, bottom line, is a projection of the body.) For long hauls in the composition of her demonology,
Acker watched movies and metabolized them, first in her sleeping,

dreaming state, then in writing. At the same time she sought to extract writing from her sexualized body, a body massively traversed by projections, including the cinematic ones to which the body skewered on a dildo was also responding before or after or during its dream response. In interview Acker answered my question about the resistance she might have encountered in turning her body into writing as follows:

> But with dreaming, if you work hard at breaking through the resistance, it gets easier every time. By the time I finished *My Mother: Demonology*, because the book is really my "Interpretation of Dreams," I was waking up five times a night so I could write down my dreams. I trained myself. I had a hard time *not* dreaming. . . . Dreaming and masturbation are different techniques of writing. The writings I get from masturbation aren't fantasy narratives but are descriptions of architectures, of space shifts, shifting architectures, opening spaces, closing spaces. . . . Right now I suspect that the language accessed during sex has some relationship to Kant's categories. (Rickels, 113)

While thus laying claim to new frontier zones of writing, Acker was also seeking, as the writing-self declares in *My Mother: Demonology*, "the power to reclaim myself" (249).

For her demonological exploration of projection, Acker ostensibly departed from her signature work of incorporation of novels with recognition value whereby even the pre-curse of originality could be lifted. In *My Mother: Demonology* even *Wuthering Heights* is in the first place a movie (146) before it passes through the dreaming, remembering, writing, reading body into demonology. The mother part of the novel's title also emerges in this series (on the other side of the "colon"): "Then I dreamed or saw a movie. . . . There was a woman holding a huge dog by a leash. She had no eyes. It was my mother. She said, 'I've been looking for you.' I woke up. As I woke up, I realized that my mother was trying to murder me through me" (251).

In "Reading the Lack of the Body: The Writing of the Marquis de Sade," Acker identifies rejection of the mother as the trait distinguishing certain female characters—at least in Sade's "patriarchy" from "Hell"—as enjoying a "propensity for freedom" (67): "The daughter who does not reject her mother interiorizes prison" (69). Acker underscores that in Eugénie's formulation of her matricidal wish lies above all certainty: "in *Philosophy In the Bedroom*, Eugénie, no longer a virgin in a number of ways, admits to her female teacher that the most 'certain impulse' in her heart, note that she does not say 'deepest,' is to kill her mother" (68). Certainty rather than passion gets the mother—the off-limits body, the missing body, the loss that one cannot lose—out of the way so the daughter (or, interchangeably, the son) can make back-end deals with the primal father (or Devil father). Dolmancé's counsel tries to make of the interchangeability of gender in this primal phase a masculinist virtue or privilege: "Women can 'transform . . . themselves into men by choosing to engage in sodomy'" (69). But "to have the breach open always" applies equally to mother, little boy, and little girl at the same time that the third-party intruder, before the advent of Oedipus and substitution, monopolizes sexual difference as his exclusive right to penetrate. With the introduction of the era of the anal theory of birth, the woman's reproductive body, conceived as article of faith, has no hold or place here. The privileging of sodomy therefore requires, in the outside chance that the wrong orifice is penetrated in the polymorphous activity of orgies, a woman's right to abortion. As Acker observes, "Only a belief in God, rather than in Nature, could lead a human to value an embryo more than herself" (70).

In league with the Devil, the writing-self in *My Mother: Demonology* can address something dead, something of her own, as the world and in the word of death: "Since my childhood is dead, in speaking of it I shall be speaking of something dead, but I shall do so in order to speak of the world of death, of the Kingdom of Darkness, or of Transparency" (185). The Devil gets the writing-self across or through or beyond—trans-—the parents, with the mother at the front of the line. The mother, a suicide, is doubly inside the writing-self trying to take her out. "That night I dreamed my last dream. In which my mother tried to kill me. She didn't succeed. Then someone else tried to murder me. When I asked who the murderer might be, the Voice told me that it wasn't my mother. It was a question of time. 'But it must be my mother,' I replied. 'Yes: it's your mother who's now inside you'" (226). To get herself out from under the

dead wait with mother, and transform the murderous merger into writing—"When I was five years old, I knew that Mother wanted me to be a
red or dead child" (52)—the writing-self passes through p-unitive relations with the pre-Oedipal father, the Devil father. This father—in whom
she recognizes that the quality of evil inheres in the quality of artistry
(101)—dutifully sets out to abuse his daughter in order to realize his ultimate work of art, a masterpiece of horror:

> "In order to see horror, I have to touch or fuck horror." (99)
>
> Father said, "To paint horror, I must violate both vision and my own
> child." (100)
>
> "I must see horror. I said that to see must be to touch or become what
> is seen." (103)

The writing-self in *My Mother: Demonology* passes from imprisonment by the mother's missing body to the sexuality the Devil father first
administers.

> I was imprisoned by my mother and had no father. My body was all I
> had. (10)
>
> I escaped my mother because sexuality was stronger than her.... The
> acceptance of this separation between sexuality and being was an
> invention of hell. (14)

The writing-self was all along telling "everything" in order that the
Devil father would "kill" her "faster" (24). Or since murder and dream
are interchangeable (via the lack viewed as central to both [35]), the
Devil father should dream her faster, hold her fast in the dream body,
bind her in projection, meet the exhaustion of "everything" said and done
with the exhaustion, wasting of the body and its projective Sensurround.
"I always want to test everything to the point of death. Beyond" (24).
But death metamorphoses or translates—back and forth—into dream,
into projection.

Red is the color of dreams, of horror, of murder, of writing. Just as
"led" follows or serves the guiding verb "to lead," so "red," for "read,"
could give us the clear text and past tense of reading, which, as Acker

underscores, is already also writing. "The more that I write my novels, the more it seems to me that to write is to read" ("Reading the Lack," 66). In the beginning was the red word, the word as deed of writing. The pact with the Devil father soon follows. But in both Goethe's *Faust* and *My Mother: Demonology,* the pact goes into effect only with the assistance of the witch. In order to enter "the library of the witch" "where there was red somewhere" (125), the writing-self drags the paternal deed of her soul's possession down into the maternal body and underworld of writing/reading/remembering. "My mother spoke: From now on, whenever I dreamed, I called it *going back to the witch*" (116). "And so I began descending, *as in my dreams,* walking down the spiral staircase that led to the witch's library" (261).

In her study of Goethe's *Faust* as transference prop that in the course of Freud's self-analysis allowed him to articulate and reexperience various relations with the Devil father, Sabine Prokhoris takes both Freud and Goethe at their word when Faust's rejuvenation as promised by Mephistopheles cannot proceed without the assistance of the witch. In Freud's summons, the witch is also named metapsychology, the ultimate articulation of those otherwise discarded self-analytic spookulations to which psychoanalysis owes its inscription and application. According to Prokhoris, every paternal function in this Faustian-Freudian discourse "is gradually transmuted into unsettling, uncontrollable maternal terrain, subject as it eventually is to the witch. What one may call 'self-analysis' is this very transformation" (74).

Goethe's *Faust* serves as station identification for transferences passing through or into Freud's self-analysis. But it is also cite-specific medium mediated by the transference it mediates. Prokhoris reads Goethe's lines of dead-ication (to the reunion with spirits for which his completed *Faust* stands) within the grid of associations and contexts wherein Freud compulsively summons them, in letter and in spirits:

> This commerce with spirits and . . . this love act consummated with them, this fort-da, governs the self analysis. It is abundantly represented in Freud's dreams. And it likewise marks off the space of every analy-

sis. That is, it clears a broad path for the transference, to cite Freud's own words, or rather Goethe's, whom Freud quotes in rather surprising fashion, leaving the impression that an irresistible force has compelled him to reproduce the poet's words—as if they had materialized from somewhere else, like the shades they speak of. This same commerce with the spirit world is in evidence . . . in the upsurge of ideas leading toward metapsychology. . . . For metapsychology is the theoretical expression of this transference; it is what brings it to light. (89)

Her focus on the supplementary turn to the witch—and to the witch metapsychology—gives Prokhoris license and motivation to lump together vampiric spirits of the departed with the Devil. But otherwise the recycled blood of undead suckers is not the spot of blood you're in when you sign the pact with the Devil. The Devil's blood spots are fecal, menstrual, a medium for signing and all the other smear tactics of certainty, Dad certainty. But then the spot of blood is out, out of this limited economy once mixed into the witch's brew, the resource for red writing. If the pre-Oedipal father as Devil must turn to the pre-Oedipal mother as witch (who is there to serve him but with powers all her own), then it is in order to give the missing body a rest or breast, the prize of doubled life that the Devil promises in his back-end deals. In turn, the only father who can be resurrected is the early father joined at this rip-and-tear line with the pre-Oedipal mother. Thus, Prokhoris argues, the ambiguous Devil in the case of the "demonological possession" that Freud analyzes is "the father . . . truly brought back to life":

> He cannot exist in this diabolical form, in which he is again endowed with the attributes and features of the primal father, until the venerated, adored, deified father has disappeared. . . . Only when this exaltation comes to an end is the diabolical father, who had been imprisoned by the majesty of the paternal function, at last set free. (117)

As becomes apparent—a parent—on the Devil's body in Freud's case study, "the attributes and features of the primal father" are those that must be shared with or returned to the pre-Oedipal mother. The part or parting objects to which the father owes his projection (notably penetrating penis and buttocks) must double the breast tumescent with milk. This realignment is the objective relation of Satanic orgiastic sexuality. It is also the significance the built body shares sexually with the fuck dolly.

All of Them Witches: "Books are unfaithful—like men."

In *The Witches* Joan Fontaine is almost out of Africa, packing up the mission schoolhouse with her two attendants while all the natives shake and bake. "Nothing can eat your soul." Then the fetish gets in her face. Blackout. She gets a schoolmarm job, even or especially because, during the interview, she begins to decompensate when pressed about her African breakdown. He says, "Someone who has worked abroad would stimulate the children." She really can't talk about it—it was the fault of the witch doctors. Once in Heddary, she decides that it's "a nice place to get over things." Her employer, Mr. Bax, only looks like a reverend. His sister, Stephanie, explains: "It's all perfectly harmless, you'll see." There isn't even a church in the town, only the ruins of one, left in ruins over two hundred years ago. Wearing reverend drag is a little off-putting—isn't it a sacrilege? But in a small town it's also just something the local eccentric likes to do. The children are all alike: inbreeding. Her star pupil falls into a coma. JF finds decapitated boy doll with pins sticking in it. Stephanie, who assures JF that she'll like it here, even if the town is primitive, septic tanks, you know, is a famous journalist. JF reads all her articles, though she disagrees with many of her viewpoints. They become fast friends. The author even proposes that they coauthor an article about the continuity shot between African fetishes and the remainders of witchcraft belief in backwoods Britain. JF is ecstatic: just like an academic, she always wanted to be a journalist. But JF is also beginning to crack. A feather duster left behind by her housekeeper looks just like one of those fetishes out of Africa. A boy wakes up from his coma after his mother talks to the girlfriend's grandmother: Hands off Linda! In exchange for the vital signs mother and son leave the village. JF figures out that the only reason Linda would need to be kept apart from boyfriends and intact would be to meet the criteria for virgin sacrifice. She asks one question too many. Then she wakes up and finds an African fetish by her bed. She jumps out of bed, rushes out of her room, but is stopped at the opened door by a hanging African mask or shield. When next she wakes up, she's in an asylum. She can only remember the mission house in Africa. When she sees a doll that a little girl brought with her on the visit to the asylum, JF starts remembering. Yes, she remembers: a virgin is the best sacrifice. She escapes from the asylum. Then from her bedroom window she watches as the villagers gather inside the ruins of the church. She follows them inside: the recognizable face of Linda is stitched onto an amorphous writhing sort of rag doll with plastic doll limbs attached. Inside she finds a cat in the bag. Stephanie turns out to be the High Priestess of the local witch cult. "I willed you to come and you came. You came to join us and you shall." The followers push JF down to the ground. After their incantation is finished, Stephanie announces: "Now you're one of us." Like Faust, Stephanie wants to live one more lifetime: another fifty years. While still pretending to be only an essayist, Stephanie had suggested as rational explanation that witchcraft was a sexual thing for women getting old who relish a secret power when other powers are waning. "All my life I have tried to push my brains to the limit and put them at the service of mankind. Only now, when the end of my life is in sight, do I feel that I am really learning." JF doubts that this extension is possible. Read this book. Here's my translation of the refrain that lifts the restraining order of mortality: "Grow me a gown with golden down. Cut me a robe from toe to lobe. After the blow be struck, give me a skin for dancing in." What about Linda?! "That little idiot. What about my brain continuing into the twenty-first century?!" Don't think of it as summoning the Devil. That's a cheap shot. It's all about getting a power or force under control. The magic book is like a trigger used in a nuclear explosion. In the orgiastic ceremony Stephanie makes her moves like Martha Graham. Linda is now introduced into the services. But the orgiastic dancers run up against her off-limits status. Stephanie remote controls her. At a crucial juncture, JF cuts herself in order to befoul the ceremony. The book says, "At the moment of sacrifice let no blood be spilled." Stephanie dies. The cult members, who had been kept out of the loop of Stephanie's more advanced plans for witchcraft, are glad that local magic can now be kept at village level. Shaking the hold of the orgy drug, Linda's grandmother is glad that the local witchcraft she was always into stopped short of murder. Now, as the local popular teacher, JF is one of them, one of them.

NOTEBOOK TWENTY-THREE

The Legacy addresses, according to its ad campaign or ectoplasm, the "birthright of living death."

A couple of interior designers in LA get offered a job in the UK. She gets a check in the mail made out to "Margaret Walsh." "Does that mean I can spend it?" To her partner she says: "I don't understand. But I want to go to England." Something is drawing her away, so come what may, she's off to places she's never been. A motorcycle accident leads the couple to accept the invitation to stay in a manor owned, it turns out, by her own distant relation, Mr. Mount Olive. She was, after all, looking for where her English blood comes from. All sorts of people start arriving. They seem to know all about her. Mr. Mount Olive is ailing fast. Who's going to be the master of the house? Via the mediation of his medical equipment, Mount Olive addresses his guests as heirs. "I have waited so many years to meet Margaret. My legacy. The ring each of you wears. To you I bequeath my knowledge and my estate. Come receive the blessing of the ring." A gnarly hand grabs Margaret's hand and gives the ring her finger. She can't get it off.

The LA couple tries to live, I mean, leave. "Honey, it's not hopeless. We just got to get onto the right road." They keep on circling back to the manor to which she, as her look-alike ancestor in the portrait, was born. Her portrait double was torched by orders of Elizabeth I.

He plays it by the book: "Satan! Select one among them to carry my soul forward." The losers are killed off. The punishments fit their crimes. Mount Olive bought their lives.

Maggie shares the same name with the witch in the portrait that becomes her."It's me, it's me. I'm the one.""It's just a name. It isn't you." When a sniper on the mansion roof starts firing, Maggie is magically protected. She says to her wounded partner: "You see, it is me." There's a showdown in the hospitalization chamber at the mansion's core. Does the legacy transmit, or does the ancient one need a new vehicle? Maggie's wounded partner destroys the ancestor. Margaret emerges in his place. "It's alright; it's all over now. I've got the power." "What are you going to do with it?" "Anything I want."

Published in 1922, Lou Andreas-Salomé's *The Devil and His Grandmother* is submitted by Luisa de Urtubey (in her study *Freud and the Devil*), together with other Devil interpretations by Freud's disciples (including Oskar Pfister, Otto Rank, and Theodor Reik) that appeared at that same time, as proof that there were indeed blanks to be filled when Freud foreclosed the Devil in his analysis of Daniel Paul Schreber's *Memoirs of My Nervous Illness*—or rather, in other words, when the Devil foreclosed on Freud. Urtubey cooks up the Schreber case with close attention to the details. Schreber's family saw to it that most of the psycho's recollection of his soul murder was excised from the memoirs. But Schreber's passing reference to soul murder's similarity to Faust's pact with the Devil was left alone as was his historical note regarding some of his own ancestors who sought to extend lifetime through pacts of soul murder. Urtubey notes that as Schreber goes on with his listing of ancestral soul murders and (since his persecutor's influence over Schreber extends through both families' histories) the consequent transformation of certain of Dr. Flechsig's ancestors into "Auxiliary Devils," Schreber uses the phrase "appetite comes with eating." Thus, the relationship of soul murder, a pact with the Devil father through which an increase in life can be obtained at, say, Schreber's expense, is, Urtubey concludes, a regressed representation of castration as cannibalism and as such a most extreme expression of one of the forms of the phantasm of seduction by the father (79–81).

Freud catches up with his disciples in 1923 with his analysis of the seventeenth-century pacts between a painter and the Devil. In his demonological neurosis essay, Urtubey argues, Freud succeeds in separating out the contradictory sentiments that compose his otherwise obscure ambivalence regarding the Devil. The Devil receives positive aspects— even admiration and love—and the painter Haitzmann gets the negative sides and asides (namely, Freud's contemptuous dismissal) (124). The only parallel between the cases of Schreber and Haitzmann, Urtubey admits, is the pact with the Devil as source both of their suffering and of their distinction and benefit. The painter is treated as the Devil's son, and Schreber becomes Prince of Hell. In both cases the connection with the Devil is filled with anguish (over the castrating, devouring conse-quences) and topped off with prestige.

To determine how the case study fits Freud, Urtubey emphasizes, one, Freud's disdain for the painter on the basis of the reality of the events, a basis that loses touch with all bases of psychoanalytical thought, and two, Freud's complete *disregard* at the same time for the historical set-ting (this case is not medieval, for example, but baroque):

> Haitzmann, placed in a sort of atemporality, never resituated in his historical and cultural context, figures as an unconscious representa-tion, hence atemporal, the representation of "the possessed." It con-cerns an unconscious representation constructed by the condensation of a series of representations: baby Sigismund, bound to his nursemaid, who tells him about Hell; young Freud, traveler along the forbidden route of auto-analysis leading to the interior underworlds of the un-conscious and admirer of the Devil as cultic object of "primitive reli-gion"; the demonic hysterics of whom Charcot, the magician, spoke; and Freud's first hysterical patients, possessed by their demonic un-conscious and seduced by their diabolical fathers. (127)

Freud is thrown out of context. Contrary to Freud's evocation of the pure ore of the case material, says Urtubey, he retreats horrified, attend-ing only to some gravel, at the prospect of a man giving himself body and soul to the Father Devil. Freud's interpretation thus refers to his own case, to the time when he, a "new Faust," entered upon his phantas-matic pact with the Devil Father (128). "The painter represents Freud seduced by the demonic at the time of his auto-analysis and since then repressed" (133). Hence Freud seizes the father reference—based on what the Latin text of the church fathers referred to as the painter's loss of a "parent" and thus filling in the parent role the Devil assumes when the painter signs up to be his or her son—in order to express the long-repressed idea that the Devil is a representation of the father (135).

Another projectile Urtubey tracks back to its source and resources concerns the Devil's alleged therapeutic powers. "This identification shows Freud's hesitation to align himself with the exorcists close to the possessed or alongside the Devil. Up to this point he seemed close to the clerics while keeping his distance from the painter. But in this passage, he appears tempted to take the place of the Devil" (138). Urtubey is struck by Freud's use of "belief" with regard, interchangeably, to the Devil and to psychoanalysis (139). Is psychoanalysis, then, also seductive and perverse? she may well ask (while loading her own question or projectile). Perhaps in Freud's fantasy psychoanalysis has become the primitive religion of the Devil described in his letter to Fliess, dated January 24, 1897. Certainly the sentence Freud passes down in the letter is comprised of two parts. It's on the second hand that repression overtakes sublimation: "I dream, therefore, of a primeval Devil religion, whose rites are carried on secretly, and I understand the severe therapy of the witches' judges."

The obscurity wherein the origin of the Devil at first appeared to lie in the individual's development, as Urtubey again summarizes the way stations of Freud's netherworld itinerary (143), is the dark that surrounded the father seducer and that arrested Freud's advance toward the Devil father. Haitzmann through his crashed manifest of outright expression of fealty permits Freud to lift the repression. Perhaps the Devil writings of his disciples that followed the Schreber case and pulled up short before "A Seventeenth-Century Case of Demonological Neurosis" assisted Freud, too.

In *One's Own God and the Foreign God (Der eigene und der fremde Gott)*, which appeared in 1923, Theodor Reik explored the metabolization of brotherhoods skewered together, prior to all opposition (as in wars of religion), by the suicidal backfire of the overthrow of the former god. World religions worship only son gods who after the fact, after the change in godship, become, if the new one, the father god and, if the toppled one, the Devil father. In *The New Testament,* Jesus is not only tempted by the Devil but also possessed, himself perhaps a demon. When the Devil tries to tempt Jesus to demonstrate his supernatural powers by throwing himself from the temple roof, he touches on suicide rebounding from rebellion against the father. "The desire of the Devil corresponds to a suicidal impulse, a reaction to the self-aggrandizing impulses to topple the heavenly father" (134). Christ not only ascends into the heavens; he also flies through the air and falls into Hell. Where was Jesus for the forty hours before ascension? The question reflects unconscious doubt. At first the legendary answer, he went to Hell, reflects a breakthrough of repressed hostile impulses toward the savior. Later on Christ was also given a mission, namely to redeem the suffering souls. "Out of the greatest triumph of the Devil emerged over time the greatest triumph over the Devil" (134 n.1).

While it is true that if you contemplate the aborigines, it seems hard to keep separate the gods, demons, and spirits of the dead, even Freud's emphasis on the death wish, and its projection onto the deceased during mourning's onset, guarantees that the premier spirits will always be the evil or, indeed, demonic ones. In the early clan religions the gods were cruel and vengeful; the raw rebound of ill wishes toward a primal father required the protection plan of sacrifice. In time the clan religions gave way to new gods. The old clan gods were either, one, assimilated to the new gods in the mode of syncretism; or, two, they became heroes, auxiliary spirits (like angels), or go-between functionaries, servants, mediators; or, three, they were demonized outright. This is a developmental countdown of stages: syncretism yields to subordination of the earlier gods, which in turn, in time, gives way to their demonization (139). "The demon thus became the other ego of the divinity, a sort of supplement that contains his earlier more primitive essence; the old object lives on in this degraded form" (141).

Thus, it was ambivalence, all in a mourning's work, that found a partial resolution in the splitting off of the beloved traits as divine and the inimical features as Devilish. With mounting guilt and the matching strengthening of the yearning for the father as well as with the growing need for reconciliation, the significance of the father god also grew, and cultural changes softened his traits. The Devil picked up the slack he was given on the projection range. This fundamental rearrangement of illicit thoughts or feelings via their projection out into the external world counts, says Reik, as the greatest accomplishment of primal man. "The animosity of the believers didn't turn against the former god; rather, the earlier god became a hostile, vengeful, and heathen being who torments mankind" (142). While the new god is a representative of the son, the old god becomes the father god who persecutes the successful rival. The first god was most likely a son god the clan brothers derived via the deification or idealization of their dead leader. A demonic rival emerged out of an unconscious sense of guilt. He carried the traits of the clan god like a mirror image but also received and reflected the traits that the clan would have preferred not to encounter again. Cruel and hate-filled, he became the opposing image of god. "We have seen that dualism is grounded in the creation of religion: against the son god emerges in the father god, whose murder is in truth impossible, an irreconcilable foe, like Banquo's ghost arising threateningly and scarily before Macbeth" (145).

The Devil's abode underwent projective reversals, too. "Hell" refers via Hel, goddess of death, to *hehlen*, "to conceal," and to *Hehl*, as in the expression *keinen Hehl daraus machen*, which means "make no bones about it." If the realm of shades became over time a place of torment, then Hell is the former heaven that in the interim is held in disdain. That countless myths send the lover hero underground to retrieve his beloved underscores that the underworld itself is cathected. According to Reik, George Bernard Shaw brilliantly exploited the happy medium of projections otherwise shuttling between extremes in the lexicon of religion when, in *Man and Superman*, he showed the heavenly character of Hell in its dual role as amusement establishment.

Dante's Inferno is a movie — and a Coney Island attraction. It is also the story twice told of the protagonist Carter's relationship to fatherhood, first as

Devil Father, then, at the end, which is a new beginning, as Oedipal father. "Pop," the owner of "Dante's Inferno," gives Carter, who's down on his luck, a break. Beginning as barker, Carter becomes the unstoppable promoter and transformer of Pop's legacy until the new top attraction on the pier proves unstable and unsafe. It's no longer only Pop's legacy. In the meantime Carter is married to the boss's daughter with his own "Sonny" to bear in mind. But rather than heed the building inspector's warnings, Carter bribes him to keep silent instead. When the ride collapses (with Pop among the wounded), Carter avoids prosecution through his wife's testimony that he never met with the inspector. But the wife, who knows better, leaves with Sonny, while the inspector, as compromised delegate of Oedipus, kills himself. But Carter, unstoppable, launches his next project, a gambling ship or floating casino, which represents an advance in risk taking and spectacle over the former ride on the pier. At its opening, on schedule in spite of the safety considerations and concerns he ignores, a drunken customer lights everyone's fire during the dance number featuring Rita Hayworth and her Pop. Sonny, who happened to be on board, also almost went down with the ship. Thus Carter is brought to his senses as family man.

Hellzapoppin' is a movie about making a movie about the Broadway show *Hellzapoppin'* (a show that's trying out to make it to Broadway, all of which is the show). Welcome to Vaudeville: "Anything can happen and it probably will." We open with the film studios and cut to the projection booth — and to the projectionist (who throughout has powers over the film within the film, which is the film, manipulating both the frames themselves and the action that keeps on going inside the frames as though live on stage). Once this interventionist or directive self-reflexivity (compatible with German Romantic drama) is established, the titles come up with the film's reopening in Hell. Devils are busy "canning" "Guys" and "Gals." Two new arrivals (who just made us gag on the slapstick of an endless procession of animals exiting the finite space of their cab) demand of the projectionist that he stop and rewind the film, in which they are recorded and which we are watching.

"Hey operator! Let me see that part of the film again.""Don't you know you can't talk to me and to the audience." But they just did. Following the replay, it's decided that, like every other picture, *Hellzapoppin'* needs a story, a love story (in which to embed its own story or metabolism about being a show and knowing it). The recognizable love story is carried away by the other love story: a slap stick it to her routine, which, continuous with *Hellzapoppin'*, admits the economy of "forepleasure" (which as its collapsus corollary, foreplay, can never enter into play where it's possible to rewind but impossible to unwind). What kind of love is this, when a girl can't even get a kiss? Martha Raye has to ask. But she asked for it: she's happily the fort-da bobbin or poppin' of quickies without end.

The regurgitated relationship to the Devil father, from the case of Schreber to that of the seventeenth-century demonological neurotic, encounters more refusal on Freud's part, as Urtubey points out. He attributes the mix of gender traits on the Devil's person to the painter's pathology; otherwise, Freud proudly, lovingly affirms, the Devil is entirely masculine, phallic. In the preceding year, in writing about the head of Medusa, Freud had ascribed all the positive traits of the Devil's masculinity to castration anxiety. Urtubey is rough writing Freud here to draw a diversion. She already referred to the unambiguous masculinity of Goethe's Mephistopheles (141) (just as Prokhoris would proclaim Goethe's Faust as thoroughgoing a father figure as you can wish for or if there ever was one [119]). There is anxiety in influence.

Urtubey doesn't turn to the mother, however, but rather to the parental combo that Melanie Klein postulated shortly after Freud's case study of demonological neurosis. "Freud didn't admit that the imago of the father represents these pregenital desires or, in short, he couldn't accept that archaic desires could be projected onto the father" (148). And yet, as Urtubey admits, this generation of the Devil father—and the son's feminine position—out of both-sex traits is where Freud does erect the bridge between the painter's case and what he learned in reading Schreber's *Memoirs:* we're dealing here with a paranoid, because homosexually charged, or rather discharged, superego. Freud's focus on the homosexual disposition in his Faust fuckers causes Urtubey's reading to identify with the "loser." Freud treats the painter as simulator on the turf of factual reality because Freud *believes* in the Devil father seducer. Thus, Freud weighs the two pacts as though they possessed factual reality. Freud's conclusion that the painter finds what he's looking for when he gets a subvention or guaranteed income is therefore an "astonishing accumulation of arguments without rapport with one another" (155). Freud's explication of an ulterior motivation of the painter's neurosis is unique in Freud's writings in its Jungian character (the preference, namely, accorded to real-life conflict), in the denial of the significance of phantasms, drives, repression—the denial, ultimately, through the attribution of significance to self-preservation, of sexuality itself (157). But something returns or turns around here: for when Freud suggests that the exorcism was therapeutic (the first installment of his subvention support), the exorcist, the Father of the church, lands the role of therapist, while the Devil gets to play the role of the bad internal paternal object.

While Urtubey's close reading of the pockets of turbulence in Freud's study of the painter and the Devil is correct and justified, Prokhoris's reminder is just as right on: for better or worse we know that Freud knows that we're on transferential turf (111). Already the "believe" word signifies as much. Ferenczi, as we saw, keeps a strict accounting of certain patients who, often because of early experiences of adult untruthfulness, refuse categorically to allow the analyst to be right. Thus, belief in God gets replaced by belief in the Devil (much as the persecutor in persecution mania is the ideal father conceived negatively). Thus, belief in the Devil organizes a phase of the transference in these cases.

Both the repressed and the repression return within Freud's infernal frame of reference. In 1931 Freud would designate the mother the prime and unwitting seducer of her children. During his auto-analysis and while writing *The Interpretation of Dreams* (and, Urtubey notes, following his reading of books of and on witchcraft [45]), Freud replaced the father as demonic seducer with the nursemaid (or witch). In his letter to Fliess dated October 3, 1897, Freud shares his latest discovery, namely, that his father plays no active role in his own neurosis. The *Urheberin* or primal mother of his neurosis was his old nursemaid who told him extensively about God and Hell and who gave him an aggrandized sense of his own abilities. In a truly remarkable formulation, Freud credits her with having given him the means to live and *to continue to live*. According to Urtubey's hypothesis or "phantasm," the nursemaid entered into a sexual pact relationship with the diabolical father seducer; the nursemaid as witch takes her powers and orders from him. Does she clear the father of the abuse charge, or does she leave him standing accused through, across, behind her? Or in the course of the auto-analysis, does she, following a bout of regression, replace the father? Isn't she also masculine or of blended parental provenance? In the course of his auto-analysis, Freud makes a transition from the father seducer (the Devil) to the woman as seduced, as seducer, as castrated, as castrator. This is the same moment when Freud approaches the discovery of infantile sexuality and thus also its punishment, castration, whereby he is guided (back) to sentiments inspired by the female genitalia and the prospect of the mother's sexuality. When, in his letter of September 21, 1897, Freud announces to Fliess his abandonment of the seduction theory, Freud's anticipation of the glories that will come his way as a result of this shift in his hysteria paradigm suggests to Urtubey just the sort of benefits one might hope for from a pact with the Devil (27).

Freud's relationship to the Devil is, already as early as, say, 1893 (the year of his Charcot eulogy), profoundly ambiguous "because he is sorcerer to the extent that he evokes the evil demonic desires and he is exorcist to the extent that he makes them disappear. Just the same, the accumulation of these two roles, to summon the demons and to send them away again, is characteristic of the sorcerer" (Urtubey, 27). Thirty years later, "he sees himself as sorcerer; the evil spirits he conjures are the unconscious of his patients and, notably, their transference, hence repetition, and above all repetition of incestuous love and the baneful experiences of the past" (167). In his 1926 article on psychoanalysis and medicine, Freud quotes Hamlet and Mephistopheles on words signifying magic: the talking cure, too, could thus be viewed as magical. The *Malleus Maleficarum*, Urtubey reminds us, underscores that curing by words is the magical act that defines witchcraft (166). But from the Christian point of view, as represented by Oskar Pfister (in his letter to Freud dated November 24, 1927), the world of Freud's *The Future of an Illusion*—the world as revealed, treated, or administered by psychoanalysis—would be Devil's island. And Satan's hand would put us there, not the random momentum of blind chance.

According to his first equation between the unconscious and the Devil, Freud set out in his auto-analysis to encounter the Devil (only several weeks after his father's death). Early on along the way (in a letter to Fliess dated January 17, 1897) he comments on the possessed:

> What would you say, by the way, if I told you that the whole of my brand-new primal history of hysteria was already well-known and had been published a hundred times over—several centuries ago? Do you remember how I always said that the medieval theory of possession, held by the ecclesiastical courts, was identical with our theory of a foreign body and a splitting of consciousness? But why did the Devil, who took possession of the poor wretches, invariably defile them, and in a revolting manner? Why are their confessions under torture so like the communications made by my patients in psychical treatment? Some time soon I must delve into the literature of the subject.

In his follow-up letter, dated January 24, 1897, Freud cuts from the chaste to the confession particulars of witches, most likely, Urtubey wagers, as encountered in the diabolical and sexual discourse of the *Malleus Maleficarum*. The meaning of witches riding broomsticks is their servitude to their master the penis. Urtubey asks: is it the paternal penis as part object? Is the witch conjoined with the paternal penis, or does she possess a penis? Or is this the composite picture of both parents at once merged in uninterrupted coitus? When Freud points out that the rites of witches are to this day child's play, he gives an advance preview of his discovery of childhood sexuality (which then makes way for the abandonment of the seduction theory). In this letter, which includes his earliest reflections on the perversions, Freud is inspired to see his future work all laid out before or behind him in primitive sexual cults from the Semitic orient, whereby Freud couples Moloch, a masculine divinity that devours children, with Astarte, a feminine erotic divinity.

In another letter to Fliess, dated June 10, 1900, Freud contemplates an intellectual Hell wherein one can discern "the silhouette of Lucifer-Amor." This Devil reunites with (and within him) all the contradictory elements: shade, light, love, death. In *The Interpretation of Dreams* Freud considers Tartini's Devil dream (and, by association, the equally inspired production lines signed by Goethe and Helmholtz) as illustrating a "demonic power" that created the desire of the dream and that we now can rediscover in our unconscious. We are here at the stabilizing end of the auto-analysis, according to Urtubey; what was at first a tumultuous encounter and "led to the discovery of infantile sexuality and of Oedipal conflict can now be theorized, explained, and sublimated. The symptom has become metaphor" (50). But it isn't conclusive; we can't be sure if the unconscious is the metaphor for the Devil, or if the Devil is the metaphor for the unconscious. What we end up with instead is "a circular relation . . . that includes at the same time metaphor and metonymy and is ready to be reborn at each instant" (50).

NOTEBOOK TWENTY-FOUR

In *The Devil and His Grandmother,* Lou Andreas-Salomé introduces us into the cycle of the deceased's digestion under the Devil's guidance. The Devil proposes marriage to a newly dead girl crawling out of her grave's decomposition to find herself alive again, alive to the prospects of Hell (4–7). In Hell her gravesite is rear-side seating up against the ass of the Devil's grandmother. In contrast, God admits souls only after they have been "de-assed" (7). At bottom, the dead in Hell are free to be themselves, to create or re-create themselves interminably. "Satanized you enjoy yourselves for the first time completely: Give yourself to me— and you have been given to yourself" (7). The love the Devil offers his bride-would-be is "selfless" as only "Devil's love" can be: "I am nothing but the space in which you burn bright, nothing but the emptiness in which you fulfill yourselves.... With my border of many thousand sparks, I proceed as illumination in order to celebrate you" (10).

The Devil's proposal is knocked out by an accidental reversal in grandmother's anal productivity: an undigested living baby falls by the rear side into the lap of the girl's untenable affirmation of reproductive life. What follows is all the show the Devil must rally against reproductive creativity: the girl's body gets laid out as waste production in the projective lab space of anal birth or animation.

The Devil summons an audience of prospective clients to view his own brand of motion picture. The good citizens agree to grant the Devil a captive audience.

> "Well then: that business is done. Let's go then! For my little dolly has likely done her business, too, in the golden pot." (Rapidly increasing darkness in which one can only vaguely make out the high smooth

wall pushing up in place of the abyss. . . . The wall surface illuminates
itself; in rapid sequence animated pictures glide across. Music starts to
play.) "Did I catch a disappointed cry: 'Just a movie'?" (27)

But no, this is the film from Hell: in it the viewers will see accomplished
"what was not yet in" them, namely, the "grinning decomposition" of
their "basic life force" (28). To this end, the Devil himself will play an
original role in this film, "not as image of something that has happened,
no: as a living embodied happening in the film": "Everything there passes
by as depiction; only I, myself mirror image and illusion, am only there
my essential self" (30).

The Devil's silent film is the remake of his marriage proposal. Poster-
sized intertitles (represented in the text as boxed-in bold-letter phrases)
are suspended in the scenes that follow when dialogue or voice-over is
called for. The Devil and the bride are all dressed up and ready to go.
"Passing by them, to musical accompaniment, artistic creations in all
media, now uniting into composite effects, now presented separately in
increasing and decreasing enlargements of the parts" (31). In writing,
then, the Devil offers his betrothed all this and more if only she would
belong to him alone. But the response that captions her dumb show: "I
am sufficiently rewarded if you just grant me life." This was of course
the sore spot they were already in. He goes on (and on) about their
eternal rule. She reformulates her wish with great modesty: just the least
proof of life would make her happy. Whereupon she begins to pluck out
a small flower by the roots: if this can be replanted in their abode and
thrive there, then she too can flourish. The Devil tries to stop her—but
it's too late too soon. Where before the plant grew in the meadow, "a
hole in the film" opens up as bright piercing light "as happens with used-
up reels" (32). The film steps back from representation into the background of rapidly alternating scenes; in the foreground the runaway bride
crashes through the projections with the Devil in hot-as-Hell pursuit. She
faints upon a bed—"the film bed." The Devil proceeds to undress her:
"This makes for a show in its own right in that the film brings each body
part before the eyes of the audience in penetrating enlargement" (32).

Next the bride makes the cut, the Devil's cut or portion. The Devil cuts her up along the dotted lines of her strip show's fragmenting projection:

> Now he pulls his tail out from behind his coat tails, grabs its end between bunches of hair and sharpens it with his pocketknife, whereupon it begins to glow red. Then he plunges it into the navel of the sleeping girl; from there he draws his cuts in star formation. Then, in similar fashion, he cuts around each of the nipples; then around the mouth; finally he slices up arms and legs. (33)

The Devil's direct address to his audience takes over where the intertitles have left off. He seeks to reassure them that when snuff is enough, the result is abstract creation (which only but especially in its cleanliness betrays the extreme anality it wipes clean). "What balm for the eyes— without blood and wounds! How clean and exact the specimen! As a wonderful mosaic of death and life, uncorrupted in forms and in colors" (33). A puzzle play with mosaic pieces—affirmed as the Devil's specialty in the area of creation—picks up where the bride's body and the consummating cutting left off. "What you call decay and dismemberment becomes for me in the first place plaything" (35). Thus, the ends are justified, from the Devil's point of view, as free beginning or creation. But for those of us out in the audience, this arresting of the end in pieces still spells: *Aus,* over and out. While crying out the "over" word over and over again, he tosses bride bits out into the audience: midair they stop to form a final intertitle, but this one is mixed media, red lettering of one big "Over." But the audience just won't take the Devil's *Aus* for an answer and rises up against and through the field of projections, landing down in the abyss in front of Hell's gates. When they pass through the gates, Hell seems only a stage or film set. Then a scream interrupts the strict silence of the silent film from Hell. This unheard of cry never should have happened, never happened before, like the living baby dropped in the bride's lap. It was the cry of one dying—and it was already more than enough to fathom Hell beyond the trappings of illusion, detour, mistake, or trickery (37). As accident and contradiction turning up the contrast with the silent-movie intertitle—"Loud and terrible were the bride's screams"—the scream of one dying, of one lost, can be heard elsewhere or otherwise, the audience concludes, as song in praise of God.

In *Mardi Gras Massacre* the serial killer is reenacting Aztec sacrifice. But the frame of reference is Christian. He hires whores to serve unwittingly as his sacrificial victims because they're "evil." As he asks one of his prospective sacrifices, "Are you sure you're really evil?" The outside world, which is all indoors, looks like a relay of 1970s-style steak houses. We keep on returning with killer and whore to a kind of examining room where she, just like the other victims, gets strapped down to a table. He lubes her with warm oil massaged into her body. So far kinky but OK. Then he goes into the next room to slip into something more High Priestly, more Satanic. He lays the long dagger on her belly. What follows is done "directly": no editing, no camera blink. He cuts into her hand. She hollers, but her bonds won't let her go. Then he goes to diagonally opposite foot and stabs the sole. Then he cuts out the heart whole from his living victim.

While the Devil was organizing the pieces of his bride into patterns of his own invention, he also piled up "spook formations." The combination prospects are endless, unlike all "works" that, like the life-forms themselves, must pass on, fall apart, "decay like spooks." The mixed metaphorizing with "spooks" gives the lie or slip to the Devil's abstract game. Because to "decay like spooks" is to come back. Thus, when the film medium projects the pieces of the bride larger than life, their images unfold "as though sharply animated by the drive to exist." What we see here we also recognize: her lidless eyeballs "out of which spectacularly clear despair without hope looks at you—grief over that which is irretrievably dead" (34). Hence, in lieu of the mourning that strikes up between the scrubbed-down lines of cutting—a blank his grandmother or mother will fulfill for him—the Devil commits suicide, which his mourners prefer to view as his becoming whole again in re-union with the Father. The pull of this promised union, however, doesn't hold a candle to the push of suicidal grief accumulated in unmourning and undeath.

The Devil first tried re-pairing his dis-pair: If an undigested living baby could slip through or past grandmother's excrementality, then why, oh, why cannot the reverse also occur and that which was already digested be again animated (39). As he again picks up, piece by piece, where the bride took leave, he is struck—down—by the weight of just one bit, heavy with "life's greatest secret" (39). He turns to his grandmother, the source of secret and secrecy's powers, to see if a slice of wife—a slashed piece he refers to as "tiny rhyme"—can recover and come alive again under her care. To reach her, the Devil projects himself outward in meglo mode over the tops of vast mountains until his supersized visitation is greeted by the "avalanche" of grandmother's "laughing voice through the night." Grandmother is willing to give one "little rhyme" new release. But, the Devil ponders bashfully, doesn't one always need two, a pair, for rhyming or conjugation? He is chided for trying to pull one over his grandmother, to get two for one—and the special request goes away without saying. If the Devil, too, requires animation, incarnation with pairing potency, then we are given to understand that he cuts up his brides for re-creation not only because he can't engender life, but also as compensation for his failure to get it up. As Norman Brown argues, and as the Osiris legend already spelled or spilled out, the resurrected body is the body again but without the genital center. Andreas-Salomé begins to dig our own grave in the gaps and overlaps between life and unlife.

According to his grandmother, it's time for her Devil boy to reunite with God the Father. The Devil still dreads the dissolution of death. But it's not about death, she reassures him, it's about becoming whole again. You wouldn't seduce a seducer, would you? To grandmother's peace he goes. Besides, she counsels, his Devil role is by now beside the pointlessness. His mission came full circle, completed itself, with Christ's mission possible: through the Devil man was deified and then through Christ God was humanized (44). He's just a leftover piece of what belongs together: he was mistaken to take up his place of exception as being apart—or to be all cut up over it.

He therefore goes ahead and exposes himself to her light—and wipes out frame by frame like a motion picture. He diminishes in stages, even passing through the stage of childhood. His grandmother always knew that her Devil son was never any different or worse than any child who out of curiosity—surgically or sadistically—takes apart containers. To grandmother's peace he goes. But will there be anyone to mourn him? the Devil wonders. Christ, he pouts, gets all the grief for the crucifixion and a mere three-day visit to Hell. But, as becomes clear by the end of Andreas-Salomé's poem or play, whoever follows Christ gets around grief—except the mother, *save* the mother. The grand mother of pre-history, the first mother of God, is also the Devil's and his brother's mother. Right before the Devil goes, he hears her crying, grieving over him. He dies crying out: "Mother!" (51).

In *Psychomania* suicide in the Devil's name isn't suicide anymore. Indifference to individual death occupies interchangeable places with the indifference to individual lives. Leave and let leave. The biker gang "The Living Dead" hangs out in a Stonehenge-like setting where in fact witches were once turned to stone for breaking their bargains with the big one. It's called "The Seven Witches." The leader of the pack is attracted to the girl with complications. "It's not me that scares you. It's the world. Let's cross over to the other side. We kill ourselves. But we'll come back. It'll be even better." In Christianity this is what believers want to do, in order really to believe: take a round-trip to Hell and back.

We attend a séance. Through the medium the clients learn that their dead daughter couldn't be happier: "It's so lovely here." The clients offer antique cross that's been in the family forever as gift in lieu of the payment the medium never takes. Horror! The manservant intervenes: "Get out! Get out!"

The medium is the leader of the pack's mother. He wants to know how the dead come back. Forget long-distance connections! "Don't go on with this, you don't know enough." He pressures her into giving him the key to the secret room. Once inside he's at the movies. He sees himself as a child riding around the primal stones. His mother also has a baby. A figure arrives. She signs document. The figure snatches the baby away. The biker son passes out and wakes up holding his father's glasses. He overhears mother lament his father's mistake. "I told him, don't cross over. You don't have the faith to come back. When you die, you've got to believe you're coming back with all your being." "Thank you, mother, thank you very much."

Biker quickly crosses over. His gang buries him at the Seven Witches. Then in no time he's back—and super powerful. "It can be done. You have to believe you're going to come back, believe enough so that you really want to die. You can only die once. After that nothing can harm you." "Man, what are we waiting for?" Only one out of the next two comes back. "Hinky isn't coming back. At the last moment he hesitated—he didn't really want to die."

Inspector interviews the medium mother. She learns for the first time from him that another member of the gang committed suicide and that the grave was next day found empty. She tells her manservant: "Please tell the inspector if that girl comes back, not to have anything to do with her— it's evil!"

Even though she now knows that suicides can come back, the girlfriend has nightmares filled with double takes and second thoughts. In her dreams she's the successful suicide. But then she's corpse, nurse, and witness. She wakes up. She's so glad she didn't die.

The suicide pack of daredevils follows leader and comeback girlfriend at the front of the line into transgression. He wants them all to drive through a brick wall just to survive what should have killed them. Girlfriend didn't leave a hole in the wall. "My back wheel skidded." "Liar—you're not dead." "That's what I was trying to tell you. I don't want to die."

Mother: "I must stop him." Manservant, minion, or master: "You made a bargain, it was for all time." "I'm going to break that bargain."

Leader confronting his girl: "If we kill you, you can't come back. If you kill yourself, we'll be together forever. You've got three minutes to decide."

Minion or Master:"You know what you will become and that it will be
for all eternity. And that your son was part of the bargain and that he will
have to pay too.""It was his own doing." Medium mother turns into big old
toad.

The gang members prepare to kill the girl stuck on the world. Suddenly
they turn into more stones to count at The Seven Witches.

It takes two codas for Andreas-Salomé to part with the affirmation contained in the closing lines of Goethe's *Faust*. The Devil's bride, now reanimated, reclaims her sensorium. As she learns once more to separate
things out in her field of vision, recognition, or even existence, she also
experiences the separation that links and limits her encounter with the
very world to which she is returning. She is given consolation and direction by a reflection she glimpses on the surface of the water: a grieving
mother cradling in her lap her dead son. It is sheer reflection without
original. "Was the surface a final depth?" (53). The revivified bride affirms
the maternal, therefore, as the tight spot of birth (and rebirth) and the
dead end of unmourning. Mother's embrace—her materiality or medi-
ality—is commensurate with our firmament. The eternal maternal draws
her onward: toward a conclusion in the image. The primacy of the image can be hitched to the ascendancy of belief. No image without belief
in it: hence the image that everything ultimately is equals image of belief. Death, too, is but an image of belief. What she saw was the corpse of
God's son—Christ or the Devil—a child again on the knees of his grieving mother. Death is, then, the image or reflection of that which will
transfigure the dead son as resurrected (54–55). But as Derrida points
out, the resurrection, importantly, can be "shown" or "proved" only via
the empty tomb: this double whammy belongs to the bride's aside that
belief in images (even or especially, Derrida adds, in live transmissions)
renders death an image *as* reflection of resurrection, of that which is in
turn, turn, turn, image of belief. All that is transitory—or, in Nietzsche's rendition, all that is intransitory, immutable—is but image. The
word Goethe uses, *Gleichnis,* resonates in German both with *das Gleiche,*
"the Same" that the overman asks to return eternally, and with, internally,

die Leiche, "the corpse," which on the stage of *Trauerspiel*, according to Benjamin, was the original allegorical margin of a difference from itself that therefore cannot but tell "another story."

Coda two places the dead Devil as subject of conversation between an old woman and the young girl with head and arm in her wide lap. With his passing, the Devil as supernatural spark, as monogram in lights, became human, maternalized in his setting (as son) and became thus mournable and unmournable. The girl awakens from a deep daydream. All these dreams, these daytime bouts of exhaustion, refer to the Devil's departure. But the old woman adds as proviso that it was the evil mode in which he took his departure—all the way up his meglo aspirations to replace the Father—that caused the breakup of their space-time continuum. But the girl understands that he would want to go where no one had gone before. The old woman recognizes words of love when she hears them and warns the girl not to deracinate herself in yearning for someone so ungrounded. But, the girl counters, rooted existence coexists with the wish or need to cut loose. The old woman advises that now that he has been restored to himself, reunited with the Father, the Devil would no longer be recognizable if he were to return. Flashing back to her last dream, in which she saw the Devil dead in the water on his mother's lap, the girl allows herself to hope that the restored or resurrected son could be accompanied to his reunion celebration, invisibly, by the departed Devil, whose return would be ghostlike rather than resurrected. But he would pass by unproven, unrecognized, the old woman points out. But I would recognize him, replies the girl, who wishes that the Devil's rebirth or comeback be her vehicle or that she, as his future, be given his ghost of a chance. What drove the Devil to suicide will pull him back: the return trajectory along which the dead clog, interrupt, and break up the transmission of union or unity. In other words: the eternal/internal maternal draws us onward.

Skeletons in open niches in the wall, a superimposed foreground of flames: that's the opening of *Demonia* for you. Sicily 1400: crucifixion of evil nuns. Toronto 1990: at the séance table a young woman, channeling the crying,

dying nuns, drops to the floor. She's an archaeology student who will be following her professor to Sicily for an excavation. Her prof advises her that
archaeologists dig into the past; they don't attend séances. "I only do it for
fun." Once in Sicily she's drawn to the ruins of the medieval convent: "These
ruins are so compelling. It feels like there is something alive in there." The
archaeologist is only interested in the finds from antiquity: he passes on the
convent in ruins, the Middle Ages crisis. But the student enters the ruined
halls. She hallucinates her double as nun, her forehead marked with what
looks like a question mark. On automatic she finds herself breaking through
the false wall covering up the vault of crucified nuns. She dreams that she
walks toward and beyond the arena, but the professor, Paul, tells her no, you
mustn't go. Liza, come back! In her dreams she attends the crucifixion. She
wakes up when the nail is hammered into her heart. Awake she still flashes
back to the crucified nuns. She goes to the Hall of Records to find out what
happened back then. But the local fortuneteller knows the story. Five nuns,
young and beautiful, each had a covenant with Satan. In the convent they
held their orgiastic rites. The young men who took part in the orgies vanished mysteriously. We see the sexual coupling coupled with murder: the
man is stabbed in the back at climax time. The blood is collected in vessels.
The fruits of those nights, babies, burn, baby. But then the townspeople
intervened, and we're back inside the crucifiction. The local butcher sees his
array of backroom animals as the crucified nuns. The slabs of meat attack
him. The meat hooks finish him off. Someone jabs the meat thermometer
into his tongue. Nun in white cloak leads away Robbie, who just wanted
some help. But then the boy is free to look for papa, who's tug-of-war-tied
between two trees held in check only by the trip wire that the son trips
over and breaks. The two trees tear papa apart right down the middle. In
the end the dead nuns, including Liza, who's also on a cross, foaming at the
mouth, are set blazing.

NOTEBOOK TWENTY-FIVE

Goethe's *Faust* establishes rhyming as Christian frame (in which the Devil also sets a spell). Faust invites Helen of Troy to join him in coupling via instruction in rhyming. Their progeny, Euphorion, inhabits the artificial abyss that rhyming contains and bridges. But then he seeks to expand the metabolism of rhyming to support flight. Even after he crashes and his mother follows him down into Hades, we never leave the artificial turf spanned and spawned by rhyme. Helena leaves behind her veil, which marks the spot of her allegorical return as cheerleader of the eternal or internal feminine of mourning. Rhyme as Eros or Lust exceeds (even while returning to) the end in sight rhyme also already projected or forecast from the starting position of Sloth.

Though Faust doesn't really die, at least not once and for all or right away, he must recognize the approach of the allegorical figure of Death as "rhyme-word" (the rhyme between *Not* and *Tod*). But this rhyme tracks back to the setting of his father's festivities where guests toasted in rhyme. Faust picks up the rhyming and toasting cup as vessel for his choice of poison (from the collection of medicines and/or poisons, which is his physician father's legacy). But the suicide Faust contemplates comes to be deferred by the trans-momentum of Faustian striving. While the rhyme-word pops up at or as the end, the end, which is not your usual death, is in turn caught in near rhyme, the metathesis keeping *sterben* (dying) and *streben* (striving) cycling through one another.

Composed in Goethean good measure—along the assembly lines comprising the portable *Faust*, lines Goethe gave (unconsciously on purpose, according to Karl Kraus) for easy recall and recitation—*The Devil and His Grandmother* is on one continuum with an otherwise surprising partner in rhyme: Michelle Smith and Lawrence Pazder's *Michelle Remembers,* in which the Devil's doggerel authorizes and authenticates the document. For better or verses, the Devil's rhymes only *seem* banal— they *are* evil, as, we are assured, only intelligent life can be. Dr. Pazder and his patient, Michelle, consult Father Guy: "If you look up Satan in a theological dictionary, it will say that he is known to speak in rhymes. And the form of the rhymes reveals his personality. They do not have an orderly structure, but they are very intelligent. And very deceptive. They all have meaning.... Satan will not humiliate himself to speak like ordinary people" (209).

The encrypted lines directed both over our heads and smack dab in the middlebrow are also the audio portion of the Devil's hands-on performance of violent cutting. While reciting his Master Plan, the Devil whittles away at the sculpted wooden body of the crucified Christ.

> During the course of the ceremony, he would whittle away at the carved statue... until nothing was left. Symbolically of the way he works in the world—undercutting—he would start his whittling at the foot of the cross and proceed upward.
>
> > "First cut away the feet;
> > Make a man feel incomplete.
> > Lose his footing, lose his ground;
> > Lose the way to walk around."
>
> ...
>
> He had reached the loins of the corpus.
>
> > "Then I chip away at the part
> > They say should be connected to the heart.
> > But I can separate it with one cut,
> > And make it separate, make it smut." (227–28)

When the chips are all off the old block—leaving nothingness and the prospect of the ritual's endless repetition—the Devil's ability "to project colossal three-dimensional images illustrating what he was saying" (223) takes over: "The sinister illusion was now a bottomless hole within a raging fire. Falling into the hole... were houses, cars, books, numbers, paintings, animals, coffins—the whole world seemed to be tumbling into the pit" (230).

Hellraiser: Inferno. At the crime scene the detective recognizes that he knew the victim in High School. "Once he tried out for the basketball team. We gave him shit. We gave him Hell." There's a cutoff finger lying around. In the meantime, the detective steals the nerd's stash of drugs. He finds a puzzle box among the effects and evidence. He gets it started. Then it opens itself. He opens the door onto his childhood bedroom. Women with smooth anal heads stick their hands, then arms up under the skin of his chest. They have long hard tongues. Pinhead opens the door and his face. Detective wakes up, intact, next to box, opens door, it's still in the meantime.

Autopsy results: when the finger was cut off, the kid was still alive. Detective takes the call. "Oh God, help me, aaah!" Slurp, slurp. Another child's finger to pick up. Video sent to detective. Butthead women whip someone to death. When he shows it to his colleagues — there's nothing on the tape.

"You're wrong about the engineer. You like guns. He likes to play. He doesn't want you to stop playing the game. He wants you to play the game." "I'm still going to find that child." "That I suspect is the object of the game."

"What do you know about the engineer?" "It was 1986, my first year as counselor, a veteran, like you, developed paranoia. In his delusions he elevated the engineer to supernatural status. These moods alternated with deep depression. He shot himself in the head." What the counselor knows about the box: according to the occult literature, it's a portal or gateway that allows the demons to come in and get you. "They didn't take me to Hell." "You opened the box?"

He's with the parents in the old rest home. "We don't like it here." Their door opens onto his childhood bedroom. Door shuts. "Mom?" Slurp sounds, shrieks, groans, blood slopping against and under the door.

We're back in the loop. Phone rings. "That was your mother. She had a visitor. I think she said he was some kind of engineer." Now the parents seem to have vanished from the nursing home. "I'm their son." "I didn't know they had a son." This time there's an address that goes with the finger.

The engineer phones him. "What do you want from me?" "I want you to go home." Wife and daughter are trussed, frozen up a shaft of deep freeze.

He picks up the obligatory child's finger. "The child's fingerprint is yours. When I told you to go home, I meant your first home. I know everything about you. Your file's almost complete." He turns into Pinhead. "Go back, go home to where you started, if you want to find the killer."

He finds his child-self strapped down in the torture chair. Fingers are missing. When he's about to shoot one of the buttheads for revenge, the cover comes off and reveals his double. Yes, every game, like chess, consists of random moves, but they move toward one single objective: to kill the king. "Who is the king in this game? That is the question you must ask yourself." "I don't understand." "How human always to plead ignorance. This is your life. You've allowed your flesh to consume your spirit. You are your own king. This is the Hell you created for yourself." There's only one finger left to go, only one life to leave, one more death to go. He wakes up alongside the box on the floor. He's back in the loop. He shoots himself at his desk. He wakes up again, same room, same loop. It's the other "forever," the one that rhymes with "never."

The bottom line of projected nothingness is the bodily cut. The Devil in *Michelle Remembers* sees to it that we—who should go forth and multiply—are all cut up over his slicing of life:

> Seizing the knife, the Beast drove it into the girl's chest. With a few violent strokes he cut out the heart and, scooping it up, he heaved it into the fire.
>
> "Twelve times two, and then add four.
> Cut it in half and then there's more."
>
> With another strong stroke he cut the body in half.... Working harder now with the knife, he cut the halves in half, then cut the segments in pieces. (217–18)

The cutting climbs over multiples to grow the body up and away into projected parts.

The Devil (in *Michelle Remembers* as in *The Devil and His Grandmother*) inhabits and wields the cut inside a field of projections recognizable as cinematic. The Devil offers, as the saying goes, to cut our losses.

To cut your loss is to accept it, let it go, but also write it off, turn it into a benign deduction that yields returns. However, in both instances of the Devil's representation, the cut runs up against a loss it otherwise tries to cut around or cut out. The loss asserted itself in Andreas-Salomé's (screen)play as suicide or, impossible to decide, as reunion with God and then as unmournable loss one of the girls offers to carry as ghostly return.

Michelle undermines the Devil's cutting and counting by concealing one of the holy relics the Devil drops during the ceremony. The principle of cutting your losses is advertised and sustained by the Devil's inner circle of followers as ritual removal of one finger. But when the missing bone relic cannot be retrieved, the Devil's economy falls a cut below the loss or missingness that only the divine love of Christianity can, apparently, redeem.

Cuts not on the screen, but secreted away, exceed the wounds on projective display, to which they nevertheless belong. The ritual mutilation marking the members of the Devil's inner circle is the last secret Michelle lets go in therapy at the end of her total recall of the projected Vision of Hell:

> "You see Hell!"... And as he spoke, the walls of the round room faded away, and it seemed to the child that she was in the middle of an enormous movie, with gigantic, soaring images.... Below them, as if in some ultimate nightmare, Michelle could see masses of starving people, bodies on battlefields, a million acts of cruelty somehow made visual all at once. "There's people with arms that are bleeding.... There's people with no eyes, and they're bleeding from their eyes. There's people that's got no noses! And there's people that got ears cut off.... An-n-n-n... and there's people with missing fing..." (213)

So there's one body part in the series that she can't part with—except by performing its cutting off. The girl just can't divulge it. But Dr. Pazder won't budge. She must tell if she wants to get well. She gives him the finger that makes the cut that gives the secret handshake: "'It's always the middle finger....' She looked at Dr. Pazder in terror. 'Oh, God, I said too much. Am I going to die?'" (215). The fuck finger goes down in the transference where it is left unanalyzed, uncut, and wholly at the service of holy healing. Now give me your hand! The figures of the Christian faith—with Ma Mère leading the procession—hover above in love during Michelle's trial and then install the repressed memory of her sojourn with Satan as up for release or revelation once a match can be made with ears to hear. In Ira Levin's *Rosemary's Baby*, the plot rewinds around the secret plot that is now proclaimed in rhyme: "The year is One, God is done! The year is One, Adrian's begun!" (298). Rosemary's anamnesis and decoding of those dream visions nine months ago are also triggered and received via stored souvenirs that operate like posthypnotic suggestions: "It *was* the linen closet. In a dream long ago she had been carried through it. That had been no dream; it had been a sign from heaven, a divine message to be stored away and remembered now for assurance in a time of trial" (287).

In *Michelle Remembers*, the religious frame of reference overlaps with the therapeutic, transferential frame. The Christian guidance back then, inside the repressed memory, leaves behind a placeholder, even a pronoun, through which the psychiatrist enters Michelle's life. Outside the book's ending Dr. Pazder takes Michelle to be his wife. The Pazders bypass the witch. "For it is the witch who makes it possible for the words which initiate the cure to become analytic, which is to say, transferential, discourse" (Prokhoris, 91).

The Devil's projective medium is subtended by the whirring network of recording devices whereby the in-session dynamic is doubled and erased as record speaking for itself. "Once the explanations were arrived at, sometime later, it all was fairly intelligible—almost impossible to conceive of, to hold in the mind, but at least intelligible. But while Michelle was reliving it—bringing it up from her depths and pouring it out for Dr. Pazder while the video camera hummed, recording her gestures and expressions—it was confusing in the extreme" (214). This admission of the setting of revelations in place of transference introduces the one memory—the missing middle finger—"that Michelle could not bring herself to divulge."

LaVey's impatient exclamation in fact addresses this live repression of memory with exacting precision: "Where was Freudian wisdom when psychiatry like *Michelle Remembers* was validated by the media?" ("To: All Doomsayers," 6). I, too, remember the 1980s, when our mass mediatization ran on the child abuse charge. The Devilish phase of the transference that Ferenczi identified in 1913 was the phase everyone was going through in the 1980s. Freud and the Satanists were codependents in cross-examination for the seduction offense.

NOTEBOOK TWENTY-SIX

Popcorpse, I mean, *Popcorn* offers a bag of teenage fun that sends the teacher home in a box first. Sarah wants to turn her scary dreams into movie material. In her apocalyptic girlhood dreams she's in the crypt with the Evil One, who wants to sacrifice her with his jagged sword.

At school the kids are putting together a horror festival as fund-raiser for their film program. "Welcome to the House of Ushers," namely, the specifically Southern Cal horror of service personnel who're just too young to know better than to ask if you're still working on it. While setting up the props, a short film is discovered. Opening shot of eye. "I am the possessor, possessor, possessed!" His head on a table: "Come into my head." In her dreams! Sarah passes out. The teacher recognizes the film titled "Possessor." It was the director's response to being laughed at for his earlier avant-garde work. At the screening he played the last scene live, murdered his family in front of the audience, set the theater on fire.

Back home: "Mom I think this is the man I've been dreaming about. I can't run away from something that's inside me. It's something psychic." Mom goes to the theater packing a gun. The letters fall down from the marquee. What's left spells "Possessor." This will be a one-film festival. She enters an automatically functioning theater. She alone screens the blast-from-the-past preview: "Coming soon, spreading retribution, death. They tried to stop it. Fifteen years in the making." Someone — or something — grabs her.

At the benefit Sarah sells tickets. Suddenly someone — or something — asks: "Will these films be as shocking as 'Possessor,' Sarah?" She follows and loses him. "I know it was him. Maybe he's still alive, he's older and his face is burned. Maybe he's lurking around, ready to strike—what a great movie this would make!"

During screening of radioactive mosquito monster movie, the teacher sends a mosquito prop flying above the audience. But the intruder overrides the teacher's remote control. The teacher gets the point of the mosquito's stinger. In the film within the film the mosquito is destroyed: "He's dead." We see the speared teacher. The intruder makes a mask from the corpse face.

"Maybe he thinks I'm his daughter. Her name was Sarah." "How do you know?" "I don't know!" You know. Sarah is listening to her ongoing tape recording of her nightmares. His voice comes on: "Sarah, wake up, your life has been a dream. You are possessed."

Backstage the intruder wears the teacher mask. One of his students, Tina, reveals the reason for her straight As. She kisses him. But the mask mouth slimes her. Soon the intruder wears Tina's face.

"No kiss for Daddy? Now it's time to join your mother."

"It's not a screenplay that I've been writing, it's my life. My unconscious has been trying to make me relive my past so that I would remember it." Mom, really her aunt, saved her back then. "Why is he here?" "To finish the film." Sarah is in the contraption for face making or saving face. It was her classmate Toby. "You might say I'm multi-identical. Sexual difference no problem. Lanyard Gates is dead." "If you're Toby, why are you doing this?" "We were sitting in the first row when your aunt shot Lanyard and set the theater on fire." He wants to re-create that night so maybe this time his mother won't die and he won't be burned. Thirty minutes before midnight. He still has "time to kill." Aunt mom is mummified holding a gun she can't fire. "I'm so glad I cast you in this part." However, the bug prop, on the rebound of negative transference, gets him in the end.

Among the parting shots of *My Mother: Demonology*, we find a cut above the rest, a cut in life that, just like bad language and puns, follows the beat of memory. "It's necessary to cut life into bits, for neither the butcher store nor the bed of a woman who's giving birth is as bloody as this. Absurdity, blessed insolence that saves, and connivance are found in these cuts, the cuts into 'veracity.'.... All these are found in the cuts.... The entire human being is found there" (267). Dario Argento's horror film *Suspiria,* one of the sustaining introjects of *My Mother: Demonology,* follows out the cutting across vision that admits demonization or projection.

One girl arrives at an all-red school only to witness another girl running. (Which school? The one where all the teachers, all of them, are witches.) We're on the outside looking in on the runaway in the bathroom. But then we're inside there with her, too. She looks out into darkness and sees herself mirrored in the pane. But then: two cat's eyes. Hirsute creaturely arms stab her without letting up, without letting go. At the end of the laundry line, her rebound breaks the glass ceiling below and splits the second victim, whose face is divided up by sharp shards. No eyewitnesses. The only outsider working at the school is a blind man walking. In time the seeing-eye dog chews out his throat. The catch to this movie, like a catch in the throat, is that the secret word the new girl overheard dead girl running cry out— "irises"—not only marks, as flower password, the secret spot of extended lifetime the witches are in every night with their centuries-old coven mistress, but also names the filmy surface of eyesight the film slices or otherwise secretes away in order to see better.

The iris, in German, is the rainbow of the eye. As the female Devil in love with the book dealer protagonist intones (in *The Club Dumas,* another novel that can barely contain between its lines the projection momentum that will get it into pictures): "The rainbow is the bridge between heaven and earth. It will shatter at the end of the world, once the Devil has crossed it on horseback" (204).

At one turning point in Arturo Pérez-Reverte's *The Club Dumas,* the protagonist, Corso, deals with a collector who must periodically sell a volume to maintain the rest. Once another sacrifice has been made, the collector goes back to playing his violin "to summon the ghosts of his lost books" (165). When Corso first makes his acquaintance, the collector is doubled over with the burden of choosing between two of his favorite collectibles, the best of the rest, a Virgil edition, featuring illustrations of Aeneas in Hell, and a first-edition copy of *De Re Metallica* by Georgius Agricola. The bottom lines of the Devil's projective medium are suspended here: between Hell and mining.

The novel drops these lines within a relay of self-reflections aggrandized through inter-reference to address all of letters—and their spirits. And yet the titular plot, which proves diversionary, not even a subplot of the Devil fiction, is the haunted text. But then even the main text devoted to the Devil—as the author or subject of Black Magic volumes that contribute not to melancholy self-collection but instead serve a certain purpose that uses them up—is subsumed at the end by a twist-off of literature's self-involvement as medium down to the fine printing. Two printers specializing in restoration of collectible ancient books were commissioned to restore without acknowledgment—in other words, to counterfeit—one of the original illustrations in the Black Magic book signed by the Devil. Only the collector who uses the pages to make the change knows for sure: he merely dies in the attempted transformation.

Roman Polanski swerves away from the book's title, the haunted plot from which it hangs, and all the reflexive loops beyond and in between, and focuses instead on the titles of his film *The Ninth Gate*. The film's opening titles and first scene open the surface wide to admit light that ultimately takes a double shining to the end, the convergence of the illuminated, illustrated book plates as of the film's titles with the binding brightness of Corso's transforming sexual union with the Devil. But all this depth or diversification never leaves the span of a projector's illumination, the surface of the filmic image.

David Seltzer wrote the novel *The Omen* after the film was already folding out of his original screenplay. As novel that one could not but write or read as basis for the film version, as artifact in the older medium handing its sentence down on the reductive newer medium to which it sells out, through which it seeks new lease on shelf life, *The Omen* is of necessity in the postproduction line of metabolizing and reclaiming projections. The movie *The Omen* included a medium-specific side effect or symptom of the Devil's occult mediation. A press photographer's shots of future victims already showed the "light writing" on the wall: the fore-cast of the future event was outlined in light smears or scratches that looked like flaws in the photographic process. The screen version recalls Spiritist photography in which ghostly presences invisible to the living participants in a séance were just the same recorded through the cam-era's eye. According to Freud, the death wish we cannot bear to acknow-ledge as our own when a living target joins the ranks of the departed dictates that what we see is what we forget. We always only have a ghost of a chance of making the connection at the mediatized remove and re-versal brought to us by haunting. In the case of the photographs inside the film *The Omen*, we witness the advance preview of the fateful fulfill-ment of the Devil's omnipotent wish is his command. The novel can't let the photographic sign or symptom go:

> It was the same sort of defect he'd had a few months ago in the shot of the nanny at the Thorn estate. This time it involved the shots of the priest. Once again it seemed to be a flaw on the emulsion.... Even more curious, it seemed linked to the subject, the strange blur of move-ment hanging above the priest's head as though it were somehow actually there.... Not only did the blemish disappear in the two shots of the Marine, but when it reappeared in the final shot, it was smaller in size, relative to the size of the priest. (63)

The photographer considers recent theories about film emulsion's sen-sitivity to heat, including that of the residual energy that ghosts can be seen to embody.

> What was the meaning of energy that clung to the outside of a human form? Did it come at random, or did it have some *meaning?* ... Anxi-ety was known to create energy, this the principle of the polygraph used for lie detector tests. That energy was electrical in nature. Elec-tricity was also heat. Perhaps the heat generated by extreme anxiety burst through human flesh and could thus be photographed surround-ing people in states of great stress. (64)

He tests the theory by photographing patients in a terminal ward who know they are dying, subjects he could presume, therefore, to be in states of extreme stress. Nothing. He redevelops the pictures of priest and nanny:

"It was plain, in enlargement, that something was actually there. The naked eye had not seen it, but the nitrate had responded. Indeed, there were invisible images in the air" (64–65). In the novel the photo speculations outnumber their matching on-screen special effects. The novel's parting shot (as seen NOT in the screen version) is staggered via Before and After photography. Out of the reporters' shots photographs are developed in which one can make out the ectoplasmic lowering of the doom on the car taking son-of-Satan to his new and improved home.

Without exception in the film *The Omen,* the markings on the photographs are cuts that are at the same time projections or forecasts: cut along the dotted line. They cut the loss that photography otherwise records on the rebound.

Photographs (like dreams) can recognize or read *as* projection and forecast what passes before the naked eye unseen. They hold the place of legibility alongside the projections that in Devil fiction must also make the cut and touch the wound.

It seems almost metapsychological fact that Devil fiction requires the loop between literary and screen media. *Rosemary's Baby, The Ninth Gate, The Exorcist, The Sentinel, Angel Heart, The Possession of Joel Delaney*—all of them, all of them, titles of films based on books. Barring the lineage of or in letters, Devil movies can turn instead to the slasher formula. The self-reflexivity of slasher movies touches the outside wounds of murderous violence that the mass media at large must be seen or watched as (in every sense) containing. In *The Devil and His Grandmother,* screen-deep projections are accompanied by cuts, losses, and screams that are as real as the audience the Devil summons. In Lamberto Bava's *Demons* a demonizing wound is transmitted via an infinite regress of screens within screens. A demon mask hanging in the lobby wounds a member of the audience who tries it on. This cut is simulcast (with only a brief delay back on the screen) as the wounding of one character by a demon mask discovered in a grave, a cut that will transform this person into the first screen demon. But in the meantime the wound on the audience's side of the spectacle demonizes one member, driving her to ravage another one. The demon epidemic on screen meets the epidemic soon raging up and down the aisles when the second demonized moviegoer rips through the screen and becomes everyone else's scream memory.

The *Scream* trilogy recycled and reclaimed this staging of self-reflexivity within the slasher Sensurround of violence of everyday life. *Scream* reverses the mythic-historic setting of *Demons:* Nostradamus, the movie inside this movie tells us, predicted Hitler's rise to power and now this demon invasion coming at us. But both *Demons* and *Scream* prey and stay together via the Mass of murder.

The loop through the wound is basic to the Devil's hold on projection: yes, it's a self-contained world after all created out of nothing, but all its terms are not generated out of itself, do not come down to nothing. Next to nothing, this world throws at least one loop through the cut that cuts in on the endless fall, its bottom line, the bottom you hit even when you fall into the abyss, into nothingness. Something literal, something projected: that's what Devil fictions are made of.

When Milton reaches across his own blindness to conjure the abyssal fall of the rebel angels and dictate his representation of unrepresentability to his seeing-I daughter, he has the falling angels hit bottom in an underworld that precedes the creation of the world as the bottom line of worldly creation. Out of the burning fecal wasteland, Milton and Lucifer extract the shining ore of mining, our primal technology: palaces of gold can be built—as well as the infernal war machines with which Lucifer arms his soldiers for the second assault upon the heavens. The writing-self in *My Mother: Demonology* conjures her own escape artistry as the abyssal immersion in language that contains itself as her fiction: "I write in the dizziness that seizes that which is fed up with language and attempts to escape through it: the abyss named *fiction*" (80). Call it the fiction in the abyss or the transference in the transmission of knowledge—it is what Acker saw red writing.

The Marquis de Sade, a Devil father in Acker's reading, seeks to seduce "us, his readers, into the labyrinth where nothing matters because, there, nothing can matter" ("Reading the Lack of the Body," 71). And again: "Every labyrinth is a machine whose purpose is to unveil chaos" (73). But peeling the veil from chaos or nothingness can also resonate as pealing it: letting it ring out and up from the bottom of your art. There is a labyrinth of bottom lines that does not fit a finite/infinite machine or logic. Acker—like Freud, like Goethe—supplements the pact psychology of Satanic doubling and nothingness with the turn to and trope of the witch. On his own the Devil father cannot grant a new beginning but can only defer the end for the finite time it takes for it to arrive after all. Turning to the witch named fiction, extending through her offices the range of the Devil's best offer, Acker takes the plunge through language, catching fire from the projections around and passing through her, until, hitting bottom lines of red writing, she begins again from scratch (from Old Scratch).

REFERENCES

Abraham, Nicolas, and Maria Torok. *The Wolf Man's Magic Word: A Cryptonymy.* Trans. Nicholas Rand. Foreword by Jacques Derrida. Minneapolis: University of Minnesota Press, 1986.

Acker, Kathy. *My Mother: Demonology.* New York: Pantheon Books, 1993.

————. "Reading the Lack of the Body: The Writing of the Marquis de Sade." In *Bodies of Work. Essays by Kathy Acker,* 66–80. London: Serpent's Tail, 1997.

Agricola, Georgius. *De Re Metallica.* Trans. H. C. Hoover and L. H. Hoover (from the first Latin Edition of 1556). Reprint of the 1912 translation published by *The Mining Magazine,* London. New York: Dover Publications, 1950.

Allen, Thomas B. *Possessed: The True Story of an Exorcism.* Lincoln, Neb.: iUniverse, 2000 [1994].

Andreas-Salomé, Lou. *Der Teufel und seine Grossmutter.* Jena: Eugen Diederichs, 1922.

Arendt, Hannah. *Eichmann in Jerusalem: A Report on the Banality of Evil.* New York: Penguin Books, 1992 [rev. and enlarged ed. of 1964].

Baddeley, Gavin. *Lucifer Rising.* London: Plexus, 1999.

Balzac, Honoré de. *La Peau de Chagrin.* 1835. *The Wild Ass's Skin.* Trans. Herbert J. Hunt. London: Penguin, 1977.

Blatty, William Peter. *The Exorcist.* New York: Harper Paperbacks, 1994 [1971].

Bogdanovich, Peter. *Who the Devil Made It: Conversations with Legendary Film Directors.* New York: Ballantine Books, 1997.

Bradley, Marion Zimmer. *The Mists of Avalon.* New York: Knopf, 1982.

Brittle, Gerald Daniel. *The Demonologist: The Extraordinary Career of Ed and Lorraine Warren.* Lincoln, Neb.: iUniverse, 2002 [1980].

Brown, Norman O. *Love's Body.* New York: Random House, 1966.

Chabon, Michael. *The Amazing Adventures of Kavalier and Clay.* New York: Picador, 2001.

Chamisso, Adelbert von. *Peter Schlemihls wundersame Geschichte.* 1813. *Peter Schlemiel: The Man Who Sold His Shadow.* Trans. Peter Wortsman. New York: Fromm International, 1993.

Clarke, Arthur. *Childhood's End.* New York: Ballantine Books, 1990 [1953].

Crowley, Aleister. *The Confessions of Aleister Crowley: An Autohagiography.* Ed. John Symonds and Kenneth Grant. London: Arkana, 1969.

Dante Alighieri. *Inferno.* 1321. *Inferno.* Trans. Robin Kirkpatrick. London: Penguin Classics, 2006.

Defoe, Daniel. *History of the Devil.* Boston: C. D. Strong, 1848 [1726].

Derrida, Jacques. *La carte postale: De Socrate à Freud et au delà.* Paris: Flammarion, 1980.

———. "Cogito et l'histoire de la folie." In *L'écriture et la différence.* Paris: Éditions du Seuil, 1967.

———. *États d'âme de la psychanalyse.* Paris: Éditions Galilée, 2000.

———. "Faith and Knowledge: The Two Sources of 'Religion' at the Limits of Reason Alone." Trans. Samuel Weber. In *Religion,* ed. Jacques Derrida and Gianni Vattimo. Stanford, Calif.: Stanford University Press, 1998.

———. *Mal d'archive: Une impression freudienne.* Paris: Éditions Galilée, 1995.

Dostoyevsky, Fyodor. *The Brothers Karamazov.* Trans. Richard Pevear and Larissa Volokhonsky. New York: Farrar, Straus and Giroux, 2002 [1880].

Ebon, Martin. *The Devil's Bride. Exorcism: Past and Present.* New York: Harper and Row, 1974.

Enzensberger, Hans Magnus. "Schwedischer Herbst." *Ach Europa! Wahrnehmungen aus sieben Ländern.* Frankfurt: Suhrkamp, 1989.

Estorick, Eric. "Morale in Contemporary England." *American Journal of Sociology* 47, 3 (November 1941): 462–71.

Ferenczi, Sándor. "Glaube, Unglaube und Überzeugung." In *Schriften zur Psychoanalyse,* ed. Michael Balint, 135–47. Vol. 1. Frankfurt am Main: Fischer Verlag, 1982 [1913].

Flaubert, Gustave. *La Tentation de Saint Antoine.* 1874. *The Temptation of Saint Anthony.* Trans. Lafcadio Hearn. Introduction by Michel Foucault. New York: Modern Library Classics, 2001.

Flusser, Vilém. *Die Geschichte des Teufels.* Göttingen: European Photography, 1993 [1965].

———. *Die Schrift. Hat Schreiben Zukunft?* Göttingen: European Photography, 1992 [1987].

———, with Klaus Nüchtern. *Ein Gespräch.* Göttingen: European Photography, 1991.

———. *Vampyroteuthis infernalis. Eine Abhandlung samt Befund des Institut Scientifique de Recherche Paranaturaliste.* Göttingen: European Photography, 1993 [1987].

Freud, Sigmund. *The Standard Edition of the Complete Psychological Works of Sigmund Freud.* Ed. James Strachey. 24 vols. London: The Hogarth Press, 1953–74. Cited in the text as *SE.*

Goebel, Eckart. *Charis und Charisma. Gewalt und Grazie von Winckelmann bis Heidegger.* Berlin: Kulturverlag Kadmos, 2006.

Goethe, Johann Wolfgang von. *Faust, in Werke.* Ed. Paul Stapf. Vol. 3. Berlin: Deutsche Buch-Gemeinschaft, 1963.

Gold, Scott, Ken Ellingwood, and H. G. Reza. "2 Killed, 13 Hurt in School Shooting. Suspect, 15, Had Made Repeated Threats before Attack near San Diego," *Los Angeles Times,* Tuesday, March 6, 2001, A1, A16.

Goodman, Felicitas D. *The Exorcism of Anneliese Michel.* Garden City, N.Y.: Doubleday and Company, 1981.

Graf, Max. *Composer and Critic: Two Hundred Years of Musical Criticism.* Port Washington, N.Y.: Kennikat Press, 1946.

———. *Deutsche Musik im neunzehnten Jahrhundert.* Berlin: Verlag Siegfried Cronbach, 1898.

———. *From Beethoven to Shostakovich: The Psychology of the Composing Process.* New York: Philosophical Library, 1947.

———. *Die innere Werkstatt des Musikers.* Stuttgart: Verlag von Ferdinand Enke, 1910.

———. "Reminiscences of Professor Sigmund Freud." Trans. Gregory Zilboorg. *Psychoanalytic Quarterly* 11, 4 (October 1942): 465–76.

———. *Richard Wagner im "Fliegenden Holländer." Ein Beitrag zur Psychologie künstlerischen Schaffens.* Leipzig and Vienna: Franz Deuticke, 1911.

———. *Wagner-Probleme und andere Studien.* Vienna: Wiener Verlag, 1900.

Hauff, Wilhelm. *Mitteilungen aus den Memoiren des Satan.* In *Werke.* Vol. 2. Frankfurt: Insel Verlag, 1969 [1825].

Hay, William Delisle. *Three Hundred Years Hence.* London: Newman, 1881.

Hjortsberg, William. *Falling Angel.* New York: St. Martin's Paperbacks, 1996 [1978].

Hoffmann, E. T. A. *Die Elixiere des Teufels.* Cologne: Könemann, 1994 [1815–16].

———. "Die Bergwerke zu Falun." 1820. "The Mines at Falun." In *Tales of Hoffmann,* trans. R. J. Hollingdale, 311–38. London: Penguin Books, 1982.

Huxley, Aldous. *The Devils of Loudun.* London: Chatto and Windus, 1952.

Huxley, Julian. "Evolutionary Humanism as a Developed Religion." In *Religion without Revelation.* London: C. A. Watts and Co., 1967.

Huysmans, J. K. *En Route.* 1895. *En Route.* Trans. W. Fleming. Sawtry, U.K.: Dedalus, 2002.

———. *La-Bas.* 1891. *The Damned.* Trans. Terry Hale. London: Penguin, 2001.

Idel, Moshe. *Golem: Jewish Magical and Mystical Traditions on the Artificial Anthropoid.* Albany: SUNY Press, 1990.

Jones, Ernest. *On the Nightmare.* London: Liveright Paperbound Edition, 1971 [Part I, 1910; Part II, 1912].

Jung, C. G. "The Significance of the Father in the Destiny of the Individual." In *The Collected Works of C. G. Jung,* ed. William McGuire, Herbert Read, Michael Fordham, and Gerhard Adler, 301–23. Vol. 4. Trans. R. F. C. Hull. Princeton, N.J.: Princeton University Press, 1989 [1909/1948].

Jürgenson, Friedrich. *Sprechfunk mit Verstorbenen. Eine dem Atomzeitalter gemäße Form der praktischen technisch-physikalischen Kontaktherstellung mit dem Jenseits.* Freiburg: Verlag Hermann Bauer, 1978.

Kapp, Ernst. *Grundlinien einer Philosophie der Technik.* Braunschweig: Verlag George Westermann, 1877.

Kieckhefer, Richard. *Forbidden Rites: A Necromancer's Manual of the Fifteenth Century.* University Park: Pennsylvania State University Press, 1998.

Kierkegaard, Søren. *Enten-eller.* 1843. *Either/Or.* Trans. Howard V. Hong and Edna H. Hong. Princeton, N.J.: Princeton University Press, 1988.

King, Stephen. *Needful Things.* New York: Signet, 1992.

Kittler, Friedrich. *Eine Kulturgeschichte der Kulturwissenschaft.* Munich: Fink Verlag, 2000.

———. "Flusser zum Abschied." *Kunstforum international* 117 (1992): 99.

———. *Optische Medien. Berliner Vorlesung 1999.* Berlin: Merve Verlag, 2002.

Konvitz, Jeffrey. *The Apocalypse.* London: New English Library, 1979 [1978].

———. *The Sentinel.* London: Wyndham Publications, 1976 [1974].

Kraus, Karl. *Dritte Walpurgisnacht.* Frankfurt: Suhrkamp Verlag, 1989 [1952].

Kris, Ernst. *Psychoanalytic Explorations in Art.* New York: Schocken Books, 1974.

Kubie, Lawrence S. "The Drive to Become Both Sexes." In *Symbol and Neurosis: Selected Papers of Lawrence S. Kubie,* ed. Herbert J. Schlesinger. New York: International Universities Press, 1978.

Kubin, Alfred. *Die andere Seite. Ein phantastischer Roman.* Reinbek bei Hamburg: Rowohlt Taschenbuch Verlag, 1994 [1909].

Lang, Fritz. *Fritz Lang: Interviews.* Ed. Barry Keith Grant. Jackson: University Press of Mississippi, 2003.

Lanz von Liebenfels, Jörg. *Theozoologie oder die Kunde von den Sodoms-Äfflingen und dem Götter-Elektron. Eine Einführung in die älteste und neueste Weltanschauung und eine Rechtfertigung des Fürstentums und des Adels.* Vienna: Moderner Verlag, 1905.

Laqua, Carsten. *Wie Micky Maus unter die Nazis fiel. Walt Disney und Deutschland.* Reinbek bei Hamburg: Rowohlt Taschenbuch Verlag, 1992.

LaVey, Anton Szandor. "A Plan." In *Satan Speaks!* 20–22. Los Angeles: Feral House, 1998.

———. "Evocation." In *The Devil's Notebook,* 76–78. Los Angeles: Feral House, 1992.

———. "The Merits of Artificiality." In *The Devil's Notebook,* 130–31.

———. "To: All Doomsayers, Head-Shakers, Hand-Wringers, Worrywarts, Satanophobes, Identity Christers, Survivor Counselors, Academia Nuts, and Assorted Tremblers." In *Satan Speaks!* 4–7.

———. *The Satanic Bible.* New York: Avon Books, 1969.

Leinenbach, Harald. *Die Körperlichkeit der Technik. Zur Organprojektionsthese Ernst Kapps.* Essen: Die Blaue Eule, 1990.

Leven, Jeremy. *Satan: His Psychotherapy and Cure by the Unfortunate Dr. Kassler, J.S.P.S.* New York: Alfred A. Knopf, 1982.

Levin, Ira. *Rosemary's Baby.* New York: Signet, 1997 [1967].

———. *Son of Rosemary.* New York: Dutton, 1997.

———. *The Stepford Wives.* New York: Harper Paperbacks, 2002 [1972].

Lewis, Matthew G. *The Monk.* New York: Grove Press, 1952 [1796].

Link, Luther. *The Devil: A Mask without a Face.* London: Reaktion Books, 1995.

Lorenz, Emil Franz. "Die Geschichte des Bergmanns von Falun." *Imago* (1914): 250–301.

Lovecraft, H. P. "The Call of Cthulhu." In *More Annotated H. P. Lovecraft,* ed. Peter Cannon and S. T. Joshi, 172–216. New York: Dell Publishing, 1999 [1928].

———. "The Dunwich Horror." In *The Annotated H. P. Lovecraft,* ed. S. T. Joshi, 103–74. New York: Dell Publishing, 1997 [1929].

Löwenstein, Rudolf. "Zur Psychoanalyse der Schwarzen Messen." *Imago* (1923): 73–82.

Luther, Martin. "Consolation for a Depressed Friend" (March 29, 1538). In *The Table Talk of Martin Luther.* Trans. William Hazlitt. London: George Bell and Sons, 1875.

Lyotard, Jean-François. "Can Thought Go On without a Body?" In *The Inhuman: Reflections on Time,* trans. Geoffrey Bennington and Rachel Bowlby [translation modified]. Stanford, Calif.: Stanford University Press, 1991.

Lytton, Edward. *The Coming Race.* Santa Barbara, Calif.: Woodbridge Press, 1989 [1871].

Macalpine, Ida, and Richard A. Hunter. *Schizophrenia 1677: A Psychiatric Study of an Illustrated Record of Demoniacal Possession.* London: William Dawson and Sons, 1956.

MacLaine, Shirley. *Dancing in the Light.* New York: Bantam Books, 1985.

Mann, Klaus. *Mephisto. Roman einer Karriere.* Amsterdam: Querido Verlag, 1936.

Mann, Thomas. *Doktor Faustus. Das Leben des deutschen Tonsetzers Adrian Leverkühn, erzählt von einem Freunde.* Stockholm: Bermann-Fischer Verlag, 1947.

Martin, Malachi. *Hostage to the Devil: The Possession and Exorcism of Five Living Americans.* San Francisco: HarperSanFrancisco, 1992 [1976].

Messadié, Gerald. *A History of the Devil.* Trans. Marc Romano. New York: Kodansha International, 1996 [1993].

Meyrink, Gustav. *Der Golem.* Berlin: Ullstein, 1915.

———. *Walpurgisnacht.* Prague: Vitalis, 2003 [1917].

Michelet, Jules. *Satanism and Witchcraft: A Study in Medieval Superstition.* Trans. A. R. Allinson. New York: Citadel Press, 1939.

Milton, John. *Paradise Lost.* New York: W. W. Norton, 2004 [1667].

Morris, Nat. *A Man Possessed: The Case History of Sigmund Freud.* Los Angeles: Regent House, 1974.

Mozingo, Joe. "Freshman Is Charged with Murder in 4 Deaths Near UC Santa Barbara," *Los Angeles Times,* February 27, 2001.

———. "Parents of Car Crash Suspect Express Sorrow," *Los Angeles Times,* February 28, 2001.

———. "Witness Describes Driver's Actions after His Car Plowed into Crowd in Isla Vista," *Los Angeles Times,* March 2, 2001.

Nietzsche, Friedrich. *Sämtliche Werke. Kritische Studienausgabe.* Ed. Giorgio Colli and Mazzino Montinari. 15 vols. Munich: Deutscher Taschenbuch Verlag, 1980.

Novalis (Friedrich von Hardenberg). *Werke.* Ed. Gerhard Schulz. Munich: C. H. Beck, 2001.

Payer-Thurn, Rudolf. "Faust in Mariazell." In *Chronik des Wiener Goethe-Vereins.* Vol. 24 (1924): 1–18.

Pérez-Reverte, Arturo. *The Club Dumas.* Trans. Sonia Soto. New York: Vintage International, 1998 [1993].

Pfister, Oskar. *Das Christentum und die Angst.* Zürich: Artemis Verlag, 1944.

———. *Religionswissenschaft und Psychoanalyse.* Giessen: Verlag von Alfred Töpelmann, 1927.

Pommier, Gérard. "Des dieux au monthéisme, des démons au diable (Examen de textes bibliques concernant la signularisation du diable á la lumière de la métapsychologie freudienne)." In *Le Diable,* 155–73. Cahiers de l'Hermétisme. Paris: Éditions Dervy, 1998.

Prokhoris, Sabine. *The Witch's Kitchen: Freud, Faust, and the Transference.* Trans. G. M. Goshgarian. Ithaca, N.Y.: Cornell University Press, 1995 [1988].

Reik, Theodor. *Der eigene und der fremde Gott.* Leipzig/Vienna/Zürich: Internationaler Psychoanalytischer Verlag, 1923.

Reisner, Erwin. *Der Dämon und sein Bild.* Frankfurt: Suhrkamp Verlag, 1986 [1947].

———. *Die Juden und das Deutsche Reich.* Erlenbach-Zürich and Stuttgart: Eugen Rentsch, 1966.

———. *Vom Ursinn der Geschlechter.* Ulm: Hesse and Becker, 1986 [1954].

Rice, Anne. *Memnoch the Devil.* New York: Alfred A. Knopf, 1995.

Rickels, Laurence A. "Body *Bildung.* Laurence Rickels Talks with Kathy Acker." In *Acting Out in Groups,* ed. Laurence A. Rickels, 109–17. Minneapolis: University of Minnesota Press, 1999 [1994].

Ronell, Avital. *The Test Drive.* Urbana: University of Illinois Press, 2005.

Sachs, Hanns. "*Die andere Seite.*" *Imago* 1 (1912): 197–204.

Sade, Marquis de. "Ernestine, a Swedish Tale." In *The 120 Days of Sodom and Other Writings*. Trans. Austryn Wainhouse and Richard Seaver. New York: Grove Press, 1967.

Schneider, Manfred. "Luther with McLuhan." Trans. Samuel Weber. In *Religion and Media*, ed. Hent de Vries and Samuel Weber. Stanford, Calif.: Stanford University Press, 2001.

Schneider, Monique. *Le Féminin expurgé: De l'exorcisme á la psychanalyse*. Paris: Retz, 1979.

Scholem, Gershom. *On the Kabbalah and Its Symbolism*. Trans. Ralph Manheim. New York: Schocken Books, 1997 [1960].

Schreck, Nikolas. *The Satanic Screen*. Los Angeles: Creation Books, 2001.

Schubert, Gotthilf Heinrich von. *Ansichten von der Nachtseite der Naturwissenschaften*. Darmstadt: Wissenschaftliche Buchgesellschaft, 1967 [1809].

Schur, Max. *Freud: Living and Dying*. New York: International Universities Press, 1972.

Schwarzenegger, Arnold, and Douglas Kent Hall. *Arnold: The Education of a Bodybuilder*. New York: Simon and Schuster, 1993 [1974].

Sekula, Allan. "Photography between Labour and Capital." In *Mining Photographs and Other Pictures, 1948–1968: A Selection from the Negative Archives of Shedden Studio, Glace Bay, Cape Breton*, ed. Benjamin H. D. Buchloh and Robert Wilkie. Halifax: The Press of the Nova Scotia College of Art and Design, 1983.

Seltzer, David. *The Omen*. New York: Signet Books, 1976.

Shakespeare, William. *Hamlet*. New York: Washington Square Press, 2003 [1601].

Shelley, Mary. *Frankenstein; or, The Modern Prometheus*. London: Penguin Books, 2003 [1818].

Smith, Michelle, and Lawrence Pazder. *Michelle Remembers*. New York: Congdon and Lattès, 1980.

Smolowe, Jill, Leslie Berestein, Maureen Harrington, and J. Todd Foster. "'It's Only Me': Andy Williams, 15, Told Friends He Was Going to Shoot Up His California High School, but Nobody Really Believed Him." *People*, March 19, 2001, 61–62.

Sprenger, Jakob, and Heinrich Institoris. *Malleus maleficarum*, 1487. *The Malleus Maleficarum of Heinrich Kramer and James Sprenger*. Trans. Montague Summers. New York: Dover, 1971 [1928].

Stanford, Peter. *The Devil: A Biography*. New York: Henry Hold and Company, 1996.

Stephens, Walter. *Demon Lovers: Witchcraft, Sex, and the Crisis of Belief*. Chicago: University of Chicago Press, 2002.

Stewart, Ramona. *The Possession of Joel Delaney*. Boston: Little, Brown and Company, 1970.

Strindberg, August. *Inferno*. 1897. *Inferno/From an Occult Diary*. Trans. Mary Sandbach. Harmondsworth, Middlesex, England: Penguin, 1984.

Theweleit, Klaus. *Male Fantasies*. Trans. Erica Carter, Stephen Conway, and Chris Turner. 2 vols. Minneapolis: University of Minnesota Press, 1987 and 1989.

Turing, Alan. "Computing Machinery and Intelligence." *Mind: A Quarterly Review of Psychology* 59, 236 (October 1950): 433–60.

Urtubey, Luisa de. *Freud et le diable*. Paris: Presses Universitaires de France, 1983.

Vernes, Jules. *Vingt mille lieus sous les mers*. 1870. *Twenty Thousand Leagues under the Sea*. New York: Scholastic, 2000.

Villiers de L'Isle-Adam, Auguste. *L'Ève future*. 1886.

Wagner, Richard. "Die Bergwerke zu Falun. Oper in drei Akten." In Hubert Ermisch, "Ein ungedruckter Entwurf Richard Wagners zu einer Operndichtung, nebst Briefen." *Deutsche Rundschau* 73 (1905): 1–14.

———. "Der Virtuous und der Künstler." In *Ein deutscher Musiker in Paris. Novellen und Aufsätze*. Berlin: Verlag der Nation, 1988.

Watanabe, Teresa. "Exorcism Flourishing Again." *Los Angeles Times*, Tuesday, October 31, 2000, A1, A16.

Wheatley, Dennis. *The Devil and All His Works*. London: Arrow Books, 1973 [1971].

———. *The Devil Rides Out*. London: Hutchinson and Co., 1972 [1934].

———. *To the Devil—A Daughter*. London: Arrow Books, 1979 [1953].

Wiener, Norbert. *God and Golem, Inc.—A Comment on Certain Points Where Cybernetics Impinges on Religion*. Cambridge, Mass.: M.I.T. Press, 1964.

Wride, Nancy, and Nora Zamichow. "Suspect Described as Troubled, Puny, and Picked-On." *Los Angeles Times*, Tuesday, March 6, 2001, A15.

Youngblood, Gene. "*Free Press* Interview: Arthur C. Clarke." In *The Making of 2001: A Space Odyssey*, 258–69. Martin Scorsese, series editor. New York: Modern Library, 2000.

FILMOGRAPHY

The Abominable Dr. Phibes. Directed by Robert Fuest, 1971.
All of Them Witches. (Sobrenatural.) Directed by Daniel Gruener, 1995.
All the Colors of the Dark. Directed by Sergio Martino, 1974.
The Amityville Horror. Directed by Stuart Rosenberg, 1979.
The Amityville Horror. Directed by Andrew Douglas, 2005.
Amityville II: The Possession. Directed by Damiano Damiani, 1982.
Angel Heart. Directed by Alan Parker, 1987.
Army of Darkness. Directed by Sam Raimi, 1992.
Asylum of Satan. Directed by William Girdler, 1971.
Bedazzled. Directed by Stanley Donen, 1967.
Bedazzled. Directed by Harold Ramis, 2000.
The Black Cat. Directed by Edgar Ulmer, 1934.
Black Circle Boys. Directed by Matthew Carnahan, 1997.
Black Sunday. (The Mask of Satan.) Directed by Mario Bava, 1960.
Bless the Child. Directed by Chuck Russell, 2000.
Bride of Frankenstein. Directed by James Whale, 1934.
The Brotherhood of Satan. Directed by Bernard McEveety, 1971.
The Brotherhood II. Young Warlocks. Directed by David DeCoteau, 2001.
Conan the Barbarian. Directed by John Milius, 1982.
Constantine. Directed by Francis Lawrence, 2005.
The Contract. Directed by Steven R. Monroe, 1999.
Curse of the Demon. Directed by Jacques Tourneur, 1957.
Damien: Omen II. Directed by Don Taylor, 1978.
Damn Yankees. Directed by George Abbott and Stanley Donen, 1958.
Dante's Inferno. Directed by Harry Lachman, 1935.
Deal of a Lifetime. Directed by Paul Levine, 1999.
Def by Temptation. Directed by James Bond III, 1990.
Demonia. Directed by Lucio Fulci, 1990.
Demon Knight. Directed by Ernest Dickerson, 1995.
Demons. Directed by Lamberto Bava, 1985.
Demons 2. Directed by Lamberto Bava, 1986.
Demon Seed. Directed by Donald Cammell, 1977.

Demon Wind. Directed by Charles Philip Moore, 1990.
Desecration. Directed by Dante Tomaselli, 1999.
Devil Dog. Directed by Curtis Harrington, 1978.
The Devil Probably. (Le Diable probablement.) Directed by Robert Bresson, 1977.
The Devil Rides Out. Directed by Terence Fisher, 1968.
The Devils. Directed by Ken Russell, 1971.
Devil's Advocate. Directed by Taylor Hackford, 1997.
The Devil's Eye. Directed by Ingmar Bergman, 1960.
The Devil's Gift. Directed by Kenneth Berton, 1984.
The Devil's Rain. Directed by Robert Fuest, 1975.
Dogma. Directed by Kevin Smith, 1999.
Dr. Phibes Rises Again. Directed by Robert Fuest, 1972.
The Dunwich Horror. Directed by Daniel Haller, 1970.
Dust Devil. Directed by Richard Stanley, 1992.
Education for Death. Disney, 1943.
The Eighteenth Angel. Directed by William Bindley, 1998.
End of Days. Directed by Peter Hyams, 1999.
End of the World. Directed by John Hayes, 1977.
Event Horizon. Directed by Paul Anderson, 1997.
Evil Dead 2. Dead by Dawn. Directed by Sam Raimi, 1987.
The Evil Within. Directed by Jeffrey Bydalek, 1998.
The Exorcism of Emily Rose. Directed by Scott Derrickson, 2005.
The Exorcist. Directed by William Friedkin, 1973.
The Exorcist II. The Heretic. Directed by John Boorman, 1977.
The Exorcist III. Legion. Directed by William Blatty, 1990.
Eyes Wide Shut. Directed by Stanley Kubrick, 1999.
Fallen. Directed by Gregory Hoblit, 1998.
Fertilize the Blaspheming Bombshell. (Mark of the Beast.) Directed by Jeff Hathcock, 1990.
The Final Conflict: Omen III. Directed by Graham Baker, 1981.
The Gate. Directed by Tibor Takács, 1986.
Gate II. Directed by Tibor Takács, 1992.
Ghoulies II. Directed by Albert Band, 1987.
Der Golem: wie er in die Welt kam. Directed by Paul Wegener, 1920.
Hellbound: Hellraiser II. Directed by Tony Randel, 1988.
Hellraiser. Directed by Clive Barker, 1987.
Hellraiser: Inferno. Directed by Scott Derrickson, 2000.
Hellraiser III. Hell on Earth. Directed by Anthony Hickox, 1992.
Hellzapoppin'. Directed by H. C. Potter, 1941.
Horror Hotel. (The City of the Dead.) Directed by John Moxey, 1960.
House of Exorcism. Directed by Mario Bava and Alfredo Leone, 1973.

The Inauguration of the Pleasure Dome. Directed by Kenneth Anger, 1954.
Incubus. Directed by Leslie Stevens, 1965.
Invocation of My Demon Brother. Directed by Kenneth Anger, 1969.
Junior. Directed by Ivan Reitman, 1994.
Last Action Hero. Directed by John McTiernan, 1993.
The Last Boy Scout. Directed by Tony Scott, 1991.
The Legacy. Directed by Richard Marquand, 1978.
Legion of the Dead. Directed by Olaf Ittenbach, 2001.
Little Nicky. Directed by Steven Brill, 2000.
Lost Souls. Directed by Janusz Kaminski, 2000.
Lost Voyage. Directed by Christian McIntire, 2001.
Love at Stake. Directed by John Moffitt, 1988.
Lucifer Rising. Directed by Kenneth Anger, 1970–80.
Mardi Gras Massacre. Directed by Jack Weis, 1978.
Mephisto. Directed by István Szabó, 1981.
The Mephisto Waltz. Directed by Paul Wendkos, 1971.
Metropolis. Directed by Fritz Lang, 1927.
Midnight Cabaret. Directed by Pece Dingo, 1988.
The Minion. Directed by Jean-Marc Piché, 1998.
Needful Things. Directed by Fraser Clarke Heston, 1993.
Night Visitor. Directed by Rupert Hitzig, 1989.
The Ninth Gate. Directed by Roman Polanski, 2000.
Nosferatu, eine Symphonie des Grauens. Directed by F. W. Murnau, 1922.
The Omen. Directed by Richard Donner, 1976.
The Omen. Directed by John Moore, 2006.
The Order. Directed by Brian Helgeland, 2003.
L'Orgueil. Directed by Roger Vadim. In *The Seven Deadly Sins,* 1962.
La Paresse. Directed by Jean-Luc Godard. In *The Seven Deadly Sins,* 1962.
Phantasm. Directed by Don Coscarelli, 1979.
Popcorn. Directed by Mark Herrier, 1991.
The Possession of Joel Delaney. Directed by Waris Hussein, 1972.
Prime Evil. Directed by Roberta Findlay, 1988.
Prince of Darkness. Directed by John Carpenter, 1987.
The Prophecy. Directed by Gregory Widen, 1995.
The Prophecy II. Directed by Greg Spence, 1998.
Psychomania. Directed by Don Sharp, 1971.
Race with the Devil. Directed by Jack Starrett, 1975.
Raging Angels. Directed by Alan Smithee, 1988.
Resurrection. Directed by Russell Mulcahy, 1999.
Return of the Blind Dead. Directed by Amando de Ossorio, 1973.
Rosemary's Baby. Directed by Roman Polanski, 1968.
Satan's Cheerleaders. Directed by Greydon Clark, 1977.

Satan's Children. Directed by Joe Wiezycki, 1974.

Satan's School for Girls. Directed by David Lowell Rich, 1973.

Scream. Directed by Wes Craven, 1996.

Scream 2. Directed by Wes Craven, 1997.

Scream 3. Directed by Wes Craven, 2000.

The Sentinel. Directed by Michael Winner, 1977.

Seven. Directed by David Fincher, 1996.

Simón del desierto. Directed by Luis Buñuel, 1965.

The Skull. Directed by Freddie Francis, 1965.

Sometimes They Come Back. Directed by Tom McLoughlin, 1991.

Sometimes They Come Back... Again. Directed by Adam Grossman, 1996.

Sometimes They Come Back... for More. Directed by Daniel Berk, 1999.

Soulkeeper. Directed by Darin Ferriola, 1964.

Speak of the Devil. Directed by Nick Bougas, 1993.

Sphere. Directed by Barry Levinson, 1998.

The Stepford Wives. Directed by Bryan Forbes, 1975.

Stigmata. Directed by Rupert Wainright, 1999.

Suspiria. Directed by Dario Argento, 1977.

The Terminator. Directed by James Cameron, 1984.

Terminator 2: Judgment Day. Directed by James Cameron, 1991.

Das Testament des Dr. Mabuse. Directed by Fritz Lang, 1933.

To the Devil a Daughter. Directed by Peter Sykes, 1976.

The Visitation. Directed by Robby Henson, 2005.

The Visitor. Directed by Guilio Paradisi, 1979.

Wishmaster. Directed by Robert Kurtzman, 1997.

Wishmaster 3. Beyond the Gates of Hell. Directed by Chris Angel, 2001.

Witchboard. Directed by Kevin S. Tenney, 1986.

Witchboard 2. The Devil's Doorway. Directed by Kevin S. Tenney, 1993.

The Witches. Directed by Cyril Frankel, 1966.

X-Men. Directed by Bryan Singer, 2000.

You Only Live Once. Directed by Fritz Lang, 1937.

Laurence A. Rickels is a licensed psychotherapist and professor of German and comparative literature, as well as adjunct professor in the departments of art and film and media studies, at the University of California, Santa Barbara. He is also Sigmund Freud Professor of Media and Philosophy at the European Graduate School in Saas Fee, Switzerland. His writing is renowned for its stylistic experimentation, and as a theorist he takes seriously the task of finding form for thought.

Other Books by Laurence A. Rickels
Published by the University of Minnesota Press

Acting Out in Groups
The Case of California
Nazi Psychoanalysis
    Volume I. Only Psychoanalysis Won the War
    Volume II. Crypto-Fetishism
    Volume III. Psy Fi
Ulrike Ottinger: The Autobiography of Art Cinema
The Vampire Lectures